The Economics of
Consumer Credit

The Economics of Consumer Credit

Giuseppe Bertola, Richard Disney, and Charles Grant, editors

The MIT Press
Cambridge, Massachusetts
London, England

© 2006 Massachusetts Institute of Technology

All rights reserved. No part of this book may be reproduced in any form by any electronic or mechanical means (including photocopying, recording, or information storage and retrieval) without permission in writing from the publisher.

This book was set in Palatino on 3B2 by Asco Typesetters, Hong Kong and was printed and bound in the United States of America.

Library of Congress Cataloging-in-Publication Data

The economics of consumer credit / Giuseppe Bertola, Richard Disney, and Charles Grant, editors.
　　p.　cm.
Includes bibliographical references and index.
ISBN-13: 978-0-262-02601-7 (alk. paper)
ISBN-10: 0-262-02601-5 (alk. paper)
1. Consumer credit. I. Bertola. Giuseppe. II. Disney, Richard. III. Grant, Charles (Charles Benedict)
HG3755.E36　2006
332.7'43—dc22　　　　　　　　　　　　　　　　　　　2005058407

10　9　8　7　6　5　4　3　2　1

Contents

Main Book Title: y20

Preface

Most of the papers collected in this volume were presented and discussed in draft form at a May 2003 conference convened at the European University Institute (Florence, Italy) by the Finance and Consumption in the EU Chair research program. For very helpful comments, the editors and authors are indebted to the formal discussants and audience at the conference, and to John Covell and four anonymous reviewers at The MIT Press.

The conference and this volume mark the end of a four-year period for the Chair's research activities, coordinated by Giuseppe Bertola and generously supported by Findomestic Banca and CETELEM. Since 1999, the Chair has pursued and disseminated research on international and cross-national analysis of consumer behavior and on the competitive, institutional, and contractual design issues in formal and informal credit provision, with particular attention to consumer borrowing and to banks' supply of credit to consumers.

Bringing together a distinguished set of specialist researchers from both sides of the Atlantic, this book offers novel perspectives on a relatively unexplored and very important set of issues. Its chapters review theoretical and empirical aspects, focusing in particular on empirical and regulatory issues from a comparative viewpoint. The material is covered from a variety of complementary perspectives, and the volume aims to serve as a valuable reference source for practitioners and policy analysis as well as to familiarize academic readers and advanced students with state-of-the-art findings and open research directions.

The Economics of
Consumer Credit

1

(US, Europe)

D14

G21

The Economics of Consumer Credit Demand and Supply

Giuseppe Bertola, Richard Disney, and Charles Grant

Credit markets are the subject of extensive research and intense policy debates, and of courses and textbooks (such as Freixas and Rochet 1997). Attention, however, is mostly focused on credit extended by banks and other market agents to firms and producers. Households are typically viewed as suppliers of funds in the financial markets, and academic research and policy discussions focus on their saving and portfolio choices (Poterba 1994; Guiso, Haliassos, and Jappelli 2001, 2003). When indebtedness does attract interest from academic and policy-oriented observers, much of the relevant research and discussion does not adopt an economic perspective. Sociological studies—such as Sullivan, Warren, and Westbrook (2000) and Manning (2000)—tend to reproach households for acquiring so much debt and policymakers for allowing them to do so, and throughout history, social perceptions of personal credit have been very mixed (Gelpi and Julien-Labruyere 2000; Calder 1999).

While borrowing and repayment are far from problem-free, opportunities to borrow can enhance economic welfare by allowing smoother consumption paths over time. Economic progress has been associated with the expansion of credit markets alongside all other markets, and a growing body of economic research fruitfully studies the large amount of information provided by cross-country differences and by time-series developments in the structure and regulation of consumer credit. Households' access to credit is more limited in Continental Europe than in the United States, but the formal consumer credit industry has been developing rapidly in all countries, and is the object of extensive policy debate. Privacy rules and the regulation of contractual responsibilities bear importantly on the functioning of consumer credit markets and are an important political concern in all countries, as are financial stability issues and the possible so-called overindebtedness of some segments of the population. In the latter respects, the policy debate is especially vibrant in the United States, and regulatory policy issues in the credit market are very prominent in Europe, where economic and monetary union may lead the credit industry to develop along lines previously followed in the United States and, more recently, in the United Kingdom. European Union authorities are in the process of actively exploring opportunities for regulation or deregulation of consumer credit relationships within and across borders, and European households' portfolios may, sooner or later, mirror the United States not only in the spread of equity on the asset side (studied by Guiso, Haliassos, and Jappelli 2003) but also in the pervasiveness of debt on the liabilities side.

This volume covers these and other theoretical, empirical, and policy aspects of a very interesting research field. It focuses specifically on consumer debt and adopts an international comparative approach, with particular attention to policy issues. In this introductory chapter, we briefly outline key aspects of consumer credit demand and supply, highlighting relationships between aspects of the following chapters to each other and to broader issues left out of the volume's scope.

Because it appears to be poorly understood by many contributions to the policy debate, the economic approach to household borrowing deserves to be covered in some detail here. Section 1.1 reviews theoretical and empirical contributions that interpret indebtedness as an optimal, possibly constrained household strategy. It also sketches formal relationships between consumption dynamics and saving or borrowing decisions, in order to acquaint readers with notions and terminology that may be unfamiliar to them but are essential to the volume's chapters. In less formal detail, and focusing especially on features that differentiate consumer credit markets from the producer credit banking relationships that may be more familiar to most readers, section 1.2 proceeds to discuss issues arising on the supply side of the consumer credit market, and sections 1.3 and 1.4 review the implications and treatment of repayment difficulties and imperfect information in the consumer credit market.

1.1   The Economics of Consumer Credit Demand

Some of the popular discussion of household debt levels is conducted in a tone of moral disapproval. Household borrowing, however, can be just as sensible as saving. To see this, it suffices to consider how dismal consumption patterns would be if individuals had to consume their earnings, with no access to assets and liabilities. The life-cycle perspective on household finances (Modigliani and Brumberg 1954) emphasizes savings for old age as the main implication of consumption-smoothing behavior. But while labor income certainly declines in old age, expectations of rising labor incomes can justify borrowing for young individuals. And the expenditure requirements of durable goods, especially at the time of household formation, can very well exceed labor income and accumulated assets in the early stages of an individual's life.

Borrowing in order to finance a more desirable consumption pattern or to finance housing purchases can be optimal from the economic point of view, and is perfectly normal nowadays. In earlier times, conversely, indebtedness was often frowned upon. From the economic point of view, a negative attitude toward indebtedness could be justified by market failure. In particular, poor repayment mechanisms could indeed make it unadvisable to incur debt. Before 1600, few English landowners mortgaged their land or property because if any scheduled repayment was missed the entire mortgaged property was forfeited regardless of the outstanding debt, and repayment entailed collecting gold and silver bullion and transporting it by cart under guard to London (Stone 1965). A view of borrowing as foolhardy behavior or evidence of moral desuetude could be justified when bad weather or robbers could easily mean a payment was missed, but a large increase in the use of mortgages unsurprisingly occurred when, in the 1620s, chancery reduced the penalty for missed payments.

Consumer credit today is much better organized, but it remains fascinatingly complex and interesting to study the determinants of household borrowing. In this volume, several chapters study the use of credit markets by households and their debt portfolios. Chapter 2 compares levels of housing and non-housing debt in different countries and the evolution of these debts over time, while chapter 3 extensively reviews and contrasts debt levels among different population groups in several different countries. Chapter 3 also reviews the many studies that estimate the proportion of constrained households, the differences across demographic groups in both the United States and Italy, and how much more such households wish to borrow.

Three of the following chapters illustrate general insights by focusing on single-country case studies and reporting relevant comparative indicators for other countries. Chapter 4 discusses the role of history and regulation in shaping consumer credit differences and dynamics in Italy, a country featuring substantial regional heterogeneity and particularly sharp regulatory developments. Chapter 5 casts light on the role of housing expenditure (the main durable good that most households own) in the cyclical pattern of borrowing and the other factors that shape borrowing decisions of households across time. It does so by analyzing macroeconomic and microeconomic evidence from the United Kingdom, a country featuring very pronounced and regionally heterogeneous house prices dynamics. Chapter 6 investigates the use of credit cards by U.S. consumers, a country where their use is particularly prevalent, and reviews some of the puzzles that are posed by the failure of many households to repay in full the debts that they accumulate each month.

In the remainder of this section, we offer a review of theoretical insights and previous literature, aiming at allowing readers to appreciate the following chapter's contribution in the context of a broader literature and set of issues.

1.1.1 Modeling Consumer Behavior

The modern economic model of consumer behavior is based on substantive and technical insights reviewed by Deaton (1992) and Attanasio (1999) and briefly summarized in what follows. We include some mathematical notation for the benefit of readers who are familiar with optimization techniques in general but not in the particular context of this volume. The gist of this and the other chapters' arguments, however, may also be appreciated without explicit formalization.

According to the Permanent Income Hypothesis, the difference between income and consumption (hence savings, or borrowing) is determined by forward-looking considerations in the presence of randomness of future income—that is, households optimally choose their level of consumption in each period, subject to an intertemporal budget constraint, in order to control its volatility.

The household's problem is to choose consumption c in each period so that utility is maximized subject to the intertemporal budget constraint. The consumption stream is chosen so as to maximize lifetime utility, a discounted sum of period utility functions $u(\ )$ in the form

$$\max E_t \sum_{j=0}^{T} \beta^j u(c_{t+j}), \tag{1}$$

where T is the (possibly infinite) individual planning horizon, E_t denotes household expectations conditional on information available at t, and $\beta = 1/(1 + \delta)$ is the household's discount factor where δ is the subjective discount rate. Maximization of (1) is subject to

$$A_{t+1} = (1 + r_{t+1})(A_t + y_t - c_t), \tag{2}$$

where A is the level of assets (or liabilities), labor income at time t is denoted y_t, and the interest rate determined in the credit market is the same r_t on assets and liabilities. This is an asset evolution equation, stating that assets in any period must equal assets in the previous period plus income (labor income and the return on assets) less consumption in that period.

The optimal solution of this problem satisfies Euler equations in the form

$$u'(c_t) = E_t u'(c_{t+1})[(1 + r_{t+1})/(1 + \delta)], \tag{3}$$

where marginal utility $u'(\ )$ is a decreasing function of consumption if consumption fluctuations are welfare-decreasing. Thus, optimization implies that marginal utility at time $t + 1$ is uniquely determined by tastes and by the interest rate, and is unrelated to anything that is predictable (and does not affect tastes) at time t or earlier, such as current and past income.

If marginal utility is (approximately) linear in consumption, consumption growth depends on the relative magnitudes of r and δ, but changes in consumption from period to period are independent of predictable changes in income, which are smoothed out by access to the credit market. Linearity of marginal utility makes it possible to combine the optimality condition and the intertemporal budget constraint to obtain a relationship among saving, income, and consumption,

$$s_t = \frac{rA_t}{1 + r_t} + y_t - c_t \tag{4}$$

and between savings and the evolution of income over time,

$$s_t = -\sum_{j=0}^{\infty} (1 + r)^{-j} E_t(y_{t+j} - y_{t+j-1}). \tag{5}$$

When the present value of income is expected to increase, it is optimal for savings to be negative: the household will run down its assets, or borrow if assets are not available, when future income is expected to be higher, for example, because the householder lost his job but expects to find another one soon. Conversely, the household will save if it predicts lower income in the future, for instance, in retirement. Lending and borrowing make it possible to redistribute spending from periods in the life cycle in which income is high to periods in which it is low. Earnings are typically hump-shaped: lower early in life and also later in life, when people fully or partially withdraw from the labor market, than in prime age. Hence, this model predicts that borrowing should be higher for young households, and that households in late middle age should be saving for their retirement. Moreover, households expecting their income to grow more quickly (college educated rather than manual workers) should borrow relatively more when they are young.

1.1.2 Extensions of the Basic Model

The model just outlined is, of course, much too simple to represent reality, and its implications are often rejected by empirical evidence. It can however be extended and made more realistic in various important directions.

1.1.2.1 Taste-Shifters and Uncertainty about the Future

The basic model's representation of individual consumption behavior is often rejected by microeconomic survey data, in that consumption is typically found to react to predictable changes in income. As discussed in Attanasio 1999 and its references, the fit of the model can be vastly improved by a more flexible specification of consumption's utility-generating role. While in equation (1), utility depends only on consumption flows, it is realistic to allow utility to depend on "taste-shifters" such as household's size and the demographic characteristics of its members. Elderly individuals may be less demanding as regards the quantity and quality of food consumption, and the quantity and composition of desired consumption by households with young children are obviously different from those of households whose head is older or younger. If consumption needs are higher in middle age than when the head of the household is young and single, or in old age when the children have left home, optimality calls for less borrowing by young households and less savings by middle-aged ones, and the model predicts closer tracking of income by consumption over the life cycle.

When discussing the basic model's predictions, we focused on the implications of a linear relationship between marginal utility and the level of consumption. Linearity makes it simple to characterize optimal behavior, but this is because it implies "certainty equivalence": only expected values of future income and consumption matter for that behavior. In reality, of course, uncertainty around expected values can play an important role in determining consumption, savings, and borrowing. Formally, if marginal utility of consumption is convex rather than linear, then an increase in consumption when consumption is low is valued more highly than the same increase when consumption is high. It is then optimal to self-insure and buffer the impact of income fluctuations on consumption by building a "precautionary" stock of wealth, to be decumulated upon the realization of negative shocks. This behavior implies more savings and less borrowing. Quite intuitively, if a household considers borrowing in the current period but fears bad news (e.g., because a promotion is expected but may not materialize, or unemployment duration is very uncertain), it will want to borrow less when the impact of repayment on marginal utility is stronger at low consumption levels than in the "certainty-equivalent" linear marginal utility case.

In general, the amounts borrowed may therefore depend importantly on uncertainty as well as on the relationship between households' impatience and lifetime income patterns. Expanding the basic model to account for the role of uncertainty makes it possible to explain why young households, for instance, borrow less than one might expect, and why individuals in risky occupations (such as the self-employed) may wish to borrow less than those in occupations with highly reliable income streams (such as, in many countries, those in the public sector). Theoretical extensions are relevant when they explain observed phenomena, and precautionary behavior can help interpret these and other cross-sectional differences, discussed and documented in the literature as well as in the chapters in this volume, among borrowing patterns across individuals within a country.

1.1.2.2 Restrictions of the Level of Borrowing

Other aspects of the evidence reviewed by chapters 2 and 3 of this volume, however, are not easy to explain in terms of uncertainty. In particular, it is hard to invoke precautionary behavior in order to explain recent increasing trends in debt levels, because labor-market deregulation and technological trends have, if anything, increased the variance of labor income shocks (the implications of this for consumption inequality and volatility in the United States are studied by Krueger and Perri 2004; see also the references therein). To interpret these aspects and the sizable differences in the borrowing behavior of similar individuals living in different countries and periods, it is important to further extend the basic model and account for the possibility that households may be "liquidity constrained," that is, unable to borrow as much as would be implied at the observed interest rate by unconstrained optimization.

The rationale for such constraints is discussed in section 1.2. Here, we focus on the impact of liquidity constraints on the lifetime consumption plans of households. While in the basic model the household was able to access the financial market to borrow at will against future income, the household could face an upper limit on its level of borrowing or face interest rates that are higher for borrowing than for lending or that increase with the amount borrowed. Liquidity constraints may be simply represented as a prohibition on borrowing, in which case maximization of lifetime utility as in (1) and (2) is further constrained to consumption of no more than currently available resources,

$$c_t \leq (1 + r_t)A_t + y_t = x_t, \tag{6}$$

where x_t is dubbed "cash-on-hand" in the literature; if positive borrowing is allowed up to some limit, total current resources are also increased by the maximum amount that can be borrowed. Additional constraints obviously reduce the welfare achievable by the household, and also influence observable behavior in obvious and less obvious ways. Formally, the Euler equation now takes the following form:

$$u'(c_t) = \max\{u'(x_t), E_t u'(c_{t+1})[(1 + r_{t+1})/(1 + \delta)]\}. \tag{7}$$

This states that, in any time period, the household will either spend its current resources, or equate marginal utilities if the borrowing constraint is not binding currently. Obviously, liquidity constraints reduce borrowing at times when they are binding. Less obviously, the path of lifetime consumption is affected even at times when the unconstrained Euler equation applies, because the anticipation of future binding constraint leads the household to try and reduce their likelihood by building a "buffer" stock of wealth (Deaton 1992, sec. 6.2).

In this and other respects, the implications of borrowing constraints are similar to those induced by precautionary behavior when marginal utility is nonlinear in the presence of uncertain income streams, as previously discussed. Liquidity constraints and precaution both imply that households borrow less on average, and that their observed consumption growth is faster on average and more sensitive to income shocks. Similar implications for borrowing, consumption, and wealth are driven by different environmental features in the two cases, however, and the two phenomena can be disentangled from each other by bringing additional information to bear on the evidence. As mentioned earlier, the volatility of households' income prospects is relevant to the strength of precautionary motives shaping their behavior, and consideration of liquidity constraints allows consumer-side modeling efforts to account for supply-side conditions (discussed later) in flexible and insightful ways.

1.1.2.3 Durable Goods

An important extension of the basic model of consumption allocation arises from the existence of durable goods (such as a house or a car) whose ownership not only yields a flow of consumption services over several periods, but also constitutes part of a household's wealth. Purchasing a durable good requires a reduction of the household's financial wealth or, if current wealth does not suffice to finance the purchase, entails borrowing.

In the presence of durable goods, the objective of the maximization problem in (1) includes the durables stock d in the utility function,

$$\max E_t \sum_{j=0}^{\infty} \beta^j u(c_{t+j}, d_{t+j}). \tag{8}$$

Like the taste-shifters discussed earlier, the stock of durables can affect the marginal utility of nondurable consumption. Unlike age and other demographic characteristics, however, durables stocks are endogenous to the household's constrained optimization problem. The wealth accumulation constraint (2) is amended to account for purchases of new durable goods (denoted i, which may be negative),

$$A_{t+1} = (1 + r_{t+1})(A_t + y_t - c_t - i_t), \tag{9}$$

and needs to be considered in conjunction with a similar asset-evolution equation for the stock of durable goods, which in any period equals the stock in the previous period, plus new durable purchases, minus depreciation. If the latter occurs at rate λ, the durables stock d evolves as follows:

$$d_{t+1} = i_t + (1 - \lambda)d_t.$$

Households need to formulate their optimal plan, given their information and expectations about the future, by equating the marginal utility of consumption between periods as in equation (3), and also by equating the marginal utility of durable and nondurable consumption. This determines a set of relationships between the level and dynamics of nondurable consumption, and the stock of the durable good in each period. In general, the presence of durables introduces a more complex and predictable link between utility and consumption flows across periods. (Other specifications that allow the household's utility to depend on a stock variable, such as those that account for habit formation, have qualitatively similar implications in some of the empirically relevant aspects.)

As to household expenditure on the durable good, i, it is intuitively predicted to fluctuate much more than nondurable consumption flows. As the household updates its predicted future income levels, it should adjust the durables stock to its "permanent" level, which—as durables' user costs include foregone asset returns—also depends on interest rates directly as well as through the construction of expected discounted labor income. Thus, durable purchases provide a further, highly variable reason for borrowing by young households that expect their income to increase in the future and have not yet been able to accumulate assets.

In the expressions above, durable good stocks were modeled as perfectly divisible, and the household was supposed to be able to increase or decrease them without incurring adjustment costs. In reality, many households own zero amounts of specific categories of durables, and adjust their stocks infrequently. Models with fixed and adjustment costs can rationalize these empirical regularities. Theoretical and empirical results (Bertola and Caballero 1990; Bertola, Guiso, and Pistaferri 2005) indicate that it is in general optimal for households to allow durable stocks to diverge from their "permanent" level when adjustment is costly, and to implement purchases (or sales) only when income, financial wealth, and depreciation and price dynamics have accumulated so as to imply a discretely large divergence between the actual and desired stocks of durables.

1.1.2.4 *Interactions between Credit Constraints and Durable Goods*

Just because durable consumption goods are part of the consumer's wealth, financial considerations play a very important role in determining their optimal sales and purchases. For example, a house is both a consumption good and a financial investment, and any housing transaction must be based not only on the consumption "dividend" provided by a house's or apartment's amenities but also on forward-looking expectations of housing prices relative to those of other assets.

Housing is often financed through mortgages. More generally, the durability of housing and other consumption goods features important interactions with credit supply conditions. (Chapter 5 specifically considers such interactions.) Recall that in equation (9) the household's level of consumption was restricted to current income and liquid wealth when borrowing was not allowed. Lenders, however, may allow households to borrow when they have collateral, such as a house or other durable good. If durable goods both provide consumption services and can act as collateral, households may choose a consumption basket with a larger durables component when credit constraints are more binding.

Empirically, households that hold more durable goods should then be observed also to owe more debt. But interactions between interest rates, credit constraints, durable goods, and adjustment costs can be complicated. Juster and Shay (1964) noted that interest rates are different on consumers' assets, liabilities, and durable purchases. They characterized qualitatively the implications of this state of affairs for consumer choices, and explored survey data empirically, focusing in particular on the sensitivity of aggregate consumption to changes in macroeconomic monetary conditions. While the extensive literature analyzing consumers' constrained borrowing mostly did not follow up on these early efforts, focusing on simple quantity constraints instead, there are a few notable exceptions: cash outlays are problematic for liquidity-constrained consumers, who are prepared to pay higher interest rates in exchange for longer loan duration (Attanasio 1995). Brugiavini and Weber (1994) and Alessie, Devereux, and Weber (1997) also analyze empirical relationships between borrowing opportunities and durable good purchases. These and other contributions, however, propose and study models in which borrowing opportunities depend on the existing stock of durable goods rather than on new purchases as would be implied by the mechanisms outlined earlier. Bertola, Guiso, and Pistaferri (2005) focus on the role of uncertainty in shaping durable and nondurable expenditure patterns; in their data, credit restrictions do not appear to be binding.

Theory and evidence indicate that individuals and households do wish to borrow (as well as save) in order to make consumption smoother than labor income. Allowing households to borrow will raise their welfare. However, access to borrowing is not always easy, and there are important empirical and welfare implications of how the household credit market operates.

1.2   The Economics of Consumer Credit Supply

Lenders to consumption-smoothing households face many of the same problems as lenders to producers. Instead of investing borrowed funds wisely, managers of firms may use them in ways that suit their objectives but make repayment impossible, or very unlikely. As with producer credit, consumer credit supply is hampered by moral hazard and adverse selection problems. If the possibility of consuming more when borrowing today and less when repaying in the future is attractive for a consumer when he or she expects to earn much more in later periods, borrowing is even more attractive if the higher current consumption is not associated with lower consumption in the future— namely, if consumers default on their repayment obligations. Hence, although the previous section explained that limited borrowing opportunities reduced consumers' welfare, credit constraints can be explained by credit suppliers' need to avoid lending funds that will not be repaid.

In general, it is imperfect information and the resulting adverse selection and moral hazard problems that make it difficult for the credit market to clear through prices. Such supply-side problems are familiar from standard and banking textbooks (Freixas and Rochet 1997) and do not need to be reviewed here in as much detail as the demand-side household problem earlier. In this section, we introduce them and discuss their relevance to consumer credit, and to the specific issues addressed by many of this volume's chapters.

1.2.1   Reasons for Lenders to Restrict Credit

When the probability of default differs across borrowers, and is known by borrowers more accurately than by lenders, then demand for credit by borrowers who are more likely to default is less sensitive to the interest rate. Adverse selection occurs because interest rate levels more strongly discourage borrowing by those who plan to repay than borrowing by those who are likely to default. Hence, higher interest rates attract fewer and worse borrowers, and higher default rates imply that higher contractual interest rates can actually result in a lower ex post return on each unit of credit extended. It is then optimal for lenders to set the interest rate so low as to be attractive to "good" borrowers, and to control the risk of default by "bad" borrowers by rationing credit to both high- and low-risk borrowers. In this setting, first analyzed by Stiglitz and Weiss (1981), rationing arises not from any market "disequilibrium" but because lenders set interest rates to obtain the right "mix" of borrowers.[1] This reasoning is theoretically and empirically relevant to consumer credit in that many households appear liquidity constrained, as discussed earlier, and are denied credit.

Moral hazard arises when borrowers can affect the likelihood of repayment. Its relevance is obvious as regards producer credit: an entrepreneur gains from any excess return in a risky project, but losses are limited by bankruptcy. Hence entrepreneurs have incentives to invest in riskier projects when a larger proportion of the cost is funded by loans, and lenders—who suffer losses if the project is unsuccessful—have incentives to limit the amount of credit they extend, so as to force entrepreneurs to bear (and control) a portion of the risk. To some extent, similar phenomena are relevant to household borrowing. Many firms are family owned and operated, which makes it difficult, not to say impossible, to distinguish producer and consumption credit. Employees' work effort on the job and search effort when unemployed can also influence the level and riskiness of their labor income and debt-repayment ability. But moral hazard is directly relevant, even to the behavior of consumption-smoothing households with exogenous labor income, if repayment reflects the willingness (rather than the ability) to honor one's debts. When deciding whether to repay, a rational agent weighs the gain of resources from nonrepayment against the punishment for default. If the punishment for default is permanent exclusion from the consumption-smoothing opportunities offered by the financial market, as in models by Kehoe and Levine (1993) and Kocherlakota (1996), quantity constraints emerge endogenously. In fact, a (finite) welfare loss from the lack of consumption-smoothing opportunities can induce repayment only up to a maximum debt level, beyond which any borrower would default and no lenders would rationally extend credit.

Equilibrium models of default recognize that all debt *could* be repaid if the punishment were sufficiently large. In reality, punishment is even less severe than perpetual exclusion from further consumption-smoothing opportunities, and more detailed modeling of borrowers' options upon default offers useful insights into the determinants of liquidity constraints. The ability of the financial market to punish default is limited by its competitive and information-sharing structure (see chapters 9 and 10 in this volume, introduced later in section 1.4) as well as by legal restrictions: For example, bankruptcy cannot be recorded in credit files for more than ten years in the United States. More generally, informal consumption-smoothing opportunities, such as those offered by friends and family, may be available even after default.[2]

Models of adverse selection/moral hazard were developed in the context of producer credit. While the insights also apply to consumer credit, there are important differences in the underlying features and organization of the producer and consumer credit markets. In both, more difficult enforcement of debt contracts makes lending less attractive for lenders and leads them to restrict credit, but the strength of this effect depends on the details of procedures enacted upon default. On the one hand, the legal provisions for personal bankruptcy on consumer loans (see section 1.3 and chapter 7, this volume) are different from those applicable to loans extended to corporations. On the other hand, and importantly, the amount of debt needed to smooth a typical household's consumption or finance its durable expenditures are much smaller than those needed for firms' investment purposes.

The small size of the debts implies that it is not cost-effective to implement ex ante screening of consumers' repayment prospects on a case-by-case basis in an attempt to control adverse selection. In highly developed credit markets, the consumer credit industry has developed sophisticated "scoring" procedures for assessing repayment risk of whole categories of customers or, indeed, of credit transactions on the basis of observable characteristics that, if statistically associated with low repayment probabilities, will lead lenders to reject credit applications. Small transaction sizes also rule out ex post monitoring of moral-hazard-prone borrowers, and intense collection efforts are not cost-effective for most consumer loans. In practice, most nonrepayments are "punished" by recording them, and using that information to score and likely refuse further loan applications by defaulting consumers.

1.2.2   The Role of Collateral

Faced with imperfect information on the risk of individual loans, lenders may be reluctant to extend credit to households lacking a repayment history that allows credit bureaus to score them favorably. Asset ownership may also enhance a household's borrowing opportunities, as collateral may allow recovery of at least part of what is owed by defaulting borrowers. For most households, the main source of collateral is housing wealth. Housing purchases are large investments, amounting to a substantial proportion of lifetime income, and usually secured by mortgages. Chapter 5 discusses the particular issues that arise in housing markets and compares them to other forms of credit to the household sector. Lenders also frequently secure their debt against other assets—for example, when the loan is specifically made for the purpose of purchasing durable goods such as cars, or in hire-purchase agreements for household goods. However, in these cases, the resale value of repossessed goods would rarely cover the outstanding debt. (Legal and other costs involved in recovery are substantial. Even for housing debt, U.K. lenders reckon to recover only 75 percent of the value of the property if they foreclose.)

1.2.3   The Role of Retailers and Other Agents in Credit Provision

Banks and other lenders have an obvious comparative advantage, compared to retailers, in processing credit applications. As discussed in chapter 9, most of the increase in indebtedness among U.S. households over the past one hundred years has been due to banks extending credit in cases where previously credit was provided directly and more informally by the retailer at the point of sale. Nevertheless, there are advantages in lenders and retailers cooperating closely. Since the costs to lenders of finding and processing credit applications are lower when transactions are processed on dealers' premises, the banks' relationship with sellers of durable goods is very important. Installment payment plans for certain durable goods purchases may be safer than cash loans from the point of view of lenders, even when they are not backed by housing or vehicle collateral, because a direct link of borrowed funds to a specific use offers valuable information to lenders. Just as the ability to monitor a firm's investment expenditures would be valuable for producer credit suppliers, a consumer's purchase of items such as household appliances may be more favorably correlated with repayment-relevant features of the borrower's lifestyle (and offer lenders more peace of mind) than purchases of, say, fast motorcycles.

Such details of credit supply are only beginning to be studied in the economics literature. Often, favorable credit terms are not granted to purchasers of durable goods by the lending institutions (banks) that bear repayment risks but by the sellers themselves in the form of familiar "zero-rate" financing deals. When such deals are advertised, and customers purchase the item, the bank is entitled to receive future installment payments from the customer. But if the advertised rate is lower than what would be required by the bank's cost of funds, processing costs, and assessment of repayment probabilities, then the amount paid by the bank to the seller's account is lower than the amount that the seller would receive had the customer paid with cash.

Seller-financed credit has been studied from a monopolistic price discrimination perspective in the context of business credit. Suppliers rather than banks may provide credit when they are in a better position to screen, select, and discipline the borrower, or to repossess and use the loan's collateral, as well as for price discrimination purposes. Brennan, Maksimovic, and Zechner (1988) study incentives for sellers of investment goods to finance their customers' purchases in the presence of ad hoc liquidity constraints, and an extensive literature (surveyed by Petersen and Rajan 1997) studies more general forms of trade credit.

As regards consumer credit, Bertola, Hochguertel, and Koeniger (2005) show that dealer subsidization of consumer credit can be explained by incentives for durable good sellers to engage in monopolistic price discrimination when potential customers face imperfect consumption-smoothing opportunities. If realistic differences between borrowing and lending rates segment the population of potential customers into distinct groups inclined to purchase on cash and on credit terms, sellers can set those terms so as to offer different prices to cash-rich and liquidity-constrained customers, in much the same way as lower prices are sometimes charged to consumers who own particularly old trade-ins or take the time to clip coupons. Hence, the structure of discriminating prices is explicitly linked to intertemporal transfers of resources, and Bertola, Hochguertel, and Koeniger use data from differently developed regions of Italy to confirm their theoretical predictions empirically. As in other models of imperfect price discrimination, some customers may benefit and others may be less well off relative to a single-price configuration. The borrowers pay less than they would if the subsidy were not available, and they pay less on a present discounted basis than those who pay cash. This arises because the intertemporal rate of return differs across these groups, the good being purchased is different across groups of consumers, and price discrimination is similar to that which routinely occurs across, for instance, classes of air travel: Business class is not only much more expensive but also more comfortable and less restricted, thus ensuring that customers self-sort in a way that is profitable for the airline. The profitability of additional sales generated by credit availability also plays a role in models of credit card usage (Murphy and Ott 1977; Chakravorti and To 2003), as well as in models of voluntary or legal provisions that make the lender jointly liable for the seller's failure to deliver suitable goods (Spence 1977; Iossa and Palumbo 2004).

While banks have many advantages in offering credit to households, doing so may require that they allocate capital to lending to the household sector for a considerable amount of time. For example, mortgage terms can exceed twenty-five years. In practice, most long-term consumer debt is securitized, that is, packaged in risk-rated instruments on the wholesale financial market: In the U.S. housing market, securitization is aided by implicit government guarantees through institutions such as Freddie Mac, chartered by congress in 1970 (see Passmore 2003); it is a newer phenomenon in Europe. As to the nonsecuritized portions of banks' consumer loans, the Basel capital-adequacy requirements allow short-term debt, such as credit card balances, to be rated according to certified internal procedures. Space does not allow treatment of such aspects here. (Readers may refer to a recent special issue of the *Journal of Banking and Finance* 28, no. 4, 2004.) Also outside the scope of this volume are other financial and industrial organization aspects of the banking industry and a discussion of producer rather than consumer debt, in which there is relatively limited scope for differentiation across countries.

1.3 Repayment Arrears and Default

An understanding of debt is incomplete without an understanding of what happens when the debtor defaults or misses a scheduled repayment. Incentives to both lend and borrow are heavily influenced by whether and under what circumstances the borrower can be made to repay—and which assets can be seized if he does not. The creditor has recourse to several actions. Collateral can be repossessed in the case of housing mortgages or car loans. But for most other consumer credit, if a consumer fails to repay a specific loan, the amounts are often too

small for a lender to try and recover them through formal legal procedures (although the amounts can be substantial when summed across
all lenders), and the punishment for debt default takes the form of
deteriorating credit scores and limitations to future access to credit.
When the debtor defaults and the creditor legally pursues the debt,
then the debtor enters bankruptcy.

When do borrowers default? Sullivan, Warren, and Westbrook
(1989) look at a sample of bankruptcy filers in the United States and
conclude that the nonrepayment of debt provides a safety net from
poverty to members of the lower middle class. Bridges and Disney
(2004) examine the phenomena of "recycling" of arrears on loans and
bill payments among low income households in the United Kingdom.
Little is known, however, about the behavior of debtors before and
after they fall into arrears. Chapter 2 in this volume offers new relevant information, reviewing surveys of households having difficulties
repaying their debts in the United States and several European countries, and concluding that default is often the result of the household
suffering some unexpected and adverse shock (such as the main earner
losing his job) that makes repayment difficult. This is consistent with
the story in section 1.1, and suggests that if there was some way to
mitigate the effects of these shocks, there would be a welfare gain to
consumers—hence motivating the regulation of default through such
things as bankruptcy law.

1.3.1 Bankruptcy

The regulation of bankruptcy has differed substantially throughout
history. Some jurisdictions in classical times sold debtors into slavery,
while fourteenth-century Florence used the criminal courts to enforce
merchant debts, fining such debtors and, if necessary, forcing their relatives to pay (see Stern 1994). Defaulting debtors were liable to be tor-
tured if caught.[3]

Modern sanctions are less draconian. The courts may manage a
bankrupt debtor's finances, aiming to repay creditors, before discharging his debts. During bankruptcy, the court will share the debtors
assets (and income if it is sufficiently high) among the creditors, and
the bankrupt consumer is barred from obtaining any more credit. U.S.
regulations are much more generous than those of other countries.
When U.S. debtors enter bankruptcy, they can not only apply for a
court-ordered repayment rescheduling (under Chapter 13 of the relevant legal code) but can also (under Chapter 7) be relieved of liabilities

while keeping many of their assets: in Texas, for instance, a married couple filing jointly can keep their house and $60,000 worth of other assets regardless of their ability to repay.[4] Concerns with sharply increasing bankruptcies in the United States prompted a restrictive reform in April 2005, stipulating substantially higher filing costs for personal bankruptcy and preventing individuals earning more than their state's median income from filing under Chapter 7. Introduction or reform of formal household bankruptcy procedures in other countries is also a difficult and relatively unexplored policy issue.

Chapter 7 provides more detail on U.S. institutions, which vary between states, and reviews theoretical and empirical insights; chapter 9 updates the U.S. institutional information and discusses the reforms enacted in 2005. Theoretically, it is clear that the possibility of bankruptcy ex ante restricts credit availability: if repayment were completely optional, no lending could ever take place. To the extent that nonrepayment reflects genuine inability to repay due to unforeseeable developments in the individual's life, however, bankruptcy procedures and less formal default opportunities offer potentially valuable consumption-smoothing opportunities across different developments of households' income paths. Lenders faced by a population of potential borrowers will need to receive a higher interest rate upon repayment in order to recoup losses on loans that are not repaid, and this will indirectly transfer resources from consumers who are ex post lucky and can repay toward consumers whose income is ex post reduced by exogenous events. Clearly, the balance of these effects is not easy to assess in practice, even in a steady-state situation.

The literature reviewed in chapter 7 draws lessons from the U.S. experience, which are very useful as the UK, France, and other European countries engage in reforms of default regulations that aim at making bankruptcy quicker, easier, and less traumatic for the debtor. Bankruptcy proceedings in England and Wales changed in April 2004, with much of the emphasis on proceedings for entrepreneurs (although these formed only a third of bankruptcies). Debtors are now normally discharged from their first bankruptcy within one year rather than after three, although they can be ordered to make payments from their income for up to three years, and these income payments were made easier to administer and could now extend beyond discharge. However, for repeat bankrupts, or for those judged to have behaved recklessly or irresponsibly, the process can last up to fifteen years.

The reforms also removed some of the restrictions that had been placed on bankrupts and seriously tried to distinguish fault with those who were deemed to be in some way culpable suffering many more penalties: previously, all bankrupts had received substantively the same treatment. It was also made easier to come to individual voluntary agreements, or court-supervised repayment plans proposed by the debtor and binding when agreed to by 75 percent of the creditors by value, in which the debtor does not suffer the full penalties of bankruptcy. Following the reform, both bankruptcy filings and voluntary agreements have risen 30 percent in the months following the change, and are the highest ever recorded in England; although at 9,000 bankruptcy orders and 2,500 voluntary agreements per quarter, this is far lower than U.S. per capita levels.

Arrangements similar to the English voluntary agreements were introduced in France in December 1989, and the law was most recently amended in August 2003. It allowed courts to propose a recovery plan, which if agreed by the debtor and creditors, would suspend the normal operation of bankruptcy (where assets were seized, and wages could be garnished until the debt was repaid) if the consumer was "over-indebted" (for example, if it was obviously impossible for the debtor to meet all his outstanding and accruing personal debts). Unlike in England, either party could stop the plan before it was completed if, for example, the debtor's situation changed. At the end of the plan, remaining debts are discharged although the debtor's name was inscribed on a national list of defaulting debtors for up to ten years.

1.3.2 Counseling

Courts can also order other measures, such as counselling, to address repayment problems. Consultation, at the debtor's expense, is now required in the United States before bankruptcy filing. Little work has been done specifically on the European regulations and despite differences in bankruptcy in Europe and the United States, there is much to learn from the U.S. experience. In France, mandatory counseling is widely imposed by courts in which small debtors can also obtain from courts a "time order provision" to rearrange their debts. Many defaulting debtors may be simply unfortunate, though others may have behaved "irresponsibly" by accumulating debt with little apparent regard for their ability to repay (Sullivan, Warren, and Westbrook 1989). Chapter 6 shows that the behavior of households that use credit cards is often difficult to reconcile with the theory of borrowing in section

1.2. Chapter 2 also shows that default may often be the consequence of debtors' limited understanding of contractual provisions. These findings suggest that debtors, especially those having problems repaying their debts, could usefully be offered advice or counseled about their use of credit. In the United States, this counseling is usually offered by nongovernment organizations—that is, credit counselors—who are cofunded by creditors and those debtors seeking advice. This contrasts with the United Kingdom, where Citizens Advice Bureaus offer free counseling and are for the most part directly funded by national and local government.

The U.S. arrangement is not problem-free. Chapter 8 charts the development of the credit counseling industry in the United States, and especially its role in negotiating repayment plans with creditors (in which the lender typically discounts the debt) on behalf of debtors who are in arrears. Counselors are only paid for these repayment plans; hence, they have a clear conflict of interest vis-à-vis the debtor (who want to minimize their repayment, taking account of the costs, including the stigma, of bankruptcy) and the creditor (who want to maximize the repayment they receive, whether or not through a formal repayment plan). While in the past, a lack of competition among counselors alleviated these agency problems, more recently, competition seems to have caused counseling firms to concentrate much more clearly on maximizing their payments (or be driven out of business). Amazingly, the NFCC, the leading purveyors of counseling advice, still advise bankruptcy in over 30 percent of cases and "educate" borrowers about planning their finances in another 30 percent of cases, services for which they are not paid. Chapter 8 also discusses some recent developments by lenders to address the agency problem, but nevertheless, this chapter shows that counseling seems to work.

1.4 Sharing Information among Lenders

As discussed in section 1.2, lenders assess credit applications on the basis of observable indicators in order to control adverse selection, and exclusion of defaulters from further borrowing can play an important role in controling moral hazard. For both purposes, historical data on past repayment behavior is very useful. It may be gathered about their own customers by individual banks or lending institutions, which thereby gain informational advantages on potential competitors. Or it may be shared by all market participants on the basis of the economic considerations and institutional constraints. Chapters 9 and 10 review historical, theoretical, and empirical aspects of information-sharing arrangements, which play a particularly important role in consumer credit supply. Pooling information offers stronger economies of scale when small amounts are involved in each transaction and extensive information on similar transactions can help predict individual repayment probabilities. And information-sharing arrangements are more pervasively shaped by official regulatory frameworks in the case of household borrowing because an individual's privacy is more likely than a corporation's to be protected by regulators. Chapter 9 discusses the history and motivation of regulating information sharing in the United States. Similar developments are observed in other countries with more recent consumer credit industries. In continental Europe, privacy concerns play an important role.[5] Chapter 2 reviews indicators of data protection regulations and, similar to chapter 10, discusses the effect that different regulation of information sharing has on credit markets in different countries. The integration of European Union credit markets introduces particular issues for information sharing, and chapter 2 assesses the likely effect of recent policy proposals from the European Commission.

1.5   Other Issues and Further Research

It is easy to model perfectly flexible credit arrangements, but, as discussed in section 1.2, they do not describe many individuals' borrowing opportunities. Realistic credit imperfections are many, varied, and interact in interesting and subtle ways with imperfections in other markets. This introductory chapter has painted a broad picture of the main specificities of consumer credit arrangements. The other chapters in the book focus on particularly important aspects of the issues that arise with consumer credit, but, of course, the volume cannot address all of the relevant issues, many of which are just beginning to be studied in the literature.

As the accessibility and volume of household credit instruments grow, the macroeconomic implications of consumer credit phenomena become increasingly important, but are relatively poorly understood.[6] This largely reflects the difficulty of disentangling changing structural features, of the type discussed comparatively by many chapters in this book, from cyclical phenomena with which supply-driven developments interact at the macroeconomic level. For example, much of the

U.K. boom during the 1980s was reflected in consumption, and financial market deregulation played an important role in that episode (Attanasio and Weber 1995); evidence from mature household-finance markets such as the United States and United Kingdom indicates that the transmission of monetary impulses works through consumption as well as through production and investment, as discussed in chapter 5 with specific attention to housing prices and consumption. This could exaggerate the business cycle, a point made by Aghion, Bacchetta, and Banerjee (2003). But these issues and the mechanism that maps consumption to the aggregate economy are an open research question.

At the industry level, interactions between supply and demand factors are also only beginning to be studied in the consumer credit context. One such study is Alessie, Hochguertel, and Weber 2005. Like chapter 4, this study examines the Italian case, exploiting both time-series and regional variation. Like chapter 5, it exploits disaggregated supply-relevant information to assess characteristics of demand: Rather than exploiting housing equity variations as a factor relaxing quantity constraints, it exploits the supply shift induced by a usury law to estimate the interest elasticity of consumer credit demand. The authors use information from a variety of sources, including administrative data made available by lending institutions.

These and other policy aspects are relevant on both sides of the Atlantic. We believe that bringing together experiences of the operation of credit markets in different countries can help academics, policymakers and practitioners better understand how credit markets can usefully help consumers smooth consumption over time, and assist in determining what measures, if any, can make markets perform better.

Notes

1. Ausubel (1991) argues that a model based on rationing of credit markets because interest rates are "too low" flies in the face of empirical evidence that credit providers, especially credit card providers, tend to levy interest rates well above those that would exist in competitive markets. Bertaut and Haliassos (chapter 6) further discuss why households borrow on credit cards (especially when they have assets earning lower interest rates).

2. Within family and other local circles, repayment is supported by informal trust mechanisms. In developing countries, Rotating Savings and Credit Associations (ROSCAs) rely on similar mechanisms.

3. Enforcing merchant debts was considered so important that the Mercanzia, the court that usually tried debt cases, conducted day-to-day diplomatic relations with foreign states in the fourteenth century: Italian city-states made great efforts to enforce debts in

foreign jurisdictions. The Mercanzia even had the right of reprisal (a kind of miniature declaration of war) against other states (especially remarkable since it was always headed by a foreigner).

4. Such generous provisions are not unique. Louis XIV of France, for instance, exempted peasant livestock from seizure for debts. What is unique about the United States is the avowed purpose of bankruptcy—namely, to allow debtors to make "a fresh start." Louis XIV wanted to ensure assets did not move from peasants, who were taxable, to nobles or townsmen, who were tax exempt (see Root 1987).

5. Throughout we talk about "privacy" rather than "confidentiality," which should properly be used. The English law countries do not protect privacy (something that is private and not known to others) but do protect confidentiality (when this private fact is necessarily disclosed as part of the relationship between two parties). In law, what matters in these countries is how the information was acquired. And banks that discuss their clients' financial circumstances are breaching confidentiality, unless this information sharing is in the interest of their client. Other jurisdictions also provide greater protection to confidential—rather than private—information. Much of the regulation defines criteria for disclosure to third parties to be beneficial.

6. Stiglitz and Weiss (1992) discuss the macroeconomic implications of rationing varying over the business cycle, but Bernanke and Gertler (1995) argue production declines follow declines in final demand and that declines in consumer spending, especially on durable purchases, are what drive the economy. The relative degree to which the household and the production sector affected recessions is documented by Perry and Schultze (1993), while Hall (1993) argues that the consumption fall caused half the fall in output in the 1990–1991 recession in the United States; see also Blanchard 1993.

References

Aghion, Philippe, Phillippe Bacchetta, and Abhijit Banerjee. 2003. "Financial Development and the Instability of Open Economies." *Journal of Monetary Economics* 51: 1077–1106.

Alessie, Rob, Michael P. Devereux, and Guglielmo Weber. 1997. "Intertemporal Consumption, Durables and Liquidity Constraints: A Cohort Analysis." *European Economic Review* 41, no. 1: 37–59.

Alessie, Rob, Stefan Hochguertel, and Guglielmo Weber. 2005. "Consumer Credit: Evidence from Italian Micro Data." *Journal of the European Economic Association* 3, no. 1: 144–178.

Attanasio, Orazio P. 1995. "The Intertemporal Allocation of Consumption: Theory and Evidence." *Carnegie-Rochester Conference Series on Public Policy* 42: 39–89.

Attanasio, Orazio P. 1999. "Consumption." In *Handbook of Macroeconomics*, vol. 1, ed. J. B. Taylor and M. Woodford, 741–812. Amsterdam: Elsevier Science B.V.

Attanasio, Orazio P., and Guglielmo Weber. 1995. "The U.K. Consumption Boom of the 1980s, Aggregate Implications of Microeconomic Evidence." *The Economic Journal* 104, no. 427 (November 1994): 1269–1302.

Ausubel, L. M. 1991. "The Failure of Competition in the Credit Card Market." *American Economic Review* 81 (March): 50–81.

Bernanke, Ben S., and Mark Gertler. 1995. "Inside the Black Box: The Credit Channel of Monetary Policy Transmission." *Journal of Economic Perspectives* 9: 27–48.

Bertola, Giuseppe, and Ricardo Caballero. 1990. "Kinked Adjustment Costs and Aggregate Dynamics." In *4th NBER Macroeconomics Annual*, 237–288. Cambridge, Mass.: NBER.

Bertola, Giuseppe, Luigi Guiso, and Luigi Pistaferri. 2005. "Uncertainty and Dynamic Durable Adjustment." *Review of Economic Studies* 72: 973–1007.

Bertola, Giuseppe, Stefan Hochguertel, and Winfried Koeniger. 2005. "Dealer Pricing of Consumer Credit." *International Economic Review* 46, no. 4: 1103–1142.

Blanchard, Oliver. 1993. "Consumption and the Recession of 1990–91." *American Economic Review* (Papers and Proceedings) 83, no. 2: 270–274.

Brennan, Michael J., Vojislav Maksimovic, and Josef Zechner. 1988. "Vendor Financing." *Journal of Finance* 43, no. 5: 1127–1141.

Bridges, S., and R. Disney. 2004. "Use of Credit and Arrears on Debt among Low-Income Families in the United Kingdom." *Fiscal Studies* 25 (March): 1–25.

Brugiavini, Agar, and Guglielmo Weber. 1994. "Durables and Non-durables Consumption: Evidence from Italian Household Data." In *Saving and the Accumulation of Wealth: Essays on Italian Household and Government Saving Behavior*, ed. Albert Ando, Luigi Guiso, and Ignazio Visco, 305–329. Cambridge: Cambridge University Press.

Calder, Lendol. 1999. *Financing the American Dream: A Cultural History of Consumer Credit*. Princeton, N.J.: Princeton University Press.

Chakravorti, Sujit, and Ted To. 2003. "A Theory of Credit Cards." Mimeo., Federal Reserve Bank of Chicago.

Deaton, Angus. 1992. *Understanding Consumption*. Oxford: Oxford University Press.

Freixas, Xavier, and Jean-Charles Rochet. 1997. *Microeconomics of Banking*. Cambridge, Mass.: The MIT Press.

Gelpi, Rosa Maria, and François Julien-Labruyere. 2000. *The History of Consumer Credit: Doctrines and Practices*. London: Macmillan Press.

Guiso, Luigi, Michael Haliassos, and Tullio Jappelli, eds. 2001. *Household Portfolios*. Cambridge, Mass.: The MIT Press.

Guiso, Luigi, Michael Haliassos, and Tullio Jappelli, eds. 2003. *Stockholding in Europe*. London: Macmillan.

Hall, Robert E. 1993. "Macro Theory and the Recession of 1990–91." *American Economic Review* (Papers and Proceedings) 83, no. 2: 275–279.

Iossa, Elisabetta, and Giuliana Palumbo. 2004. "Product Quality, Lender Liability and Consumer Credit." *Oxford Economic Papers* 56: 331–343.

Juster, F. Thomas, and Robert P. Shay. 1964. "Consumer Sensitivity to Finance Rates: An Empirical and Analytical Investigation." NBER Occasional Papers no. 88, Cambridge, Mass.

Kehoe, Timothy J., and David K. Levine. 1993. "Debt-constrained Asset Markets." *Review of Economic Studies* 60, no. 4: 865–888.

Kocherlakota, N. R. 1996. "Implications of Efficient Risk Sharing without Commitment." *Review of Economic Studies* 63, no. 4: 595–609.

Krueger, Dirk, and F. Perri. 2004. "On the Welfare Consequences of the Increase in Inequality in the U.S." In *18th NBER Macroeconomics Annual*, 83–121. Cambridge, Mass.: NBER.

Manning, Robert D. 2000. *Credit Card Nation: The Consequences of America's Addiction to Credit*. New York: Basic Books.

Modigliani, Franco and Richard Brumberg. 1954. "Utility Analysis and the Consumption Function: an Interpretation of Cross-Section Data." In *Post-Keynesian Economics*, ed. K. K. Kurihara. New Brunswick, N.J.: Rutgers University Press.

Murphy, Michael M., and Mack Ott. 1977. "Retail Credit, Credit Cards and Price Discrimination." *Southern Economic Journal* 43, no. 3: 1303–1312.

Passmore, Wayne. 2003. "The GCE Implicit Subsidy and Value of Government Ambiguity." Federal Reserve Board Finance and Economics Discussion Series no. 2003-64, Washington, D.C.

Perry, George L., and Charles L. Schultze. 1993. "Was the Recession Different? Are They All Different?" *Brookings Papers on Economic Activity* 1: 145–211.

Petersen, Mitchell A., and Raghuran G. Rajan. 1997. "Trade Credit: Theories and Evidence." *Review of Financial Studies* 10, no. 3: 661–691.

Poterba, James M., ed. 1994. *Public Policies and Household Saving*. Chicago: University of Chicago Press.

Root, Hilton L. 1987. *Peasants and King in Burgundy*. Berkeley, Los Angeles, and London: University of California Press.

Spence, Michael. 1977. "Consumer Misperception, Product Failure and Producer Liability." *Review of Economic Studies* 44, no. 3: 561–572.

Stern, Laura. 1994. *The Criminal Law System of Medieval and Renaissance Florence*. Baltimore and London: Johns Hopkins University Press.

Stiglitz, J. E., and Weiss, A. 1981. "Credit Rationing in Markets with Imperfect Information." *American Economic Review* 71 (June): 393–410.

Stone, Lawrence. 1965. *The Crisis of the Aristocracy 1558–1641*. Oxford: Oxford University Press.

Sullivan, Teresa, Elizabeth Warren, and Jay Lawrence Westbrook. 1989. *As We Forgive Our Debtors: Bankruptcy and Consumer Credit in America*. New York and Oxford: Oxford University Press.

Sullivan, Teresa, Elizabeth Warren, and Jay Lawrence Westbrook. 2000. *The Fragile Middle Class: Americans in Debt*. New Haven and London: Yale University Press.

2

Consumer Credit Markets in the United States and Europe

D14

Nicola Jentzsch and Amparo San José Riestra

621 628

This chapter provides an overview of the current state of consumer credit markets and credit-reporting systems in Europe and the United States. It shows that, on both sides of the Atlantic, the ratio of consumer credit to gross domestic product (GDP) has increased in the last two decades. As the stock of debt has risen, so too has the repayment burden. An increasing number of households report repayment difficulties or file for bankruptcy. This has sparked a debate across these countries as to the role of regulation, and as to the forms that regulation might take. These include increasing consumer protection, consumer counseling, and information sharing among creditors with a view to forestalling or providing "early warning" of households' debt difficulties. The chapter examines these reporting and regulatory systems, as well as moves toward cross-border information flows, whether through cooperation or through the internationalization of the activities of credit bureaus.

The chapter is structured as follows. Section 2.1 reviews aggregate statistics on the level and composition of household sector debt in the United States and in several European countries. An important caveat is that the data are collected from national sources such as the annually published national accounts, as described in the appendix to this chapter. Definitions and level of disaggregation are not always consistent across these national data sources.

Section 2.2 discusses comparative statistics on reported repayment difficulties for a number of countries. Again, the sources for these data and definitions are discussed in the appendix. Since survey information is only collected on an ad hoc basis by an array of institutions, the reported extent of "repayment difficulties" in national surveys ranges from objective criteria (such as data on the fraction of households with at least three months' delay in payment of installments due) to wholly subjective self-reported criteria (such as asking indebted individuals about their perceived capacity to repay outstanding debt). Moreover, only in some studies are these numbers representative of all households. For these reasons, we can only draw rather general conclusions from the data, as discussed further in that section. The data show that the majority of individuals who have consumer debt meet their obligations. Among those that do not, unexpected life events such as unemployment, divorce, or illness appear to be important sources of default or bankruptcy (see also the discussion in chapter 7). Many respondents, however, also report that poor financial management or excessive borrowing have contributed to default events and to their perceived difficulties in repaying debts.

These findings suggest that limited information, and some form of limited rationality, may also play important roles in shaping consumer credit demand and supply. Accordingly, the credit industry is subject to extensive regulation, and section 2.3 explores in some detail the empirical evidence on the regulation of information sharing and information provision. As described in chapter 1, sharing data on the behavior of borrowers between creditors reduces informational asymmetries, provides a better picture of the actual financial situation of the household sector, and disciplines borrowers by allowing default to affect credit supply from all sources. We review data protection regulations affecting credit reporting in sixteen industrialized countries, including most of the EU members as of 2004, the 2005 accession states, and the United States.

Section 2.3 also constructs a summary index of the regulation of credit reporting based on a variety of regulatory indicators. It examines the relationship between this composite index and a range of indicators of national indebtedness and industry credit reporting. Finally, section 2.4 discusses the possible impact of EU-level legislation on credit-reporting systems, since credit systems differ in their national regulation. It also briefly describes other channels by which credit reporting make take on an international dimensions.

2.1 Credit Markets in Europe

2.1.1 Some Facts about Consumer Credit
This section examines the growth of consumer credit at a national level in a number of European countries, providing selective comparisons with the United States and Japan. Consumer credit grew rapidly

throughout Europe in the second half of the 1980s. This development was driven by several factors, including not only a favorable macroeconomic climate with declining interest rates but also increasing competition and deregulation. (See Diez Guardia 2000 for a discussion of country-specific developments; the appendix to chapter 4 reports Italian deregulation measures in detail). Interest rate ceilings were abolished in all countries, albeit at different times (around 1980 in the United Kingdom, Belgium, and Germany, but only about ten years later in France, Italy, and Spain; see table 5.1). Remaining regulations only apply to usury rates and are still determined at the national level, while transparency requirements as regards the cost of credit are mandated by EU legislation.

Consumer credit growth continued in many countries into the 1990s and the early 2000s (table 2.1). As a result, as table 2.1 shows, in the 1990s, some countries had extraordinarily high average growth rates in consumer credit as a percentage of GDP, including Greece and Ireland. Other countries—such as the United Kingdom, Luxemburg, and Italy—also saw sharp increases in lending. Countries differed in

Table 2.1
Consumer credit growth, 1991–2002 (percentage of GDP)

	1991	1992	1993	1994	1995	1996	1997	1998	1999	2000	2001	2002
Austria	n/a	n/a	n/a	n/a	n/a	n/a	n/a	n/a	−4.4	44.8	7.7	−0.4
Belgium	7.1	6.9	2.6	−9.0	6.8	0.3	3.7	10.2	6.9	6.6	3.9	2.1
Germany	14.5	9.5	9.0	3.9	4.7	1.0	1.8	6.0	−0.4	3.2	−0.1	0.9
Denmark	n/a	−4.9	−10.1	−2.2	4.6	5.1	6.6	9.0	4.0	11.7	−3.2	−3.2
Spain	3.4	−1.0	−1.7	−7.2	5.7	5.2	5.4	26.7	17.2	7.8	−4.6	6.2
Greece	1.9	20.5	21.4	54.0	89.7	34.6	13.8	38.3	30.7	42.4	42.5	24.2
France	−1.8	6.2	4.6	18.8	2.2	8.6	10.0	11.9	10.9	8.4	4.2	1.2
Finland	n/a	n/a	n/a	−10.5	−5.9	−4.0	6.0	0.6	−8.0	1.3	1.8	4.8
Italy	6.4	−7.0	−18.5	2.9	−9.9	11.7	30.7	12.1	18.8	16.5	10.4	10.4
Ireland	n/a	n/a	6.8	3.9	10.1	11.4	12.5	34.3	35.1	13.8	20.0	7.1
Luxembourg	n/a	n/a	n/a	n/a	n/a	n/a	n/a	20.0	66.7	0.0	10.0	0.0
Netherlands	10.0	17.6	7.1	5.0	7.3	3.0	4.9	−10.9	8.4	25.5	−6.0	16.6
Portugal	n/a	n/a	n/a	n/a	n/a	n/a	0.2	23.4	9.9	20.4	−1.7	−2.1
Sweden	−12.1	−8.7	−29.4	−5.0	−2.3	1.1	−6.7	5.5	9.0	17.9	−3.1	2.2
United Kingdom	1.8	−1.7	−0.4	8.9	17.5	13.6	13.7	16.0	13.6	−1.7	10.7	10.6
EU	7.6	3.7	1.7	5.1	6.2	6.2	7.9	14.3	8.0	6.2	4.1	4.9
United States	−1.5	0.6	7.2	14.5	14.4	7.6	4.4	5.4	7.1	1.7	6.9	3.4
Japan	n/a	−0.4	−6.3	−6.8	−6.5	−5.3	−5.2	−10.2	−9.4	−2.8	−6.4	−10.2

Source: European Credit Research Institute 2003.

the level of debt with which households started in 1991: typically, the Mediterranean countries started from a relatively lower level of credit/GDP ratio than countries such as the United Kingdom. For the period as a whole, Europe's consumer debt as a percentage of GDP grew at a slightly faster rate than that of the United States (6.3 percent growth per year compared to 6 percent). Nevertheless, even among the countries in table 2.1, there were some countries that showed trends very divergent from the average: In Finland, Sweden, and especially Japan, growth rates were negative for much of the period. These countries' factors seem largely to stem from specific adverse financial and macroeconomic shocks and the loss of consumer confidence arising from such episodes.

Despite these changes, there are, in general, considerably lower levels of lending to consumers in EU countries when compared to the United States, as well as a greater dispersion. This is illustrated in figure 2.1, which compares level of consumer credit as a proportion of private consumption and as a proportion of GDP across various countries. Only the United Kingdom shows a similar level of consumer credit to GDP as the United States; the discrepancy in the ratio to private consumption for the United States may stem from differences

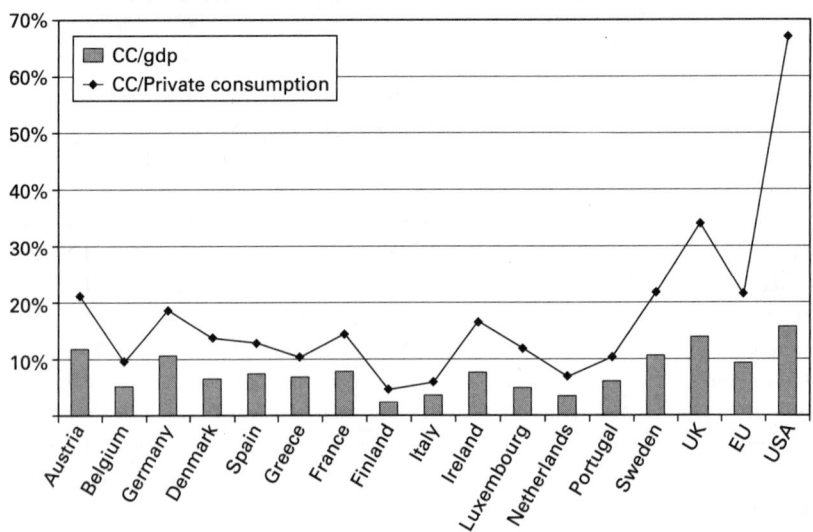

Figure 2.1
Consumer credit as a percentage of consumption and GDP (2002)
Source: European Credit Research Institute 2003; see the appendix.

in statistical definitions, since, in other respects, the two measures track closely across countries. After the United Kingdom, figure 2.1 shows that Germany, Austria, and Sweden have the highest levels of consumer debt. Other countries—such as Finland, Italy, and the Netherlands—report significantly lower levels of lending.

In most of the countries reviewed here, housing debt constitutes the major proportion of debt. Table 2.2 shows that home ownership rates in Europe were high in 2002, certainly comparable to the United States in a number of countries (see also table 5.1). However, as figure 2.2 shows, the proportion of housing-related debt in total household debt varies substantially from country to country. Some countries with below-EU average rates of owner occupation, such as the Netherlands, appear to have shares of housing debt comparable with those with the highest levels of owner occupation, such as Spain. These differences may stem from differences in housing prices, from the extent of the market in nonhousing debt (such as the spread of credit cards) and, again, from differences in definition. In general, housing debt is largest in the Netherlands, Denmark, and United Kingdom, and it is comparably low in Italy and Luxemburg. The EU average breakdown of debt into its components is 71.6 percent for housing debt, 17.8 percent for consumer credit, and 10.6 percent for other credit. For the United States, the comparable proportions are 70 percent for housing debt, 22.1 percent for consumer credit, and 7.9 for other debt, which are very similar.

Table 2.2
Home ownership rates in Europe (%)

Austria	53.7
Belgium	72.9
Denmark	65.0
France	62.7
Germany	43.4
Greece	83.6
Italy	75.5
Luxembourg	70.8
Netherlands	54.4
Portugal	65.0
Spain	85.3
Sweden	59.9
U.K.	70.6

Source: Eurostat (data for 2000).

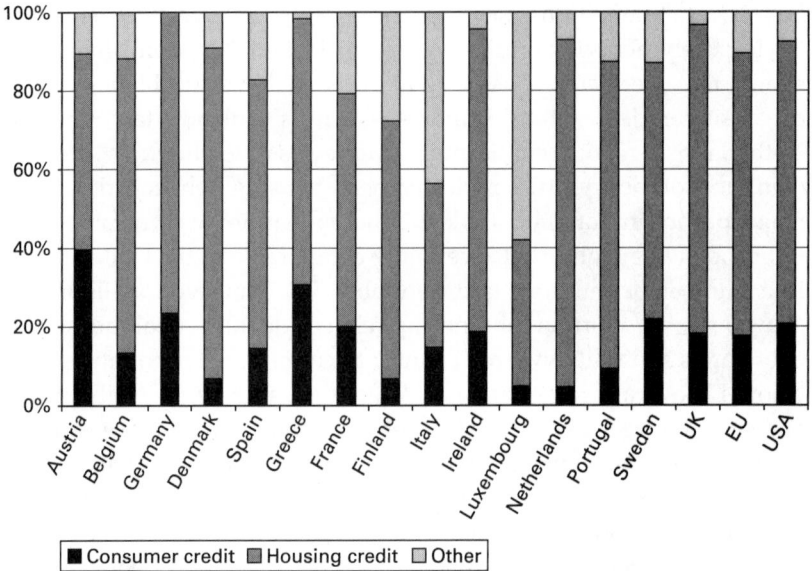

Figure 2.2
Composition of lending to households in 2002 by type of loans (EU countries)
Source: European Credit Research Institute 2003; see the appendix.

Figure 2.3 documents the level of debt as a proportion of house-holds' disposable income for twelve countries for two separate years, 1995 and 2001. The most striking feature of figure 2.3 is that the pro-portion has increased in all the countries displayed here, albeit to a varying extent. There is some evidence of convergence of debt levels, insofar as in 1995, the Mediterranean countries such as Spain, Italy, and Greece displayed far lower levels of debt than countries such as the Netherlands, Sweden, the United Kingdom, and the United States. By 2001, although the debt in the high-debt countries continued to grow (especially the Netherlands), other countries, and notably Portu-gal and Spain, saw very rapid growth in the debt/disposable income ratio. Note also that by 2001, in the United Kingdom, United States, and the Netherlands, the levels of debt exceeded the households' dis-posable income.

Some commentators and policymakers have become concerned that these increases in debt over recent years increase the sensitivity of households' finances to adverse economic shocks. If the household's income stream is interrupted, serious repayment difficulties might occur. Some commentators also believe that high current debt ratios

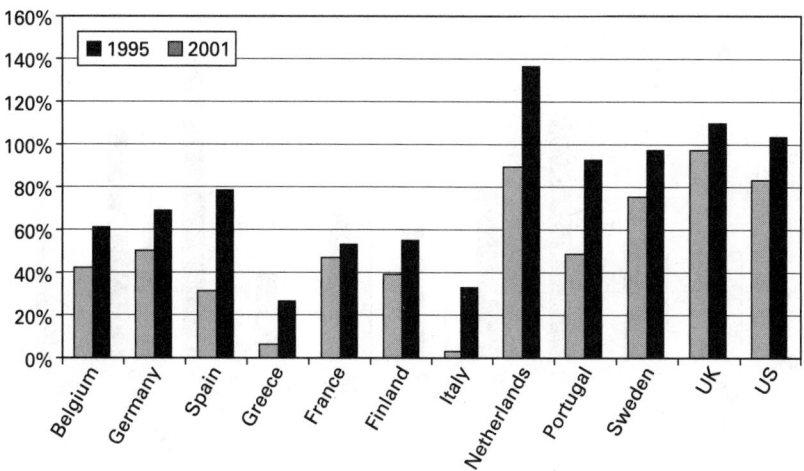

Figure 2.3
Household debt as a percentage of disposable income
Source: European Credit Research Institute 2003; see the appendix.

must lead to a reduction in household spending at some time in the future. As discussed in chapter 1, however, the standard permanent income theory of consumption would view sustained growth in indebtedness as a prediction of future income growth. Maki (2000), for instance, documents how high levels of debt are associated with faster growing incomes among households in the United States. (Cross-section household evidence on debt is also available for some European countries in chapter 3.)

What are the repayment obligations associated with this growing consumer debt? Figure 2.4 provides data for selected countries on the proportions of household income that are devoted to interest rate payments and minimum repayments to service debt in 1997 and 2001. The household debt-service burden is probably a better indicator of consumer credit risk than the level of debt. Debelle (2004) observed that an increase in the household debt-service burden will make the household sector "more sensitive to movements in interest rates, particularly if they are unexpected, and to changes in income, most notably arising from unemployment." Moreover, Maki (2000) showed that for U.S. households, a high debt-service burden is a good predictor of bankruptcy.

The data show that the debt-service burden increased between 1997 and 2001 in all the countries considered here. The increase was

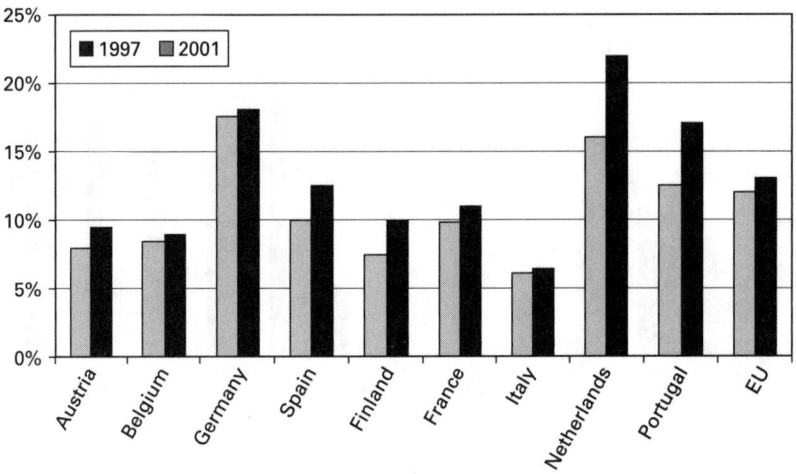

Figure 2.4
Household debt-service burden in selected European countries
Source: Banco de España 2003.

especially strong in the Netherlands, Portugal, and Spain. In 2001, the countries with the highest debt-service burdens were the Netherlands (over 20 percent of disposable income), Germany, and Portugal (both over 15 percent of disposable income). However the average debt burden across European countries only grew from 12 percent of disposable income in 1997 to 13 percent in 2001. Comparable numbers calculated for the United States by the Federal Reserve showed an increase from 12.4 percent in 1997 to 13.3 percent in 2001, an almost identical increase. The European household debt-service burden has not increased as fast as consumer credit volume. This is not surprising in the light of lower nominal interest rates at the macroeconomic level, as well as, perhaps, increasing competition among credit providers leading to smaller lending-rate spreads over the cost of funds.

2.2 Reasons for Repayment Difficulties

Statistics of average debt burdens suggest that debt-service problems are not pervasive among households. However some households might well experience difficulties, and so we proceed to examine evidence on specific factors underlying households' financial difficulties. Little consistent cross-country information is available, and differences in the definition of "excessive debt" and "repayment problems"

Table 2.3
The extent of repayment problems in selected EU countries (percentage of total population)

Country	Default cases	Country	Default cases
Austria	2.7	Netherlands	2.9
Belgium	2.5	Norway	5.5
Finland	3.7	Spain	2.0
France	2.0	Sweden	4.5
Germany	7.0	U.K.	1.6

Notes: Data for Austria refer to 1992, for Finland to 1994, for Norway to 1996.
For definitions and sources, see the data appendix for this chapter.

in the different surveys make it difficult to compare countries (see the appendix).

Some aggregate statistics on the incidence of "over-indebtedness" are reported in table 2.3. In Belgium, France, the Netherlands, Spain, and Germany, the surveys refer to random samples of individuals who experience difficulties in repaying their contracted debts. In the United Kingdom, the statistics are based upon people being advised by consumer associations on how to overcome default incidents. The Swedish data refer to individuals included in credit bureau data who have not yet settled their default incidents. All the data refer to the year 2000 except for Austria, for which we have 1992 data, Finland, which refer to 1994, and Norway, which refer to 1996. A look at table 2.3 shows that around 2 percent of individuals in France and Spain are experiencing repayment difficulties. This fraction is only 1.6 percent in the United Kingdom. These statistics are considerably higher for Germany, Norway, and Sweden; indeed, about 7 percent of German respondents report debt problems. But these numbers have to be viewed cautiously, as they refer to different years and different stages in the business cycle.

How do these numbers compare to the aggregate statistics on debt and debt-service ratios? When comparing proportions of individuals having repayment problems from table 2.3 with the debt burdens in figure 2.4, the cross-country pattern does not reveal any clear relationship between household debt burdens and repayment problems. Recall as well figure 2.3, which showed debt as a proportion of households' disposable income. To illustrate the point, Germany has an average level of debt/GDP but higher-than-average debt burdens and repayment problems; the Netherlands has a high level of debt and also a

high debt burden, but few households report repayment problems;
Portugal, from figures 2.3 and 2.4, has high indebtedness ratios, but
unfortunately, we have no evidence on repayment problems for that
country; the United Kingdom data is not fully comparable, since it
only refers to individuals that are in the counseling process.

Overall, high levels of debt do not necessarily translate into repayment difficulties, whether measured subjectively or objectively by the
incidence of default or bankruptcy, at least when measured on a cross-
country basis. It seems likely that macroeconomic shocks, in particular
to interest rates, are an important determinant of whether a debt burden is transformed into repayment difficulties. Undoubtedly, however,
institutional differences and statistical measurement discrepancies are
also relevant to interpretation of these data.

At the household level, what are the reasons for repayment difficulties for particular households? A populist approach may view at least
some households as myopically running up debt that they have no
prospect of later repaying. This would not necessarily be inconsistent
with optimizing behavior by households that have time-inconsistent
preferences such as the hyperbolic discount rates discussed by Harris
and Laibson (2001). More conventional models would instead suggest
that difficulties might arise because, ex post, households experience unexpected (and perhaps permanent) income shocks that make it much
more difficult to maintain the payments for a given level of debt that
would otherwise have been manageable. Macroeconomic shocks enter
the picture insofar as they affect households differently (e.g., in the
incidence of unemployment).

Table 2.4, for four EU countries, and figure 2.5, for the United States,
investigate the reported reasons for repayment difficulties from individual household responses. The four EU countries all display "low
default" statistics in table 2.3 and low debt volumes in figure 2.1, in
contrast to the higher default rates and more intense borrowing of the
United States. In the U.S. survey, borrowers could cite multiple reasons
that contributed to their situation. Noticeable among the reported reasons are explanations such as "credit card debt" or "housing debts,"
but these should properly be seen as answering what type of debt became a problem rather than an underlying cause, and will play no part
in the discussion.

Table 2.4 suggests that few borrowers report simply having accumulated too much debt. Indeed, the main reasons that borrowers report
excessive debt are unpredictable external events that made it difficult

Table 2.4
Reported reasons for default in payment obligations in selected countries

Country	Reason	Percentage
Austria	Poor household management	26
	Unemployment	21
	Divorce	20
	Housing debts	16
	Other	17
Belgium	Unemployment	19
	Excessive charges	16
	Nonfinancial causes	15
	Divorce	18
	Illness	7
	Decease	5
	Unexpected charges	3
	Other	17
France	Unemployment	42
	Divorce or decease	20
	Illness	11
	Reduction of social benefits	4
	Other	23
Spain	Income reduction (due to unemployment, divorce...)	58
	Bad financial management	12
	Lack of information	26
	Other	4

Source: See the data appendix.
Note: Data corresponds to years 1998 (Austria), 1996 (Belgium), 2000 (France), and 2003 (Spain).

for the individual or family to repay their debts. Consistently, across these countries, divorce, unemployment (or underemployment), and illness are among the causes of the majority of defaults. For instance, in France, 42 percent of borrowers report unemployment as motivating their problems. The proportion blaming divorce for repayment difficulties is also remarkably high, ranging up to 18 percent in Belgium and France and 20 percent in Austria. A small percentage of families report difficulties due to taxation or to clearing legal procedures. Data for the United States show that job insecurity and medical debts are the most important reasons, followed by divorce. In the other countries, roughly from 70 to 80 percent of borrowers with financial problems report similar reasons. These borrowers have suffered some shock that they did

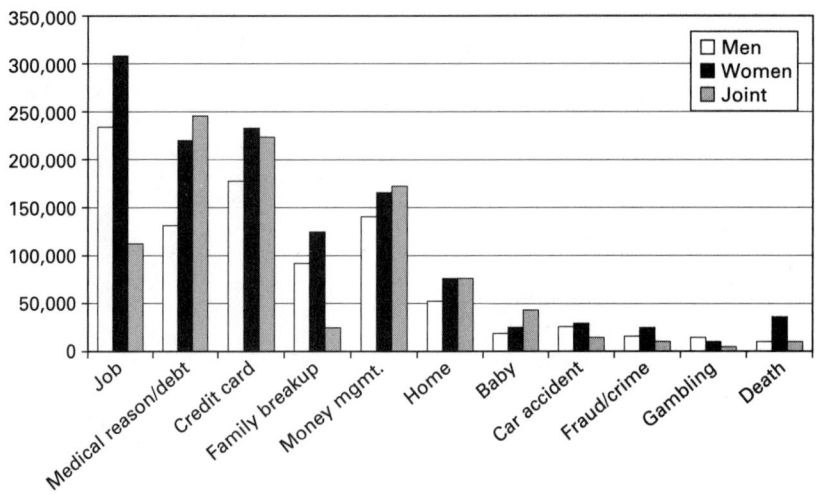

Figure 2.5
Reasons given for consumer bankruptcies extrapolated to national bankruptcy filings, by
filing status, 1999
Source: Warren, Sullivan, and Jacobs 2000. Data originally from Consumer Bankruptcy
Project, III; bankruptcy filing from Administrative Office of the U.S. Courts, 1999.
Note: Numbers do not add to total filings because debtors gave multiple responses.

not reasonably anticipate and that affected their ability to repay their
debts.

However, all these factors still leave many borrowers who report
other reasons. For instance, in Austria, 26 percent of individuals admit
that their difficulties are due to "poor financial management," and 12
percent of Spanish borrowers report that their problems are due to the
same fact. Excessive charges may also be categorized as poor financial
management, which would imply that this caused 16 percent of Belgian borrowers to suffer difficulties. Just as striking is the number of
individuals reporting that their problems arose from poor information
or unexpected charges, including some 26 percent of respondents who
reported debt problems in Spain. Many U.S. borrowers also report bad
financial management as an important factor among the five most important reasons for being in financial difficulties.

Inadequate information might be consistent with life-cycle or permanent income models of debt, but reporting poor financial management
or excessive charges cannot be consistent with such models. Indeed,
these facts about household borrowing suggest that not all households
behave consistently with the assumption of rational optimizing agents.

It remains an open question as to whether the incompletely anticipated factors for repayment implies an extended role for regulation.

2.3   Information Sharing in Credit Markets

Other chapters review evidence on various institutional aspects of the household credit market, and a few recent studies assess information-sharing issues in the light of data protection regulation. (See chapters 9 and 10 in this volume for a more general discussion.) Other sources include Avery et al. 2000; Barron and Staten 2003; Bostic and Calem 2003; Jentzsch 2003a, 2003b. This section offers some comparative statistical and regulatory information as regards information sharing among lenders and information providers' regulation.

Information sharing among creditors has become prevalent in the consumer credit markets both in the United States and in the European Union, where information on millions of borrowers is sold in the market on a daily basis. The expansion of credit reporting is partly due to improvements in information technologies over recent decades. In a highly developed market such as that of the United States, most credit-active consumers have a report with one, two, or all three of the major credit bureaus (Equifax, Experian, TransUnion). The spread of credit reporting has several effects. Information asymmetries are reduced thereby potentially minimizing adverse selection and potential moral hazard problems. Data sharing induces a disciplinary effect on borrowers as likely future repayment behavior can be better predicted. Given the quantity of information held on individuals, most countries have attempted to regulate what kind of data may be collected and for how long. Additionally, the regulatory schemes assign certain rights to consumers such as the right to access information and to have errors corrected. Such regulations might have effects on credit market outcomes, in particular in affecting individual access to credit facilities.

2.3.1   Data Protection Regulation in Europe and the United States

Around the world, there is an increasing trend to the establishment of credit-reporting systems as well as to enacting data protection laws. Many industrialized countries have enacted laws that regulate the activity of information sharing, some through general data protection legislation and others through legislation specifically directed at the credit-reporting industry. Table 2.5 lists data protection laws enacted in the individual countries as well as transnational guidelines. The U.S. legal basis is discussed at some length in chapter 9. The scope for and extent of these legal restrictions varies across countries. Within the European Union, credit-reporting regimes still differ, although there is an increasing trend to convergence, and the differences from the U.S. regime are substantively larger. Varying legal traditions among the countries of the European Union may hamper complete convergence of the data protection regimes in different countries (see section 2.4). Moreover, a simple comparison of the legal basis of data protection might not tell us anything about the reality of the enforcement of such laws. Despite these caveats, an assessment of the impact of the law in different regimes can be attempted, and we do this by constructing an index that summarizes some of the most important features of each regime. Apart from the national laws, there are also several important international guidelines on data protection. In the past, the Organization for Economic Cooperation and Development (OECD) promulgated a number of guidelines and policy reports for electronic commerce. In 1980, the OECD Guidelines on the Protection of Privacy and Transborder Flows of Personal Data were published. These principles were intended to ensure both privacy and the free flow of information among the OECD members. They have also heavily influenced national legislation. These principles include (1) the right to notice before collection takes place; (2) the right of access to personal data; (3) the right to have the data corrected or deleted; (4) the right to object to certain data-processing methods; and (5) the right to exclude variables that denote race, religious beliefs, or political opinion from being recorded.

In December 1990, the UN adopted the UN Guidelines Concerning Computerized Personal Data Files. Just as in the case of the OECD guidelines, the UN established certain principles for the protection of privacy, such as the Principle of Lawfulness and Fairness, which states that personal information should not be collected or processed in unfair or unlawful ways. According to the Principle of Accuracy, the individual has the right to accuracy, completeness, and relevance of the data recorded. Other principles cover "purpose specification" (no usage of data for purposes incompatible with the original purpose), access to the data, and security measures to protect the data. Moreover, these principles state that when two or more countries offer comparable safeguards for the protection of privacy, information should be able to circulate freely between them.

Table 2.5
Overview of data protection regimes (2003)

Regime	Resource
OECD guidelines	OECD Guidelines on the Protection of Privacy and Transborder Flows of Personal Data
UN guidelines	United Nations Guidelines Concerning Computerized Personal Data Files
COE convention	Convention for the Protection of Individuals with Regard to Automatic Processing of Personal Data (ETS No. 108, 1981, in force 1985)
EU DPD	Directive 95/46/EC of the European Parliament and of the Council of 24 October 1995 on the protection of individuals with regard to the processing of personal data and on the free movement of such data
Austria	Bundesgesetz über den Schutz personenbezogener Daten (federal law for the protection of personal data)
Belgium	Loi relative à la protection des données à caractère personnel du 8 décembre 1992 (law for the protection of personal characteristics)
Czech Rep.	Act on the Protection of Personal Data of 2000
Denmark	Act on Processing of Personal Data of 2000
Finland	Personal Data Act of 1999
France	Loi N° 78–17 du 6 Janvier 1978 relative à l'informatique, aux fichiers et aux libertés (Law No. 78–17 of 6 January 1978 relative to the information concerning personal files and freedoms)
Germany	Federal Data Protection Act of 2002
Greece	Law on Protection of Individuals with Regard to the Processing of Personal Data of 1997
Hungary	Protection of Personal Data and Disclosure of Data of Public Interest of 1992
Ireland	Data Protection Act of 1988
Italy	Law 675 on Protection of Individuals and Other Subjects with Regard to the Processing of Personal Data of 1996
Latvia	Law on Personal Data Protection of 2000
Lithuania	Law on Legal Protection of Personal Data of 1996
Netherlands	Personal Data Protection Act of 2000
Poland	Law on the Protection of Personal Data of 1998
Portugal	Act on the Protection of Personal Data of 1998
Romania	Law on the Protection of Individuals with Regard to the Processing of Personal Data and the Free Movement of Such Data of 2001
Slovakia	Act on Personal Data Protection of 2002
Slovenia	Law on Personal Data Protection of 1990
Spain	Organic Law 15/1999 of 13 December on the Protection of Personal Data
Sweden	Personal Data Act of 1998
United Kingdom	Data Protection Act of 1998
United States	Fair Credit Reporting Act of 2003

In Europe, the first legally binding international instrument for data protection was the Convention for the Protection of Individuals with regard to the Automatic Processing of Personal Data Convention of 1981 (COE), which required the signatories to transpose its principles into national law. The COE had worldwide significance and drew its inspiration directly from the European Convention on Human Rights and Fundamental Freedoms. The COE is open to any country, including those that are not members of the Council of Europe. However, it is mandatory for countries to enact adequate data protection legislation before becoming a party. The COE mandates certain rights for individuals (such as access, correction, and "stop marketing") and the duties of data controllers (e.g., to specify the purpose of collection and the purpose of disclosure).

International guidelines only stipulate a minimum level of protection, hence many countries have stricter laws than those suggested by them. In the United States, the Fair Credit Reporting Act (FCRA) mandates federal guidelines that may be modified by state legislation. A comparison of that federal U.S. legislation to its EU counterpart is therefore of some interest.

The United States has fewer regulations in the supervisory authority category. The reason for this is that U.S. authorities do not have the competence to monitor the public sector (a competence that European authorities usually have), and there is no obligation for this authority to maintain a list with the names and addresses of data controllers in America. Hence, it is not possible for data subjects to access these lists. Additionally, unlike in the European Union, there is no legal basis in the United States for auditing, whereby the supervisor is allowed to check the data-processing practices of firms (e.g., by entering their premises). In the category of property rights to information, by far the most important difference is that while the European approach to privacy issues mandates explicit "opt-in" approval by consumers for commercial use of their personal information, only some of the U.S. states have laws that make similar provisions. Several other fundamental privacy rights, however, are codified in the laws on both sides of the Atlantic—namely the right to access, correction, deletion of false information, blocking in case of disputes, the right to know to whom the information was disclosed, and special restrictions on sensitive information. The United States also provides in its FCRA time frames for deletion of obsolete information, which is not the case in the EU Data Protection Directive.

In terms of the obligations of credit bureaus, the picture is uneven. For example, in Europe, but not in the United States, bureaus are obliged to notify the subject that data are being collected. Conversely, in the United States, but not in Europe, there are rules regarding the time frames within which bureaus must respond to requests for information, or within which they must settle disputes. Information furnishers are obliged to observe fewer "principles" in the United States, where, for a long time, they were not specifically regulated. The information furnisher (usually a financial service provider) need not disclose the credit report to the consumer. However, consumers must be informed if they are adversely affected (e.g., if they are denied credit). This is a right that does not exist under the EU Data Protection Directive. However, common ground is the obligation for truthful reporting, a dispute settlement procedure with the furnisher (data controller), and the obligation to report up-to-date and complete data. Last, in the case of sanctions and remedies, both statutes provide for these although to a varying degree.

We have not displayed cross-border data regulations since they are currently technically unimportant. Nevertheless, this is one of the most striking differences between Europe and the United States: The United States denies consumers the right to give consent to the export of their personal data, and the authorities do not have to be notified if data are exported abroad. In particular, there is no obligation for countries to which data are exported to provide at least the same standard of protection as in the United States; the opposite is true for the European Union.

It is possible to summarize the differences across countries' regulatory frameworks with a simple index. Table 2.6 lists thirty-five different restrictions or obligations that might affect information sharing in different countries. They are organized into five different categories: (1) supervisory authority (SA); (2) property rights to information (PR); (3) the obligations of credit bureaus, or those who collect information (OB); (4) the obligations of information furnisher tasks, or those who supply information (IF); and (5) sanctions and remedies (SC). For each of the provisions listed in table 2.6, we defined a dummy variable that takes the value of one if the regulation had been enacted in the national laws and zero otherwise.

Table 2.7 reports the resulting summary scores for the countries considered. Overall, the United States features twenty-eight separate regulations in the index, which is fewer than the United Kingdom, for

Table 2.6
Indicators of the Credit Reporting Regulatory Index (CRRI)

Supervisory authority (SA)
General existence of an authority in data protection
Legal competence in oversight over the public sector
Legal competence in oversight over the private sector
Legal competence in oversight over the credit-reporting industry
Legal competence to investigate cases of abuse
Legal competence to hear complaints
Legal competence to administer lists of data controllers
Legal competence to conduct audits

Property rights to information (PR)
Data subject has the right to opt in data collection
Data subject has the right to access the data stored about her/him
Data subject has the right to correct the personal data
Data subject has the right to have false information deleted
Data subject has the right to block information
Data subject has the right to know to whom information is disclosed
Data subject has the right to stop marketing
Special restrictions on sensitive data exist
Special restrictions on historical data exist

Obligations of credit bureaus (in EU, data controller) (OB)
Credit bureaus have to register with the appropriate authority
Credit bureaus have to have a purpose for collection of data
Credit bureaus must notify data subject before collection
Credit bureaus have to disclose specifications
Credit bureaus have restrictions on cost of disclose to consumers
Accuracy is required from credit bureaus
Credit bureaus have to maintain up-to-date records
Regulation of reaction time in answering consumer requests
Regulation on dispute settlement time frame

Tasks of the information provider (in EU, data controller) (IF)
Accuracy of reports required
Notification of consumer about disclosure to credit bureau
Notification of consumer in case of an adverse action
Dispute settlement mechanisms
Requirement to disclose own information (or credit report)
Requirement to update data
Requirement to report complete data

Sanctions (SC)
Fines
Imprisonment

Table 2.7
Regulations and Credit Reporting Regulatory Index, 2003

Country/Contract	Absolute number of credit reporting regulations	Credit Reporting Regulatory Index (CRRI)
OECD guidelines	15	0.842026
UN guidelines	20	1.230573
COE convention	16	0.925017
EU Data Protection Directive	29	1.700566
Austria	32	1.826307
Belgium	28	1.238676
Czech Rep.	29	1.648937
Denmark	32	1.844216
Finland	32	1.844216
France	33	1.901959
Germany	33	1.894132
Greece	29	1.691012
Hungary	31	1.640678
Ireland	33	1.894132
Italy	31	1.788226
Latvia	29	1.526781
Lithuania	n.a.	n.a.
Netherlands	31	1.801280
Poland	35	1.766056
Portugal	30	1.724194
Romania	n.a.	n.a.
Slovakia	28	1.466053
Slovenia	27	1.433317
Spain	32	1.844216
Sweden	29	1.684053
U.K.	33	1.869840
U.S.A.	28	1.623751

Note: The CRRI is calculated for each country j as a Jevons index geometric mean,

$$\mathrm{CRRI}_j = \sqrt[5]{\frac{x_{SA}^j}{x_{SA}^b} \cdot \frac{x_{PR}^j}{x_{PR}^b} \cdot \frac{x_{OC}^j}{x_{OC}^b} \cdot \frac{x_{IF}^j}{x_{IF}^b} \cdot \frac{x_{SC}^j}{x_{SC}^b}},$$

of actually observed regulations in each country j for each of the five categories: supervisory authority (SA), property rights (PR), obligations of credit bureaus (OC), information furnishers (IF), sanctions (SC). Country-specific regulation counts are normalized by half of the maximum number of regulations in each category (e.g., for the supervisory design category, SA, there are eight indicators; so x_{SA}^b equals four).

example, at thirty-five regulations. Similar indicators can be computed and reported for each regulatory area. Of course, the scores just enumerate the regulations without weighing them in terms of importance or stringency, hence, a score twice as high only means that there are twice as many data protection regulations. This can serve as a proxy for the strength of data protection but certainly does not necessarily indicate that data protection is twice as strong.

We also compute and report in the last column of table 2.7 a Credit-Reporting Regulatory Index (CRRI). As defined in the table's note, a country's CRRI takes low values when very few among the regulations listed in the table are in place, and high values when many of the potential regulations are imposed across all of the five regulatory areas listed in the other columns of the table. This summary index of the pervasiveness of regulation can be useful for cross-country comparison purposes. There are too few data for running a full regression, but table 2.8 reports a number of pairwise correlations between the CRRI and some credit indicators. The sample consists of the countries in table 2.5, and, for the correlations, we chose the following credit indicators: consumer credit/GDP, the existence of a private credit registry, and a coverage index calculated by the World Bank that includes the number of individuals and/or firms listed in private credit bureaus as of January 2003, scaled to each country's population (see World Bank, 2004). Additionally, we included the estimated numbers of credit reports sold in a country in either 2002 or 2003 scaled by the population in that country. All statistics reported control for GDP growth rates.

Table 2.8
Partial correlation coefficients (p-values in parentheses)[*]

	Consumer Credit/ GDP	Existence private registry	Coverage index of private registry	Credit Reports sold Scaled by population	Credit Reporting Regulatory Index (CRRI)
Consumer credit/GDP	—	0.0503 (0.859)	0.6533 (0.008)	0.4212 (0.118)	0.1511 (0.591)
Existence private registry	—	—	0.3732 (0.171)	0.1484 (0.598)	−0.0005 (0.999)
Coverage index private registry	—	—	—	0.5119 (0.051)	0.2068 (0.460)
Credit reports sold scaled by population	—	—	—	—	−0.2471 (0.375)

[*]Correlations for twenty-one observations. We control for GDP growth rates.

In table 2.8, we see that consumer credit as a percentage of GDP is not correlated with the existence of a registry and with the CRRI at conventional confidence levels. However, there is an association between consumer credit as percentage of GDP and the coverage index of the private registry: the coefficient is 0.65 (p-value 0.008). This suggests that in those countries where lending is proportionately higher, there is greater coverage of the population. This association is not necessarily causal, since greater access to credit increases information sharing and vice versa. Table 2.8 also shows that there is no positive correlation with the credit reports sold in the markets, at least not at conventional levels of significance. In general, it can be stated that in countries with more lending, credit bureaus have incentives to store records on more people, however, there is not a discernible relationship of credit report sale and volume of lending. This might be due to aggregation of data or the fact that other factors are more important for the development of credit markets (such as GDP growth). Coverage of the population is also associated with the number of credit reports sold in the market, the coefficient is 0.51 (p-value 0.051). If more records on people are stored in the databases of the registry, then more information can be distributed in the market.

We are primarily interested in the effects of the regulation of credit reporting. Since tighter regulations might hamper the distribution of the reports, leading to a reduction in access to consumer credit, one could have hypothesized a negative relation among the CRRI summary and credit reports and the consumer credit/GDP variable. In this line of reasoning, a correlation would also be expected between the CRRI and information-sharing outcomes, as measured by the coverage index and credit report sale. In actual fact, the CRRI is not statistically significantly correlated with the outcome variables of interest when we control for GDP growth. This could mean that regulation of credit reporting aimed at data protection does not have any major negative effects on credit-reporting activities. In the European countries, data protection laws have been enacted to address many other problems, not only credit reporting. Hence, this explains why there might not be an association. Moreover, other factors such as GDP growth, consumer confidence, and positive expectations about the personal job prospects might be more important predictors of the development of consumer credit markets. Lack of significance, however, may also simply imply that the data are not informative, and that a larger sample including industrialized and developing countries may offer more precise results (see chapter 10 in this volume).

2.4   Consumer Credit Market Integration in the European Union

European and U.S. consumer credit markets are very different, but, as tables 2.3 and 2.7 illustrate, respectively, reported repayment problems and credit-reporting regulations are quite heterogeneous across European countries. One reason may be the lack of integration of the European credit market. Despite different countries sharing a common currency within the euro zone, few consumers either use a bank account or have a mortgage other than in the country in which they are resident. Many studies document this lack of integration of credit markets, including Adam et al. (2002) and the references contained therein. Several reasons are suggested for the fact that the different national credit markets are poorly integrated. Many reflect "natural" barriers to integration, such as differences in language, geographic distance, and possible cultural differences in attitudes toward saving and borrowing. Other variations are due to differences in the legal frameworks that govern credit contracts and uncertainty on the part of consumers about what these differences are.

In 2001, the European Opinion Research Group asked consumers what barriers existed to using financial services elsewhere in the European Union: 32 percent cited "a lack of information"; 28 percent reported problems due to language; 22 percent explained "it was too risky"; 19 percent reported poor legal protection in the event of problems; 18 percent cited poor reporting; while difficulties due to distance was the answer given by 14 percent of households. Harmonizing the legal framework across countries is seen as a way of encouraging integration by making it easier for consumers to approach lenders outside their home country. Although in the European Opinion Research Group survey, as many as 42 percent of households reported language or distance discouraging cross-border banking, there is clearly considerable scope for the integration of consumer credit markets.

One measure of integration is the degree to which consumers use banks outside their home locality. For example, households across the United States share both a language and a regulatory environment, yet even within the United States, many banking services are overwhelmingly supplied by local institutions. Elliehausen and Wolken (1992) showed that in the late 1980s, 50 percent of households lived or worked within two miles of the institution where they had their checking account, and 75 percent within eleven miles. Moreover, the majority of households tended to "cluster" their services at their primary institution, where they had more than one account or loan. More recently, Amel and Starr-McCluer (2001) supported this earlier evidence. They showed that although there was a growing trend of using institutions located at greater distances, the percentage of households who use local institutions still remains high. Although there has been some movement to nondepository institutions, local institutions' share of the market for home equity loans and other lines of credit remains above 80 percent.

Kiser (2002) notes that the primary reason for changing banks is a household's relocation, while location and customer service are the primary reasons for staying with the local depository institution. In the United States, approximately 3 percent of households change the region in which they live per year, whereas it is 1 percent or even below in Germany, Great Britain, and France (Nickell 1997). This suggests that perhaps there is limited scope for encouraging cross-border banking relationships on the part of consumers.

The European Commission has increasingly stressed that Europe needs to harmonize the regulation of consumer credit if it is to facilitate a common European market for consumer credit. It proposed a directive proposal on the issue in 2003, aimed at increasing consumer protection across the board and to rebalance the rights and duties of borrowers and creditors (for a discussion of these implications, see Jentzsch 2003c). The proposal was given a first reading at the European Parliament in April 2004 and, as a result of strong criticism from the industry, from consumer groups, and from experts, extensively revised by the commission. The revised draft directive, presented in October 2004, is likely to be further revised before eventual adoption.

2.4.1 International Information Flows

The primary articles in the EU draft directive are concerned with consumer protection in general and responsible lending. As to information sharing, the original draft directive included measures aimed at fostering a structured framework for the exchange of creditworthiness information. The measures were dropped in the revised draft, perhaps in light of the fact that data sharing aimed at assessing creditworthiness of consumers can already be assessed across European countries on the basis of the principle of reciprocity and existing national arrangements.

In many European countries, there are private registries that collect information from a wide range of creditors (such as finance companies, telecommunication providers, and retailers). They distribute more detailed data and have a higher coverage of individuals compared to public registries. Public credit registries in Europe work together in the Working Group on Credit Registers. Many of these registers have been established for monitoring the major trends in the overall level of debt in the private sector (at least debts above a certain threshold). Directly comparing them to private credit registries is not admissible as they have been set up for other purposes. Private registries in Europe, however, cooperate through BigNet, Eurogate, and EurisConnect: an infrastructure for data exchange is available but transnational data exchange is of marginal importance to the industry, signaling lack of demand for foreign credit by consumers.

An alternative mechanism for information sharing is the establishment of large-scale international credit-reporting agencies through cross-border mergers and acquisitions. This strategy is pursued by Equifax and Experian, whose networks already reach across borders both within and outside the European Union. Currently, however, the information is rarely reported across borders.

Information may also be shared with companies operating from outside the European Union. Articles 25 and 26 of the EU Data Protection Directive allow the export of data provided that the recipient country ensures "adequate data protection standards," and where this status is evaluated by the European Commission. By May 2003, the status was only awarded to Hungary, Switzerland, the United States, and Canada. The data exchange with the United States was allowed after the "safe harbor" agreement with the European Commission, whereby U.S. companies could register with the Department of Commerce to verify that they obey data protection principles that provide an equivalent level of protection as in the European Union. The member states and the three EEA members (Norway, Liechtenstein, and Iceland) are allowed to export data to those nations. The status of other countries is unclear. Currently cross-border credit information transfers are of marginal importance.

2.5 Conclusions

This chapter has outlined the current state of consumer credit markets and credit-reporting systems in Europe and the United States, focusing specifically on the use of credit and the regulation of credit reporting. Consumer credit is higher in the United States and the United Kingdom than in most European countries. The major part of lending is housing debt. Consumer credit growth over the last ten years had been high in some of the countries, such as Greece, Italy, and Spain, where consumer credit had previously been relatively unimportant. But it had also been high in the United Kingdom, which already had very high levels of consumer credit. The overall level of household debt as a proportion of disposable income has been growing in all the EU countries, and in some cases, it grew dramatically, such as in Italy, Greece, and Portugal.

On both sides of the Atlantic, the household debt-service burden has also increased. In some countries, such as the Netherlands, debt repayments amount to over 20 percent of income in 2001. However, the cross-country correlation of the proportion of households reporting repayment problems with the level of debt or the debt-service burden seems to be low. The chapter also discussed some of the reasons why households or individuals experience repayment difficulties. The majority of households in the reviewed countries get into repayment difficulties because they experience some unexpected trigger event (such as illness, unemployment, or divorce) that disrupts their income stream, and for which there is no mechanism for insuring these shocks. However, a minority of households report reasons that are more difficult to reconcile with standard models of saving and borrowing over the life cycle: They report their difficulties are due to poor financial management or to unexpectedly large repayments. All of these explanations suggest a role for regulation.

We discussed next some of the main differences in the regulation of credit bureaus that collect and disseminate information on the repayment history of potential borrowers. By constructing an index for each individual country that allows the comparison of one country with another, the differences in the regulatory framework can be analyzed. This quantitative approach allowed us to investigate the relationship of the index with information-sharing variables as well as with a variable describing access to consumer credit. The results, obtained from admittedly limited information, show that increasing coverage in credit reporting is associated with increasing access to credit, but the regulatory index is not associated with the existence of a credit bureau, the coverage index, or the credit reports scaled by population. Overall, there is no evidence that data protection restrictions (as we have measured them) greatly hamper information allocation in consumer credit markets.

Retail credit markets are poorly integrated across European countries. We discussed a pending EU consumer credit directive, whose explicit objective is to integrate retail credit markets in the European Union and harmonize the regulation of the national credit markets. Of course, there are many additional barriers in the European Union, such as differences in languages or legal traditions. And even in the US—a largely integrated market—the extent of cross-state lending is small in certain segments of the retail market. Whilst public credit agencies exist that could exchange information, and the large credit bureaux are increasingly internationalizing their operations, the extent of cross-border credit and credit reporting still remains limited in Europe.

2A Data Appendix: Sources and Definitions

The chapter uses data collected by ECRI from central banks, national statistical institutes, and European institutions and associations. GDP and private consumption (equal to the final consumption expenditure of households) data were taken from national accounts published by national statistical institutes and checked against Eurostat harmonized statistics when possible.

Definitions are not fully consistent across countries (see the note on Statistics). The household sector often includes households (individuals and self-employed persons) and nonprofit institutions serving households (NPISH). Loans to the private sector (that is, the household sector and private nonfinancial businesses) usually refer to lending by monetary financial institutions (MFIs) and not to total lending (which includes in addition loans from central and local government and the rest of the world).

All data are in current market prices. Data in euros for countries outside the euro zone are obtained using central banks' average annual exchange rates for different currencies.

Austria

Definition of financial sector used:

Monetary financial institutions (the OeNB and other MFIs/banks)

Other financial institutions (banks that do not qualify as MFIs, financial holding companies, financial umbrella companies, pension fund and mutual fund management firms)

Insurance corporations

Pension funds

Source for financial data: National Bank of Austria. Focus on Statistics—chapter 2, Austrian Financial Institutions. Consumer credit data are in table 2.0.2.0. "Credit to sole proprietors and individuals."

Note on statistics: Household net disposable income is used instead of household gross disposable income.

Belgium

Definition of financial sector used:

Credit institutions (banks, savings banks, securities banks, and communal savings societies)

Investment firms and investment advice companies

Exchange offices

Consumer credit is defined as "hire-purchase and installment-payment loans, leasing and opening of credits."

Overindebtedness is defined as individuals "who experience difficulties to repay the debt contracted."

Source for table 2.3: Groupe Action Surendettement de Belgique (Belgium Overindebtedness Action Group).

Source for table 2.4: ABB (1996), Enquête statistique sur les causes de défaillance en matière de prêts et de ventes à tempérament (Statistical inquiry into the causes of default on loans and installment purchases).

Source for financial data: NSI National Statistical Institute, Bulletin de la Banque Nationale de Belgique.

Note on statistics: Data for household disposable income for 2002 will only be available at the end of the 2003.

Germany

Definition of financial sector used:

Commercial banks

Land banks

Savings banks

Regional institutions of credit cooperatives

Credit cooperatives

Mortgage banks

Building and loan associations

Banks with special functions

Foreign banks

Source of financial data: Bundesbank, Banking Statistics.

Consumer credit is defined as "credit for personal use in the consumption of goods or services (including bank overdrafts on wage and pension accounts)"; hence, it results from the addition of two categories— installment credit and debit balances on wages, salaries and pension accounts.

Overindebtedness is defined as individuals "who experience difficulties to repay the debt contracted."

Source for table 2.3: IEIC, "Etat du surendettement: Eléments statistiques," September 2000.

Note on statistics: Self-employed persons represent a part of the private business sector and not of the household sector. Consumer credit does not appear as such and could be assimilated to "other funding to households, including 'installment credit' and 'debit balances.'"

Denmark

Definition of financial sector used:

Banks (commercial and savings banks)

Mortgage credit institutes

Other credit institutions

Money market funds

Danmarks Nationalbank

Spain

Definition of financial sector used:

Banco de España

Other monetary financial institutions (credit institutions and money market funds)

Credit institutions comprise banks, savings banks, credit cooperatives, specialized credit institutions (SCIs) or financial credit entities, and Official Credit Institute.

Source for financial data: Banco de España, Boletín Estadístico.

Consumer credit is defined as loans for the acquisition of current and noncurrent goods and services (motor vehicles, electrical goods, and so forth).

Overindebtedness is defined as individuals "who experience difficulties to repay the debt contracted."

Source for tables 2.3 and 2.4: Cuadernos del CEACCU, N° 1, Los españoles y el sobreendeudamiento, Madrid 2003.

Note on statistics: In national financial accounts, the category "other resident sectors" designates either household sector or private sector (financial private business included). Household disposable income includes nonprofit institutions.

Greece

Definition of financial sector used:

Bank of Greece

Commercial banks

Agricultural bank

Mortgage banks

Hellenic Industrial Development Bank

Postal Savings Bank

Deposits and Loans Fund

Investment banks

Cooperative banks

Source for financial data: Bank of Greece, Monthly Statistical Bulletin.

Note on statistics: The 2002 figure for household disposable income is calculated on the basis of the annual percentage growth of real disposable income adjusted for inflation.

France

Definition of financial sector used:

Banks

Cooperative or mutual banks

Communal credit societies

Financial societies

Specialized financial institutions

Source of financial data: Banque de France, the national financial accounts, quarterly monetary statistics.

Consumer credit is defined as loans up to EUR 1,524, overdraft facilities, revolving credit and installment credit loans over EUR 1,524, personal loans, and other loans over EUR 1,524.

Overindebtedness is defined as individuals "who experience difficulties to repay the debt contracted."

Source for tables 2.3 and 2.4: IEIC 2000.

Households include nonprofit institutions in the service of households.

Finland

Definition of financial sector used:

Bank of Finland

Resident credit institutions

Branches of foreign credit institutions

Money market funds

Overindebtedness is defined as "the number of households who declare their inability to pay interests and repayments on their loans at the very last reminder."

Source for table 2.3: Korczak, D. 1998. "Overindebtedness in Germany and Other European States and Credit Counselling." *Money Matters* 2 (June): 7–10. http://www.english.konsumentverket.se/Documents/in_english/money_matters/MM98_02.pdf./

Source of financial data: Bank of Finland, Monthly Bulletin.

Note on statistics: Household net disposable income is used instead of household gross disposable income.

Italy

Definition of financial sector used:

Monetary financial institutions or banks (Banca d'Italia, banks S.p.A., credit cooperative and mutual banks, central refunding institutions, branches of foreign banks)

Other financial corporations (including money market funds)

Financial auxiliaries

Insurance corporations and pension funds

Source of financial data: Banca d'Italia, Bolletinno Statistico.

Consumer credit refers to consumer credit and the opening and management of credit cards. It includes credit granted to individuals in the context of commercial or professional activities, might it be in the form of longer payment periods, financing, and any other financial facility to an individual person (art. 121, Testo Unico Bancario). Consumer credit and credit cards borrowing is included largely within the category of consumer families ("famiglie consumatrici").

Households do not include self-employed persons who are within the category of private nonfinancial business.

Note on statistics: The 2002 figure for households' disposable income is not directly available but calculated on the basis of the annual percentage growth.

Ireland

Definition of financial sector used:

Licensed banks

Building societies

ACC banks

Source of financial data: Central Bank and Financial Services Authorities of Ireland; Credit, Money, and Banking Statistics.

Consumer credit figures include other loans. Credit to households is divided into housing loans and consumer credit and other loans.

Note on statistics: Lending to the private sector corresponds to "total advances to resident nongovernment sectors." Lending to households corresponds to "personal credit," which includes "house mortgage finance" and "other personal credit."

Luxembourg

Definition of financial sector used:

Luxembourg Central Bank

Banks (banks, rural banks, banks issuing mortgage bonds, branches of foreign banks)

Collective investment societies

Pension funds

Other financial intermediaries (financial advisers, commission agents, private portfolio managers, distributors of investment funds, brokers, and so forth.)

Note on statistics: Luxembourg does not produce statistics about household disposable income.

The Netherlands

Definition of financial sector used:

Universal banks

Banks organized on a cooperative basis

Savings banks

Security credit institutions

Mortgage banks

Overindebtedness is defined as individuals "who experience difficulties to repay the debt contracted."

Source for table 2.3: IEIC 2000.

Source of financial data: De Netherlandsche Bank, Statistical Bulletin.

Note on statistics: Data for household disposable income for the previous year will only be available at the end of the current year.

Households comprise all natural persons and any businesses they may have (self-employed).

Portugal

Definition of financial sector used:

Banco di Portugal

Other monetary financial institutions (credit institutions such as banks, savings banks, Mutual Agricultural Credit Bank, financial credit institutions, investment societies, money market funds)

Source of financial data: Bank of Portugal, Monetary and Financial Statistics.

Note on statistics: "Private individuals" correspond to the household sector. "Nonfinancial corporations" comprise private and public nonfinancial corporations. Lending to private individuals comprises housing and consumer credit. Before September 1997, consumer credit was included in credit to other purposes.

Sweden

Definition of financial sector used:

Banks (banking companies, savings banks, member banks)

Mortgage (housing) credit institutions

Finance companies

The AP Fund (National Pension Fund)

Insurance companies

State credit funds

Overindebtedness is defined as "individuals included in credit bureaus who have not yet settled their default incidents."

Source for tables 2.3 and 2.4: Korzack 1998.

Source of financial data: Statistics Sweden, The Riksbank's financial market statistics. The Riksbank commissions Statistics Sweden (SCB) to produce financial market statistics on its behalf. Statistics appear on SCB Web site.

Note on statistics: The statistical institute of Sweden does not produce a statistical breakdown of lending to households by purpose (consumer credit, housing loans, and other); it will start to gather this information only in 2004. "Lending of housing credit institutions" stands for housing loans in ECRI statistics. According to information available, 50 percent of bank lending and other MFIs' lending are granted for consumer purposes. "Lending to public" does not refer to the private sector but to all nonfinancial sectors.

United Kingdom

Definition of financial sector used:

Bank of England

Other monetary financial institutions (U.K. banks, U.K. building societies)

Financial corporations other than MFIs

Financial quasi-corporations

Source: Bank of England, Monetary and Financial Statistics.

Consumer credit shows in the breakdown of lending to individuals (for all items comprised in lending to individuals, see the covering note to the March 1993 *Monetary Statistics* release, or pages 316–317 of the August 1992 *Quarterly Bulletin*).

Households comprise individuals, namely, all the residents of the United Kingdom as receivers of income and consumers of products, unincorporated businesses other than unlimited liability partnerships (sole traders), Nonprofit institutions serving households such as charities and universities.

Overindebtedness is based upon people being advised by consumer associations on how to overcome default incidents.

Source for table 2.3: NACAB publishes statistics that quote one million inquiries, not actual people. It is often the case, however, that a person with a debt problem will phone several times. In a letter to the editor of Credit Finance 2001, Nick Pearson, a former employee of NACAB calculates the number of enquiries at roughly 200,000.

Note on statistics: "Other U.K. residents" corresponds to the household sector. Sterling lending by U.K. MFIs to the private nonfinancial sector is also called "M4 Lending." Housing loans appear as "lending secured on dwellings," which include sterling mortgage portfolios, loans fully secured on residential property and on land to individuals.

Norway

Overindebtedness is defined as "the number of households who declare their inability to pay interests and repayments on their loans at the very last reminder."

Source for table 2.3: Korzack 1998.

United States

Definition of financial sector used:

Monetary authority

Commercial banking (consumer credit)

Savings institutions (consumer credit)

Credit unions

Bank personal trusts and estates

Life insurance companies

Other insurance companies

Private pension funds

State and government retirement funds

Money market mutual funds

Mutual funds

Closed-end funds

Exchange-traded funds

Government-sponsored enterprises

Federally related mortgage pools

ABS issuers

Finance companies (consumer credit)

Mortgage companies

REITs

Brokers and dealers

Funding corporations

Japan

Definition of financial sector used:

Domestically licensed banks

Foreign banks

Shinkin banks

Other financial institutions

Note on statistics: Japan produces two statistical series, one for the calendar year and one for the fiscal year. ECRI statistics correspond to the calendar year statistics. GDP is also called Gross Domestic Expenditure (GDE).

Note

The authors thank conference participants for discussion and gratefully acknowledge financial support by the European Credit Research Institute (ECRI). Nicola Jentzsch also thanks Yale University for the generous financial support as Fox International Fellow 03-04.

References

Adam, K., T. Jappelli, A. Menichini, M. Padula, and M. Pagano. 2002. "Analyse, Compare, and Apply Alternative Indicators and Monitoring Methodologies to Measure the Evolution of Capital Market Integration in the European Union." European Commission, Brussels. http://www.europa.eu.int/comm./internal_market/en/update/economicreform.

Amel, D. F., and M. Starr-McCluer. 2001. "Market Definition in Banking: Recent Evidence." Working paper, Federal Reserve Board of Governors, Washington, D.C.

Avery, B. R., R. W. Bostic, P. S. Calem, and G. B. Canner. 2000. "Credit Scoring: Statistical Issues and Evidence from Credit-Bureau Files." *Real Estate Economics* 28, no. 3: 523–547.

Barron, J. M., and Michael Staten. 2003. "The Value of Comprehensive Credit Reports: Lessons from the U.S. Experience." In *Credit Reporting Systems and the International Economy*, ed. M. Miller, 273–310. Cambridge, Mass.: The MIT Press.

Bostic, R., and P. Calem. 2003. "Privacy Restrictions and the Use of Data at Credit Registries." In *Credit Reporting Systems and the International Economy*, ed. M. Miller, 311–335. Cambridge, Mass.: The MIT Press.

CEACCU. 2003. Cuadernos del CEACCU, N° 1, Los españoles y el sobreendeudamiento, Madrid. http://www.ceaccu.org/docspdf/Cuaderno%201.pdf.

Debelle, G., 2004. "Household Debt and the Macroeconomy." *BIS Quarterly Review* (March): 51–64.

Diez Guardia, Nuria. 2000. "Consumer Credit in the European Union." ECRI Research Report no. 1, European Credit Research Institute, Brussels.

Elliehausen, G. E., and J. D. Wolken. 1992. "Banking Markets and the Use of Financial Services by Households." *Federal Reserve Bulletin* 78, no. 169: 169–181.

European Credit Research Institute. 2003. "ECRI Statistical Package Consumer Credit and Lending in the EU and the CEECs for the Period 1990–2002." European Credit Research Institute, Brussels.

Harris, C., and D. Laibson. 2001. "Hyperbolic Discounting and Consumption." Draft, February. http://post.economics.harvard.edu/faculty/laibson/papers/hlfeb19.pdf.

Jentzsch, N. 2003a. "The Regulation of Financial Privacy: A Comparative Study of the United States and Europe." ECRI Research Report no. 5, European Credit Research Institute, Brussels. http://www.ecri.be/HTM/research/ecripublications.htm.

Jentzsch, N. 2003b. "The Regulatory Environment for Business Information Sharing." Background paper for the World Bank Doing Business in 2004 report. http://rru.worldbank.org/DoingBusiness/TopicReports/CreditMarkets.aspx.

Jentzsch, N. 2003c. "The Implications of the New Consumer Credit Directive for EU Market Integration." Testimony before the Committee on Legal Affaires and the Internal Market, European Parliament, April 29. http://www.europarl.eu.int/hearings/20030429/juri/jentzsch1_en.pdf.

Kiser, E. K. 2002. "Household Switching Behavior at Depository Institutions: Evidence from Survey Data." Working paper, Federal Reserve Board of Governors, Washington, D.C.

Maki, D. M. 2000. "The Growth of Consumer Credit and the Household Debt Service Burden." FEDS working paper 2000-12, Washington, D.C.

Nickell, S. J. 1997. "Unemployment and Labor Market Rigidities: Europe versus North America." *Journal of Economic Perspectives* 11, no. 3: 55–74.

World Bank. 2004. *Doing Business in 2004*. Oxford: Oxford University Press.

3   Household Debt Demand and Supply: A Cross-Country Comparison

Jonathan N. Crook

Economists have been interested in the demand and supply of household credit for many decades. However, the volume of literature on these topics has rapidly expanded, especially since the 1980s. The interest has been stimulated by developments in both microeconomic and macroeconomic theory—the credit channel by which monetary policy is transmitted (as in Bernanke and Blinder 1988) by Hall's (1978) modeling of the microeconomic theory of the consumer using Euler equations, and from Stiglitz and Weiss's (1981) analysis of credit constraints.

Most empirical work using microdata relates to the United States, but studies using microdata recently have also been carried out for Italy and to a smaller extent for the United Kingdom. The need for further studies of how credit markets affect households, especially in Europe, and for analysis to underpin policy is heightened within Europe by the ongoing discussions in the European Union as to how to regulate the Europe-wide consumer credit market. This chapter is intended to review and to compare the results of studies that have examined the demand and supply of credit across countries at this apparently opportune moment.

The structure of this chapter is as follows. Section 3.1 starts with some descriptive statistics concerning access to and use of credit by households in several different countries. It is designed to complement the aggregate statistics on the credit industry provided in chapter 2, and discusses briefly the extent to which the facts are in agreement with the theory of household debt demand reviewed in chapter 1. Section 3.2 reviews issues arising in bringing theoretical perspectives to bear on the data. Observed outcomes arise from the interaction between household demand and the policies of lenders. Several methods for disentangling the demand aspects from supply, and, in particular, to identify the possibility of credit constraints, have been utilized in the literature and are discussed here. The main results from studies of the demand for credit are discussed from a cross-country comparative perspective, and a brief overview is also offered of credit-supply studies (a topic discussed more extensively elsewhere in this volume). Section 3.3 reviews in greater detail the evidence on whether households are credit-constrained, and section 3.4 provides a brief summary of the main findings.

3.1   Household Debt Facts

3.1.1   The Incidence of Household Debt

Adequate data on household debt are only available for a limited range of countries. Table 3.1, column (1), shows the proportion of households in selected countries that have at least some debt. This proportion is highest in the United States, where three-quarters of households have some debt. Debt levels are also high in Canada, the United Kingdom, and the Netherlands, and only slightly lower in France, Sweden, Australia, and Japan. Although Germany has a relatively high debt to GDP ratio, it shares with Spain a lower figure of around one-third of households in debt. Italy, with only 17 percent of households in debt, shares a low ratio with Greece where only 13 percent are in debt. Clearly, international differences in the development and liberalization of capital markets play a part in explaining these cross-country differences (Jappelli and Pagano 1989).

Columns (2) and (3) of table 3.1 show the proportions of households with mortgages and with nonhousing (consumer) debt for the subset of countries where such data are available. Here there are again roughly three groups. Among European countries, more households in the United Kingdom and the Netherlands have a mortgage or other housing loan than elsewhere, and figures are similarly high in the United States, Canada, and Japan. In the middle group, Germany, France, Sweden, and Spain all have between 18 percent and 27 percent of households with a mortgage. Although high mortgage debt is broadly associated with high consumer debt across countries, the cross-country rankings are not completely identical. Again the "Anglo-Saxon" countries stand out as having high consumer debt, but the Netherlands has lower consumer debt relatively to its mortgage debt. The three Mediterranean countries are characterized by both low consumer debt and low housing debt.

Table 3.1
Incidence of household debt

	(1) Proportion of households with debt	(2) Proportion with mortgages	(3) Proportion with consumer loans
United States	75	45	49
Canada	68	35	
Australia	46		
Japan	51	34	
United Kingdom	55	40	34
Netherlands	59	43	26
France	48	25	33
Sweden	46	27	30
Germany	34	18	23
Spain	32	18	19
Italy	17	11	8
Greece	14	7	9

Sources:
Australia: Australian Bureau of Statistics (ABS), *Australian Social Trends 2002;* income and expenditure data from ABS, *1998–9 Household Expenditure Survey.* Data excludes credit card debt.
Canada: Net wealth Table 3.10a from *Survey of Financial Security 1999* and Bank of Canada.
United States: Aizcorbe, A., A. B. Kennickell, and K. B. Moore, *Federal Reserve Bulletin* January 2003, from SCF 2001 and *Annual Report 2001* Bank of Italy. Cols. 1 and 2 refer to 2001, col. 3 to 1998.
Japan: *National Survey of Family Income and Expenditure 1999.* Japanese data refers only to households headed by a couple.
Note: The proportions for the European countries is calculated by the authors from the European Community Household Panel for 1996.

3.1.2 Debt by Socioeconomic Characteristics

Table 3.2 shows the proportions of households with any type of debt by household characteristics for seven different countries for which data are available. There is some variation in the timing of these surveys: The earliest study cited here is that of the Netherlands in 1997, while Germany's is the latest in 2002. Again, the surveyed countries vary widely from high-debt economies (such as the United States) to low-debt countries (such as Italy). The first part of the table looks at the proportion of households that has at least some debt by age of head of the household. Consistently, in all countries, younger households are more likely to be in debt than older households. A life-cycle

Table 3.2
Percentage of households with debt by sociodemographic characteristics

Year	United States[1] 2001	Canada[2] 1999	Japan[3] 1999	Italy[4] 2000	Nether-lands[5] 1997	United King-dom[6] 2000	Ger-many[7] 2002
Age							
<30	80.0	67	49.3	27.8	66.5	83.8	75.8
30–39	86.5	84	61.2	30.9	72.6	87.5	75.7
40–49	87.9	81	67.4	27.9	77.0	83.4	74.8
50–59	80.2	77	57.4	20.6	74.0	68.4	67.1
60–69	69.1	62	32.5	12.7	54.5	36.4	48.9
≥70	36.4	27	19.0	2.1	28.3	12.6	24.8
Income percentile							
<20	49.3		32.4	6.2		31.7	40.0
20–40	70.2		46.7	13.3		43.9	60.1
40–60	82.1		55.7	18.8		68.5	71.0
60–80	85.6		61.7	24.6		80.9	74.0
80–90	91.4		62.6	27.3		85.6	69.5
90–100	85.3		62.1	29.9		86.9	68.7
Wealth percentile							
<25	68.7			14.3	37.8		58.8
25–50	80.8			17.6	62.6		63.3
50–75	77.9			20.0	81.7		65.7
75–90	75.0			22.5	80.7		63.1
90–100	70.1			23.2			52.6
Work status							
Employed	86.5			29.1		84.2	72.7
Self-employed	81.7			24.6		76.7	65.7
Retired	44.3			7.8		19.8	28.1
Unemployed	61.5			14.4		65.0	64.9
Other				7.5		64.1	65.8

Notes:
[1] Authors calculations using the *Survey of Consumer Finances*. The employment category "other" includes the unemployed.
[2] Net Worth using data from the *Survey of National Security*, 1999. Age groups for Canada are <25, 25–34, 35–44, 45–54, 55–64, 65+.
[3] Results taken from *National Survey of Family Income and Expenditure*, Tables 25, 26, and 35.
[4] Constructed using 2000 wave of the *Survey of Household Income and Wealth*.
[5] Numbers taken from Alessie, Hochguertel, and van Soest 2002. For wealth, 75–90 percentiles means 75–100.
[6] Constructed using the 2000 wave of the *British Household Panel Survey*.
[7] Figures calculated using 2002 wave of the *German Socio-Economic Panel*.

pattern is apparent in each country by which the proportion of house-holds having debt peaks when household heads are in either the age range 30–39 or 40–49. The proportion with debt falls sharply after age 60. The peak is attained earlier in the life in Canada, Italy, the United Kingdom, and Germany than in the other countries.

The difference between the peak age group's debt proportion and the lowest also differs across countries. In the United States and Canada, for example, proportions in debt remain high until age of head of household reaches the late fifties and never falls below a quarter of the population, even in the oldest age group. The United Kingdom has a comparable incidence of debt until age 60, but the oldest age groups have much lower incidence of debt. The same pattern is true for Italy, albeit from a much lower peak.

Table 3.2 also compares the proportion of households with debts by their level of income. In all countries, richer households are more likely to have debt than poor households. This may reflect differential access to credit as well as differences in the demand for credit, insofar as poorer households typically have little housing wealth, and housing wealth is a key factor in obtaining access to both secured and un-secured debt (see chapter 5 for further discussion). This may explain why the proportion of households with debt increases dramatically in the bottom half of the distribution, and more slowly in the upper part of the distribution.

In Germany, more debt is held by middle-income households (with income between the fortieth and eightieth decile) than by households in the top 20 percent of the income distribution. At these high-income levels, almost all households in the United Kingdom and the United States have some debts, but in contrast, only one-third of high-income households have debts in Italy. In fact, the incidence of debt is lower among rich households in Italy than among the poorest 20 percent in all the other countries for which we have data.

Debt by the distribution of wealth varies more substantially, perhaps reflecting differences in the composition and measurement of wealth across countries. The Netherlands has a significant gradient of debt incidence from lowest wealth to highest; the United States and Germany are more uniform. Italy again has a low gradient and much lower levels of debt across wealth categories.

The final part of the table looks at indebtedness by the work status of the household head for the few countries where such data are available. In all cases, employed households are the most likely to be in debt, followed closely by self-employed households. Retired households are the least likely to borrow, as we might expect if households engage in life-cycle and precautionary saving. These households cannot expect their income to increase in the future, and hence, they should not be borrowing; moreover, risks attached to working income are in their past. Nevertheless, nearly half of U.S. households, nearly 20 percent of U.K. households, and over a quarter of German households still have outstanding debts when they are retired. In three of those countries for which figures are available, unemployed households are around 20 percent less likely to be in debt than employed households. In Germany, these households are only 8 percent less likely to hold debts.

Table 3.3 shows values of the total level of debt per household in the United States, the United Kingdom, Italy, and Japan by socioeconomic characteristics. With the exception of Italy, these are averages over all households whether they hold debt or not, but by combining tables 3.2 and 3.3, it is also possible to calculate average indebtedness for households that hold debt. The average value of debt held by those who hold debt is least in Italy and highest in the United States, with the United Kingdom and Japan lying between the two extremes (the figures for Japan, however, refer only to households with two or more persons). When comparing age groups, debt levels peak in the middle of the life cycle, in line with the result for the incidence of debt in table 3.2. Note, however, that debt levels by age do not exactly match the distribution of probabilities of holding debt by age. For example, in the United States, while 80 percent of those under 30 years old have debt compared to 86.5 percent in the 30–39 category, the level of debt for the under-30-year-olds is less than half that of the 30–39 category.

The comparison across income groups in table 3.3 shows that the amount of debt, in absolute terms, increases with current income in all four countries. It is, however, interesting to compare across countries the level of debt of the poorest compared to the richest households. The top decile has over twenty times the level of debt of the poorest group in the United States, but only eight times the level of debt among the poorest in Japan. For the United Kingdom and Italy, the ratio is between these two extremes. Debts also increase with the level of net wealth for the two countries for which we have data. In both the United Kingdom and the United States, increases in wealth are associated with increases in debt levels. This mirrors the pattern for the proportion of households by wealth category with any debt in

Table 3.3
Mean household debt by sociodemographic characteristics

	United States[1]	Japan[2]	Italy[3]	United Kingdom[4]
	54,500	5,674	3,440	18,261
Age				
<30	31,505	3,120	4,959	21,463
30–39	69,053	7,804	5,865	35,528
40–49	76,627	8,449	5,767	30,821
50–59	72,636	5,796	3,295	14,665
60–69	41,974	2,758	2,364	3,003
≥70	13,683	1,734	212	708
Income percentile				
<20	8,200	1,453	659	2,982
20–40	19,500	3,917	1,091	4,843
40–60	38,600	5,793	1,858	14,625
60–80	64,900	7,492	4,286	25,327
80–90	101,200	8,042	4,785	37,431
90–100	181,500	11,731	9,137	48,308
Wealth percentile				
<25	15,700		985	
25–50	40,600		3,314	
50–75	59,200		3,011	
75–90	76,202		5,158	
90–100	141,774		8,989	
Work status				
Employed	36,800		5,002	30,501
Self-employed	63,600		6,848	30,277
Retired	4,300		1,068	8,198
Unemployed			1,166	1,336
Other	20,800		1,073	7,313

Notes:

[1] Constructed from the 2001 Survey of Consumer Finances, in $1,000 of U.S. dollars. The employment category "other" includes the unemployed.

[2] Data from tables 25 and 26, *National Survey of Family Income and Expenditure 1999* in thousands of Japanese yen and relate to households with two or more persons.

[3] Constructed using the 2000 wave of the Survey of Households Income and Wealth, in euros.

[4] Constructed from the British Household Panel Survey, 2000 wave, in British pounds.

table 3.2, as does the fact that the level of debt increases more slowly with changes in wealth than changes in income. Finally, when comparing employment status, debts are much higher among employed and self-employed households than for other types of households. The self-employed have the greatest value of debt per household in both the United States and Italy. Table 3.2 suggested that self-employed households were less likely to be in debt than employed households, so this result suggests that when they have debts, these debts are much larger. In the United Kingdom, the overall levels of debt for self-employed and employed households are remarkably similar, but the self-employed are less likely to be in debt, so that the average debt of indebted self-employed people slightly exceeds that of employed people. However, an important caveat is that debt among the self-employed is particularly problematic to measure, since it is often difficult to distinguish between business and personal debt. The data for the United States pertains to any form of debt—including business debt—whereas that for Italy relates to debt only for personal use. As before, debt levels among the unemployed and among retired households are much lower.

3.1.3   Theoretical Perspectives on the Debt Facts

Cross-country evidence on disaggregated debt holdings is broadly consistent with the permanent-income and life-cycle approaches to household demand for debt (see chapter 1), which also offers clues as to what might determine differences across countries. The positive relationship between income and debt is not surprising if, as is likely, current income is positively correlated in cross-section with permanent income. And the different strength across countries of that relationship, and of the relationship between wealth and debt, may reflect differences in the inequality of permanent income in different countries.

As regards employment status, some of the facts might seem surprising if we apply the basic version of the Permanent Income Hypothesis (PIH). In households where the head is unemployed, current income is relatively low compared to income in the future, when the household might hope to be employed (Friedman 1957). The PIH would then predict that periods of low temporary income are exactly when we would expect such households to be borrowing, but in table 3.2, we find that they are less likely to borrow in those countries where data are available. It seems probable that constraints on the supply of debt to unemployed households explain this disparity. In other respects the impact of employment status on indebtedness is consistent with the permanent-income hypothesis. For example, it is not surprising to find that the self-employed have larger average debts when they are in debt, because consumption-smoothing motives for holding debt are stronger when incomes are more volatile.

As regards comparison across age groups, levels of indebtedness are generally perhaps not as high as might be predicted by a stylized life-cycle saving model in the early part of the working life, when consumption smoothing might easily predict debts amounting to several years' worth of income. The absolute level of debt reported in table 3.3 is lower than theory predicts—even in the United States, where the majority of people have some debt. In Italy, the most extreme case, debt levels are small among the relatively few households that do have debt: Even between the ages of thirty and fifty, households would on average take only a few months to repay all their debts. In summary, consumption tracks income rather closely over the early portion of households' lifetime. As discussed in chapter 1, this either reflects supply constraints in the credit market or additional motives for net saving in addition to consumption smoothing, such as precautionary or bequest motives.

3.2 Demand and Supply Explanations

Motives for household acquisition of debt were discussed in chapter 1. One motive derives from consumption smoothing over the life cycle and in the face of income volatility. Another arises from financing durable goods purchases and perhaps investments in health and education. In general terms, a demand function can be written as

$$D_{it}^{*d} = f^d(x_{it}) + \varepsilon_{it}^d, \tag{1}$$

where D_{it}^{*d} is the ith household's desired stock of debt at time t, x_{it} are observable characteristics, and ε_{it}^d is an error term that arises since some of the determinants of demand are not observable. The PIH suggests that, given the information available to the household in any time period, there is an optimal or desired stock of assets that can be positive (assets) or negative (debts). In reality, the existence of heterogeneous types of assets and debts and transaction costs implies that the household may have both positive assets (such as housing equity) and debt (such as a mortgage) simultaneously.

The desired stock of assets and debt changes as relevant factors evolve over time. These include the household's composition and new information about the household's future income, as well as interest rates and other financing costs. Credit market constraints in the form of a difference between lending and borrowing interest rates will also affect the volume of desired household debt. Changes in expected future wealth will affect the prospective annuity income that can be received from the household's assets and so affect the stock of debt the household wishes to hold in each current and future period. Net acquisition of debt over the lifetime will therefore arise from new information on prospective wealth, from any discrepancy between the desired and actual stock of durables, from changes in household characteristics, from changes in the current and expected interest rate, and from unanticipated fluctuations in income.

Of course, the amounts of debt observed in practice (and discussed in the previous section) are those that result from the interaction of demand and supply. In very general terms, the supply of debt equation can be written as

$$D_{it}^s = f^s(x_{it}^s) + \varepsilon_{it}^s, \tag{2}$$

where x_{it}^s is a collection of observable variables used by financial institutions and other suppliers to decide whether to lend to an individual and if so, how much and at what rate of interest. Again ε_{it}^s describes errors in observing the behavior of financial institutions. This supply function is discussed further in this chapter.

In many circumstances households can acquire their optimal stock of debt at each point in time, with the average interest rate on that debt reflecting the perceived riskiness of the household. In other circumstances, households obtain less debt than they desire, and hence can be termed credit-constrained. We discuss definitions of credit constraints later; so at this stage, a household is defined to be credit-constrained if its desired stock of debt is greater than the maximum amount lenders are willing to lend at the current risk-adjusted interest rate: that is, $D_{it}^{*d} > D_{it}^s$. If, for some reason (discussed in chapter 1 and elsewhere in this volume) interest rates do not adjust to equate demand and supply, the volume of debt that we observe for any household is the smaller of D_{it}^d and D_{it}^s. This can be written (following Grant 2003) as

$$D_{it} = f^d(x_{it}^d) - \pi_{it}[f^d(x_{it}^d) - f^s(x_{it}^s)] + \varepsilon_{it}, \tag{3}$$

where π_t equals 1 if an individual faces a binding credit constraint so that $D_{it}^d > D_{it}^s$ (and desired debt is positive) and zero if it does not, and ε_{it} is an error term.

3.2.1 Demand for Credit: Empirical Findings

In estimating the demand for credit two methodologies can be distinguished. In one, π_{it} is assumed to be observed directly using survey data, or can be reasonably proxied; in the other, π_{it} is not observed but can be estimated by a more "structural" approach. We will call the first method the sample selection method and the second the "disequilibrium" method.

In the sample selection method, which has been used by, for example, Duca and Rosenthal (1993), Cox and Jappelli (1993), Gropp, Sholtz, and White (1997), Crook (2001), and Magri (2002), equation (3) is estimated using only the sample of households that both desire debt and who do not face binding credit constraints. This is because desired debt can be observed only for this group. But this may result in sample selection bias if there is correlation between the errors in the demand equation—that is, the process explaining whether demand is positive—and in the equation explaining whether a household is credit-constrained (Heckman 1976). Therefore, two selection equations (one for whether debt is positive, the other for whether the household is constrained) are jointly estimated with equation (3).

In the disequilibrium method, we can exploit the fact that π_{it} equals 1 when $D_{it}^d > D_{it}^s$ and $D_{it}^d > 0$, and is equal to zero otherwise, to write down a fully parametric model. Grant (2003) estimated such a model, in which D_{it}^d, D_{it}^s, and π_{it} are jointly estimated as a function of the demand and supply characteristics by maximum likelihood. As in the two-stage selection model, however, exclusion restrictions are required to identify the model.

The household demand for debt has been extensively studied only for the United States and Italy. Table 3.4 summarizes the results from the United States and Italy in terms of the relationship between parameter estimates of the demand for debt and household characteristics. A number of factors may explain differences in the results between the studies. These include differences in data sets between countries, in the institutional characteristics of countries, differences in the type of debt for which the demand is modeled, and differences between time periods. For example, in the United States, the proportion of household debt made up of mortgages in the Survey of Consumer Finances (SCF)

Table 3.4
Estimates of the household demand for debt

	Cox and Jappelli U.S.A. SCF 1983 level/1000	Duca and Rosen-thal[1] U.S.A. SCF 1983 level/1000	Gropp, Sholz, and White[2] U.S.A. SCF 1983 log	Crook[3] U.S.A. SCF 1995 log	Grant[4] U.S.A. CEX 1988–1993 log	Magri[5] Italy SHIW 1989–1998 log	Fabri and Padula Italy SHIW 1998 level
Current income	−0.29*	1.03*	0.14*	2.64*	0.22*	−0.32*	0.15*
Income squared		−0.003	−0.004*	−0.87*	−0.11*		
Permanent earnings	0.42*						
Pension income		0.13				0.012	
Self-employed						0.32*	
Unemployed		−0.60*		−0.48*		−0.16*	
Net worth	0.23*	0.12*	0.28*	−0.01*		0.26*	0.03*
Homeowner				1.97*			
No. of children					ns	0.07	
Household size	1.05	2.69*	0.12*	0.15*			
Married	−3.40	1.93	0.02	−0.1	0.34*	−0.06	
Female	0.43	−3.35	−0.15	−0.2	0.47*		
Nonwhite	3.15	−5.23	0.15	ns	−0.31*		
Age ≤ 25	2.37		0.13*	0.07	−0.32		
Age 25–34	0.99*		−0.006	−0.03	−0.11	−0.012	
Age 35–44	−1.04*		−0.04*	−0.02	−0.15		
Age 45–54	−1.82*		−0.04*	−0.01			
Age 55–64	−0.65		−0.05*	−0.10*			
Age > 65	−1.29*		−0.06	−0.15*			
Education		2.97					0.39*
High school diploma			0.12		0.51*	0.17*	
Some college			0.40*		0.63*		
College degree			0.52*	0.22*	0.59*		

Notes:
*Significant at the 5 percent level. All results included a selection equation.
[1] Duca and Rosenthal selected households under age 35 and used estimated wealth instead of net worth.
[2] Gropp, Scholz, and White use total assets rather than net worth.
[3] Crook reports a result for working rather than unemployed, and for different racial groups, none of which were significant.
[4] Grant reports results for age, age-squared, and age-cubed. He excluded housing debt, measured income in logs, and used age divided by 10 rather than age. The results reported coefficients for one, two, or "three or more" children, which were not significant. His sample excluded the self-employed and those whose age was over 55 or below 25.
[5] Magri measured income and net worth in logs. Pension income was total retirement income. Coefficient for 25–34 refers to under 35. She also reported results for "number of earners."

has consistently been around 80 percent throughout the 1980s and 1990s, whereas in the Italian Survey of Household Income and Wealth (SHIW), it has consistently been around 60 percent. The studies by Cox and Jappelli (1993), Duca and Rosenthal (1993), and Gropp, Scholz, and White (1997) relate mainly to mortgage demand in the United States in the 1980s. Crook's study covers mainly mortgage demand in the United States in the early 1990s. Grant's study refers to the same time period but considers only the demand for unsecured debt. The two Italian studies (with a lower proportion of debt devoted to mortgages) relate to the 1990s.

Interesting conclusions can be drawn from the results of these different studies of different countries as regards the role of crucial variables. First, consider the role of current household income. Most studies of the United States find a positive but nonlinear effect of income on debt, regardless of the type of debt. The only exception to this finding, the study by Cox and Jappelli (1993), includes a direct measure of permanent income, which they found was positively related to the demand for debt. Given that the majority of demand is for mortgage debt, the most likely interpretation of Cox and Jappelli's finding is that families with higher permanent income have a greater demand for housing. Also, families with higher permanent income may also be more confident of their job security and hence have lower savings and higher borrowing because of precautionary motives (Duca and Rosenthal 1993). The separate and negative effect of current income found by Cox and Jappelli may be interpreted as reflecting an expectation that income will rise in the future, and so families with low current income are borrowing to smooth consumption.

For Italy, the results of the studies simply disagree on the effects of current income. Magri (2002) finds a negative effect, whereas Fabri and Padula (2002) find a positive effect. The latter study may have the same interpretation as in the U.S. studies and might be preferred to that of Magri because it is less likely to suffer collinearity between income and age. However, Magri argues that her negative effect may be due to the fact that high-income households in Italy use less debt to finance housing and consumer-durable purchases than low-income families.

The effect of net wealth (or total assets) is generally positive for both countries when the demand is mostly for mortgages. Unfortunately, Grant's study for unsecured debt did not include a direct measure of wealth. Households that expect their income to be higher in the future (their permanent income is higher) would be expected to consume more, and this includes consumption on housing and other durable goods—hence, we might expect high assets and high borrowing to be correlated. Moreover, these assets would provide collateral for more borrowing, and high-asset households may be supplied with more credit.

Turning to education, generally, the higher the level of education received by the head of household the greater the demand for debt. This is true for both countries and for both mortgage and unsecured debt. Higher educational attainment may be an indication of higher future income and greater job security and so is consistent with the PIH/life-cycle theory. Grant (2003) showed that in the United States, the earnings of college-educated household heads increase with their age by less than more poorly educated households. All the studies except that of Duca and Rosenthal (1993) (whose sample is restricted to those under 35) in the United States found that the demand for debt by age follows the familiar life-cycle pattern, at least for mortgage-dominated debt. Demand increases with age up to the middle thirties and decreases at higher ages of heads of households. For unsecured debt, the decrease in demand with age occurs only for those with a college degree; otherwise, age has no detectable effect.

Generally, controlling for being married, family size increases the demand for mortgage-denominated debt in the United States. But in Italy, having more children has no effect. United States and Italian studies relating mostly to mortgage demand find that being married has no effect, conditional on family size and household income. This is surprising since again one might expect that being married would increase the marginal utility of the consumption of durables. In contrast, the demand for unsecured debt (Grant 2003) is positively affected by being married in the United States. Gender and race of the head of household appear to have no effect on the demand for mortgage dominated debt in the United States. But households whose head is non-white appear to have lower demand for consumer credit than those with a white head of household. Also, households whose head is unemployed demand less debt in the United States, which is surprising since the PIH predicts that those who expect their income to increase will wish to take credit. An obvious explanation is that the unemployed are pessimistic about their expected future income prospects. As suggested earlier, this result suggests that credit does not act as a consumption-smoothing insurance mechanism when an income earner looses his or her job.

Some additional conclusions, which are not comparable across the two countries from the research to date, may be drawn. First, for the United States, Gropp, Scholz, and White (1997) find that wealthy households will increase their desired stock of debt when they can retain more of their assets if they go bankrupt, whereas less wealthy households decrease their stock. This is consistent with intuition: Those with the most to lose in bankruptcy will benefit more by high exemptions. Gropp, Scholz, and White interpret the negative effect at low-asset values as indicating a supply effect rather than an effect on desired debt. This is possible, but there is ambiguity as to whether Gropp, Scholz, and White are modeling demand or merely the ex post volume of debt. In their studies of Italian households, Magri (2002) and Fabri and Padula (2002) consider the effects of enforcement costs on desired debt. Fabri and Padula show that actual debt possessed by unconstrained households is positively related to the efficiency of the judicial system in the region of residence. Areas that are more efficient may have lower costs and charge lower interest rates. This is consistent with their theoretical model. Magri finds that demand is greater in regions where a greater percentage of debt is recovered.

3.2.2   The Supply of Credit

Estimating differences in the supply of credit to households is even more difficult. There are few empirical studies that estimate cross-sectional debt supply functions explicitly; many studies infer supply conditions from demand functions and from models identifying constrained households. One exception is that of Grant (2003), who used the methodology explained in section 3.2 to estimate a supply of credit function for the United States. However, only three variables were found to be significantly related to supply: Being married, having a college degree, and income are all positively related to supply. Gender, age, number of children, the interest rate, and being nonwhite are not significant.

However, there is a rapidly growing literature on credit scoring (see, e.g., Thomas, Edelman, and Crook 2002 and the special January 2001 issue of the *Journal of the Operational Research Society*). One variant of this literature examines how household characteristics are associated with the probabilities of default. If the probability of default is associated with the subsequent supply of credit to a given household, then this literature provides one route to understanding supply conditions.

Some words of warning are however in order. These models are designed to predict default, subject to being "statistically derived" and "empirically valid" (as required by U.S. law). They are not models of household behavior as such, and they predict supply conditional on demand being positive rather than estimating the unconditional supply of credit. Moreover, such models typically include a large number of variables, often entered nonlinearly, in interactions or discontinuously. In short, covariates may be highly collinear and it is difficult to draw simple conclusions as to the impact of any particular household characteristic on the outcome. Nevertheless, some general conclusions can be drawn.

Boyes, Hoffman, and Law (1989), using a constrained bivariate probit model of the accept/reject decision in a first-stage model, and the default or good payment outcome since being granted a loan in the second stage, find that the probability of default is negatively related to age and to being married, and positively related to the number of deposits and having some years of college but not a college degree. Being a homeowner is associated with a lower chance of default, a renter with a higher chance, a high expenditure: income ratio is positively associated with default. Having a major credit card reduces the probability of default, having a store card increases it. Particularly significant are items supplied by credit bureau: The number of inquiries or various derogatory accounts elsewhere were positively associated with higher probability of default, and having satisfactory accounts elsewhere was negatively correlated with probability of default.

Using the SCF for 1998, Stavins (2000) models the probability that a household was two or more months behind with any debt repayment. As in Boyes, age and being married were negatively related to default. The number of credit cards and income, net wealth, and debt: Income ratio and years of education were also related. As with Boyes, family size was positively related. Although Boyes, Hoffman, and Law 1989 is often cited, both of these papers yield very simple scoring models. As mentioned, score card builders typically use more complicated functions to predict default. Nonlinearities for each variable are allowed for; in some, the estimated probability of default need not be monotonically related to continuous variables (Crook, Hamilton, and Thomas 1992; Desai, Crook, and Overstreet 1996). In general, models that are more closely allied to those of lenders find that in addition to bureau information, measures indicating household stability—such as years at address and years at current bank—are negatively related to default and therefore to the supply of credit (see, e.g., table 5.3). For example, Crook, Hamilton, and Thomas (1992), using a sample of credit card holders, found these variables to be significant as well as employment category, residential status, spouse's income, and having a phone.

  It has been possible to identify some cross-country differences in the ability of certain household characteristics to predict default probabilities. Platts and Howe (2004) considered data relating to the United Kingdom, Germany, Greece, Belgium, and Italy. Not only are different variables collected and different nominal categories used in different countries, but the same variable sometimes has very different predictive power in different countries. For example, not having a home phone was more predictive in the United Kingdom than in other countries, and having a bad credit bureau report was more predictive of default in Italy, Germany, and the United Kingdom than in Greece. It should be emphasized that whilst the selection of these variables is not based on a priori economic theory, they are the types of variables that institutions actually use to decide whom is granted credit and whom is not, and they, therefore, do have predictive power.

3.3   Credit Constraints

Earlier in this chapter, supply-side considerations were summarized by a standard supply schedule, linking the quantity and price of credit. To explore further some of the issues, however, it is useful to recall that, as discussed in chapter 1, quantity constraints play an important role in the credit market. Theoretical explanations of how these constraints arise are provided in the seminal papers by Jaffee and Russell (1976) and Stiglitz and Weiss (1981). However, empirical studies use different meanings of the term. Hayashi (1987), for instance, proposes that credit constraints exist if either a household is unable, for whatever reason, to borrow against future earnings beyond a certain limit that can be positive or zero, or the rate at which households can borrow differs from the rate at which they can lend. Most studies have focused on the first of these two definitions, seeking empirical indicators of debt demand exceeding supply at the household level.

  A large number of empirical definitions derived from survey data have been proposed. A common definition (Jappelli 1990; Crook 1996;

Cox and Jappelli 1993; Jappelli, Pischke, and Souleles 1998; Ferri and Simon 2002; Crook 2001) is that a household is credit-constrained if the household was either "rejected" or "discouraged" from applying for credit. For example, a household might be regarded as having been rejected if (using information in the Survey of Consumer Finances for the United States) it reported that in the past five years (or past few years in the 1983 wave), a particular lender had partially or completely turned down any request for credit, and the respondent was unable to gain the full amount by reapplying elsewhere. A household was regarded as "discouraged" if it had not been rejected, but there was a time in the past five years that the respondent or his or her spouse thought of applying for credit but changed their minds because they thought they would be turned down. This definition has also been used by studies using the Survey of Household Income and Wealth (SHIW) for Italy (such as in the studies of Magri 2002, and Guiso, Jappelli, and Terlizzese 1996), which contain similar questions, but the time period to which the questions relate is just the previous year.

This definition is not universally accepted, however. One obvious weakness of indicators of being credit-constrained that use survey questions of this type is that a household may apply for such a large loan that they have no realistic chance of repaying it. They would then be identified as credit-constrained. This is even more problematic when discouraged borrowers are included. A further difficulty with this definition is how to treat discouraged borrowers, and how to decide whether they would have been refused had they applied. These households might not have been refused, and hence perhaps should not be included in the constrained group. Ferri and Simon (2002) argue that since the interest rate on credit cards is higher than on most other types of loans, those with positive credit card balances must have been unable to gain loans from cheaper sources. Their measures consist of the possession of a positive credit card balance or no card (the latter may be unable to gain a card). Given the evidence from U.S. consumers described by Bertaut and Haliassos in chapter 6, however, these may not be plausible indicators of a constraint. Duca and Rosenthal (1993) use the same measure as Jappelli (1990), but in their analysis, attention is limited to those households that had at least some debts—this being an indicator of positive demand. In effect, rather than estimating how π_{it} changes with the household's characteristics, they have instead estimated the effect of these indicators conditional on observed demand: that is, $E(\pi_{it} | D_{it}^d > 0)$. Fabri and Padula (2001) and Magri (2002) both adopted a similar approach for Italian data, restricting their sample to those who asked for a loan.

3.3.1 Aggregate Relevance of Credit Constraints

This section considers two measures of the significance of credit constraints: first, the proportion of the population that is constrained, and, second, estimates of the effect on the demand for credit of removing credit constraints.

The starting point is the extensive consumption literature that hypothesizes that rejections of the PIH in Euler equations arise because at least some consumers are credit-constrained and cannot borrow to smooth consumption in the way predicted by theory. Instead, they consume their current income (for further details, see chapter 1). For example, Hall and Mishkin (1982) found excess sensitivity of consumption to current income occurred for 20 percent of consumption; Jappelli and Pagano (1989) estimated that the proportion of income that was subject to credit constraints ranged from 12 percent in Sweden and 21 percent in the United States to 40 percent in the United Kingdom and 58 percent in Italy; Mariger (1987) estimated that just under 20 percent of the U.S. population in the early 1960s were liquidity constrained. There is, of course, an extensive debate (as in Deaton 1992 and Attanasio 1999) as to whether these results in fact constitute "rejections" of the PIH and as to whether credit constraints are the correct explanation for the rejection.

Studies of the responses to direct questionnaires are shown in table 3.5. It turns out that these results from household-level studies are very similar to those of aggregate studies that have tried to estimate the proportion of a population for which the Euler equation does not hold. The table shows that in the 1990s, the proportion of the United States population that was rejected or discouraged from applying for credit in a five-year period was around 25 percent, whereas in the early 1980s, it was around 19 percent. These figures are slightly lower than estimates from Grant (2003), who used a disequilibrium model to find that between 26 percent and 31 percent of the U.S. population was constrained in the early 1990s, but he only included households whose head was under age 55 (who may be more likely to be constrained) and also excluded the self-employed. Both estimates for the United States have weaknesses. The survey results rely on an accurate recall by the respondent on his or her own behalf and on behalf of his or her partner. Grant's model depends heavily on the exclusion

Table 3.5
Credit-constrained households as a percentage of the total population

	Consumer debt	Apply	Rejected	Rejected or discouraged	Rejected/ discouraged if applied
Italy					
1989	31.0	6.2	0.7	1.5	4.6
1991	26.3	—	1.2	3.8	13.4
1993	27.9	—	1.0	2.8	9.7
1995	31.3	5.7	0.8	2.2	6.9
1998	36.1	6.9	0.6	3.2	8.5
United States					
1983	80.0	—	9.8	15.1	18.2
1989	82.1	—	8.2	14.9	17.2
1992	83.0	—	12.9	18.4	20.7
1995	85.1	64.4	9.9	18.3	19.6
1998	82.7	63.5	10.7	18.6	20.4

Note: The U.S. data comes from the Survey of Consumer Finances, while the Italian data is obtained from the Survey of Households Income and Wealth. "Consumer debt" means that the household either holds at least some debt at the end of the year, or holds a credit card. "Apply" means applied during the last year in Italy but applied in past five years in the United States (except in 1983 where the question referred to the past few years). Data on accepted applications is not available in Italy in 1991 or 1993, or in 1983, 1989, and 1992 in the United States. The last column is conditional on either rejected/discouraged, or having consumer debt.

restrictions and may not be correctly identified. (The interest rate is not significant in either the demand or supply equations.) The true percentage may therefore lie somewhere in between the two values.

Table 3.5 also shows that in the 1990s, the proportion of the total population that was rejected or discouraged from applying to financial institutions was higher in the United States than in Italy. However, the proportion that applied for debt appears to be much higher in the United States than in Italy (63.8 percent and 7.86 percent, respectively) and so is the proportion that is rejected. That the Italian figures relate to the proportions within one year and the U.S. figures relate to the proportions over the previous five years would probably not alter this conclusion. This suggests that the greater incidence of debt shown in table 3.1 in the United States may be associated with a greater propensity for households to apply for debt in the United States than in Italy and a lower reject rate in the United States than in Italy.

3.3.2 Who Is Credit-Constrained?

Between the early 1980s and mid 1990s, the use of formal credit scoring became more widespread in most countries. Additionally, changes in U.S. banking legislation with the passing of the Reigle-Neal Act in 1994 allowed banks to operate branches in many states. There followed a wave of banking mergers that has altered the competitive structure of the U.S. retail loan market. These two factors may have altered the maximum amount of credit an individual with given characteristics could gain between the early 1980s and late 1990s. Italian banking has also been liberalized in recent years, and there may have been changes on the demand side. Hence, it is interesting to compare studies for earlier and later years.

The results of studies explaining the probability that a household of a particular type is constrained are shown in table 3.6. In the 1990s, in both Italy and the United States, current income was negatively related to the probability of being constrained. In fact a one thousand dollar increase in income would reduce the probability of being constrained by between 0.1 and 6 percentage points in the United States but only 0.004 percentage points in Italy. With the exception of the study by Cox and Jappelli, the same relationship was found for the United States in the 1980s and also in Italy. Unlike the Italian studies, three of the U.S. studies included income-squared and found it to have a positive effect, so as income increases the decrease in the chance of being constrained was reduced. Permanent income was also included in three U.S. studies but in only one was it found to be significant.

For both the 1980s and 1990s, the results for the effect of wealth in the United States are unclear: About half of the studies find a positive effect and half a negative effect. While Duca and Rosenthal's (1993) study has methodological advantages over the other studies and finds that wealth had no effect on the chance of being constrained in the 1980s, this may not be a finding that can easily be generalized because their sample consisted only of young households. Conflicting results are also found for Italy. Interestingly, home ownership has a strong negative effect on being constrained in the United States (but is not included in the Italian studies). Theoretically, we might expect that an increase in wealth would reduce lenders' risk and so increase supply. Empirically, wealth has a strong positive effect on demand (table 3.4) for both countries, so perhaps the equivocal result on the chance of being constrained is not surprising.

Table 3.6
Models of the probability that a household is credit-constrained

Data	Guiso, Jappelli, and Terlizze Italy 1987 SHIW Coefficients	Magri[1] Italy '89–'95 SHIW Marginal effects	Fabri and Padula[2] Italy '89–'98 SHIW Coefficients	Jappelli U.S.A. 1983 SCF Marginal effects	Gropp, Sholz, and White U.S.A. 1983 SCF Marginal effects	Cox and Jappelli[3] U.S.A. 1983 SCF Coefficients	Duca and Rosenthal[4] U.S.A. 1983 SCF Coefficients	Ferri and Simon[5] U.S.A. 1983 SCF Marginal effects	Ferri and Simon[5] U.S.A. '89–'98 SCF Marginal effects	Crook[6] U.S.A. 1995 SCF Coefficients
Income[7]	-0.006*	-0.002*	-0.010*	-0.55*	-0.032*	0.0136	-0.12	-0.011*	-0.012*	-0.061*
Income squared[7]					0.001*		0.00348			0.002
Perm. income[7]						-0.0763		-0.07	-0.009*	
Pension income[7]		-0.041								
Self-employed		0.054*								
Unemployed	0.902*		0.729*	0.027		0.142	0.007			-0.195
Net worth[7]		0.000	-0.008*	-0.15*		-0.043*	-1.33	0.001*	0.04*	-0.008*
Homeowner				-0.046			-0.442*	-0.090*	-0.094*	-0.174*
No. children		0.021*								
Household size	0.080*		0.043	0.011*	0.010*	0.044*	0.070	0.007	0.018*	0.078*
Married		-0.074*	-0.398*	-0.034	-0.057*	-0.147	-0.354	-0.027	-0.006	-0.102
Female	0.200*			0.007	-0.003	-0.026	0.060	0.004	-0.043	-0.038
Nonwhite				0.054*	0.087*	0.375*	0.339*	0.072*	0.093*	0.428*
Age	-0.013*	0.001	-0.013	-0.005*	0.012	-0.020		-0.005*	-0.005*	
Age squared			0.023		-0.617*	-0.000				

Education	−0.025*		0.015*	−0.0003	−0.001	0.013	0.197	0.002	0.003
High school diploma		−0.004*							
College									−0.105

Notes:

* Significant at the 5 percent level.

[1] Magri investigated only those households applying for a loan.

[2] Fabri and Padula investigated only households applying for a loan. Moreover, they look at the level of collateral rather than net worth.

[3] Cox and Jappelli selected households with assets less than $1,000,000.

[4] Duca and Rosenthal investigate households whose head was aged under 35, with wealth below $1,000,000 and who applied for a loan.

[5] Ferri and Simon report separate results for 1983, 1989, 1992, 1995, and 1998. We report those for 1983 and report the mean results across the following periods.

[6] Crook selected households whose income was less than $300,000 p.a. and wealth below $1,000,000, and used age splines rather than an age polynomial. He finds that older households are significantly less likely to be constrained, and reports a coefficient for working rather than for unemployed.

[7] Results for the United States for income, income squared, permanent income, and net worth have been adjusted so that income, permanent income, and net worth are measured in units of $10,000.

Surprisingly, the studies suggest that age does not always have a significant effect on the probability of being credit-constrained—for example, it is insignificant in Italy in the 1990s, according to Magri 2002 and Fabri and Padula 2002. However, older households are less likely to be constrained in the United States. Moreover, in the 1980s, age reduces the probability of being credit constrained in both countries. Credit-scoring models (Banasik, Crook, and Thomas 1996; Boyes, Hoffman, and Law 1989; Stavins 2000) show that older households are less likely to default. With age beyond the middle thirties being associated with less demand for debt in the United States, the evidence suggests that when the head of a household is older than, say, 35 years, the supply of debt remains the same or even increases whereas demand falls.

Being married was found to reduce the probability of being constrained in Italy, but most studies found it has no effect in the United States either for the 1980s or 1990s. Household size was included in all studies for both countries and had positive and generally significant effects. The gender of the head of household had no significant effect in the United States. Since the 1976 Equal Credit Opportunities Act 1976 forbids the use of gender in credit-scoring models in the United States and since gender has no detectable effect on demand, this result is expected. Only one Italian study included gender and found that having a female head of household increased the chance of being constrained.

Most studies found that, whereas in the United States, education appears to have no effect on being constrained in either period, in Italy, greater education reduced the chance of being constrained. All of the U.S. studies found that a nonwhite head of household increased the chance of being constrained, but this variable has not been included in studies for Italy. If the head of the household is unemployed, there is a higher chance the household will be credit-constrained in Italy, and no significant effect in the United States. From table 3.4, we see that if the head is unemployed, the family will demand less debt, so being unemployed reduces the supply of debt too.

All the papers discussed here include a number of additional variables that reflect the particular purpose and interest of the study. Gropp, Scholz, and White investigated the effect of bankruptcy rules in the United States, and this aspect of their study is discussed in chapter 7. Ferri and Simon for the United States found that variables that are typically predictive of default in credit-scoring models—such as homeownership, years lived at address, and years employed—reduce the chance of being constrained while previous delinquency increased the chance. Duca and Rosenthal found that attitudes to risk and borrowing seemed to have no effect. Crook finds no evidence that expectations about future interest rates had any effect, but found that holding credit cards from many lenders reduced the likelihood of being constrained. For Italy, Magri found that the average recovery share of debt in the region where the household lives has no effect, but longer debt recovery times do have an effect.

All of the studies in table 3.6 used the turndown measures of the SCF or SHIW, in which it was assumed π_{it} of equation (3) could be directly observed. In contrast, as explained in section 3.3.1, Grant (2003) estimates the proportion of households constrained indirectly using maximum likelihood techniques and used data from the Consumer Expenditure Survey (CEX) for 1988–1993. Grant's results are expressed as a proportion of households that are constrained for different subgroups, but it is difficult to see if the differences between the categories are statistically significant. While he finds, in common with other studies, that younger and better educated households were more likely to be constrained, he also finds that this is also true for white households in contrast to the studies in table 3.6. The effect for women is also large and positive, but there is not much effect from family size. Income effects, in his study, were highly nonlinear, with middle-income households the most likely to be constrained. One should bear in mind again that Grant's results related to unsecured debt. Moreover, whether results are obtained in a selection framework or by modeling disequilibrium, results are always sensitive to exclusion restrictions.

Despite differences in data selection and in definitions of constraints, estimates of how household characteristics affect the proportion of credit-constrained households are broadly similar across countries. In both countries, there seems to be a consensus that constrained households are younger with lower incomes. Home-owning households seem to have better access to credit, perhaps due to their increased collateral, but there seems to be no consensus on the effect of wealth. Unmarried, and in the United States, Afro-Caribbean households are also more often constrained.

3.3.3 The Level of Unmet Borrowing

In considering what would happen to demand if those who face constraints found them removed, estimates are only readily available for the United States. Using the 1983 wave of the SCF, Cox and Jappelli (1993) estimated that the average constrained household possessed only 57 percent of the credit that it wished to have. But with constrained households making up only 17.3 percent of households, Cox and Jappelli found that, considering the population of households as a whole, the average amount of desired household debt only exceeds actual debt by 9 percent. This translates into a reduction of only 2 percent in the wealth-income ratio if credit constraints were removed because their removal would increase not only debt but purchased assets as well.

However, Cox and Jappelli's prediction of the volume of desired debt ignores sample selection effects arising from the fact that they calculated the desired debt for those who were constrained by using the simple estimates of desired debt from those who were not constrained. Grant also points out that selection effects make the uncorrected demand equation for unconstrained households differ from that for constrained households. Use of the former to predict demand for the latter group therefore induces bias. Duca and Rosenthal's (1993) results, using the same data, correct for this, and they find that the average constrained household, with head aged under thirty-five years, had only 48 percent of its desired debt. Grant uses the CEX for the early 1990s, finding that an average U.S. household wished to borrow $3,882 more than it was currently able (the mean level of debt for those with debt was $3,984). Overall then, the magnitude by which households are credit-constrained may be quite significant.

3.4 Conclusion

This chapter has considered the incidence of debt and the reasons for household debt in a number of countries. It has surveyed models of methods for estimating the demand for debt, and also examined some of the (less extensive) literature that explicitly models the supply of debt. Finally, it has considered measures of the extent of credit constraints and their prevalence across households with different characteristics.

The main findings can be summarized. First, holdings of mortgages are greater in the United States, Netherlands, and the United Kingdom than in New Zealand, Germany, and Japan, with Italy having an even lower incidence. The proportion of households with consumer loans follows a broadly similar pattern. Debt holdings by age follow the life-cycle pattern in all of the countries observed, although the age range where the incidence and volume of debt peaks differs among countries. In Canada, the incidence peaks at an earlier age than in the United States. Italy follows, with incidence reaching a maximum at the oldest age range in the Netherlands and Japan. The incidence of debt decreases more rapidly as age increases in Italy than in the United States. Surprisingly, the relationship between the value of debt per household and income, age, and net wealth is much less steep in Italy than in other Western countries.

Studies that have estimated equations to explain interhousehold differences in demand and the characteristics of households that are most likely to be credit-constrained have been published only for Italy and the United States, probably due to the lack of data as to which households are credit-constrained in other countries. The evidence shows considerable variation in the determinants of demand and in marginal effects within countries as well as between countries. For instance, the effect of current labor income on demand has been found to have positive and negative effects in different studies in each of the two countries. Plausible explanations can be given to justify each finding. The effects of net wealth and of education both appear to be positive. The life-cycle relationship exists for the United States but, surprisingly, has not been found for Italy. Greater protection in the event of bankruptcy probably increases the demand for debt for those in the top half of the wealth distribution in the United States. In Italy, demand is greater in regions with a more efficient judicial system, which probably lowers the costs of borrowing.

Cross-sectional supply functions have been estimated only for the United States and so cannot be compared across countries. Studies of credit-scoring models rarely report parameter estimates. Those that do indicate that measures of household stability (such as duration of household, of residence, and of financial arrangements) reduce the probability of default. Details of previous defaults—credit bureau data—are always very predictive of default in the future, but are not related to the probability of default by an economic theory of optimizing economic agents. Evidence shows greater variation in the availability of credit bureau data between countries.

Recent studies suggest that the probability of facing actual or perceived credit constraints has changed over time, and is lower for higher-income households both in Italy and in the United States, but with a much lower elasticity in Italy than in the United States. Higher

rejection rates may arise simply because a higher proportion of households apply for credit, rather than because constraints become "more
binding." The estimated effect of net wealth is unclear in both countries. Age appears to reduce the chance that a household is creditconstrained in Italy but has no independent effect in the United States.
Being married reduces the chance of being constrained in Italy but not
in the United States. Greater education appears to have no independent effect in the United States, whereas in Italy, conflicting results
have been found. Household size and number of children increase the
probability of being constrained in both countries. Studies of the 1980s
broadly confirm those of the 1990s for both countries, albeit with a few
exceptions. For the 1980s, older heads of households in Italy appear to
have a lower chance of being constrained. (Age had no effect in the
1990s.) In addition, having a female head of household in Italy in the
1980s increased the probability of being constrained but was not investigated for the 1990s.

   Overall, a large number of further research questions are raised by
these studies. We need to have measures of whether a household is
credit-constrained for many more countries. We need to investigate
the issue of collinearity in variables and try to standardize the variables
used across countries so that comparisons can be made. There needs to
be more research to explain the observed differences between countries: Italy and the United States appear to have very different patterns,
and it would be interesting to broaden these comparisons results to see
whether these differences are broad disparities between "Anglo-Saxon"
and "Mediterranean" countries, or whether there are other dimensions
by which such disparities are observed.

Note

I would like to thank the participants of The Economics of Consumer Credit: European
Experience and Lessons from the U.S. conference, EUI, Florence, May 2003, for very
many helpful comments, and the editors for many suggestions and additional information. I would also like to thank Charles Grant, Stefano Gagliarducci, and Anzelika Zaiceva for excellent assistance in locating U.K., Italian, and German data, respectively.

References

Aizcorbe, A., A. B. Kennickell, and K. B. Moore. 2003. "Recent Changes in U.S. Family
Finances: Evidence from the 1998 and 2001 Survey of Consumer Finances." *Federal Reserve Bulletin* 89 (January): 1–32.

Alessie, R., S. Hochguertel, and A. van Soest. 2002. "Household Portfolios in the Nether-lands." In *Household Portfolios*, ed. L. Guiso, M. Haliassos, and T. Jappelli, 340–388. Cambridge, Mass.: The MIT Press.

Attanasio, O. P. 1999. "Consumption." In *Handbook of Macroeconomics*, vol. 1, ed. J. B. Taylor and M. Woodford, 741–812. Amsterdam: Elsevier Science B.V.

Banasik, J., J. N. Crook, and L. C. Thomas. 1996. "Does Scoring a Sub-population Make a Difference?" *International Review of Retail Distribution and Consumer Research* 6: 180–195.

Bernanke, B., and B. Blinder. 1988. "Is It Money or Credit, or Both, or Neither?" *American Economic Review Papers and Proceedings* 78: 435–439.

Boyes, W. J., D. L. Hoffman, and S. A. Law. 1989. "Econometric Analysis of Bank Scoring Problems." *Journal of Econometrics* 40: 3–14.

Cox, D., and T. Jappelli. 1993. "The Effect of Borrowing Constraints on Consumer Liabil-ities." *Journal of Money, Credit and Banking* 25: 197–213.

Crook, J. 1996. "Credit Constraints and U.S. Households." *Applied Financial Economics* 6: 477–485.

Crook, J. 2001. "The Demand for Household Debt in the U.S.A.: Evidence from the 1995 Survey of Consumer Finance." *Applied Financial Economics* 11: 83–91.

Crook, J. N., R. Hamilton, and L. C. Thomas. 1992. "Alternative Definitions of Default: A Comparison of Discriminators under Alternative Definitions of Credit Default." In *Credit Scoring and Credit Control*, ed. Thomas, L. C., J. N. Crook, and D. B. Edelman, 217–245. Oxford: Oxford University Press.

Deaton, A. 1992. *Understanding Consumption*. Oxford: Oxford University Press.

Desai, V., J. Crook, and G. Overstreet. 1996. "A Comparison of Neural Networks and Lin-ear Scoring Models in the Credit Environment." *European Journal of Operational Research* 95: 24–37.

Duca, D. J., and S. S. Rosenthal. 1993. "Borrowing Constraints, Household Debt and Ra-cial Discrimination in Loan Markets." *Journal of Financial Intermediation* 3: 77–103.

Fabri, D., and M. Padula. 2002. "Does Poor Legal Enforcement Make Households Credit Constrained?" Working paper no. 65, Centre for Studies in Economics and Finance, Uni-versity of Salerno.

Ferri, G., and P. Simon. 2002. "Constrained Consumer Lending: Methods Using the Sur-vey of Consumer Finances." Working paper, University of Bari.

Friedman, M. 1957. *A Theory of the Consumption Function*. Princeton, N.J.: Princeton Uni-versity Press.

Grant, C. 2003. "Estimating Credit Constraints among U.S. Households." Mimeo., Euro-pean University Institute, Florence.

Gropp, R., J. K. Scholz, and M. J. White. 1997. "Personal Bankruptcy and Credit Supply and Demand." *Quarterly Journal of Economics* 112: 217–251.

Guiso, L., T. Jappelli, and D. Terlizzese. 1996. "Income Risk, Borrowing Constraints, and Portfolio Choice." *American Economic Review* 86, no. 1 (March): 158–172.

Hall, R. E. 1978. "Stochastic Implications of the Life-Cycle Permanent Income Hypothesis: Theory and Evidence." *Journal of Political Economy* 80: 971–987.

Hall, R. E., and F. S. Mishkin. 1982. "The Sensitivity of Consumption to Transitory Income: Estimates from Panel Data on Households." *Econometrica* 50: 461–481.

Hayashi, F. 1987. "Tests for Liquidity Constraints: A Critical Survey and Some New Observations." In *Advances in Econometrics: Fifth World Congress*, vol. II, ed. T. F. Bewley, 91–120. Cambridge: Cambridge University Press.

Heckman, J. J. 1976. "The Common Structure of Statistical Models of Truncation, Sample Selection, and Limited Dependent Variables and a Simple Estimator for Such Models." *Annals of Economic and Social Measurement* 5: 475–492.

Jaffee, D., and T. Russell. 1976. "Imperfect Information and Credit Rationing." *Quarterly Journal of Economics* 90: 651–666.

Jappelli, T. 1990. "Who Is Credit Constrained in the U.S. Economy." *Quarterly Journal of Economics* 105: 219–234.

Jappelli, T., and M. Pagano. 1989. "Consumption and Capital Market Imperfections: An International Comparison." *American Economic Review* 79: 1088–1105.

Jappelli, T., J.-S. Pischke, and N. S. Souleles. 1998. "Testing for Liquidity Constraints in Euler Equations with Complementary Data Sources." *Review of Economics and Statistics*: 251–262.

Magri, S. 2002. "Italian Households' Debt: Determinants of Demand and Supply." Mimeo., Bank of Italy, Rome.

Mariger, R. P. 1987. "A Life-Cycle Consumption Model with Liquidity Constraints: Theory with Empirical Results." *Econometrica* 55: 533–557.

Platts, G., and I. Howe. 2004. "A Single European Scorecard." In *Readings in Credit Scoring*, ed. Thomas, L. C., D. Edelman, and J. Crook, 109–122. Oxford: Oxford University Press.

Stavins, J. 2000. "Credit Card Borrowing, Delinquency, and Personal Bankruptcy." *New England Economic Review* (July/August): 15–30.

Stiglitz, J., and A. Weiss. 1981. "Credit Rationing in Markets with Imperfect Information." *American Economic Review* 71: 393–410.

Thomas, L. C., D. B. Edelman, and J. N. Crook. 2002. *Credit Scoring and Its Applications*. Philadelphia, Penn.: SIAM.

4

Regulation, Formal and
Informal Enforcement, and
the Development of the
Household Loan Market:
Lessons from Italy

Luca Casolaro, Leonardo
Gambacorta, and Luigi Guiso

The Italian household loan market has three significant features. First, it is much smaller than those of other countries at a comparable stage of economic development (see also chapter 3). In 2000, in Italy, total household debt amounted to some 40 percent of disposable income, which is about half the average of the euro-area countries and much smaller than the U.S. figure of 107 percent.

Second, over the past decade, lending to households has been growing very fast, at rates higher than those in the other main European countries. Setting the stock of outstanding loans to households in 1997 equal to one hundred, the index jumps to 183 in 2003 in Italy, compared with 152 in the euro area. The difference also holds when consumer credit and mortgages are considered separately. However, the Italian growth was not fast enough to close the gap in market size, and the Italian market remains small by international standards.

The third relevant feature is that households' ease in obtaining credit differs greatly and systematically across local markets. Guiso, Sapienza, and Zingales (2004a) use data from the Italian Survey of Household Income and Wealth (SHIW) to construct an index of households' access to the credit market across Italian regions. Controlling for individual characteristics and for market risk, the probability to obtain a loan in Marche, the region with easiest access, is 50 percent higher than in Calabria, where access is most difficult. Put differently, there is considerable dispersion across Italian regions in the degree of development of the market for household loans, as measured by this gauge.

In this chapter, we use these features to examine the determinants of the size of the household loan market, which varies across regions of Italy and over time about as much as across typical cross-section samples of country observations (such as the ones considered in chapters 2 and 3 in this volume). This makes it possible to look at the determinants of household loan market development in an environment where a large number of potentially relevant factors, which in a cross-section of nations cannot be controlled due to a lack of degrees of freedom, are naturally held constant. Hence, the results of the analysis have a chance to identify variables that most likely affect the development of the consumption loan market, shedding light on why it differs so much across countries.

First, we document the three features that characterize Italy's household loan market and explain them in a unified framework. Needless to say, the size of the market may be small, either because demand for loans is small or because supply is limited. With reference to Italy, in the 1980s and the 1990s, Jappelli and Pagano (1989) and Guiso, Jappelli, and Terlizzese (1994) have concluded that small size is not due to a low propensity of Italian households to incur debt, but rather to a backwardness in the development of credit supply, as reflected in the traditionally wide interest rate spreads in the mortgage and consumer credit markets and the large down payment required to obtain a mortgage.

These papers, however, have not inquired into the causes of the limited supply of loans or explained its rapid recent growth. Interest rate spreads and credit availability, in fact, are endogenous variables that reflect the structure and functioning of markets. This is what we focus on in this chapter. Our contention is that the sharp increase in lending to households over the past decade (at annual rates above 10 percent) was spurred by financial liberalization starting in the early 1990s. Competition has substantially boosted the supply of loans to households in local markets, reducing the cost of debt and making credit more easily available. A household's probability of having a loan application accepted was much higher at the end (and the cost of the loan much lower) than at the beginning of 1990s. The share of consumers refused and that of discouraged borrowers (households that did not apply because they expected rejection) diminished by four times and two times respectively. The interest rate spread on mortgages has narrowed significantly, accounting for almost half the reduction in mortgage rates in the second half of the 1990s.

To explain these trends, we argue, and simple correlations support our thesis, that the main factor that has limited the market's development is inadequacies in formal and informal loan contract enforcement, which have substantially impaired supply. The Italian judicial system is much less efficient than other countries. The time to decision in a trial or to recovery of funds following default is much longer than elsewhere, which discourages lending. Differences in informal enforcement have analogous effects. Several indicators show that Italy has a smaller average endowment of "social capital," defined as the set of relationships that tie people together in a community and bind them to obey to rules of conduct, above all honoring informal commitments. These correlations suggest that lax protection of lenders' rights has been an effective impediment to the development of the supply of credit to households in Italy.

Fortunately, the wide geographical variation in the degree of development of the market across Italian regions makes it possible to highlight the role of these variables while holding many others constant, such as the level of taxation and debt subsidies, the laws, religious beliefs, and history that may affect individuals' preferences for debt. Judicial efficiency differs substantially across provinces and is closely correlated with access to credit. It is easier and less costly to obtain a loan in regions where courts are more efficient than where they function poorly. Similarly, social capital and trust differ markedly across Italian provinces, and the areas better endowed with social capital and generalized trust have more highly developed markets for household loans. Nor is inefficient legal enforcement countered by stronger informal enforcement; in fact, areas with better functioning courts also have more social capital so that lack of both formal and informal enforcement combine to limit the incentives to extend credit. While appropriate reforms could improve judicial efficiency (see Marchesi 2002), the endowment of social capital cannot easily be modified. It evolves only slowly over time and may remain dormant for centuries. As is argued by Williamson (2000), social capital is one of the constraints on a reform program, not an objective. Moreover, as Putnam, Leonardi, and Nanetti (1993) suggest and Djankov, Glaeser, La Porta, Lopez-de-Silanes, and Shleifer (2003) formalize, social capital may be an ingredient of well-functioning institutions, including courts, and its absence may jeopardize any reform. If this is so, the underdevelopment of the household loan market in Italy could constitute a comparatively persistent feature.

While the study refers to Italy, it carries some general lessons. First, countries differ considerably in their endowment of social capital and the working of the judicial system, and our analysis suggests that these factors should be of prime importance in explaining international differences in the size of the household loan market. Second, the Italian case suggests that while a pure program of financial liberalization can improve credit availability, it may not succeed in closing the gap in financial development if some basic infrastructure for a smooth, working financial market—such as an efficient judicial system—is not simultaneously provided.

The rest of the chapter is structured as follows. Section 4.1 documents the small size, fast growth, and interregional heterogeneity of the household credit market in Italy in the second half of the 1990s. Section 4.2 discusses the factors that could potentially account for its smallness, drawing on the existing literature. Section 4.3 focuses on the effect of supply factors and exploits the variability of local credit markets to identify some determinants. Section 4.4 looks at the role of financial regulation, while section 4.5 examines the growth of the market in the 1990s and argues that much of the expansion was due to financial liberalization. Section 4.6 concludes.

4.1 The Features of the Household Loan Market in Italy: Small Size, Fast Recent Growth, and Geographical Heterogeneity

4.1.1 Fast Growth but Small Size

Figure 4.1 shows household lending as a share of GDP in Italy over the past twenty years for various types of loans and for the total. There are three noteworthy features. First, total lending tripled between 1984 and 2003, reaching 17.4 percent of GDP from 5.6 percent in 1984. Second, most of the increase came after 1995, following moderate growth in the first half of the 1990s. After 1997, loans to households grew on average at 11 percent per year, much faster than in the past. Finally, more than two-thirds of the expansion was accounted for by mortgage lending, the share of which in GDP increased from less than 4 percent in 1984 to 13 percent at the end of 2003. In this case, too, growth was concentrated after 1995. As is shown in figure 4.2, the growth in lending to households has been faster in Italy than in the euro area.[1] Setting the volume of loans outstanding in 1997 to 100, we find that in 2003, it was 183 in Italy, compared to 152 in the euro area, 141 in France, and 120 in Germany. Only Spain showed faster growth than Italy. If we consider the ratio of household loans to GDP the results are similar.

Yet despite this fast growth, the household loan market in Italy remains small by international standards. As a ratio to disposable income, the volume of household liabilities in Italy in 2000 was 43 percent, one-half the figure recorded in France and one-third of that in

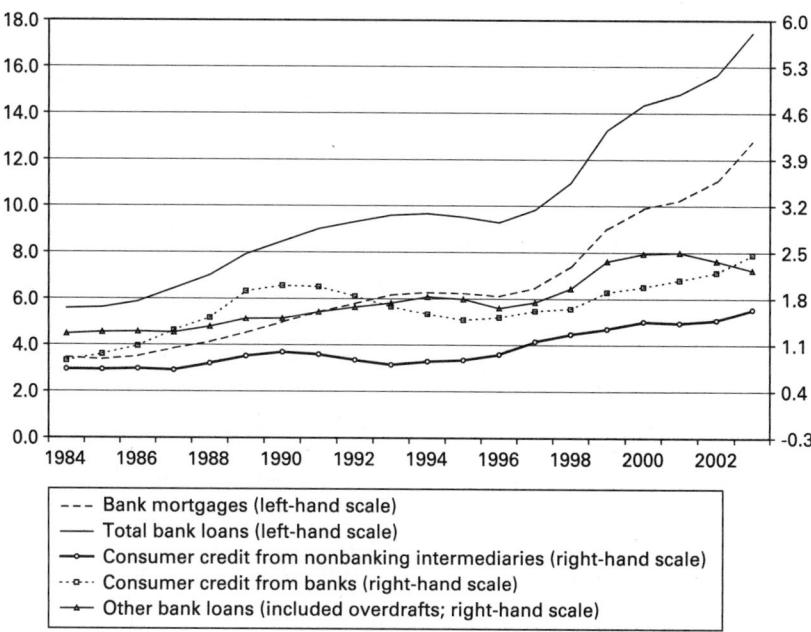

Figure 4.1

Loans to households as a percentage of GDP

The figure shows the evolution of household loans as a share of GDP by type of loan. Data are from the national statistical institute (ISTAT) and the Bank of Italy. The right-hand axis refers to consumer credit and other loans.

Germany or the United Kingdom (table 4.1, panel A). At the beginning of the 1990s, before financial liberalization, households' liabilities in Italy came to just 29 percent of disposable income, between one-quarter and one-third of the figures registered in the other G7 countries; most of the gap was and still is due to the different size of the mortgage market, equal to about 26 percent of disposable income in Italy, compared with values ranging between 55 percent and 108 percent in the other G7 countries. Data on the various components available for the euro-area countries show that as a share of GDP, the Italian consumer loan market is less than one-third as large as in the euro area, while other consumer credit components are on par with the rest of Europe (table 4.1, panel B).

To conclude, the size of the household credit market in Italy has been historically small; it grew fast in the second half of the 1990s, partly narrowing the gap with the other euro-area countries, but it remains comparatively small.

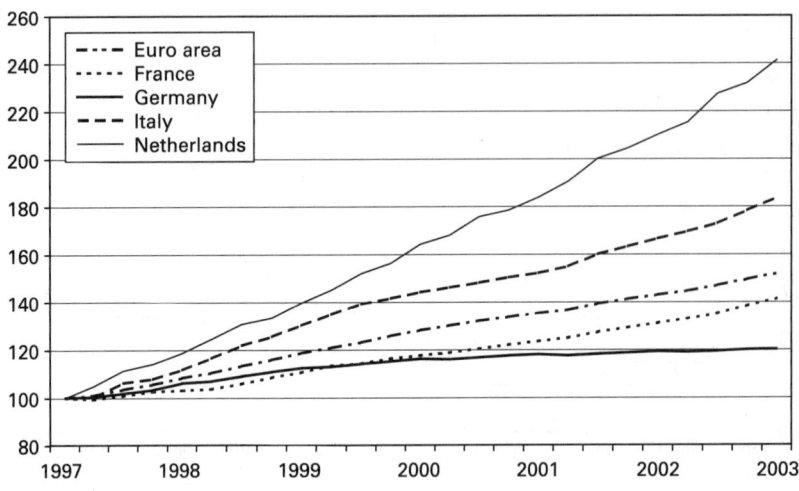

Figure 4.2
Credit to households in the main euro-area countries
The figure shows the trend in household loans in the main countries of the euro-area
after the middle 1990s. Data on consumer credit are end-of-period stocks; 1997 = 100.
Source: Our computations on ECB and national statistics.

4.1.2 Heterogeneity in the Development of the Local Markets

The second relevant feature of the household loan market in Italy is
its remarkable geographical heterogeneity across provinces. Figure 4.3
shows the variation across Italian provinces in the volume of households' mortgages (the main component of household loans) as a share
of GDP in 1995. The size of the market can be taken as a proxy of its
development. The figure shows great dispersion: The ratio ranges
from a low of 1.22 percent in the province of Vibo Valentia to a high of
9.49 percent in the province of Genoa. This dispersion is about the
same as one finds in a cross-section of countries. It allows us to inquire
into the determinants in an environment where a large number of national characteristics, which in a cross-section of countries would need
to be controlled for, are naturally held constant. These include taxation,
banking regulation, culture, and so forth. Dispersion has a clear pattern: Provinces in the center and, even more, those in the north tend to
have larger markets than those in the south. However, there is also
variation across provinces within the same areas, suggesting that the
differences do not simply reflect a north-south divide. A similar conclusion is reached using an alternative indicator proposed by Guiso,
Sapienza, and Zingales (2004a) based on data on households' access to

Table 4.1
Household indebtedness

A. Total indebtedness in the G7

	Canada	France	Ger-many	Italy	Japan	United King-dom	United States
1990							
Liabilities	92.6	88.3	70.0	29.1	131.5	115.7	87.3
of which: mortgages	59.0	51.9	53.6	13.7	50.7	104.7	60.9
1997							
Liabilities	108.2	64.9	107.6	33.8	136.4	105.0	97.6
of which: mortgages	71.2	52.0	66.5	20.0	54.4	95.5	65.6
2000							
Liabilities	112.0	70.8	115.1	42.9	133.1	117.3	106.8
of which: mortgages	70.5	54.7	71.3	25.6	58.5	107.7	71.9
Growth rate: 2000/1997	3.51	9.09	6.97	26.92	−2.42	11.71	9.42
Growth rate: 2000/1990	20.95	−19.81	64.43	47.42	1.22	1.38	22.47

B. Loans from banks by type of loan in the euro area

	Italy	France	Germany	Spain	Euro area
1997					
House purchase	5.2	20.3	37.3	21.2	23.9
Consumer credit	1.3	6.7	10.9	5.9	6.6
Other	9.7	5.6	14.9	7.2	9.5
Total	16.2	32.5	63.1	34.2	39.9
2003					
House purchase	11.8	24.3	43.6	37.1	31.4
Consumer credit	2.5	8.1	8.1	7.4	6.4
Other	9.0	4.5	14.9	10.4	9.0
Total	23.3	36.9	66.6	54.9	46.8

Sources: OECD Economic Outlook, no. 71, 2002 (Panel A). ECB and national statistics (Panel B).
Notes: Panel A shows household indebtedness outstanding at the end of the period as a percentage of disposable income. Households include nonprofit institutions serving households. For France, mortgages are defined as long-term loans; for Italy, as medium and long-term loans. Panel B refers to loans from banks as a percentage of GDP for different types of loans, and the data are available for the euro-area countries on a comparable basis since 1997.

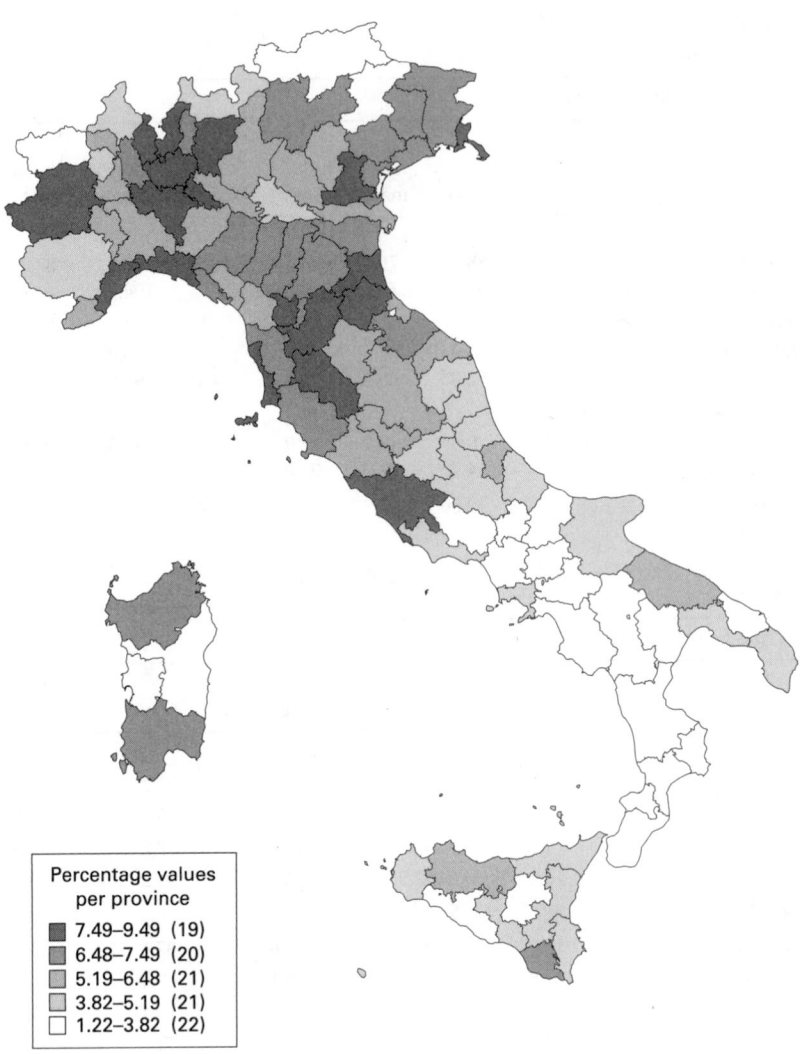

Figure 4.3

The size of the households loans market across provinces

The figure illustrates the differences in the development of lending to households across Italian provinces in 1995. It shows the end-of-period stock of medium- and long-term loans to households as a percentage of GDP in the province. Medium- and long-term data are from the Bank of Italy while data on provincial GDP are computed from Istituto Tagliacarne. Darker shaded provinces are those with higher loan/GDP ratio.

the credit market collected in the Bank of Italy Survey of Household Income and Wealth (SHIW). The indicator relies on the idea that in a
more developed credit market, it will be easier to get a loan. The
SHIW allows one to identify consumers who are credit-rationed because they have failed to get a loan or failed even to apply, though
they would like credit (discouraged borrowers). With these data,
Guiso, Sapienza, and Zingales (2004a) estimate the probability of credit
rationing as a function of a series of observable household characteristics, seemingly correlated with the quality of borrowers; the regression
included regional dummies that capture the level of financial development. The values of the coefficients on the regional dummies, after
being transformed into a financial development index, are reported in
figure 4.4. The picture again shows strong geographical dispersion in
access to credit, with the southern regions typically lagging behind
those in the center and the north, but with significant differences even
within these macroareas.

4.2 Can Demand Factors Explain the Size and the Dynamics of Lending to Households?

The differences in the size and growth of the household loan market
between Italy and other European countries could theoretically be due
to differences in the demand for loans. Following this interpretation,
one could argue that Italian households have traditionally relied little
on the loan market, but recently, due to some developments, households' demand for credit has increased faster than in other countries,
where the level of demand has held constant (or moved less). In other
words, if we plot a country's demand for household loans in the interest rate-loan demand space (adjusting for the size of the country), then
household demand for loans in Italy up to the early 1990s would (the
story goes) be closer to the origin than the Europe average but would
shift considerably upward to the right in the second half of 1990s.

   In what follows, we review some of the factors that could possibly
explain the low level of household demand for credit in Italy. All in
all, this thesis finds no empirical support.

4.2.1 Propensity to Incur Debt
One possibility is that in the past, Italian households were strongly
debt-averse and that this aversion has declined in recent years, boosting the demand for loans. A partial test of this hypothesis can be

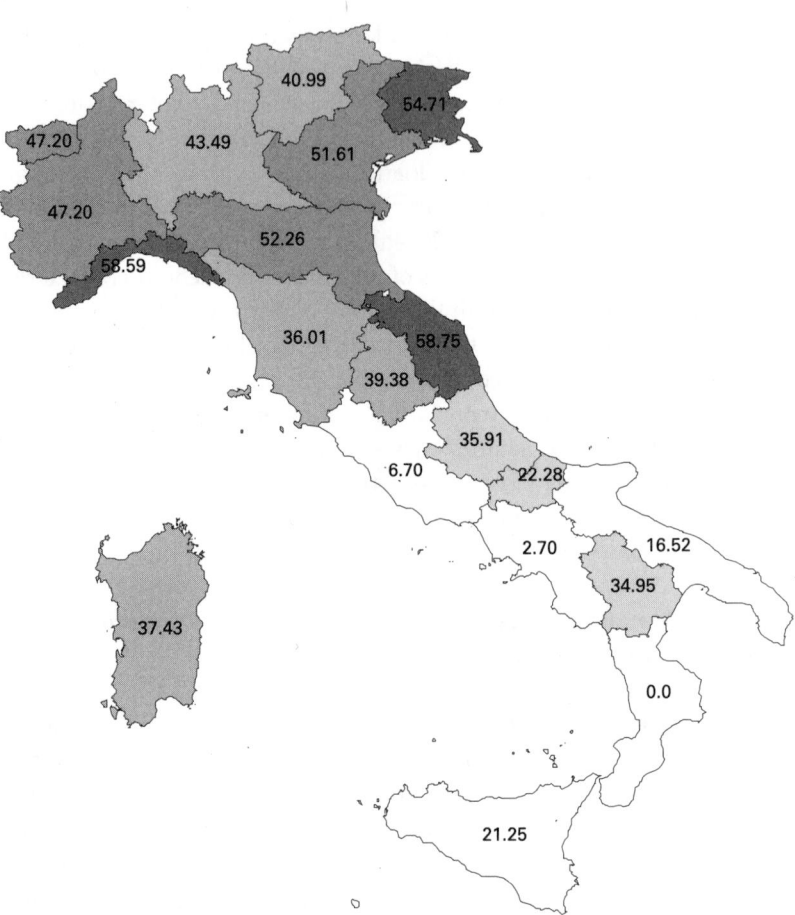

Figure 4.4
Ease of access to the household credit market by region
The figure shows an indicator of the ease with which a household obtains a loan across regions. It was produced by Guiso, Sapienza, and Zingales (2004a) regressing an indicator for whether a consumer was rejected for a loan or discouraged from applying on a number of personal characteristics and regional dummies. The coefficients of the regional dummies are then used to obtain the indicator, computed as one minus the ratio of the regional dummy's coefficient to the largest regional dummy coefficient. Access to credit is easier in darker regions.

performed using the World Value Survey (WVS), which contains information on how consumers view saving and frugality in many countries, including Italy and the rest of the European Union. Presumably, an individual who views savings and frugality as important will be more debt-averse. To gauge this, we use the responses to a question concerning the importance of instilling the "virtue" of thrift in children. The question reads, "Here is a list of qualities that children can be encouraged to learn at home. Which, if any, do you consider to be especially important?" We code a one if the respondent lists as important "thrift, saving money, and objects."[2] We pool data for the 1981 and 1990 waves and compute the share of individuals in each country who regard saving as important. In Italy, it is 23 percent, no different from the rest of Europe (24 percent). Moreover, between the 1981 and the 1990 survey, the share of individuals who answered positively rose from 20 percent to 27 percent (in the 1995 survey, the latest available to us, the question was not asked), suggesting, if anything, an increase in debt-aversion, which is hardly consistent with the upward trend in indebtedness. In sum, the WVS data suggest that the smaller size of the Italian household loan market is just not a reflection of debt-aversion. These data, though not available for more recent years, also suggest that the increased size of the market is unlikely to be due to an increased preference for debt.

A related explanation for the 1980s and the early 1990s is the thesis that the small market depends on Italian households' practice of "saving to buy," which discouraged consumer credit and mortgages and boosted the propensity to save. As figure 4.5 shows, there is a clear negative correlation between the aggregate propensity to save and the size of the consumer credit market. However, as is argued by Jappelli and Pagano (1994) and Guiso, Jappelli, and Terlizzese (1994), the causality runs the other way: It is the difficulty of getting a loan— measured by the small size of the market—that causes the high saving rate. Countries where households find obstacles in accessing the credit market naturally have a lower level of debt and a higher saving rate.[3]

4.2.2 Welfare State

In Italy the government provides some education and health services that could affect households' demand for credit. In countries with a partly private higher education system, such as the United States, households incur debt to finance investment in education. Similarly, the loan market can be used to smooth health shocks when the state

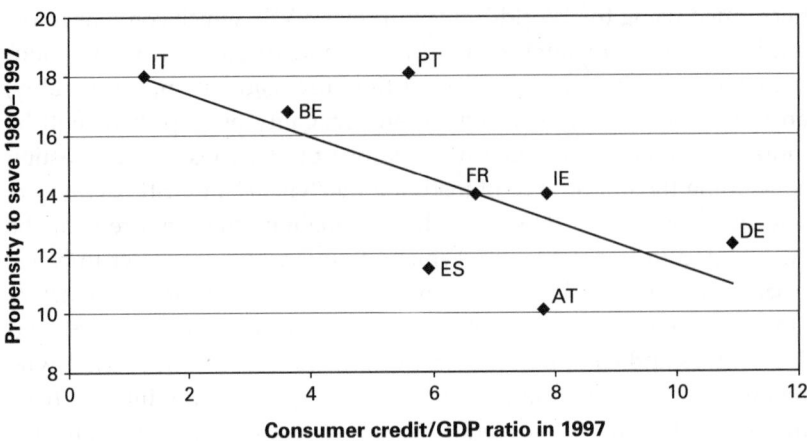

Figure 4.5
Households' propensity to save and consumer credit
The figure shows the relation between households' saving rate and the size of the consumer credit market. Data on consumer credit are from the ECB; data on households' propensity to save are from ISTAT.

provides only partial health care, again as in the United States. More generally, government provision of education and health services crowds out private insurance and credit markets. But while this explanation could account for the gap in the size of the household loan market vis-à-vis the United States, it cannot explain why the market is small relative to other European countries, such as Sweden, where the welfare state is definitely larger than in Italy.

4.2.3   Age-Income Profile and Individual's Discount Rate

According to the life-cycle theory (see chapter 1), households borrow to smooth expenses when facing an upward-sloping age-income profile. In addition, their subjective discount rate will affect how much of their lifetime resources they prefer to consume in the current period and how much in the future. Accordingly, other things being equal, the demand for loans is greater, the steeper the age-income profile and the higher (for given level of the market interest rate) the rate of time preference. Guiso, Jappelli, and Terlizzese (1994) show that the income profile of households in Italy does not differ from that in other countries, while the WVS data show no significant differences in preferences for saving, suggesting that this route, too, cannot account for the small size of the Italian household loan market. A related channel is earnings uncertainty. The more variable earnings are, the more likely households are to need the credit market to smooth consumption. Thus, if earnings uncertainty is substantially lower in Italy, this could help explain the smaller size of the market. Dominitz and Manski (1997) and Das and Donkers (1999) show that perceived income uncertainty is much higher in the United States than in Europe, represented by Italy and the Netherlands, which might explain why the household loan market is larger in the United States, but cannot explain why it is smaller in Italy than in the Netherlands, where earnings uncertainty is similar.

4.2.4   Informal Lending and Intergenerational Transfers

Intergenerational transfers and informal loans from relatives and friends could crowd out formal household credit. If informal markets were deeper in Italy than in other countries, they might impede the development of formal markets. However, the data reveal that Italy is not exceptional in this respect compared to other countries. According to the 1989 SHIW, 2.7 percent of households had loans from relatives and friends, about the same as in the United States.[4] Again, in fact, reliance on informal loans could well be an effect rather than a cause of the underdevelopment of the household loan market. Informal loans and intergenerational transfers may be a way of overcoming impediments to market lending. Consistent with this interpretation, Guiso and Jappelli (1991) find that households that were turned down for loans or discouraged from applying for one were more likely to receive a transfer or a loan from a relative or a friend. And Guiso, Sapienza, and Zingales (2004b) show that informal loans are more likely to develop in areas where there is less social capital—itself an important ingredient for the development of the credit market as we argue in section 4.3. Additional evidence for this interpretation is the decline in the share of households receiving loans from friends or relatives during the 1990s (down to 1.5 percent in 2000), consistent with the easier credit access in the second half of the 1990s, as we argue in section 4.4.

4.2.5   Taxation

The fast expansion of lending to households in the second half of the nineties could also have been triggered by fiscal changes. In Italy, as in other countries, households can deduct home mortgage interest from tax liability.[5] Recently, tax incentives for house renovation (Law 449/1997) and for first-time home buyers (Law 448/1998) have been passed. These changes could have affected households' demand for housing and the demand for mortgages: Between 1998 and 2002, the volume of real estate transactions increased by 18 percent, and the share of mortgages in total outstanding household credit jumped from 32 percent to 46 percent. It seems, however, that this effect—which is also found in other countries, such as the United Kingdom and the Netherlands (Banks and Tanner 2002; Alessie, Hochguertel, and Van Soest 2002)—can explain only a small part of the growth in mortgages. Casolaro and Gambacorta (2004) find that the contribution of tax incentives to the growth of household loans between 1998 and 2003 is no more than one-tenth. Concerning consumer credit, in Italy, as in the other major countries, no tax deduction is allowed.[6]

In short, while in theory many factors—including extensive welfare state programs and informal lending—can affect households' demand for loans, on closer scrutiny they are unable to explain the relatively smaller size of the consumer credit market in Italy. Moreover, these factors do not seem to have changed significantly in recent years and so cannot account for the rapid growth in lending to households especially after 1997.

4.3   Why Is the Household Loan Market So Small and Variable across Regions

Now let us turn our attention to the other side of the market and focus on the factors that may restrain or shift the supply of credit. In particular, we focus on three factors that have been responsible for the smallness of the Italian market (the third, also for its recent growth): (1) the cost and the inefficiency of judicial system; (2) the limited endowment of social capital (resources that are available to individuals via their social linkages); (3) the tight regulation of the credit market and subsequent deregulation. Here we focus on the first two factors, postponing the discussion of financial regulation and liberalization to section 4.4.

4.3.1   The Cost and Efficiency of the Judicial System
Since a loan is an exchange of an amount of money today against the promise of more money at a specified date in the future, a crucial requirement is that the lender attaches sufficiently high probability to the borrower's keeping the promise. The credibility of the promise, or the probability of its being honored, depends on the formal institutions

that enforce contracts—typically the courts—as well as on informal mechanisms for the enforcement of promises based on the punishment that members of a community receive from other members when they breach a promise (e.g., forms of social ostracism). Compared to other European countries, Italy is deficient on both accounts: Formal and informal institutions for enforcing contracts, including credit contracts, are much weaker than in other countries at a similar stage of economic development. Table 4.2 reports four indicators of the degree of legal protection, and the cost and efficiency of the judicial system for a

Table 4.2
Cost and efficiency of judicial systems and lenders' legal protection

Country	Creditors' rights	Length of trials (number of days)	Cost of trials	Rule of law
Austria	3	434	1	6
Belgium	2	365	9.1	6
Denmark	3	83	3.8	6
Finland	1	240	15.8	6
France	0	210	3.8	5.39
Germany	3	154	6	5.53
Greece	1	315	8.2	3.71
Ireland	1	183	7.2	4.68
Italy	**2**	**645**	**3.9**	**5**
Netherlands	2	39	0.5	6
Norway	2	87	10.4	6
Portugal	1	420	4.9	5.21
Spain	2	147	10.7	4.68
Sweden	2	190	7.6	6
United Kingdom	4	101	0.5	5.14
EU	1.93	240.8	6.23	5.42
Euro area	1.63	286.9	5.89	5.44
United States	1	365	0.4	6

Note: The table reports various indicators of lenders' legal protection in a number of countries. "Creditors' rights" is a synthetic measure of the protection of lenders' rights as guaranteed by law, obtained from La Porta et al. 1998. "Length of trials" is an index of courts' efficiency, measured by the number of days to recoup a bounced check, computed by Djankov, La Porta, Lopez-de-Silanes, and Shleifer 2003. "Cost of trials" is an indicator of the cost of a civil action, given by the cost of justice divided by GDP, computed from the World Bank. "Rule of law" is an indicator of the law and order tradition in the country; the variable ranges from 1 (weak) to 10 (strong) and is published by the International Country Risk Guide. The table reports the average value of the period 1982–1995.

number of European and non-European countries. The first indicator is a synthetic measure of legal protection of creditors' rights, constructed by La Porta et al. 1998. The second is an index of court efficiency, as measured by the number of days it takes to recoup a bounced check, taken from Djankov, La Porta, Lopez-de-Silanes, and Shleifer (2003). The third is an indicator of the cost of judicial proceedings, gauged by the cost of the judicial system as a percent of the country's GDP, drawn from the World Bank Doing Business Indicators.[7] The fourth is a measure of "rule of law," which is an "evaluation of the law and order tradition in the country"; the variable ranges from 1 (weak) to 10 (strong) and is published by the International Country Risk Guide (ICRG). We use the average of the 1982–1995 values. In the international comparison, Italian laws in principle grant creditors a degree of legal protection that, though on the low side, is higher than in countries such as the United States and France, suggesting that the problem is not one of weak regulation. In terms of the cost of judicial proceedings and rule of law, too, Italy is no different from the average European country. Where the difference is dramatic is in the actual functioning of the judicial system, namely, the time needed to retrieve a loan: While in the European Union as a whole, on average, it takes 240 days to collect a bounced check; in Italy, it takes 645 days, the longest in Europe, nearly three times the average and half again as long as even the second most inefficient country, Austria.[8]

4.3.2 Social Capital

Table 4.3 compares across EU countries two indicators of the level of trust—which is directly related to social capital—computed by Guiso, Sapienza, and Zingales (2004c) using various waves of the Eurobarometer survey. The first indicator (shown in the first column) is the share of individuals who report that they fully trust their fellow citizens; the second (second column) is the average share of citizens of other countries who report that they fully trust the citizens of a specific country. Both measures indicate Italy as the country with the lowest level of social trust, with a huge difference with respect to the other European countries: Only 19 percent of Italians fully trust other Italians, compared to a European average of 48 percent. Moreover, only 11 percent of the individuals from other EU countries report they fully trust Italians, half as many as the average for other EU citizens.

To strengthen the argument that limited formal and informal enforcement is important in explaining the development of the house-

Table 4.3
Social trust and reliability of Italians and EU citizens

Country	Trust toward own citizens	Trustworthiness according to other EU nationals
Austria	65	24
Belgium	40	23
Denmark	46	29
Finland	72	25
France	33	20
Germany	57	24
Greece	51	15
Ireland	43	20
Italy	**19**	**11**
Netherlands	37	26
Norvey	61	29
Portugal	44	15
Spain	49	16
Sweden	64	27
United Kingdom	39	20
EU	48	21.6
Euro area	41.25	18.75

Note: The table shows two measures of social trust in the European countries. Data are obtained from various waves of the Eurobarometer survey. Individuals are asked to indicate how much they trust their fellow citizens and the citizens of each of the other EU countries. They can answer in one of four possible ways: "not at all," "a little," "enough," "fully." The first indicator—"trust toward own citizens"—is the percentage of individuals in each country that report they trust their fellow citizens fully. The second indicator—"trustworthiness according to other EU nationals"—is the average share of respondents in the other EU countries who declare they fully trust the citizens of the given country. Thus, for example, 24 percent of EU citizens, excluding Austria, say they fully trust the Austrians.

hold loan market, we can exploit the marked differences in Italian local markets and correlate them with measures of court efficiency and social capital. Interestingly, the efficiency of the judicial system and the endowment of social capital, however measured, differ considerably across provinces with a pattern similar to that of the size of the household loan market and the accessibility of credit. Figure 4.6 shows the average number of years it takes to complete a lower court trial in the province, using data released by the Ministry of Justice. Darker areas correspond to provinces with a less efficient judicial system. There is wide variation, ranging from 1.4 years to 9.7 years, with a mean of 3.6

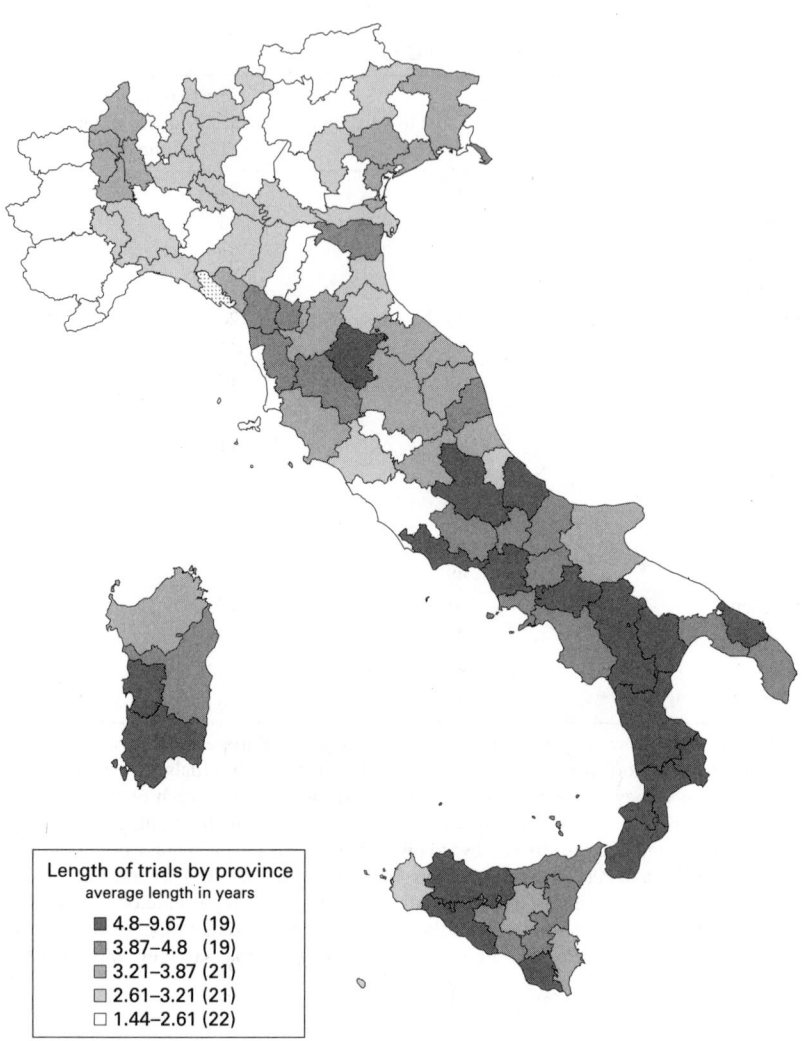

Figure 4.6
Average length of trials by province
The figure shows the number of years it takes to obtain a judgment in a civil suit in Italian provinces. Darker areas correspond to less efficient courts. Data are obtained from the Ministry of Justice.

and a standard deviation of 1.25. Figure 4.7 shows an outcome-based index of social capital across provinces as measured by the volume of blood donation (number of blood bags per inhabitant) computed by Guiso, Sapienza, and Zingales (2004b). Darker provinces are those better endowed with social capital. In this case, too, there is great geographical variation; the average level of donation is three bags per one hundred people, but there is a lot of cross-sectional variability. Some provinces have no donations, others as many as eleven bags per one hundred inhabitants. Furthermore, formal and informal enforcement measures have a clear pattern: Provinces in the north and in the center have more social capital and more efficient courts. Fabbri and Padula (2001) show that where courts are more efficient, households have easier access to the loan market, and loans can be obtained at lower rates and with less collateral. Guiso, Sapienza, and Zingales (2004b) show that, even after controlling for differences in court efficiency, the endowment of social capital has a strong additional effect on households' access to credit: A household in the province with the highest level of social capital has a probability of being credit-constrained that is three times lower than one in the province with the lowest. Also, in areas with more social capital, households are less likely to take loans from friends and relatives, which jibes with the idea that informal loans substitute for poorly working credit markets. In addition, Guiso, Sapienza, and Zingales (2004b) show that the effect of social capital does not capture some unobserved local characteristic that is correlated with the availability of credit; in fact, social capital retains its effect on access to credit, even when they use the level of social capital in the province of origin for those in the sample who have moved, and add to the regressions dummies for the province of residence to control for unobserved heterogeneity. In sum, poor legal enforcement (length of trials) and limited informal enforcement through social trust independently constrain the supply of loans to households. Furthermore, since areas where the courts are less efficient are also those with little social capital, the two channels of enforcement cumulate to increase interregional differences. Since, as tables 4.2 and 4.3 show, countries differ markedly both in quality of creditors' legal protection and in endowment of social capital, the evidence for Italy suggests that these features are likely to be important determinants of the international differences in the degree of development of the household loan market.

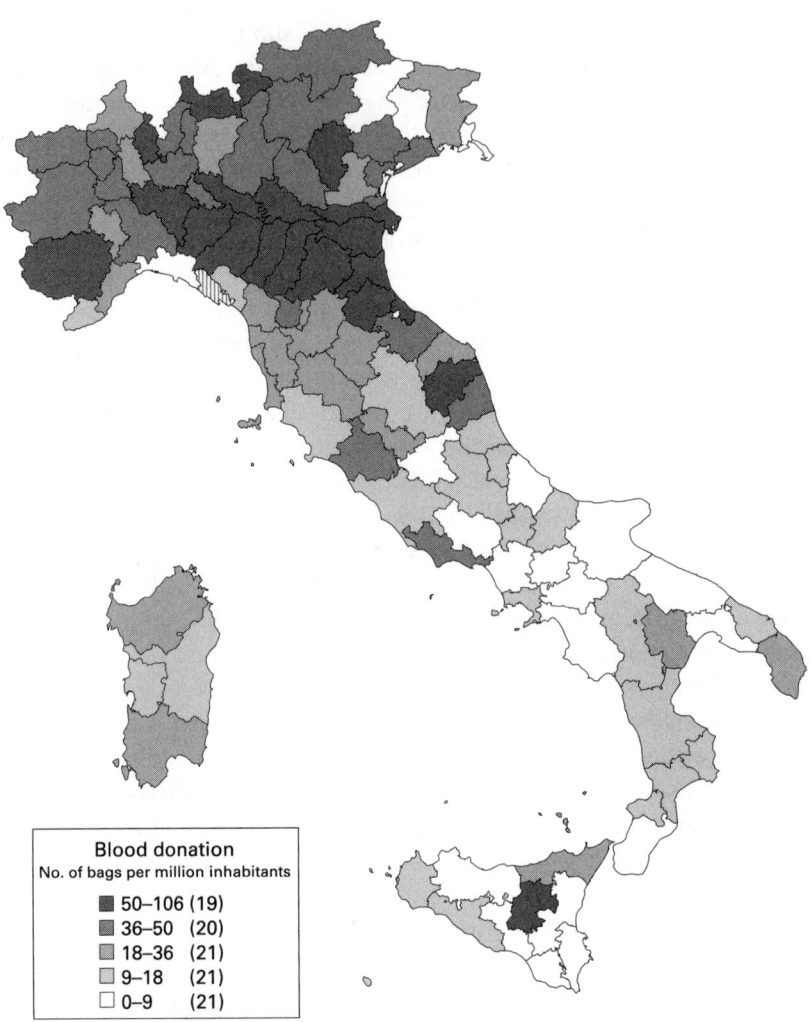

Figure 4.7
Social capital by province
The figure shows an outcome-based measure of social capital given by the number of
bags of blood donated per million inhabitants in a province. Darker areas correspond to
provinces with more social capital, based on data collected by Guiso, Sapienza, and Zingales (2004a).

4.4   Financial Regulation, Financial Liberalization, and the Supply of Household Loans

The factors listed in the previous section discourage credit supply and help explain the small size of the household loan market in Italy. However, they cannot explain why the Italian market grew faster than that of the euro area in the second half of the nineties. There is no evidence that the Italian judicial system has become more efficient in the 1990s: The average number of years to obtain a lower court sentence remained constant at 3.45, and the endowment of social capital evolves very slowly. Hence, this factor helps us to understand differences in financial development across regions or countries, but it cannot explain swift changes in credit supply, such as those observed in Italy in the past decade.

To fully explain the smallness of the household loan market in Italy and its dynamic recent growth, we must consider the regulation to which the Italian credit markets have long been subjected and the deregulation of the nineties. Following our interpretation, credit to households in Italy was limited in the past not only by poor enforcement of loan contracts but also by strict regulation that made credit scarce and interest rates high. Prompted by the financial deregulation of the 1990s, increased competition in the banking and financial markets brought a sharp decline in interest rates, greatly easing access for many households. Therefore, in the interest rate-loan demand space, Italy experienced a movement along the households' demand for loans in the second half of the 1990s, without any shift in its location due, say, to a structural change in consumers' preferences. This effect was compounded by the fall in interest rates common to all European countries, which accounts for the upsurge in household loans in the second half of the 1990s, even in countries with large and well-developed markets. In other words, financial liberalization in a strictly regulated economy such as Italy before the process began, explains the faster growth of household loans in Italy relative to the other EU countries.

First, we trace the role of strict regulation and the subsequent financial liberalization and then discuss the impact of the latter on the cost and availability of credit to households.

4.4.1   Credit Market Regulation and Financial Liberalization

Over the past two decades the Italian credit market has experienced massive deregulation, progressively removing all the restrictions and limits to competition imposed by the 1936 Banking Law. The main features of that law were strict regulation of entry, limitations in the geographical span of lending by type of bank, and complete separation of short- from long-term lending. This had two consequences: First, a severe limitation on competition in local credit markets; second, with specific reference to lending to households, a limited number of mortgage lenders, since only the few banks specialized in long-term lending, could extend mortgages.

The 1936 Banking Law essentially froze the opening of new branches; entry regulation ended up having a different impact across regions, which has affected the development of local credit markets. For example, areas with many savings banks were less affected by the limits on branching (hence less influenced by regulatory limits to competition) because savings banks were allowed to open branches in a wider geographical area—the region—than mutual banks, typically operating within the boundaries of a province. Guiso, Sapienza, and Zingales (2003) show that these geographical differences in regulation explain a good part of the regional variation in the availability and cost of credit to households (figure 4.4). Overall, their results strongly support the notion that the freezing of bank expansion imposed by the 1936 Banking Law was a major institutional bottleneck in the supply of credit, which compounded the poor quality of the judicial system and the limited endowment of social capital to discourage lending to households.

Regulation of entry remained substantially unchanged until the 1980s. The first step toward deregulation was taken only in 1978, when the Bank of Italy approved a plan setting a "desired" number of branches in each province. Authorizations, then, were determined on the basis of this plan. In 1984, the geographical restrictions to lending were broadened so greatly as to become nonbinding (Costi 2001). Then, in 1986, the branching procedure was eased by introducing tacit consent with a sixty-day deadline for response. However, it was only in 1990 that authorizations and restrictions on entry and the opening of new branches were formally lifted, giving rise to a massive increase in the number of bank branches. As figure 4.8 shows, between 1990 and 2003, the number of branches almost doubled, from 16,000 to 30,000 and, as Guiso, Sapienza, and Zingales (2003) argue, the increase was larger in the regions that had been more exposed to the 1936 regulation. The rise in the number of branches is all the more remarkable as the number of banks decreased by 20 percent (figure 4.8), prompted by

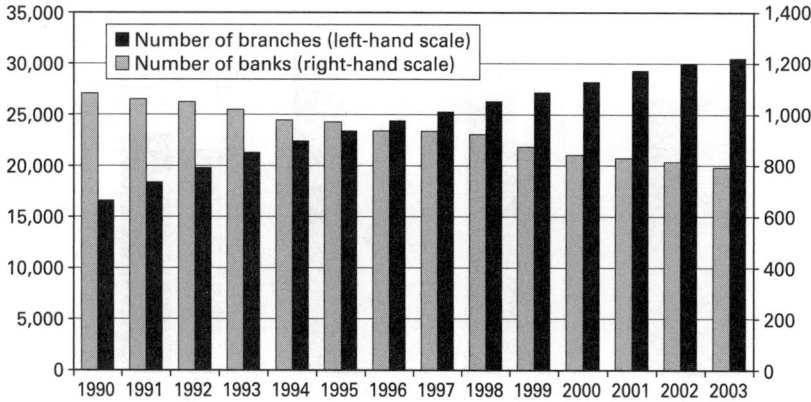

Figure 4.8
Banks and branches in Italy
The figure shows the evolution during the 1990s in the number of banks (right-hand scale) and in the number of bank branches in Italy. Data are from the Bank of Italy.

the wave of restructuring and mergers and acquisitions in the banking industry. As a consequence, the number of different banks present in each local market has increased in all geographical areas (figure 4.9), assuring that the benefits of increased competition spread out geographically. One piece of evidence consistent with this view is reported in figure 4.10, which shows a strong positive provincial correlation between the share of households with debt and the number of bank branches per inhabitant over the period 1996–2003.

The second important step in the liberalization process was the 1993 Banking Law, which ended the operational and maturity specialization of Italian banks and adopted universal banking. For our purposes, the most important effect is that participation in the mortgage and consumer credit markets was extended to all banks, dramatically sharpening competition and increasing the supply of credit to households. This was made possible by massive privatization, which, in a few years, put half of the previously state-owned banking industry under private control, providing strong incentives for profit maximization. Table 4.4 summarizes the main features of the old regulations and of the deregulation process, and illustrates the most important changes in the household loan market. The appendix details the changes introduced by liberalization and its effects on household credit market, as a well as a number of features of household credit contracts in Italy compared to other countries. One noteworthy consequence of liberalization was the

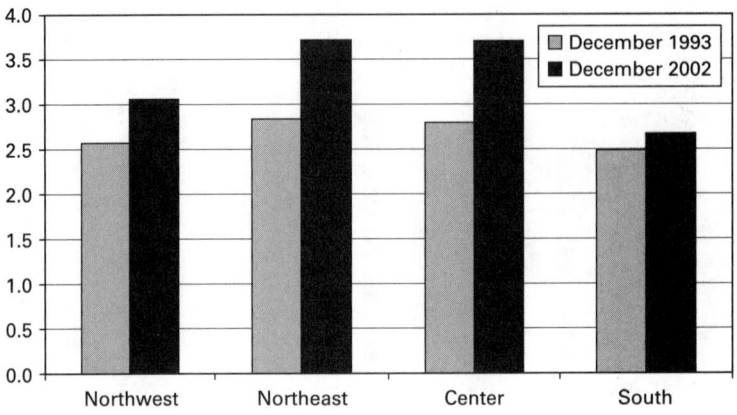

Figure 4.9
Number of banks in the banked district
The figure shows the average number of different and independent banks that are present in each local market by geographical area in Italy at the start of the liberalization process (1993) and ten years later.
Source: Our computations on Bank of Italy data.

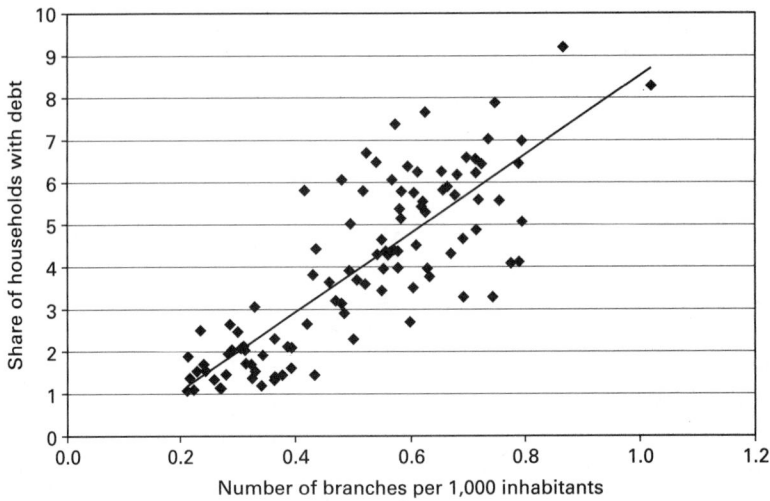

Figure 4.10
Households' debt and degree of banking development
The figure shows the correlation between the share of households with debt and the number of bank branches per thousand inhabitants across provinces over the period 1996–2003.
Source: Our computations on Bank of Italy data.

Table 4.4
The effects of the liberalization process in Italy

	Major changes introduced by financial liberalization
Competition and market structure	
Structure of the banking system	Between 1993 and 2003, the number of banks in Italy declined from 1,019 to 788. Most of the decrease is accounted for by the drop in the number of mutual banks. Mergers and acquisitions also played an important role. Over the same period, the number of bank branches increased from 22,298 to 30,504, and the number of different banks present in each local market also increased.
Market concentration	At the end of 2000, the five largest banks accounted for 23 percent of total assets in Italy, against 39 percent in the euro area. Considering the first five banking groups, the degree of concentration (54 percent of total assets) is closer to that in the euro area. Concentration of the household mortgage market, measured by the Herfindahl index, is no different in Italy from the main industrialized countries.
Market participation and market entry	Before the 1993 Banking Law, there was mandatory maturity specialization, with special credit institutions operating at medium-long term and commercial banks at short term. Under the 1993 Banking Law, all intermediaries can operate on all maturities. Since the middle nineties, both the mortgage and the consumer credit markets have experienced mobility in market shares and rapid changes in the characteristics of the banks operating in the market, consistent with massive entry of new intermediaries; entry of foreign banks has increased competitive pressure and prompted adoption of frontier screening and monitoring techniques and product innovation.
Role of government	In the nineties, the government essentially left the financial intermediation industry. The share of total assets held by state-owned banks declined from 68 percent in 1992 to 12 percent in 2000, one of the lowest levels in Europe.

Table 4.4
(continued)

	Major changes introduced by financial liberalization
Product variety and contract flexibility	
Product choice	Product variety has increased greatly in the past ten years. The interest rate on mortgages can be fixed, variable, mixed, capped, balanced. Mortgages are offered on a menu of maturities varying between 5 years and 20 years. Longer maturities are also offered but require additional conditions. Mortgages are readily available not only for home sole proprietorship but also for other purposes.
Product distribution	Distribution of mortgages in Italy is almost completely branch-driven (as in France and Germany). Independent advisors or direct purchase of mortgages via phone or the Internet is thus far a small share of the market.
Renegotiability of interest rates	The share of variable-rate mortgages or with rates renegotiable in less than one year remained quite stable in the period 1993–2003 in all the countries of the euro area. In Italy, it is around 75 percent, a figure similar to that in Spain (79 percent) but much higher than in Germany (15 percent) and in France (22 percent). Differences in the incidence of variable interest rates for consumer credit are much smaller: In 2003, one-fourth of total consumer credit in Italy was variable-rate, against 27 percent in the euro area.
Downpayment and transaction costs	
Downpayment	In recent years, the loan-to-value ratio (LTV) in Italy has risen from 50 percent to 80 percent, reaching a level close to that in the other industrialized countries. Now downpayment constraints, when binding, can often be accommodated in such a way that LTV can exceed 80 percent of market value. In this case, additional guarantees are required.
Early payments	Early repayment on mortgages is possible but quite costly so that, in practice, the option is rarely exercised. This is true in the vast majority of industrialized countries. The only countries where early repayments are costless are Denmark and the United States.

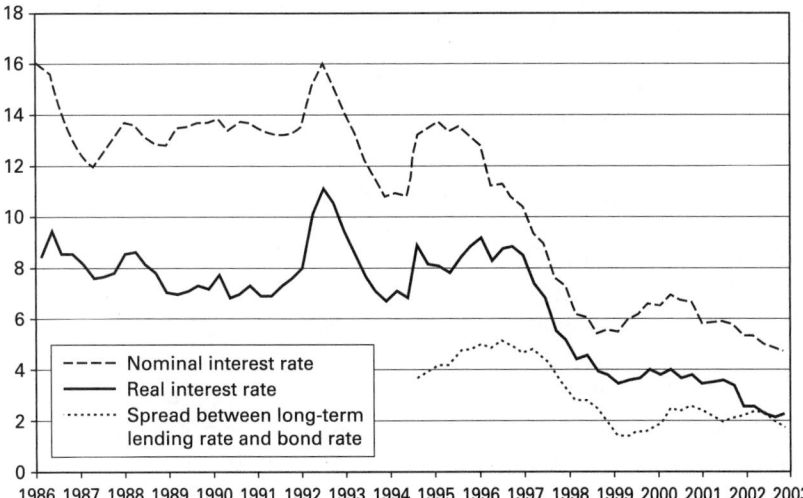

Figure 4.11
Interest rates on medium- and long-term loans to households
The figure shows the nominal interest rate, the real interest rate, and the spread on medium- and long-term loans to households. The spread is computed with respect to banks' cost of medium- and long-term funds. This measure is available on a comparable basis only since 1995.
Sources: Bank of Italy; ISTAT.

entry of foreign intermediaries that specialized in mortgage and consumer credit, which increased competitive pressure and improved the "state of the art" of Italian banks in screening loan applicants and monitoring clients by use of advanced credit-scoring techniques and warning systems.[9] As a consequence of increased competition, credit to households has become more easily available and its cost has been drastically reduced. Now let us discuss the impact of financial liberalization on the rate of interest on household loans and on the availability of credit.

4.4.2   Interest Rates on Loans

It takes time for financial liberalization to show its effects; this is because entry into new markets, either by opening new branches or by operating a new line of business, such as household mortgages, comes some time after the regulatory impediment has been removed. In fact, the effects of the liberalization on the household loan market are visible after the mid-1990s. Figure 4.11 shows the evolution of the interest rate on long-term household loans and its spread vis-à-vis the average interest rate on long-term bank funding (CDs and bonds). The nominal interest rate starts dropping after 1995, followed with a lag by the real rate. Over the three-year period (1997–2000), the real interest rate on long-term loans falls from about 8.5 percent to 4 percent. The interest rate spread follows the same pattern, with a sharp decline from around 5 percent in 1996 to 2 percent in 2000. Since then, it has held approximately constant. Thus, a sizeable part—between one-half and two-thirds, depending on the reference period—of the fall in the real interest rate on mortgages in the second half of the 1990s is due to the reduction in the spread. This is consistent with our interpretation that increased competition following liberalization brought about a significant drop in households' cost of borrowing and increased the demand for loans. The rest of the fall in the interest rate is due to changes in macroeconomic conditions, and in particular, to the decrease in nominal and real interest rates realized to achieve the Maastricht criteria for admission to the single currency and to the worldwide reduction in interest rates during the 1990s.

4.4.3   Credit Availability

The positive effect of financial liberalization on the supply of household lending is also supported by evidence on changes in credit availability. Table 4.5 reports data on households' access to credit collected in the SHIW for the period 1989–2002. The first column shows the share of households that applied for a loan, either for home purchase or to smooth consumption. This share increases markedly after 1995. The second column shows the share of individuals whose application was rejected, and the third shows the share that was discouraged from applying by expectations of rejection. The fourth column groups together rejected consumers and discouraged borrowers—that is, all those consumers who can be classified as liquidity-constrained—and reports them as a fraction of the total sample interviewed. The last column shows the share of applicants who have been turned down. Interestingly, after 1995, access to credit becomes much easier. For instance, while about half of those applying for credit were turned down up to 1995 (last column), in 1998, only one applicant out of four was denied, and in 2002, only one out of ten. Furthermore, the share of discouraged borrowers is halved between the early 1990s and 2002 (third column), suggesting that consumers were quick to realize that loans were now easier to get. This result shows that, besides the significant reduction

Table 4.5
Access to credit for Italian households

Year	Share of households applying for a loan (1)	Share of applicants rejected (2)	Discouraged borrowers (3)	Share of credit-constrained households (4)	Share of rejected households among those applying for a loan (5)
1991	—	.0117	.031	.0427	—
1993	.0219	.0100	.022	.0320	.457
1995	.0145	.0079	.015	.0219	.545
1998	.0256	.0062	.026	.0322	.242
2000	.0490	.0029	.014	.0169	.059
2002	.0386	.0037	.0166	.0203	.099

Note: The table shows various indicators of a household's ease of access to the loan market. They are obtained from various waves of the Bank of Italy Survey of Household Income and Wealth and are based on the following two questions: "During the year, did you or a member of the household think of applying for a loan or a mortgage to a bank or other financial intermediary but then changed your mind on the expectation that the application would be rejected?" We classify "yes" as "discouraged borrowers." The survey also asked, "During the year, did you or a member of the household apply for a loan or a mortgage to a bank or other financial intermediary and have the application totally or partially rejected?" We classify answers "yes totally" and "yes partially" as "rejected consumers." In the first four columns, the shares are computed with respect to the whole sample of households; in the last column, the share of rejections is relative only to loan applicants.

in the cost of debt, competition also made access to the loan market much easier.

To sum up, financial liberalization has benefited consumers because they can borrow at a significantly lower cost and because they can get a loan much more easily than when markets where tightly regulated. These two features explain the fast growth of household loans that otherwise could be difficult to account for.[10]

4.5   Financial Liberalization, Households Savings, and Regional Loan Availability

To offer additional evidence that financial liberalization was the main force behind the development of the consumer loan market during the 1990s, we focus on two additional events deriving from liberalization: the reduction in households' saving rate and the faster development of credit in the parts of Italy that had been more financially repressed, namely, where regulation had been more binding.

4.5.1 Financial Liberalization and the Household Saving Rate

If before liberalization households were subject to liquidity constraints either through rationing or because of the large spread between the lending and borrowing rate, then their consumption plans were constrained by availability of funds, inducing them to save more than they would have wished. Financial regulation thus had the effect of boosting the overall saving rate, which has traditionally been high. Following the same logic, financial liberalization should have lowered the saving rate either because previously credit-constrained households increased current consumption or because they had less need to accumulate funds to purchase a home or a durable good. In both cases, greater availability of consumer or mortgage credit reduces current saving. This is consistent with the sharp reduction in the households' saving rate during the nineties. Figure 4.12 shows a clear negative trend starting in the second half of the eighties, but after 1996, following liberalization, the saving rate drops by more than 8 percentage points in just three years. This is the sharpest fall in the period covered and is consistent with episodes of financial liberalization in other countries, such as the United Kingdom and the United States (see, among

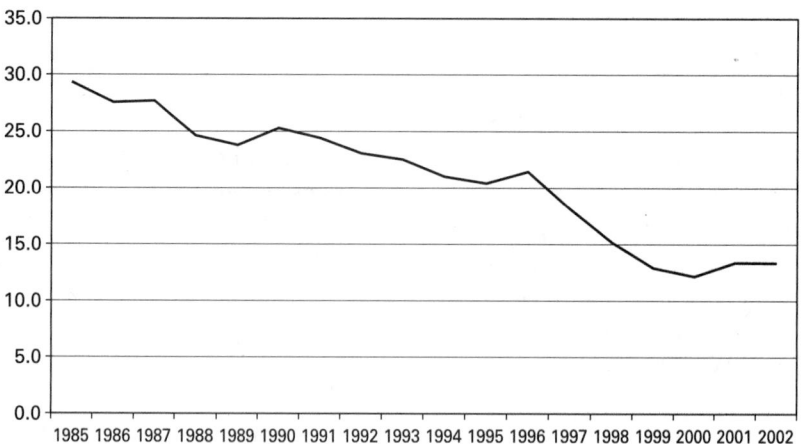

Figure 4.12
Household saving rate in Italy
The figure shows Italian household saving as a percent of disposable income since 1985. Data are from ISTAT.

others, Muellbauer and Murphy 1997; Follain and Dunsky 1997; Leece 2000).

4.5.2   Growth of Mortgages and Financial Liberalization: Differences across Local Markets

If the growth of household debt in the nineties was due mainly to the increased supply of credit thanks to liberalization, then households' debt should have grown most rapidly in the most financially repressed areas, where liquidity constraints were more binding. To check this, we exploit the considerable differences in the degree of development of the household loan market across provinces, which, as we have seen, are driven partly by differences in social capital and legal enforcement but partly by differences in the stringency of the 1936 Banking Law, as is shown by Guiso, Sapienza, and Zingales 2003. Financial liberalization should have triggered a process of convergence in the degree of development of the market for household loans because after deregulation, the areas most penalized by the 1936 law show more entries implying that, other things equal, the growth rate of loans to households in the years after liberalization should be higher in the more financially repressed provinces. Consistent with the foregoing, we assume that financial liberalization reveals its effects only in the second half of the nineties. We have thus regressed the cumulative growth rate of medium- and long-term household loans in a province between 1996 and 2003 on the ratio between the stock of medium- and long-term household debt and GDP at the beginning of 1996. Table 4.6 reports the results of the estimates. There is a significant negative correlation between the growth rate of household loans and the size of the pre-deregulation market (scaled by GDP). This result is robust to the inclusion of the level of GDP per capita in 1995 or the growth rate of provincial GDP; moreover, the effect is also robust and actually increases if we insert a dummy variable for the southern provinces to account in a simple way for differences in the initial level of development of the market due to differences in social capital and judicial efficiency. Furthermore, the effect is economically relevant: In the provinces with the highest value of the household-debt/GDP ratio prior to liberalization (Genoa and Siena), the volume of lending to households increases by 11.5 percentage points less than in the province with the lowest ratio (Catanzaro), supporting the idea that, at the margin, financial liberalization has benefited more the most financially repressed areas.

Table 4.6
Liberalization and convergence in households' access to credit

Variable	(1)	(2)	(3)
Outstanding loans/GDP$_{1995}$	−29.884***	−42.049***	−42.654***
	(−4.770)	(−7.110)	(−7.160)
GDP per capita$_{1995}$			3.92e-06
			(0.52)
GDP growth$_{1996-2003}$			0.713
			(1.380)
South dummy		−0.936	−0.893
		(−5.450)	(−5.570)
R^2	0.197	0.393	0.470
Number of observations	95	95	95

Notes: The table tests whether financial liberalization has fostered loan supply more in the areas with a smaller household loan market. The left-hand side variable is the rate of growth of mortgages in a province between 1996 and 2005; outstanding loans/GDP is the value of the stock of medium and long-term loans to households at the end of 1995. *t*-statistics in parenthesis. *** coefficient significant at the 1 percent level.

4.6   Conclusions

This chapter has surveyed demand and supply factors to explain three important features of the household credit market in Italy: (1) small size, (2) marked geographical differences in access, and (3) remarkable growth in the second half of the nineties.

We have argued that the smallness of the market cannot be ascribed to compressed demand, driven either by adverse preferences for borrowing by Italian households, crowding out by government supply of debt-intensive services, or by a large informal market for loans from relatives and friends. We have shown that there are no significant differences in households' propensity for debt between Italy and the other developed countries. We conclude that, in the past, the size gap depended on supply bottlenecks due to an inefficient judicial system, limited informal enforcement, and strict regulations. Italy's geographical heterogeneity in the availability of household credit enables us to test this hypothesis in an environment where a number of potentially important variables that affect demand or supply can be held constant: The efficiency of the courts, the availability of social capital, and the strictness of regulation all vary significantly across regions and provinces, and the pattern correlates with the degree of development of the local household credit market.

The remarkable growth of household credit in the second half of the nineties mostly reflects the liberalization process, which got under way in the mid-eighties and was formally completed with the 1993 Banking Law. Financial liberalization spurred the opening of many branches and massive new entries in all local markets, and the shift to the universal banking model produced a significant increase in the number of banks and other intermediaries offering mortgages and consumer credit. This, together with entry of foreign banks, has greatly increased competition, lowered interest rates, and made loans much more readily available.

The study focuses on Italy but its conclusions are of a more general validity. The considerable international variation in the degree of protection of creditors, in social capital, and in regulatory strictness strongly suggests that these are likely to be major factors explaining international differences in the development of the consumer credit market.

4A   Appendix: Financial Regulation and Liberalization in Italy

In Italy, important measures to liberalize and deregulate financial markets began in 1985. Complete liberalization was achieved with the 1993 Banking Law (Testo Unico Bancario, TUB).[11]

At the start of the 1980s, the Italian banking system was still strictly regulated. Foreign exchange controls were in place; the establishment of new banks and the opening of new branches were subject to authorization;[12] competition was curbed by mandatory maturity specialization, with special credit institutions operating at medium-long term and commercial banks at short term; the quantity of bank lending was subject to a ceiling.

Between the mid-1980s and the early 1990s, all these restrictions were gradually removed (Cottarelli, Ferri, and Generale 1995; Passacantando 1996; Angelini and Cetorelli 2002). In particular, the lending ceiling was abolished in practice in 1985; foreign exchange controls were gradually lifted between 1987 and 1990, branching was liberalized in 1990; and universal banking was adopted with the 1993 Banking Law, allowing all intermediaries to engage in all forms of banking business, completing operational and maturity despecialization.[13] The mortgage and consumer credit markets have benefited greatly. The main characteristics of Italian banking deregulation are summarized in table 4.4.

Banking Structure

The rationalization of the Italian banking system and the more intense competition that followed the 1993 Banking Law resulted in a steady decline in the number of credit institutions. From 1993 to 2003, the number of banks declined from 1,037 to 788, while the number of branches rose from 22,298 to 30,504 (figure 4.8).[14] Despite the decline in the total number of banks, the number of different banks present in each local market increased in all geographical areas (figure 4.9). Mergers played an important role in this transformation. Between 1996 and 2000, bank mergers accounted for nearly 40 percent of the total value of merger activity in Italy, compared with 22 percent in the euro area.

Market Concentration

At the end of 2000, the five largest Italian banks accounted for 23 percent of total assets, while the weighted (by number of banks) average-across euro-area countries of that concentration index was 39 percent (ECB 2002). Considering the largest five banking groups, the degree of concentration (54 percent of total assets) is closer to that in the euro area. Even from the specific perspective of the mortgage market, concentration in Italy, measured by the Herfindahl index, is now more or less on a par with the main industrialized countries (Mercer Oliver Wyman 2003).

Market Participation and Entry

Until the 1993 Banking Law, there was mandatory maturity specialization; "special credit institutions" operated at medium-long term and commercial banks at short term. Now all banks can extend mortgages and grant consumer credit.

The Italian mortgage market experienced high mobility in the second half of the 1990s, with sharp changes in market shares and modification of the characteristics of the intermediaries. These changes were more pronounced than in the other European countries, suggesting that, despite M&A activity, the Italian market was experiencing a formidable increase in competition (Mercer Oliver Wyman 2003). In particular, the entry of British and German mortgage specialists significantly increased competitive pressure and prompted product innovation. As for consumer credit, Law 142/1992 mandated greater transparency in contractual conditions and in the computation of the "actual" interest rate (which includes accessory and administrative expenses). These changes fostered resort to consumer credit on the part of households, which had been particularly averse to this form of debt. The experience of foreign intermediaries (especially French ones) that hold stock in Italian banks and other intermediaries specialized in consumer credit has improved the "state of the art."

Government Intervention
Government intervention in the Italian banking system has been steadily declining. The share of total assets held by state-owned banks and groups plunged from 68 percent in 1992 to 12 percent in 2000, one of the lowest in Europe. Concerning the mortgage and consumer credit markets, there are few relevant public measures. Subsidized loans or borrower guarantees are very limited; in 2003, only 2 percent of medium- and long-term lending carried subsidized (capped) interest rates. On the ranking proposed by Mercer Oliver Wyman (2003), together with Spain and the United Kingdom, Italy is one of the countries with the least direct government involvement in the banking sector.

Product Choice
Both in the mortgage and in the consumer credit market, the range of products has expanded considerably over the past ten years. The increase in product variety has facilitated households' reliance on mortgages and consumer credit. At the beginning of the nineties, mortgages were mainly variable-rate, with a standard ten-year maturity, and were granted only for house purchase. The range of contract characteristics has widened greatly since then. The interest rate can now be fixed, variable, mixed (allowing the borrower to switch from fixed to variable and vice versa at a specified date), capped, balanced (partly fixed-rate and partly indexed). Contracts generally range from five years to twenty years. Longer maturities are granted but with additional conditions. Mortgages are readily available not only for home sole proprietorship but also for other purposes, in practice, allowing the possibility of second mortgages. Additional conditions are generally

required for shared ownership. To limit credit risk, mortgages are not granted to consumers whom have declared bankruptcy in the past or whose income is not demonstrable.

Product Distribution
Distribution of mortgages in Italy is almost completely branch-driven (as in France and Germany). Recent regulations issued by the Bank of Italy allow financial companies to promote and place mortgage loans, by signing agreements with banks. This product distribution system mainly reflects the fact that, before extending a loan, banks build a deposit relationship with the client. Placement via an independent advisor and direct purchase of mortgages via phone or Internet still account for a small share of the market, because by law mortgage contracts must be registered with a notary. These channels are well developed only in the United Kingdom and the Netherlands.

Renegotiability of Interest Rates
More than three-quarters of new credit for house purchase in 2003 in Italy was at variable rates or rates renegotiable in less than one year. This structure is strongly influenced by Italy's long tradition of variable rates, due especially to recent periods of high inflation and a funding model for Italian banks that is mainly based on current accounts and deposits repayable at notice.

As figure 4A.1 shows, the incidence of variable interest rates in Italy is similar to that in Spain (79 percent), Ireland (78 percent), Finland (89 percent), and Portugal (99 percent), but much higher than that in Germany (15 percent) and in France (22 percent); see chapter 5 for a discussion of U.K. evidence. Except for France, these figures are quite similar to those reported in Borio (1996) for 1993, indicating that the renegotiability of interest rates in mortgage markets follows specific national patterns. In the United States, more than three-quarters of mortgages are at fixed rates, but this is substantially influenced by the fact that early repayment is generally possible without penalty. Differences in the weight of variable interest rates for consumer credit are less evident: One-quarter of total consumer credit in Italy is at variable rate, against 27 percent in the euro area.

Transaction and switching costs have been rapidly reduced in Italy: Down payment and early repayment costs are now in line with those applied in other banking systems.

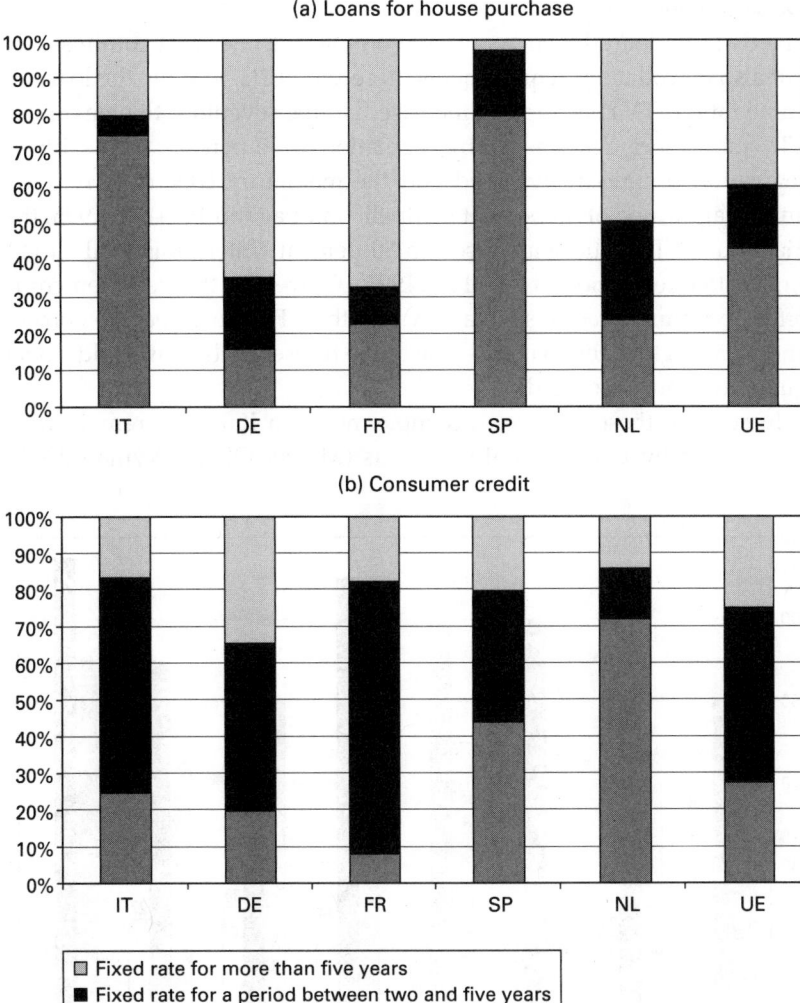

Figure 4A.1

Distribution of household loans by type of interest rate

The figure shows the composition of household lending in various European countries by type of interest rate arrangement (fixed-rate, variable-rate) for mortgages (panel A) and consumer credit (panel B). Data are from the ECB and the Bank of Italy.

Downpayment

The cost of a loan depends not only on interest rates and commissions but also on collateral requirements. In recent years, in Italy, the loan-to-value ratio (LTV) has rapidly increased. In the seventies, the maximum LTV for a mortgage was set by regulation at 50 percent; in the 1980s, regulation progressively eased and the maximum LTV ratio reached an average value of 56 percent (Jappelli and Pagano 1994). In 1995, the maximum LTV ratio was raised to 80 percent (Interministerial Credit Committee resolution of April 22, 1995). Currently, this requirement is often accommodated in such a way that the LTV can exceed 80 percent and be as high as the market value of the house. In this case, additional guarantees are requested.

In spite of these changes, downpayments in Italy still remain relatively large by international standards (Mercer Oliver Wyman 2003).

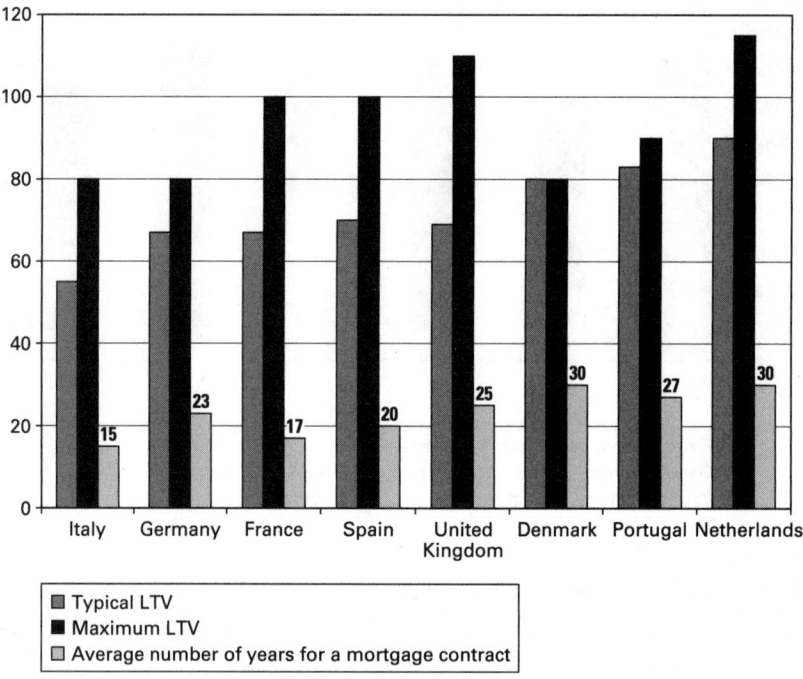

Figure 4A.2
Loan-to-value ratio and maturity of mortgage contracts
The figure shows the typical loan-to-value ratio, its maximum value, and the typical maturity of a mortgage for several European countries. LTV ratios are in percent, maturity in number of years.
Source: Mercer Oliver Wyman 2003.

In 2001, the typical LTV ratio ranged from a low of 55 percent in Italy to a high of 90 percent in the Netherlands (figure 4A.2); in Germany, the United Kingdom, and Spain, it was intermediate (67–70 percent). The high Dutch LTV partly reflects tax incentives. It is worth noting that in Denmark and Germany, though the LTV is relatively low, the constraint can often be accommodated by using a secondary loan, so that the lending cap can be as high as 80 percent to 100 percent of the market value of the house. The typical mortgage maturity is positively correlated with the loan-to-value ratio, averaging fifteen years in Italy, for example, and thirty years in the Netherlands.

Early Repayments

In Italy, early repayment of a mortgage is possible but at a high cost so that, in practice, few consumers exercise the option. Borio (1996) argues that this feature is shared by the vast majority of industrialized countries. At the two extremes are Austria, where early repayment is virtually impossible, and Denmark and United States, where it is cost-free. This means that the relatively high share of long-term and fixed-rate financing in the United States (respectively, 85 and 75 percent of the total) overstates the effective maturity of the contracts and understates the freedom to adjust terms.

Notes

1. We focus on the period 1997–2003, for which comparable data for the euro-area countries is available. Comparability, however, is obtained for the set of households that includes "producer households" (sole proprietorships and partnerships with fewer than twenty employees); in Italy, this last category accounts for 25 percent of total lending to households and almost 10 percent of mortgages.

2. The person interviewed is given eleven alternatives, ranging from imagination to obedience, and can select five as important.

3. The implication is that a financial liberalization, relaxing financial constraints, reduces the household saving rate. In section 4.5, we show that this implication is consistent with the drop in the saving rate that has taken place in Italy following financial liberalization.

4. The figure for Italy may be somewhat biased downward due to the high incidence of families with working-age, live-in children, and transfers within the family are not picked up in the survey.

5. For a survey of tax treatment of interest rate payments across nations, see Poterba 2002.

6. The only exception is the Netherlands, where tax deduction for consumer credit is allowed but subject to a cap.

7. This is available on the Web at http://rru.worldbank.org/DoingBusiness/ TopicReports.

8. A survey run by the Bank of Italy on a sample composed of ninety major Italian banks reveals that the time required to recoup a loan following default varies from a minimum of two years, in the case of private settlements, to seven years, if done through a court. The portion recovered is about 38 percent, with high variation depending on the characteristics and the conditions of the loan, such as the existence of collateral (Generale and Gobbi 1996).

9. The use of credit-scoring techniques for extending mortgages and consumer credit has spread greatly in recent years: At the end of 2002, in each Italian province, there were (on average) eleven banks that relied upon credit-scoring techniques, compared with just five in 1999. There is evidence that credit-scoring techniques have a positive effect on the supply of loans in local credit markets. For instance, Bofondi and Lotti (2003) find that banks that use credit-scoring techniques to screen applicants have increased their mortgage supply more than other banks.

10. To get a sense of the contribution of financial liberalization to the growth of household loans, Casolaro and Gambacorta (2004) estimate a reduced-form model for household loans using time-series data for the period 1984–2003 and letting the growth in household loans depend on the real interest rate, GDP growth, and other controls that affect the demand (tax incentives, the average price of housing, and so forth). They capture the effect of financial liberalization on household credit not reflected in a lower interest rate with a dummy variable that is equal to 1 after year 1997. According to the model's estimates, more than a third of the growth of household loans between 1997 and 2003 is due to the reduction in the real interest rate, and a quarter is explained by financial liberalization. Thus, if half the drop in the cost of household credit is due to increased competition, financial liberalization alone can explain almost half the growth in lending to households after 1996.

11. Italian financial reforms during the 1980s and early 1990s are discussed in Gambacorta 2003. For an analysis of the main differences between the Italian banking system and the other main countries of the euro area, see Gambacorta, Gobbi, and Panetta 2001.

12. Before 1987, the opening of new branches was authorized by the Bank of Italy on the basis of a four-year plan that established the number of branches in each local market on the basis of estimated local needs for banking services.

13. For more details on the 1993 Banking Law, see the Bank of Italy Annual Report for 1993.

14. Most of the decrease in the number of banks is accounted for by the decline in the number of mutual banks, which fell from 671 to 456 between 1993 and 2003; in terms of market share, at the end of 2003, mutual banks covered about 6 percent of total loans, compared with 0.3 percent in December 1993.

References

Alessie, R., S. Hochguertel, and Van Soest A. 2002. "Household Portfolios in the Netherlands." In *Household Portfolios*, ed. L. Guiso, M. Haliassos, and T. Jappelli, 219–250. Cambridge, Mass.: The MIT Press.

Angelini, P., and N. Cetorelli. 2002. "Bank Competition and Regulatory Reform: The Case of the Italian Banking Industry." *Journal of Money Credit and Banking* 35: 663–684.

Banks, J., and S. Tanner. 2002. "Household Portfolios in the United Kingdom." In *Household Portfolios*, ed. L. Guiso, M. Haliassos, and T. Jappelli, 219–250. Cambridge, Mass.: The MIT Press.

Bofondi, M., and F. Lotti. 2003. "Bad Loans and Entry in Local Credit Markets." Mimeo., Bank of Italy, Rome, February.

Borio, E. V. 1996. "Credit Characteristics and the Monetary Policy Transmission Mechanism in Fourteen Industrial Countries: Facts, Conjectures and Some Econometric Evidence." In *Monetary Policy in a Converging Europe*, ed. K. Alders et al., 77–115. Dordrecht: Kluwer Academic Publishers.

Casolaro, L., and L. Gambacorta. 2004. "Un modello econometrico per il credito bancario alle famiglie in Italia" (An econometric model for bank credit to households in Italy). Mimeo., Bank of Italy.

Cottarelli, C., G. Ferri, and A. Generale. 1995. "Bank Lending Rates and Financial Structure in Italy: A Case Study." IMF Working Papers no. 38.

Costi, R. 2001. *L'ordinamento bancario*. Bologna: Il Mulino.

Das, M., and B. Donkers. 1999. "How Certain are Dutch Households About Future Income? An Empirical Analysis." *Review of Income and Wealth* 45: 325–338.

Djankov, S., E. L. Glaeser, R. La Porta, F. Lopez-de-Silanes, and A. Shleifer. 2003. "The New Comparative Economics." NBER Working Paper no. 9608, Cambridge, Mass.

Djankov, S., R. La Porta, F. Lopez-de-Silanes, and A. Shleifer. 2003. "Courts." *Quarterly Journal of Economics* 118: 453–517.

Dominitz, J., and C. F. Manski. 1997. "Perceptions of Economic Insecurity: Evidence from the Survey of Economic Expectations." *Public Opinion Quarterly* 61: 261–287.

ECB. 2002. *Report on Financial Structures*. Frankfurt am Main: European Central Bank.

Fabbri, D., and M. Padula. 2001. "Judicial Costs and Household Debt." Mimeo., Università di Salerno.

Follain, J. R., and R. M. Dunsky. 1997. "The Demand for Mortgage Debt and the Income Tax." *Journal of Housing Research* 8, no. 2: 155–199.

Gambacorta, L. 2003. "The Italian Banking System and Monetary Policy Transmission: Evidence from Bank Level Data." In *Monetary Policy Transmission in the Euro Area*, ed. I. Angeloni, A. Kashyap, and B. Mojon, 323–334. Cambridge: Cambridge University Press.

Gambacorta, L., G. Gobbi, and F. Panetta. 2001. "Il sistema bancario italiano nell'area dell'euro." *Bancaria* 57: 21–32.

Generale, A., and G. Gobbi. 1996. "Il recupero dei crediti: costi, tempi e comportamenti delle banche." Temi di discussione, Banca d'Italia, No. 265.

Guiso, L., M. Haliassos, and T. Jappelli. 2002. *Household Portfolios*. Cambridge, Mass.: The MIT Press.

Guiso, L., and T. Jappelli. 1991. "Intergenerational Transfers and Capital Market Imperfections: Evidence from a Cross Section of Italian Households." *European Economic Review* 35: 103–120.

Guiso, L., P. Sapienza, and L. Zingales. 2003. "The Cost of Banking Regulation." Mimeo., Bank of Italy, Rome.

Guiso, L., P. Sapienza, and L. Zingales. 2004a. "Does Local Financial Development Matter?" *Quarterly Journal of Economics* 119, no. 3: 929–969.

Guiso, L., P. Sapienza, and L. Zingales. 2004b. "The Role of Social Capital in Financial Development." *American Economic Review* 94, no. 3: 526–556.

Guiso, L., P. Sapienza, and L. Zingales. 2004c. "Cultural Biases in Economic Exchange," NBER Working Paper no. 11005, Cambridge, Mass.

Guiso, L., T. Jappelli, and D. Terlizzese. 1994. "Why Is Italy's Saving Rate So High?" In *Saving and the Accumulation of Wealth: Essays on Italian Household and Government Saving Behavior*, ed. A. K. Ando, L. Guiso, and I. Visco, 23–69. Cambridge: Cambridge University Press.

Guiso, L., T. Jappelli, M. Padula, and M. Pagano. 2004. "Financial Market Integration and Economic Growth in the EU." *Economic Policy* (October): 523–577.

Jappelli, T., and M. Pagano. 1989. "Consumption and Capital Market Imperfections: An International Comparison." *The American Economic Review* 79: 1088–1105.

Jappelli, T., and M. Pagano. 1994. "Saving, Growth, and Liquidity Constraints." *The Quarterly Journal of Economics* (February): 83–109.

Jappelli, T., and M. Pagano. 1999. "The Welfare Effects of Liquidity Constraints." *Oxford Economic Papers* 51: 410–430.

La Porta, R., F. Lopez-de-Silanes, A. Shleifer, and A. Vishny. 1998. "Law and Finance." *Journal of Political Economy* 106: 1113–1155.

Leece, D. 2000. "Choice of Mortgage Instrument, Liquidity Constraints, and the Demand for Housing in the UK." *Applied Economics* 32: 1121–1132.

Marchesi, D. 2002. "Giustizia civile e sistema economico." In *La competitività dell'Italia*, ed. O. M. Petracca, 146–172. Milan: Il Sole 24 Ore.

Mercer Oliver Wyman. 2003. "Study of the Financial Integration of European Mortgage Markets." Report published by the European Mortgage Federation, Brussels.

Muellbauer, J., and A. Murphy. 1997. "Booms and Busts in the U.K. Housing Market." *Economic Journal* 107: 1701–1727.

Passacantando, F. 1996. "Building an Institutional Framework for Monetary Stability." *BNL Quarterly Review* 49, no. 196: 83–132.

Poterba, J. 2002. "Taxation, Risk-Taking and Household Behavior." In *Handbook of Public Economics*, vol. 3, 1109–1171. Amsterdam: North-Holland.

Putnam, R., R. Leonardi, and R. Y. Nanetti. 1993. *Making Democracy Work. Civic Traditions in Modern Italy*. Princeton, N.J.: Princeton University Press.

Williamson, Oliver E. 2000. "The New Institutional Economics: Taking Stock, Looking Ahead." *Journal of Economic Literature* 38, no. 2: 595–613.

5

Housing Wealth and the
Accumulation of Financial
Debt: Evidence from U.K.
Households

Sarah Bridges, Richard Disney,
and Andrew Henley

This chapter explores the role that home ownership and, in particular, the accumulation and decumulation of housing equity has played in underpinning recent household financial behavior. Although it provides some cross-country evidence on the importance of home ownership and on the extent of borrowing for house purchases, the chapter focuses primarily on household-level data from the United Kingdom. The United Kingdom is an interesting case study both for institutional reasons (it has a high level of home ownership relative to many other countries in the European Union, significant house price volatility, high levels of mortgage and other financial indebtedness, and because it was an early "deregulator" of financial markets) and for data reasons, since new data sets for the United Kingdom allow us to explore the relationship between housing wealth and various forms of financial indebtedness at the household level.

The consequences of booms and busts in house prices on household behavior—in particular, on spending on nonhousing consumption, and on the acquisition of financial debt—have been widely debated in the United Kingdom, the United States, and elsewhere. The consequences for macroeconomic stability of the interaction between volatile housing markets and house price sensitive household behavior have been of particular concern to central bankers in a number of countries in recent years (see Barnes and Young 2003; Borio and McGuire 2004; Debelle 2004; Reserve Bank of Australia 2003; and references cited therein). One specific concern in the United Kingdom is the possible impact of future entry to the European Monetary Union (EMU). The U.K. housing market is perceived as exhibiting greater sensitivity to monetary policy than other EMU countries, both because U.K. consumer spending appears to be relatively interest rate elastic (HM Treasury 2003) and because of the prevalence of variable-rate mortgages.

Miles (2004) reports that 25 percent of households have fixed-rate mortgages in the United Kingdom, and discusses the contractual details of the remaining share of mortgages; the incidence of fixed-rate mortgages is much higher in France and Germany—albeit similar to that in the United Kingdom in Italy, Spain, and Ireland, and even lower in Finland and Portugal (see appendix 4A in this volume).

The basic "building block" in modeling consumer spending and wealth acquisition, as described in chapter 1 and elsewhere in this volume, is the life-cycle hypothesis of saving by which individuals accumulate wealth, both in the form of housing and nonhousing wealth, in order to smooth consumption over the lifetime. The decision as to how much wealth to allocate to housing at any point in time depends on preferences, on the stage of the life cycle, and on the relative returns to housing and other wealth. These factors will also underpin the consumption response of any given household to unanticipated changes in their housing wealth arising from house price volatility, as well as households' subjective perception as to whether (and for how long) changes in house prices will persist. For example, rising house prices will tend to benefit older home owners (who have low outstanding mortgages) but be detrimental to young households who are trying to enter the homeownership market. These relative wealth effects may cause offsetting changes in saving behavior across households and substitution between consumption of housing and other goods. The net effect on consumer spending might be large, or zero (Case 2000; Carroll 2004).

But while the life-cycle model focuses on consumption smoothing and on the role of the intertemporal budget constraint, rising housing prices may have other effects on the asset position of households. If the borrowing constraint of indebted households is tied to the value of their home, rising housing wealth may underpin higher indebtedness by permitting households to increase their secured (collateralized) borrowing. And unsecured debt, such as credit card borrowing, may also be higher if households "feel" more wealthy as a result of house price rises. Moreover, where credit providers and credit bureaus treat home ownership and/or the value of housing equity as a signal of current and future household wealth, this permits home owners access to forms of credit that would not be available if they rented their home rather than owning it. Several studies have used aggregate simulations to suggest that there is a sizeable fraction of credit-constrained consumers, even in deregulated financial settings, and that for these consumers, the elasticity of consumption, with respect to changes in house prices, can exceed unity—the so-called financial accelerator (Aoki, Proudman, and Vlieghe 2002; Iacoviello 2004).

Households with rising housing wealth may also withdraw housing equity in order to finance consumption as an alternative to maintaining equity value and using other lines of credit. Remortgaging is the obvious route by which to withdraw equity from the home, but downsizing and even shifting out of owner occupation altogether are alternatives. To the extent that housing equity withdrawal is an alternative to acquiring additional unsecured debts, rising housing wealth might have an offsetting impact on total financial indebtedness, as well as affecting the ratio of secured to unsecured loans.

The links between housing wealth and access to various forms of financial credit, and the trajectory of household indebtedness are issues examined in this chapter. It uses new household panel data sets in Britain to measure household-specific values of housing equity and of housing equity withdrawal, to examine their influence on the credit channels used by households, on the extent of household indebtedness, and on arrears of financial debt. Specifically, the chapter examines a number of questions:

• How does home ownership and the household's value of housing equity affect its access to sources of credit, such as bank loans, credit cards, and so forth? Can any impact of home ownership on access to unsecured debt be construed as evidence of credit rationing in the credit market?

• Are differences in housing equity across households associated with different values of household debt and changes in the composition of that debt?

• What factors induce households to exhibit indicators of "debt distress" such as arrears in debt and self-reported difficulties in paying off debt? In particular, is there any evidence that home owners have run into difficulties from borrowing excessively in recent years as a result of perceived increases in their housing wealth?

• What are the determinants of housing equity withdrawal (HEW)? Is there evidence that households with cumulated high values of HEW have ended the period with greater or lower financial wealth than would otherwise be the case?

The format of the chapter is as follows. Section 5.1 gives a brief overview of housing markets in Europe and then examines the macroeconomic evidence on key variables in recent years in the United Kingdom—namely, the trend and volatility of house prices, consumer expenditure, the growth of personal financial debt (and, in particular, of credit card debt), and the value of housing equity withdrawal. Some of the macroeconomic episodes underlying these trends are described and explained.

Several of these data series are highly collinear, not least in part because they are derived from national income accounting and are, by construction, closely related. So it is important not to confuse correlation with causation. This point is discussed later as a justification for augmenting existing aggregate analyses by evidence from household data sets, since variables constructed at the household level avoid associations deriving from aggregate balance sheet requirements.

Section 5.2 briefly surveys theories of credit constraints and of household access to financial markets. The particular focus, differentiating the analysis from the discussion in chapter 1 (especially section 1.2), is on the circumstances in which being a home owner and having housing equity impacts access to different types of credit and asset and debt portfolios. It then briefly describes the macroeconomic evidence on the relationship between housing wealth, the acquisition of financial assets, and consumer spending. It argues that, whilst the macroeconomic evidence is insightful, there are again difficulties of interpretation arising from reduced form estimation of aggregate relationships. For example, increases in house prices may increase spending on consumption of both housing and other goods (and therefore income), but house prices are themselves responsive to changes in income (see HM Treasury 2003, Table 4.2). Disentangling these issues is tricky in practice.

One response to this potential problem of simultaneity in the aggregate data is to simulate impulse shocks, or to attempt quasi-structural estimation. However, an alternative tack is to examine the behavior of households at the disaggregated level—for example, to see whether households that obtain above-average gains in housing wealth exhibit above-average gains in consumer spending (as in Attanasio and Weber 1994). Section 5.3 therefore utilizes two household data sets for the United Kingdom, matched by household characteristics, to examine the relationships between home ownership and housing equity values, and access to different types of credit and accumulation of debt. It provides evidence that home ownership is used as a screening or signaling device for some kinds of credit but not other channels, and thereby affects the portfolio of assets and the magnitude of debts held by households with different housing tenure and housing equity. This sheds some light on a question implicit in much recent policy discussion of the association between rising housing wealth and rising debt levels, namely, the extent to which rising housing wealth may induce financial debt overhang and generate early signals of stress among heavily indebted households.

Section 5.4 examines the sources of HEW in the United Kingdom. The major departure from the existing macroeconomic evidence is that we construct HEW from the observed actions of households, such as downsizing and remortgaging, rather than from aggregate balance sheet calculations. Most episodes of HEW seem to derive from house moves and from remortgages of relatively small magnitude, the latter is almost certainly utilized to finance moving costs and home improvements. Events in which substantial housing equity is released seem to be associated with the stage of the life cycle at which households are decumulating assets. There is little clear evidence that rising housing wealth in recent years is inducing households at all stages of the life cycle to release significant housing equity in order to boost consumption. The main results of the chapter are summarized in section 5.5.

5.1 Some Preliminary Evidence on Housing Markets

5.1.1 Housing Markets in Europe

Figure 5.1 documents the extent of home ownership and mortgage debt as a percentage of GDP in a number of EU countries. The home ownership rate in 2000 as a percentage of total households varies from around 40 percent in Germany to just over 80 percent in Spain. The United Kingdom lies toward the higher end of the distribution (although it is not the highest) at just under 70 percent. Home ownership rates rose significantly in the 1980s in the United Kingdom (due to government-sponsored "right to buy" policies that subsidized the purchase of social housing by tenants) and also significantly in Sweden in the 1990s (see HM Treasury 2003, Chart 3.1). Rates have drifted upward in most other countries in the 1980s and 1990s (a notable exception is Germany, although this divergent trend may represent a consequence of unification). By way of comparison, the proportion of the U.S. residential housing stock that was owner-occupied in 1999 was 58 percent

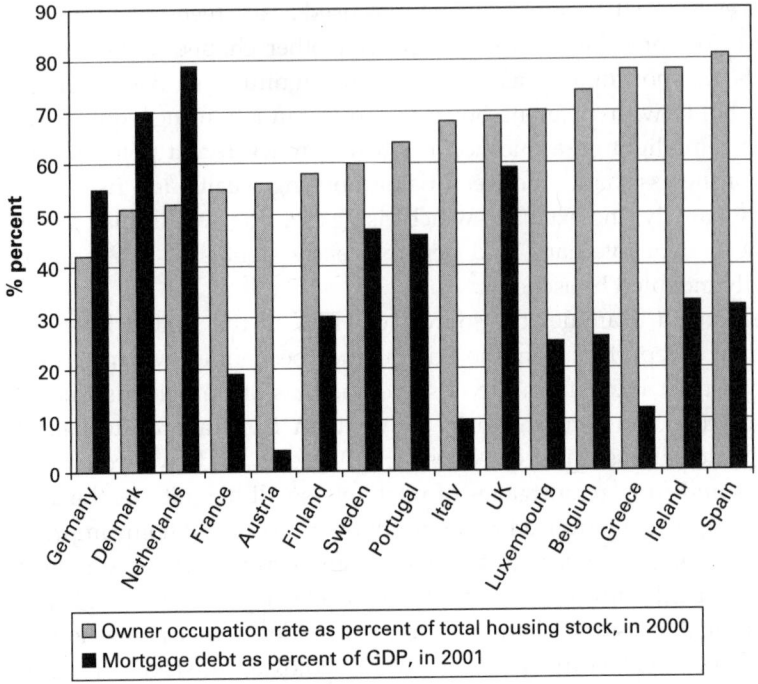

Figure 5.1
Owner occupation rates and mortgage debt to GDP ratios

(Case 2000), although since around 10 percent of the stock was "seasonal or vacant," the underlying proportion is closer to two-thirds.

The EU cross-country pattern of home ownership is not mirrored in differences in the values of outstanding residential mortgage debt as a percent of GDP. Some countries have lower-than-average owner occupation rates accompanied by a high mortgage debt-GDP ratio (such as the Netherlands), others the reverse (such as Spain). The United Kingdom is near the top end of the distribution of mortgage debt. Cross-country variation reflects differences in downpayment conditions, in the prices of new houses, in capital market constraints, and in within-family sources of finance for home purchase.

Table 5.1 illustrates other indicators of cross-country variations. Column 1 illustrates some disparity in real house price growth across countries, with stagnant real house prices (over the whole period) in Sweden contrasting with rapid real house price increases in the Netherlands, Spain, and the United Kingdom. Given that the supply of

Table 5.1
Basic indicators of EU members' housing and financial markets

Country	(1) Annual real house price inflation, 1971–2001 (percent)	(2) Long-run income elasticity of house prices	(3) Volatility: average percentage deviation of real house price from trend, 1970–2001	(4) Date of interest-rate deregulation
Germany	0.1	0.0	11.1	1981
Denmark	1.3	n.a.	13.4	1988
Netherlands	2.8	1.2	25.1	1981
France	1.2	0.6	7.6	1990
Finland	0.7	0.5	19.0	1986
Sweden	0.0	−0.7	13.5	1985
Italy	1.5	0.4	15.5	1990
United Kingdom	3.3	1.0	15.1	1979
Belgium	2.1	1.0	14.3	1990
Ireland	3.1	1.1	17.4	1993
Spain	3.3	1.9	17.3	1992

Source: HM Treasury 2003. Column 1, Table 4.1; Column 2, Table 4.2; Column 3, Table 4.5; Column 4, Tables 5.3 and 5.5.

houses is relatively inelastic, the U.K. Treasury has calculated reduced form elasticities of house prices with respect to GDP growth, which are depicted in column 2. These estimates may reflect differences in the income elasticity of the demand for owner-occupied housing across countries, although, of course, other factors, such as changes in household composition and differing supply elasticities, may also play a role.

Column 3 suggests that there may be differences in volatility of house prices around the underlying trend. Again, the Netherlands stands out as having very high volatility; the United Kingdom, despite the cyclicality discussed further in the next subsection, lies somewhere in the middle of the distribution. (The same result applies if other measures of dispersion, such as a coefficient of variation, are used.) Finally, column 4 gives a date of significant deregulation for each country— that is, broadly, the date at which quantity controls and interest rate restrictions were relaxed for domestic consumers. However arbitrary it is to set a single such date for a process of deregulation, the data give a clear pattern of three early "deregulators" (the United Kingdom, followed by Germany and the Netherlands) followed by the rest of the EU in the late 1980s and early 1990s.

5.1.2   The United Kingdom: Evidence on Housing and Financial Markets

The existing literature in the United Kingdom on housing wealth, the accumulation of debt, and household spending has tended to focus on macroeconomic trends. In some periods, such as the decade since 1994, these trends have been highly collinear, tempting analysts to assert causal links that may or may not be present. Despite our reservations on this interpretation, discussed further in later sections, macroeconomic trends serve as a background to what follows, and it is useful to examine briefly the aggregate data on some of the key variables. The data series used here are derived from data either downloadable from the Bank of England or the Office of National Statistics Web sites.

5.1.2.1   *House Prices in the United Kingdom, 1970–2003*

Figure 5.2 describes the average annual change in house prices in the United Kingdom since 1970, both nominal and real. The indexes are calculated for a representative house reflecting the mix of owner-

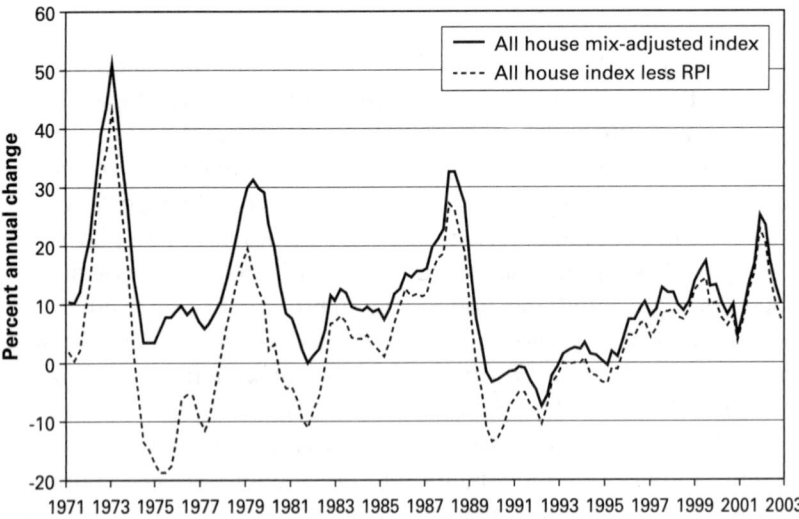

Figure 5.2
Changes in nominal and real house price indexes, 1971–2003
Source: Office of National Statistics online data for house price index and retail price index.

occupied houses in the United Kingdom. Nominal growth is contrasted with the growth of house prices minus the change in the retail price index (RPI). The chart shows that there have been four distinct booms in house prices in that period: the early 1970s; the late 1970s and early 1980s (although this was the weakest and most short-lived of the upturns); the "Lawson" boom of the mid-to-late 1980s, and the period from the mid-1990s to 2003.

The two early booms in the period since 1970 were associated with incoming conservative administrations, but the "dash for growth" in the early 1970s was curtailed by the real oil price rise—and then around 1980, by rapidly rising unemployment, with consequent effects for the housing market. Both the early 1970s and mid-1980s booms were also associated with increased liberalization in capital markets— in the first case, with the elimination of a good deal of quantity rationing and bank reserve requirements; in the latter case, with greater competition among providers. Controversy, particularly around the mid-1980s boom, has centred on whether rising income expectations are sufficient to explain the upsurge of house prices during that period, or whether the asset market liberalization in that period produced a classic asset "bubble," reflected in the boom-bust feature of the housing market over the decade (see Muellbauer and Murphy 1990; Attanasio and Weber 1994).

The boom in house prices that persisted from the mid-1990s to 2003 had some unusual features. It was longer lasting than previous episodes. Although, in general, real incomes rose over the period, the upsurge in house prices was not accompanied by above-trend increases in other asset and consumer prices, so that the real and nominal house price indexes tracked each other more closely than in past booms. Moreover, the upsurge in prices occurred despite measures to reduce the favorable tax treatment of owner occupiers relative to renters, and higher effective taxes ("stamp duty") on moving home. Real mortgage rates are not at historically low levels (at least, relative to the period from 1970 onward), and in any event, house prices seem to be rather real interest-inelastic (Meen 1996). In fact, the two recent periods of falling real interest rates occurred during the early-to-mid-1970s, when "stagflation" had been induced by rising oil prices, and in the early 1990s, when house prices were still falling.

One possible explanation for the post-1995 upsurge in prices is that historically low nominal interest rates, and therefore lower nominal mortgage payments on a loan of a given size, have induced home owners to increase the average value of the loan. Higher loans have then been capitalized in the form of higher house prices. Higher prices themselves may have concealed an underlying increase in the loan-to-value ratio. Moreover, there may be an additional selection effect insofar as first-time and low-income buyers, who may have lower loan-to-value ratios than average, are driven out of the market. These factors, quite apart from the unusual duration of the boom, have raised some concerns as to whether the post-1995 house price surge is also sustainable (Farlow 2004).

5.1.2.2 House Prices, Consumption, and Income Growth

Whatever the specific factors behind house price movements, rising house prices have typically been associated with periods of growing income expectations and with consumption spending. The accumulated evidence suggests that house price movements, both real and nominal, are highly pro-cyclical. This is confirmed in figure 5.3, which depicts the four quarter-on-quarter growth of real household consumer spending (to eliminate seasonality) and the quarterly change in the real

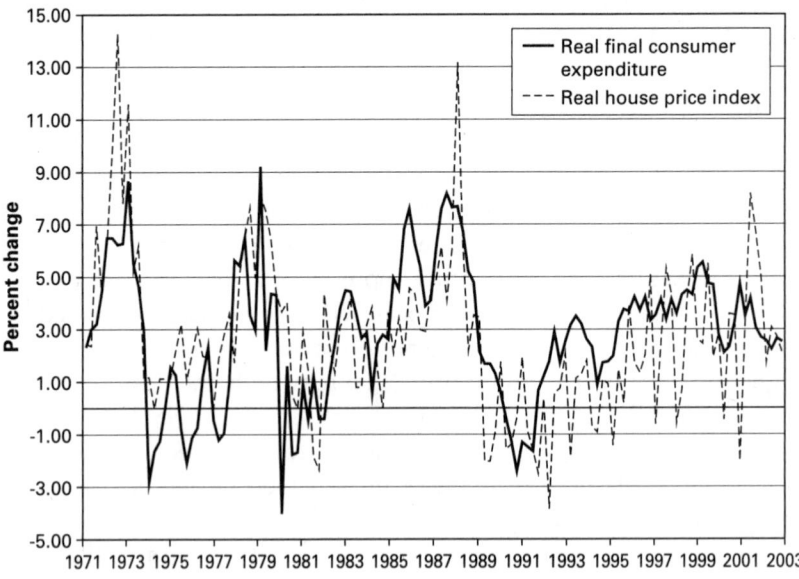

Figure 5.3
Final consumption expenditure (annual changes) and real house prices (quarterly changes)
Source: Calculated from Office of National Statistics online data.

house price index over the 1971–2003 period. There is a strong correlation between the series. Although this is consistent with evidence that rises in housing wealth increase consumption in the short run, it is also consistent with the reverse causation that consumption and income growth affect the demand for housing wealth. The overall long run income elasticity of real housing demand in relation to changes in real income has been estimated to be in the region of 1.7 to 3.0 (Meen 1996). Since housing supply tends to be highly inelastic in the short run, this translates into a high volatility of house prices over the economic cycle.

5.1.2.3 The Growth of Consumer Credit from the Late 1980s Onward

Rising housing wealth in the decade since the mid-1990s has been accompanied by a significant rise in consumer borrowing through other secured and unsecured sources. Figure 5.4 illustrates "stock" measures of outstanding consumer credit (excluding net housing debt), and of outstanding credit card balances, as a proportion of post-tax income, from 1987 onward.

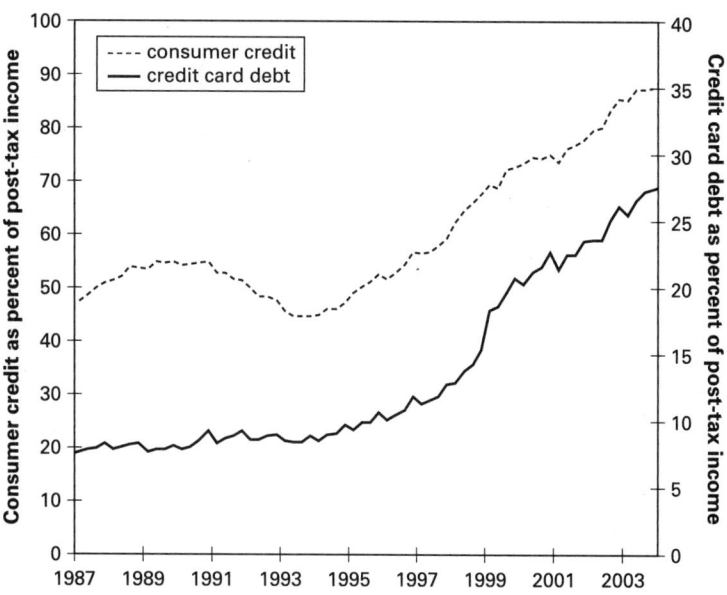

Figure 5.4
Outstanding consumer credit as percent of post-tax income, 1987–2003
Source: Calculated from Office of National Statistics online national accounts data.

The trends are somewhat different for consumer credit as a whole and for credit cards balances. The cycle for consumer credit as a whole matches the business cycle closely—that is, rising in the mid-1980s, followed by a downturn coincident with the fall in house prices and final consumption expenditure at the end of the 1980s, and a subsequent surge from the mid-1990s onward. In contrast, the trend in credit card balances is almost flat until the mid-to-late 1990s, after which there is a rapid rise in outstanding credit card debt. This trend may be associated with the more aggressive competitive strategy of credit card providers in the latter period, which involved both greater marketing to existing cardholders but also targeting income groups that had previously been excluded from credit card access either because of their income or credit histories.

Figure 5.5 describes a flow measure of consumer credit over the same period, illustrating the pattern of net lending (repayments versus new credit) as a proportion of post-tax income. It illustrates the strong seasonality of consumer credit, rising in the fourth quarter and negative in the first quarter. Again, the trend of net consumer credit follows the pattern of consumer spending and house prices, although the pattern of net credit card lending seems to show a rather undramatic secular upward trend, probably exhibiting a slow growth in seasonal

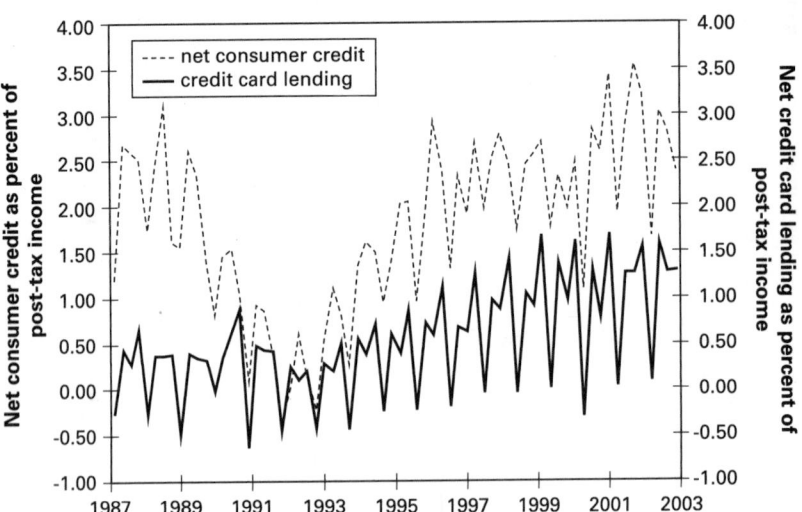

Figure 5.5
Net lending as percent of post-tax income, 1987–2003

volatility over the period. Thus, the clear growth in outstanding credit card balances in Figure 5.4 may simply illustrate greater use of credit cards to shift consumption between quarters rather than any secular trend in indebtedness. We come back to this important point when we examine household access to credit cards in a subsequent section.

5.1.2.4   Housing Equity Withdrawal

The final macroeconomic aggregate that has provoked interest in relation to housing equity, consumer spending, and indebtedness is housing equity withdrawal. Housing equity withdrawal describes explicit efforts by households to release part of the equity value of their home, either by re-mortgaging or by downsizing, and is typically associated with periods in which house prices are rising. The equity released may be used to invest in other assets, in order to rebalance the household's portfolio, or in consumer spending. Since HEW is strongly associated with moving house, HEW may in fact be used to finance specific expenditures such as moving costs or home improvement—the latter will, presumably, ultimately affect the value of the house so that the measured HEW is only transitory.

In the aggregate statistics provided by the Bank of England (Davey 2001), HEW (there known as mortgage equity withdrawal) is defined as the difference between total net secured lending on the housing stock and investment in the housing stock. If net secured lending exceeds investment, HEW occurs. The bank's measure is defined specifically as the difference between lending secured on dwellings (mortgage advances) plus grants for housing, less investment in housing, defined as the sum of the value of new houses and the net transfer of houses into the home ownership sector (primarily sales of social, or public, housing to tenants), plus the value of home improvements and house moving costs (including stamp duty and legal fees). Figure 5.6 illustrates the bank's calculated measure of housing equity withdrawal from 1970 to 2003.

The chart illustrates that HEW, as measured by the Bank of England, has been strongly procyclical, but not as closely linked to the path of household consumer spending as, say, house prices. In fact, HEW, although positive, was of lesser significance in the 1970s and rose sharply in the early 1980s, despite the recession of the early 1980s. HEW became negative during the collapse of house prices in the late 1980s and early 1990s but has been steadily rising since that time.

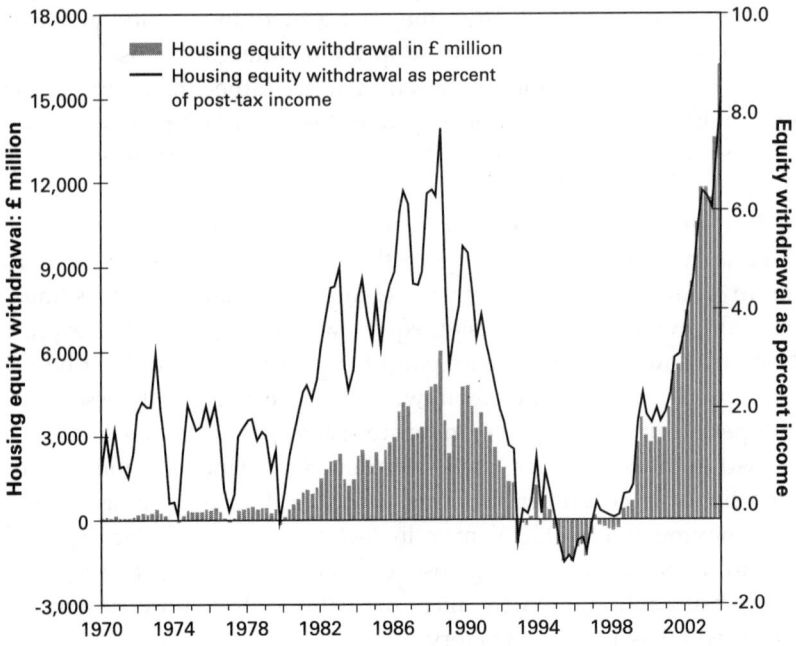

Figure 5.6
Housing equity withdrawal in United Kingdom, 1970–2003
Source: http://www.bankofengland.co.uk/mfsd/mew/mew.htm.

Davey (2001) points out that, if gross saving rates are less volatile than consumer borrowing, there will be a strong link between changes in real consumption, real income, and the net change in borrowing (HEW) simply from the underlying accounting relationship. In effect, there must be a positive correlation between the two series, even if the degree of comovement varies over time. Moreover, there will also be a strong link with house-moving rates, since moving costs are a component of measured investment in housing, and moving tends also to be procyclical. Changing costs of moving home will also affect measured HEW—for example, a fall in legal and selling costs, other things being equal, would show up as an increase in HEW, whereas increases in the tax on moving (stamp duty) would show up as the reverse. Since the aggregate series is therefore dominated by accounting and institutional relationships, examining household-level decisions to withdraw equity gives more insight into underlying household behavior (see section 5.4).

5.2 Access to Credit and Housing Wealth: General Considerations

5.2.1 Housing Wealth, Lifetime Wealth, and Spending

How do house price increases affect the lifetime budget constraint? Why should there be any relationship between housing wealth and other forms of debt, both secured and unsecured? This section considers theses issues in general, before focusing on patterns of debt from household data from the United Kingdom.

House price fluctuations affect the value of lifetime wealth. In the life-cycle saving "story," permanently higher house prices increase the value of the lifetime wealth of home owners, reduces their need for additional borrowing, and, on the margin, increases consumer spending. However, the net impact on overall spending and lifetime wealth of a given period of increasing house prices may be less clear-cut: The increase may be regarded as transitory or, if perceived as likely to continue, induce consumers to substitute spending on housing consumption for spending on other goods. Moreover, there are distributional effects: would-be buyers face a greater hurdle as house prices rise and may have to increase their indebtedness in order to enter the market, whereas housing wealth gains can only be obtained by downsizing or remortgaging. Overall, as Carroll (2004) points out, fluctuations in house prices redistribute wealth in the economy rather than increasing the overall real income of the economy, although this redistribution may increase spending in the short to medium term.

Modifications of the basic life-cycle consumption model arise if a proportion of consumers is liquidity-constrained, in which case the standard Euler equation approach to consumption modeling (see chapter 1) has to be modified by the addition of variables that capture additional constraints besides the intertemporal budget constraint (Campbell and Mankiw 1989). In particular, households may be liquidity-constrained because they lack collateral against which to borrow or, for unsecured borrowing, evidence of asset ownership or a credit history (such as mortgage debt) that allows credit bureaus to provide a credit score for the household.

Home ownership and housing equity may therefore impact asset holdings in other ways than through the intertemporal budget constraint. Formally, in a competitive capital market with perfect information, household decisions as to the amount of financial debt and the pattern of net wealth (including debt) should be unaffected by changes in housing wealth—the main source of collateral on borrowing—other than through the impact of house price changes on lifetime wealth (the permanent income) of the household. The divergences from this stylized model (credit constraints) stem from imperfect markets, asymmetric information, and the consequent use of screening and signaling mechanisms.

5.2.2   Screening and Credit Constraints

The seminal paper by Stiglitz and Weiss (1981) described in chapter 1 developed a model in which uncertainty over which individuals' default induces lenders to set the interest rate too low and to ration credit. Rationing implies that some low-risk borrowers will not get credit and that interest rates act as a screening device. The rationing arises not from any market "disequilibrium" but because lenders set interest rates to obtain the right mix of borrowers over the risk-return continuum.[1]

Faced with imperfect information on risks of individual loans, requesting collateral seems a sensible way of reducing the risk to the lender. The main source of collateral, to households and to small businesses alike, is housing wealth. The absence of collateral may therefore be a binding constraint on lending, which is why exogenous rises in the value of collateral—such as increased house prices—may increase observed lending on secured assets (see Black, de Meza, and Jeffreys 1996; Aoki, Proudman, and Vlieghe 2002; and Iacoviello 2004).[2]

The presence of borrowing constraints may in turn affect the portfolio choice of households, as in Paxson 1990. If the constraint takes the form of an exogenous ceiling on the loan amount, the borrower will hold more liquid assets to avoid credit constraints in the future. But when the constraint takes the form of an interest rate ceiling for given loan amount, illiquid assets can serve as collateral to reduce the interest rate on the loan and/or to increase the maximum amount that can be borrowed. The potential use of housing wealth as collateral therefore has two effects on spending on consumption goods relative to housing: it may induce households to substitute spending on housing for consumption of other goods as a source of future collateral, but by reducing the cost of credit, it will increase the total demand for borrowing to finance consumption expenditure.

5.2.3   Signaling and Credit Scoring

Housing wealth can act as a signaling device as well as a screening device as it can also be used to "signal" creditworthiness. Credit constraints may not just restrict the ability of households to smooth consumption but also limit their capacity to invest in more risky activities (i.e., that increase the probability of default, such as purchases of lumpy durables, or investments, such as retraining or changing jobs). If low-risk borrowers (for given income level, and so forth) can signal their low risk by offering greater collateral, then a separating equilibrium with different interest rate–collateral combinations, but without credit rationing, could occur, as in Bester 1985. Milde and Riley (1988) make a similar point concerning the size of the loan amount. If banks offer increasing loan size-interest rate "packages," then under certain circumstances, applicants with less risky projects select larger rather than smaller loans.

Ownership of assets such as housing also affects access to unsecured debt. Credit bureaus exist to reduce information asymmetries and have two specific functions. First, they attempt to screen out "bad" risks to lenders by searches over credit histories. Second, they provide credit scores for individuals based on household characteristics, including prospective income and the value of household assets. Home ownership, in particular, is given substantial weight as a signal of creditworthiness, even for unsecured credit such as access to credit cards.

In the market for both secured and unsecured debt, therefore, lenders offer different contracts (screening), and borrowers offer collateral and credit records (signaling). New borrowers may find it more difficult to acquire credit, either mortgages or unsecured credit, because they have neither the collateral nor the credit history. (Duca and Rosenthal [1993] suggest the young are typically credit-constrained; see also chapter 3.) So it may be worthwhile for new borrowers, such as young households, to invest in obtaining a credit "history" in order to reduce the probability of being refused long-term loans such as a mortgage. A way of signaling a lack of default risk is to acquire a clean credit record (Ben-Sahar and Feldman 2003).

5.2.4 From Micro to Macro

The focus of policymakers is on macroeconomic trends in the housing market, in consumer spending, and on how consumers finance that spending. The remainder of this chapter uses household data to examine these issues. Why follow this strategy, and how can microdata be used to underpin macroeconomic policy? As mentioned in the introduction, aggregate series of housing expenditure, housing equity withdrawal, and consumer expenditure are highly collinear, making inference as to behavioral responses conjectural. For example, household income in the accounts is allocated to consumption and investment expenditures, with investment differentiated between housing and financial assets (as noted by Davey 2001). Since HEW is measured as negative investment, this rules out anything other than a positive association between consumer spending and equity withdrawal, unless we are prepared to assume implausibly high substitution elasticities between asset holdings. In contrast, household-level measures of equity withdrawal allow us both to identify associated actions (for example, changes in equity values associated with moving home versus additional mortgages) and consequences (on household spending, saving decisions, and so forth).

There are studies that utilize time series data to examine the links between housing wealth and aggregate consumption spending in the United Kingdom. (Several are surveyed in Disney, Henley, and Jevons 2003 and in HM Treasury 2003.) In addition, vector autoregression methods have been used to examine the role of the housing market in the transmission of monetary policy as a "financial accelerator" (Aoki, Proudman, and Vlieghe 2002). Time series techniques can handle collinearity but are necessarily restricted in handling the structural aspects of the problem—in particular, when housing demand is income elastic and supply of housing is inelastic, consumption, income, and housing wealth will be simultaneously determined. Iacoviello (2004) makes some effort to overcome this problem using instruments.

But there remains the serious problem, described by Carroll 2004, that house price "shocks" have very different effects on different types of households, and that aggregate response parameters may conceal a good deal of the heterogeneity of responses across households. By way of illustration, Disney, Henley, and Jevons (2003) use the British Household Panel Survey to examine the relationship between housing wealth and consumption. Since investment in housing is endogenous in the life-cycle saving model, they examine the relationship between house price shocks (measured as residuals from an AR2 process using county-level house price changes as the instrument) and the consumption behavior of households. The authors test whether propensities to consume from additional housing wealth differ according to whether those shocks are positive or negative, and also according to the value of housing equity held by the household. The heterogeneity of responses is therefore of great importance.

We do not attempt any structural econometric modeling here, but the data sets described in the next section do allow us to examine behavior at the household level. We can investigate households by their ownership status and by the value of housing equity to see how this affects access to credit and credit-financed spending. We can investigate what types of households utilize housing equity withdrawals and draw some inferences as to whether it is used to finance certain kinds of activity. We can see whether indicators of "excessive" borrowing correlate with access to collateral in the form of housing wealth. As with the caveats arising from earlier work testing the link between consumer spending and changes in housing equity values using household data, our analysis urges caution in applying models derived from company finance such as the "financial accelerator" theory to households. Such models, in general, suggest that agents with above-average increases in collateral are more likely to see more rapid increases in debt-financed borrowing. Our analyses suggest that the ownership of a house does indeed act as a means of acquiring additional debt, but that the value of the house is of much less significance.

5.3   The Microeconomic Evidence

5.3.1   Data and Methods
This section examines households' access to financial credit, their levels of outstanding debt, and self-reported difficulties in repaying debt (including records of arrears). Given the specific focus of this chapter on the role of home ownership, and housing equity in particular, it examines the relationship between home ownership and the household's value of housing equity and also evidence that the magnitude of either affects access to and use of sources of credit such as bank loans and credit cards, conditional on other household characteristics.

We use two household surveys to examine these issues: the British Household Panel Survey (BHPS) and the Families and Children Survey (FACS). The BHPS is representative of all households within the geographical area of Britain that is covered (which excludes part of Scotland and Northern Ireland for much of the period), whereas the FACS covers only households with children. In this section, therefore, we construct a subsample of the BHPS that has the same selection criterion as the FACS. The constructed subsample of the BHPS has roughly 2,500 households, and FACS has around 7,000 households.

5.3.1.1 The British Household Panel Survey

The BHPS is a panel survey of approximately 10,000 adults in around 5,000 households that has been running annually since 1991. Apart from questions concerning household demographics, health, and economic status, the BHPS asks about wealth and indebtedness in two of the currently available eleven waves, 1995 and 2000. It also asks in those waves about the sources of household debt and the total value of this debt. We focus primarily on the 2000 wave.

The data on the amount of financial debt are collected in two stages. In the first stage, individuals are asked to give a precise value for the total amount they owe. Individuals who say that they do not know how much that they owe are then asked to give a banded answer. In this analysis, we impute a continuous value for those households who report banded information.[3] It also asks sufficient questions to allow us to estimate the current value of the house, as well as year-on-year self-reported house values. We experimented both with using self-reported values and with proxying the changing values among nonmovers by an index of house prices disaggregated to the county level (as in Disney, Henley, and Jevons 2003). We use the former series to construct housing equity, although results using the latter are available on request.

5.3.1.2 The Families and Children Survey

The FACS is a relatively new U.K. household data set. First established as the Survey of Low Income Families in 1999, the survey was designed to elicit information on household characteristics and their economic and financial status for a sample of low-income families with children. Separate samples were constructed for lone parents and for low-income couples with children. (Therefore, the former are over-represented in the sample.) The financial status of households in that first wave are analyzed in Bridges and Disney 2004. The same sample of families was reinterviewed in 2000. In 2001, the sample was increased to encompass a representative sample of all families with children, and has continued thereafter in this format. Here we focus on the 2001 survey. The main aim of the FACS was to examine the effectiveness of new government work-incentive measures (particularly Family Credit and its replacement, Working Families Tax Credit), and in doing so, it asked the standard questions on household demographics and income sources. However, it also asks both qualitative and quantitative questions on financial hardship, together with questions on the extent of credit and borrowing arrangements. Some of these questions are similar to those in the BHPS, but they are asked in every wave rather than at irregular intervals. Moreover, some of the FACS information on debt arrears and other indicators of financial stress are not available in other surveys. The major weakness of FACS, however, is that it does not have sufficient questions to permit us to construct a value of housing equity for each household. This limitation is unfortunate, because with housing equity measures, we could exploit the panel dimension to examine the "financial accelerator" hypothesis explicitly. As it is, we have to rely on cross-sectional differences in debt and home ownership to examine the question.

A full list of questions asked in the two surveys is provided in the appendix for this chapter.

5.3.2   Evidence on Use of Types of Financial Credit: The Role of Home Ownership

Table 5.2 depicts cross-tabulations of access to unsecured debt among households from the 2000 wave of the BHPS and from the 2001 wave of the FACS. It differentiates households in two dimensions—whether they are home owners or tenants, and whether they are single parents or couples with children. An important difference between the surveys is that, whereas the BHPS generally asks whether households owe money on each credit arrangement, the FACS asks about use or owing money. For credit cards, the BHPS asks both questions separately, and the comparison of response in the two surveys concerning usage suggests very similar patterns. Not surprisingly, across all types of credit, usage is higher than the probability of owing money, but the proportionate differences in responses across household types are common whether the question concerns usage or owing money.

There are striking differences in access to credit cards and store cards between home owners and tenants (row 1, panels A and B). The probability of home owners having such cards is over twice that for tenants. Single-parent tenants are even less likely to have cards. This suggests prima facie evidence that access to such cards is related to home ownership. (Unless it solely reflects differences in preferences across households.) We reject the possibility that it arises from omitted covariates (such as income) in the next table. Conditional on having a card, the reported probabilities of having card debts are almost constant across household types.

Table 5.2
Percentages of households using or owing money on a given credit or borrowing arrangement

Question to household	Home-owning couples	Tenant couples	Home-owning singles	Tenant singles	Total
A. *BHPS 2000*					
Have a credit card (and/or store card)?	74.87	32.66	70.74	23.81	57.86
Owe money on a catalogue purchase?	9.49	20.77	17.55	33.60	16.22
Owe money on a personal loan?	27.65	19.15	26.60	15.61	23.93
Base	1,349	496	188	378	2,411
Owe money on a credit card (given you have a credit card)?	38.02	41.36	45.86	48.89	39.86
Base	1,010	162	133	90	1,395
B. *FACS 2001*					
Use a credit card?	78.88	36.08	61.11	20.27	57.57
Use a catalogue?	42.35	46.79	36.99	45.64	43.23
Used loan from bank?	19.61	12.63	11.84	5.49	14.63
Building society to borrow money?					
Base	3,712	1,045	684	1,584	7,025

Sources: (A) Percentages in each category calculated from British Household Panel Survey, Wave 10, 2000, for sample of households with children only. (B) Percentages in each category calculated from Family and Children Survey 2001.

The second row illustrates another common source of credit—using mail order catalogues. These can be regarded as close substitutes for purchases of durables, clothing, and so forth using credit cards, but effective interest rates are usually less transparent (and sometimes higher) on catalogue purchases than on credit cards and store cards. Generally, using mail order catalogues is not subject to credit scoring, although defaults and arrears on such purchases will generally be flagged by credit bureaus. The use of catalogues is pervasive among all types of households, but outstanding debts on mail order catalogues are much more prevalent among tenants than home owners. This suggests strong evidence that households substitute catalogue purchases for credit card- and store card-financed debts when the latter are not available; note, however, that some households often use both credit/store cards and catalogues in making credit-financed purchases (Bridges and Disney 2004).

Finally, the table reports the probability of owing money on a personal loan. The higher proportions in the BHPS may reflect the broader nature of the question (including, for example, finance companies and other financial institutions) rather than the specific sources mentioned in the FACS. Home owners have a greater preponderance of loans than tenants, although the difference is not as pervasive as in the case of credit cards and store cards.

We now examine the household probabilities of using or owing money on unsecured credit arrangements in a multivariate regression framework using the BHPS.[4] What hypotheses underlie the analysis? First, from the cross-tabulations, we might anticipate that home ownership will be a significant predictor of credit card usage (but not necessarily the size of debt on the card), and also of owing money on personal loans, but will have no impact on owing money on mail order catalogues, as in table 5.2. However, we can now condition this finding on other characteristics—household income, education, demographics, and so forth—to test explicitly the screening/signaling hypothesis that it is home ownership that permits access to certain credit arrangements. It is also interesting to see how this effect is modified if the household has significant housing equity. In the collateral model, it is the value of housing wealth that increases access to credit. We can examine whether a positive relationship holds for access to unsecured credit or whether it is home ownership per se that matters. Finally, it is useful to see what other household characteristics are associated with both access to and owing money on unsecured credit arrangements.

The first column of table 5.3 provides the marginal effects from a probit of the household having a credit or charge card, estimated on household characteristics. The probability of having a card is related positively to the individual having a higher income, working, being better educated, and being single, and reduced if the individual is on a greater number of welfare benefits. Being a home owner, independent of the value of housing wealth, raises the probability of having a credit or charge card by 16.7 percent.[5] The probability is also positively related to having more housing equity, given home ownership. Home ownership is therefore an important determinant of access to one form of unsecured debt.

Column 2 examines the probability that the household uses credit or charge cards to borrow, rather than simply rotating balances from month to month, conditional on having a card. An unrestricted probit is not the appropriate estimator for an economic model in which

Table 5.3
Probit models of access to credit and types of debt—marginal effects

	(1) Credit card	(2) Owe money— credit card	(3) Owe money— catalogue	(4) Owe money— personal loan
Owner	0.167***	0.108**	−0.003	0.070***
	(6.06)	(2.22)	(0.14)	(2.93)
Owner*housing equity	0.001***	−0.001***	−0.001***	−0.001***
	(4.12)	(3.66)	(3.89)	(4.83)
Couple	−0.137**	−0.059	−0.185**	0.026
	(2.48)	(0.41)	(2.51)	(0.36)
Couple*married	0.032	−0.111**	−0.050**	0.066**
	(1.13)	(2.09)	(2.19)	(2.37)
Number of benefits	−0.011***	0.020***	0.013***	−0.002
	(3.47)	(3.10)	(5.20)	(0.50)
ln(income)	0.097***	0.039	−0.018	0.059***
	(6.31)	(1.06)	(1.39)	(3.46)
Respondent working	0.124***	−0.011	0.016	0.063**
	(4.22)	(0.22)	(0.81)	(2.38)
Couple*partner working	0.013	0.100***	0.038*	0.071***
	(0.59)	(3.20)	(1.93)	(3.13)
Respondent's age	0.002	−0.002	−0.004***	0.001
	(1.22)	(0.88)	(3.66)	(0.38)
Couple*partner's age	0.003	0.001	0.003**	−0.004**
	(1.35)	(0.37)	(2.17)	(2.06)
Other	−0.072	0.279*	−0.027	−0.149**
	(0.94)	(1.96)	(0.46)	(2.52)
A-level	0.069**	−0.019	0.023	−0.012
	(2.27)	(0.37)	(0.82)	(0.36)
Degree	0.094***	0.017	−0.002	0.036*
	(4.45)	(0.48)	(0.10)	(1.73)
Higher degree	0.153***	−0.003	−0.054	−0.024
	(3.18)	(0.06)	(1.27)	(0.52)
Children	0.009	0.052***	0.008	0.029***
	(0.84)	(2.82)	(0.95)	(2.77)
Log likelihood	−1,206.283	−1,347.917	−900.406	−1,216.010
Number of observations	2,321	1,518	2,321	2,321

Source: Calculated from British Household Panel Survey 2000.
Notes: t-statistics in parentheses. *** significant at the 1 percent level; ** significant at the 5 percent level; * significant at the 10 percent level.
Columns 1, 3, and 4 illustrate the marginal effects, evaluated at covariate means in the case of the continuous variables, and evaluated at the effect of a discrete change in the case of all other binary variables. Column 2 illustrates the marginal effects from an equation reporting credit debt estimated as a probit with sample selection (estimated with a selection equation of similar specification to 1 but including time at address for model identification). The ρ (testing sample correlation between equations) = −0.950, se = 0.108.

borrowing on a credit card is conditional on having a card. Column 2 is therefore estimated as a probit with sample selection (using time at address in the credit card access equation as the exclusion restriction). Here, being a home owner has a significant impact on the probability of owing money, conditional on having a card, although higher housing equity reduces that probability (presumably a wealth effect). Few other coefficients are significant, although higher numbers of children in the household and being on a greater number of welfare benefits increases credit card borrowing.

Column 3 examines borrowing using credit through mail order catalogue purchases. As implied in the discussion of table 5.1, this form of borrowing is an alternative for individuals who are unable to acquire a credit card and is particularly prevalent among tenants. The question is whether, once we control for characteristics associated with tenancy (single parent, youth, a lower likelihood of working, a greater propensity to receive welfare benefits, lower wealth, and so on), housing status has any independent effect on the probability of owing money by this route. There is no particular reason why housing status should have any independent effect, once we control for characteristics, since our contention is that tenancy status plays no signaling or screening role in accessing this form of credit. And this is exactly confirmed by the multivariate analysis. There is, however, some evidence of a wealth effect arising from having housing equity.

Finally, column 4 illustrates the probit estimates for the other type of debt identified in table 5.2—that is, credit in the form of personal loans. Again, home ownership seems to act as a screening device, insofar as there is a positive association with the probability of having such a loan in addition to the positive impact of current income. As before, higher housing equity reduces the probability of owing money on a personal loan, again perhaps illustrating a wealth effect.

Overall, therefore, home ownership does seem to play an independent role in enabling householders to acquire some forms of unsecured debt. Home ownership acts not just as collateral for secured loans but also allows the household access to a wide variety of unsecured credit arrangements (although some personal loans may be secured on the home). However, tenants are also able to acquire unsecured credit, such as mail order purchases, albeit often on unfavorable terms. There is, however, no evidence of a "financial accelerator," at least in the cross-section of households—that is, having greater housing equity, conditional on owning a house, is not associated with higher levels of outstanding unsecured debt. Indeed, typically, higher housing wealth is associated with lower outstanding debt. This is shown clearly in the next subsection. However the caveat needs to be stated, and is reiterated in that section, that cross-sections are of limited value in understanding the response, in terms of acquisition of debt, of home owners to an unexpected increase in their housing wealth.

5.3.3 Home Ownership, Total Unsecured Debt, and Arrears

What is the overall impact of home ownership and the value of housing equity on the total stock of financial (largely unsecured) debt? And how does home ownership affect self-reported arrears on debt? The "financial accelerator" model utilized by Aoki, Proudman, and Vlieghe (2002) suggests that rising housing equity values permit households to increase their secured debt. Evidence from the previous subsection suggests that home owners can also gain access to sources of unsecured debt less easily available to tenants, even allowing for differences in current and permanent income. The obvious risk in such a home equity debt scenario is that households can rapidly find themselves with a debt overhang, since, as Iacoviello (2004) points out, "Consumers [primarily, homeowners] are actually inundated by offers of car loans, credit cards, home equity loans, and so on" (2–3). The risks arising from downturns in property values are then self-evident.

As described previously, cross-sections do not permit us to test whether changes in property values or tenure status change the value of household debt or arrears. But we can examine between-household variations in debt and debt arrears, and see whether these differences are simply explained by characteristics other than the source of housing wealth.

Column 1 of table 5.4 provides a tobit analysis of the logarithm of the amount of reported financial debt, comprising debt accumulated on the credit arrangements described in table 5.1 plus money owed on DSS social fund loans, hire purchases, overdrafts, and student loans. Again, the marginal effects are cited and can be interpreted as elasticities. Various measures of higher income (household income, partner working, more welfare benefits) are associated with a higher value of debts. The most interesting finding, however, is the insignificant impact of home ownership and the negative and significant impact of housing equity on the value of outstanding debt. Higher housing wealth is not associated with higher unsecured debt, at least not in the cross-section.

Table 5.4
Determinants of (the log of) total household debt, and arrears on debt (Tobit specifications)

	1	2
	Total debt (£) Marginal effect	Total arrears on debt (£) Marginal effect
Owner	−0.091	−0.926***
	(0.36)	(15.01)
Owner*housing equity	−0.007***	—
	(4.27)	
Couple	1.642**	0.550***
	(2.41)	(3.60)
Couple*married	0.006	—
	(0.02)	
Log (income)	1.222***	−0.001***
	(7.17)	(5.85)
Number of benefits	0.087***	0.141***
	(2.57)	(5.43)
Respondent working	0.465*	0.024
	(1.70)	(0.47)
Couple*partner working	0.880***	−0.107
	(3.84)	(1.25)
Respondent's age	−0.004	−0.012***
	(0.24)	(3.86)
Couple*partner's age	−0.048**	−0.023***
	(2.46)	(5.67)
Number of children	0.344***	0.090***
	(3.26)	(4.21)
Highest qualification		
GCSE grade A–C	0.491[a]	−0.128***
	(0.62)	(2.82)
A-level	0.424	−0.314***
	(1.22)	(4.73)
Degree	0.349	−0.346***
	(1.64)	(4.22)
Higher degree	−0.876*	−0.329***
	(1.84)	(2.79)
Number of observations	2,411	7,025

Sources: Column 1 calculated from British Household Panel Survey 2000.
Column 2 calculated from Family and Children Survey 2001.
Default categories: tenant, single householder, not working with no children, and no qualifications.
Notes: *t*-statistics in parentheses. *** significant at the 1 percent level; ** significant at the 5 percent level; * significant at the 10 percent level.
Columns 1 and 2 illustrate the marginal effects, evaluated at covariate means in the case of the continuous variables, and evaluated at the effect of a discrete change in the case of all other binary variables.
[a] This educational category in BHPS is "other qualifications."

This is not a refutation of the housing-financial debt model. To test it, we need to construct a measure of household house price shocks (as in Disney, Henley, and Jevons 2003) and examine how household financial debt reacts to these unanticipated wealth shocks. Unfortunately, the BHPS does not contain panel data on debt—the two waves that contain debt data (1995 and 2000) are not strictly comparable in their measures of debt, and a long difference cannot sensibly be constructed with this data. But the cross-section evidence is also consistent with a story that it is wider access to credit arrangements and rising real incomes, rather than housing wealth per se, that lies behind the rapid increase in unsecured debt in recent years.

A similar story emerges when we examine arrears on financial debt among comparable families using the 2001 wave of the FACS. As mentioned earlier, FACS does not contain information on housing equity, but we can exploit a home ownership variable, and a slightly different set of additional regressors.

Column 2 of table 5.4 estimates a tobit of the log of the total value of arrears reported by households in the 2001 FACS. The debts covered comprise debts on cards and catalogues, on financial loans, on utility bills and local taxes, and on housing payments, including mortgages (see the appendix). The regression shows that being a couple with children rather than a single parent, being less educated and younger, as well as having a lower income and receipt of a greater number of welfare benefits, are all associated with higher arrears on debts. However, owning a house is negatively associated with total arrears on debt. The analysis of the FACS suggests that low income, rather than access to housing equity, lies behind household problems with debt.

We do not discuss arrears on particular kinds of credit arrangement and bill paying separately here. Typically, mail order and catalogues charge high implicit rates of interest, reflecting less discrimination over clients and greater probabilities of default. Rates of arrears among low-income families on mail order/catalogues are indeed typically higher than on credit cards, but this largely reflects the greater default rate of tenants relative to home owners, with the latter much less likely to have a credit card. Among home owners, default rates appear to be roughly comparable on credit cards and catalogues (Bridges and Disney 2004, Tables 2 and 3).

Overall, therefore, in analyzing patterns of debt and arrears on debt, and focusing in particular on home ownership, a mixed analysis emerges. Home ownership undoubtedly allows households access to credit, and not just debt secured on housing equity. Home owners and tenants therefore have different portfolios of debt. However, higher housing equity is not associated with greater levels of unsecured debt, and home ownership is not associated with greater arrears on debt. The source of concern with rising house prices, if there is one, may therefore lie in the relationship between growing housing equity and the growth of secured debt. This is the topic of the next section.

5.4 Housing Equity Withdrawal: Evidence from Household Data

5.4.1 Sources of Housing Equity Withdrawal

This section examines the growth of debt secured on housing equity in the United Kingdom. It focuses on the extent of HEW in the mid to late 1990s in the BHPS rather than from the aggregate national accounts, as in section 5.2. There are two attractions to calculating HEW from household data. First, equity withdrawal can be compared with observable household-specific individual behavior rather than deriving HEW from the difference between two macroeconomic accounting measures. Second, it is possible to investigate the contribution to average HEW per household derived from different methods of equity withdrawal. We also investigate whether these calculated cumulated values of housing equity withdrawal by households correlate with measures of financial wealth and financial debt at the end of the period. Unfortunately, as described in the previous section, the latter variables are only measured on a consistent basis in 2000, and we can only compare the cumulated flows with the cross-section differences in holdings of wealth and debt rather than pursuing a dynamic analysis of the evolution of housing equity withdrawal, household financial wealth, and financial debt.

5.4.2 Sources of Housing Equity Withdrawal in the BHPS

The literature (such as Reserve Bank of Australia 2003) typically delineates several "routes" of HEW. In that source, the methods are

1. "downtrading," when a seller moves to a cheaper property but reduces the mortgage by a lower amount;

2. "overborrowing," when a house move increases the mortgage by more than the difference between the value of the sale and the purchase;

3. "remortgaging," that is, taking out an extra mortgage without moving house; and

4. "final sale," when the proceeds from a sale are not used to buy a new house—for example, when the owner dies and the estate sells the property, or when a household switches from owning to renting.

By analogy, housing equity can be injected into a property by reversing these actions.

These different methods of withdrawing equity are likely to occur for different reasons and to impact the household balance sheet in different ways. Additional mortgage debt on (2) moving and (3) remortgaging are often undertaken to finance moving costs (in the first case) or home improvements (both cases). Essentially, the HEW thereby obtained may be short term only and matched ultimately by "investment" in housing on the other side of the balance sheet, which may or may not result in low housing equity over a longer horizon. Nevertheless, rising house prices may have led to sharp increases in remortgaging, and this can be investigated using our data. In contrast, "downtrading" and "final sales" may well lead to permanent changes in the portfolio of household assets.

This section examines HEW by using evidence from the BHPS for the years since 1993. We make use of self-reported information on house values, on moving decisions and moving motives, data on self-reported initial mortgage amounts, and calculated values of outstanding mortgages, as well as a variety of demographic controls. Unfortunately, the BHPS has very imperfect data on the value of home improvements.

Table 5.5, columns 1–4, looks at what happens to the outstanding mortgage when households move (owner-occupation to owner-occupation). Around 6 percent or 7 percent of the sample move in any year. Of these moves, column 1 shows that around 22 percent are associated with a reduction in the outstanding mortgage principal—that is, households injecting equity (presumably from other sources of capital in the household balance sheet, or from the proceeds of inheritance or a windfall gain).

Column 2 shows that 10 percent of households withdraw equity by "trading-down," in that their outstanding mortgage remains constant while their self-reported house value falls. It may be, of course, that some of these respondents may have overestimated the initial value of their home before the sale, and thus have not traded down (Although,

Table 5.5
Percentage of households according to change in mortgage and moving status

Households (%)	Movers as % of all households of which:	(1) Outstanding mortgage reduced	(2) Outstanding mortgage unchanged, house value fell	(3) Outstanding mortgage unchanged, house value rose	(4) Outstanding mortgage increased	Non-movers as % of all households of which:	(5) Outstanding mortgage increased
1993–1994	6.7	19.6	7.6	9.4	63.4	93.3	3.1
1994–1995	5.8	18.8	9.2	8.3	63.7	94.2	2.9
1995–1996	5.6	23.0	14.0	13.1	50.0	94.4	3.6
1996–1997	7.3	25.3	8.5	13.9	52.3	92.7	3.9
1997–1998	6.4	22.3	7.8	13.3	56.7	93.6	2.9
1998–1999	6.4	25.8	5.8	9.3	59.2	93.6	3.9
1999–2000	6.4	18.9	11.1	16.5	53.6	93.6	4.3
2000–2001	6.7	25.5	14.5	10.0	50.0	93.3	5.3
Average all years	6.4	22.4	9.8	11.7	56.1	93.6	3.7

Notes: Columns 1 to 4 may not sum exactly to 100 percent due to rounding, proportions are weighted using BHPS household weights, house value is self-reported. Column 1 identifies households that used a house move to reduce mortgage debt; column 2 identifies households that used a house move to trade down and withdraw equity; column 3 identifies households that used a house move to trade down and inject equity; column 4 identifies households that used a house move to increase mortgage debt; column 5 identifies households that did not move house and increased mortgaged debt.

if this were the case, we might expect this proportion to have fallen as realism in self-reported house values improved through the 1990s.) Column 3 shows that, on average, 12 percent of households held their mortgage constant but increased the value of their home by moving. These could be equity injectors. Again, some of these may be misvaluations—households who underreport the true market value of their home prior to selling. Again, there is no consistent temporal pattern to this potential misvaluation although it tended to increase in the latter part of the period when house price increases started to accelerate.

Column 4 shows that the vast majority of movers take out larger mortgages to finance a move from a smaller to a larger property. Column 5 is the only part of table 5.5 that considers nonmovers. Consistently, about 4 percent of stayers (who comprise 93 percent to 94 percent of the sample each year) remortgage or extend their mortgage. As suggested, this may be because many of these nonmovers use the withdrawn housing equity to finance purchases on consumer durables or home improvement. One reason for thinking that releasing housing equity is not a primary motive for remortgaging is that, despite rising house prices in the latter part of the period, the proportion of remortgagers has stayed constant. On the other hand, as the next table shows, amounts withdrawn have increased as house prices have risen.

How much equity is withdrawn, on average, by each activity? Table 5.6 provides the key results: It shows the average level of calculated equity withdrawal (given the caveats above) for each of the first three "routes" (table 5.5, column 2, "downtrading"; table 5.5, column 4, "overborrowing," and table 5.5, column 5, "remortgaging").

In the case of "overborrowers," the equity withdrawal is calculated by netting out the change in the house value before and after the move. For a given HEW "event," the most equity is withdrawn by "downtraders" (a nominal average of £42,000 withdrawn). The amount withdrawn through this route increases substantially over the period, particularly in the past two years, and is consistent with the upturn in the housing market. "Overborrowing" is far more pervasive during moves, but the average amount withdrawn is generally small and does not increase over the period, despite falling interest rates and rising housing equity. Again, this absence of any temporal pattern may suggest that such borrowing is utilized to cover moving expenses and other related expenses. Whilst legal fees and other expenses have risen over time, increased competition among estate agents (realtors) may have kept nominal moving costs down.

Table 5.6
Average nominal mortgage equity withdrawal by year and source

	(1) Mover households with no change in outstanding mortgage, house value fell ("downtraders")	(2) Mover households who increased outstanding mortgage ("over- borrowers")	(3) Non-mover households who increased outstanding mortgage ("remortgagers")
1993–1994	£15,468	£3,450	£2,209
1994–1995	£14,680	£3,310	£2,225
1995–1996	£36,862	£1,865	£2,737
1996–1997	£26,834	£1,066	£3,957
1997–1998	£40,300	£2,078	£2,482
1998–1999	£34,266	£2,116	£4,563
1999–2000	£56,217	£3,056	£5,250
2000–2001	£72,575	£1,995	£8,563
Average all years	£41,723	£2,355	£3,997

Source: BHPS using household weights.
Note: Computed as nominal (nonnegative) change in outstanding mortgage principal, adjusted for trading down effect on house value for house movers.

"Remortgagers" who do not move have the second-highest average level of withdrawal per "event." This route is the most popular form of equity withdrawal, simply because nonmovers outweigh movers (from table 5.5). The average amount withdrawn, while much lower than through "trading down" (it averages £4,000), has increased significantly in the past few years of the period in question, again consistent with the housing market upturn.

Table 5.7 provides some limited information on the scale and effect of "final sales" in the BHPS. Equity withdrawal through the final sales of the property of deceased households is likely to be rather small. Less than 1 percent of BHPS households are recorded in any year as disappearing from the sample because the household dies. Equity withdrawal through the final sale of property belonging to households who move out of owner occupation is also on a very small scale, albeit at a rather higher rate. Table 5.7 also reports the average level of household housing equity for such households. Given the very small numbers involved, it is difficult to make any reliable interpretation in these averages from one year to the next.

Finally, from 1997, the BHPS has asked all household members whether they have received an inheritance during the previous year.

Table 5.7
Equity withdrawal on transition out of owner occupation and receipt of bequests

	1 % transition out of owner occupation	2 Average fall in housing equity (1995 prices)	3 % owner- occupiers receiving an inheritance	4 Average value of inheritance (1995 prices)
1993–1994	1.2	£39,269		
1994–1995	1.9	£37,406		
1995–1996	1.4	£31,428		
1996–1997	1.6	£31,453	3.7	£18,252
1997–1998	1.3	£66,608	4.9	£15,387
1998–1999	1.3	£43,611	3.2	£19,669
1999–2000	1.1	£38,551	4.0	£27,154
2000–2001	1.4	£61,308	3.7	£26,122
Average all years	1.4	£43,704	3.9	£21,317

Table 5.7 also reports that around 4 percent of households in any year contain at least one household member in receipt of an inheritance. Such inheritances may be financial as well as being in the form of property. The average reported value of the inheritances is also given in the table, and does appear to have risen along with house prices.

5.4.3 Housing Equity Withdrawal and Financial Assets

In this section, the determinants of HEW by households are examined. The relationship between the cumulated totals and the distribution of financial wealth and debt at the end of the period are then assessed. The objective is to see if there is evidence that cumulative withdrawal affects the household's financial position at the end of the period, ceteris paribus.

Table 5.8 reports two estimated tobit equations. The tobit is an appropriate estimator for a reduced-form model to capture the feature that only a subset of households withdraw any housing equity. The dependent variable is the estimated cumulative amount of equity withdrawn per household between 1993–1994 and 2000–2001. For a mover household, equity withdrawal (EW) is adjusted for the effect of moving to a more valuable house (HV) on the size of the mortgage (M), and is computed as:

$$EW_t = -((M_t - HV_t) - (M_{t-1} - HV_{t-1})) \quad \text{if } EW_t < 0 \text{ and 0 otherwise}$$

Table 5.8

Tobit models of mortgage equity withdrawal (dependent variable: household nominal mortgage equity withdrawal, mover households adjusted for trading down)

		1 1993–2001		2	
		Coefficient	Standard error	Marginal effect conditional on being uncensored	Standard error
Initial status					
Age		2,791.7	982.9***	545.4	192.0***
Age squared		−30.0	10.1***	−5.86	1.98***
Female household head		−7,489.7	3,550.8**	−1,436.0	693.7**
Married household head		7,971.9	7,337.4	1,516.7	1,433.5
Divorced household head		15,775.2	7,532.3**	3,426.5	1,471.6**
Widowed household head		13,125.9	9,201.3	2,786.6	1,797.6
No. of adults		872.2	2,640.3	170.4	515.8
No. of children 0–2 yrs.		9,679.7	5,252.3*	2,024.1	1,026.1**
No. of children 3–4 yrs.		−617.4	4,544.3	−120.6	887.8
No. of children 5–11 yrs.		−122.7	2,341.9	−24.0	457.5
No. of children 12–15 yrs.		−297.5	3,588.2	58.1	701.0
No. of children 16–18 yrs.		4,605.8	8,384.4	931.6	1,638.0
Change in status					
Married		9,380.2	7,584.4	1,963.0	1,481.7
Divorced		14,049.6	8,988.8	3,058.0	1,756.1*
Widowed		−613.2	10,282.7	−119.3	2,008.9
Change in household size (persons)		−1,176.6	2,039.7	−229.9	398.5
Housing					
Outright owner		−20,351.0	4,966.1***	−3,817.7	970.2***
Downtrading	1994	63,427.7	17,334.1***	21,344.2	3,386.5***
	1995	70,397.6	17,693.0***	25,204.1	3,456.6***
	1996	85,532.5	15,099.2***	34,831.3	2,949.9***
	1997	100,905.5	19,303.6***	46,526.6	3,771.3***
	1998	106,241.9	23,091.5***	50,976.8	4,511.3***
	1999	88,424.8	22,872.9***	36,992.8	4,468.6***
	2000	104,297.9	15,999.2***	49,227.2	3,125.7***
	2001	115,623.4	12,198.0***	58,733.0	2,383.1***

Table 5.8
(continued)

		1 1993–2001		2	
		Coefficient	Standard error	Marginal effect conditional on being uncensored	Standard error
Overborrowing	1994	41,498.5	6,381.1***	11,286.5	1,246.7***
	1995	23,609.2	7,644.7***	5,550.9	1,493.5***
	1996	27,618.5	9,465.4***	6,733.6	1,849.2***
	1997	9,797.6	7,591.8	2,060.8	1,483.2
	1998	25,604.3	8,280.4***	6,128.7	1,617.7***
	1999	16,610.4	8,328.6**	3,692.0	1,627.1**
	2000	8,252.5	9,875.8	1,717.4	1,929.4
	2001	20,410.1	8,071.5**	4,676.2	1,576.9**
Remortgaging	1994	27,140.0	6,209.8***	6,552.0	1,213.2***
	1995	22,784.8	6,285.1***	5,310.4	1,227.9***
	1996	27,092.3	6,044.4***	6,532.8	1,180.9***
	1997	27,807.8	5,685.1***	6,733.6	1,110.7***
	1998	29,430.8	7,340.5***	7,267.2	1,434.1***
	1999	25,709.0	5,647.7***	6,119.1	1,103.4***
	2000	45,305.3	5,374.9***	12,647.4	1,050.1***
	2001	46,440.3	5,526.8***	13,106.4	1,079.8***
Sigma		37,539.8	1,386.7***	37,539.8	1,386.7***
Intercept		−113,024.0	22,873.3***	−22,081.2	4,664.1***
N		1,636		1,636	
N (uncensored)		413		413	
Log likelihood		−5,214.7		−5,214.7	

Note: Marginal effects are evaluated at covariate means in the case of the continuous variables (age, number of adults, number of children in each age category, change in household size), and evaluated as the effect of a discrete change in the case of all other binary variables.
*** significant at the 1 percent level; ** significant at the 5 percent level; * significant at the 10 percent level.

For a nonmover household it is computed as:

$EW_t = -(M_t - M_{t-1})$ if $EW_t < 0$ and 0 otherwise.

The dependent variable is $\sum_{t=1994}^{2001} EW_t$. While it is feasible to estimate the equation as a panel, the proportion of household-year observations censored at zero will be high. The right-hand side of the equation includes covariates to capture initial household demographic status (age of household head, age squared, female household head, marital status, number of adults in household, and number of dependent children in various age categories), to capture change in demographic status (head married, head divorced/separated, head widowed, change in number of persons in household), and for outright home ownership (i.e., no initial mortgage). A series of dummy variables are also included that interact the type of equity withdrawal activity ("downtrading," "overborrowing," "remortgaging") with year dummy variables. We experimented with an equation for the subperiod from 1997 to 2001 that included interaction dummy variables for inheritance (available annually only from 1997, see table 5.3), but the results are not significant, so this specification is not reported.

Examining the demographic variables, housing equity withdrawal increases sharply with the age of the household head and peaks at 46.7 years old. Households with a female head are less likely to withdraw equity. Being divorced appears to be associated with equity withdrawal, becoming divorced weakly so. In the first equation, the presence of very young children in the household is also associated with increased equity withdrawal, probably to finance home improvements.

The sets of interaction dummies between years and types of withdrawal have strongly positive and significant coefficient estimates. As described in section 5.3.2, the strongest form of HEW is downtrading. The scale of HEW on downtrading appears to have grown through the 1990s, and, in nominal terms, a typical downtrade withdrawal is nearly twice as large in 2000–2001 as it was in 1993–1994. (Cumulative consumer price inflation over this period was about 18 percent.) Overborrowing and remortgaging appear to be associated with much lower levels of equity withdrawal, other things equal. The degree of overborrowing fluctuates substantially from year to year, with little or no consistent pattern over time. As noted earlier, this may reflect low sample numbers. The average scale of remortgaging, on the other hand, grows over time, and again, almost doubles between the start and end of the period. This last result is the most consistent evidence obtained in this

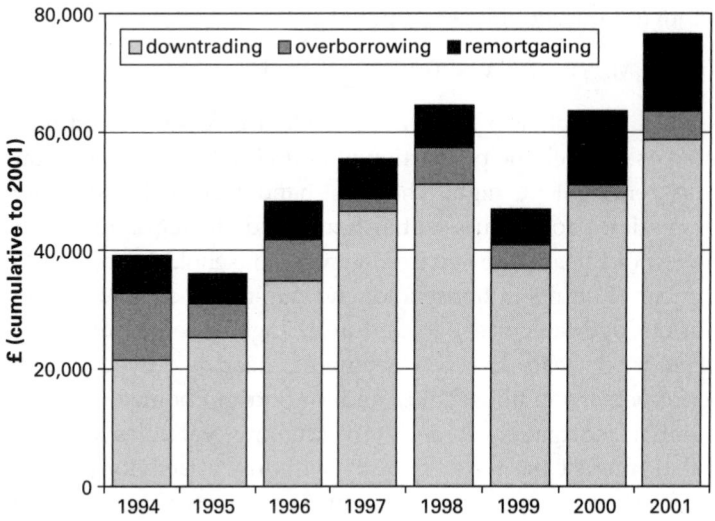

Figure 5.7
Sources of cumulative HEW, 1994–2001
Source: Calculations from British Household Panel Survey.
Note: For definitions of terms and methods, see text and methods.

chapter that rising housing wealth has led to significant increases in secured borrowing. Even so, as suggested in table 5.5, the number of home owners utilizing this route has remained constant.

Figure 5.7 plots the marginal effects from the year-equity withdrawal interactions from column 2 to illustrate the sources of, and trends in, average amounts of equity withdrawn over the period. There is a rising trend in absolute HEW over the period, as in figure 5.6, although the latter does not contain the "blip" in household HEW observed for 1998. Release of equity by downtrading is by far the strongest contributory factor to HEW. A caveat from the data is that we are unable to model precisely the amounts of equity withdrawal arising from dissolution of owner occupation at death using the data set. Such events are of low frequency in the sample as a whole but are typically the largest absolute sources of equity withdrawal. The impacts of bequests on holdings of financial wealth and on debt lie beyond the scope of this paper, however.

We can now investigate the relationship between cumulative HEW and the information in 2000 in the BHPS on holdings of financial wealth and debt. Unfortunately, year-on-year measures of household

Table 5.9
Relationship between housing equity withdrawal and the household balance sheet

	Average equity withdrawal 1993–2001	Proportion of sample
Financial assets in 2000		
Less than £500	£5,875	50.9%
£500–£999	£12,605	2.4%
£1,000–£4,999	£5,769	11.9%
£5,000–£9,999	£5,223	8.9%
£10,000–£49,999	£7,387	18.7%
£50,000 or more	£3,967	7.2%
Nonmortgage debt in 2000		
Less than £500	£4,507	69.3%
£500–£999	£7,227	4.9%
£1,000–£4,999	£6,584	15.4%
£5,000–£9,999	£17,446	7.0%
£10,000–£24,999	£16,187	2.9%
£25,000 or more	£7,515	0.5%

financial assets and debts are not available in the data set; questions on assets and debt were asked in 1995, but they are not directly comparable with 2000.

To undertake the investigation, we divide the self-reported data on total amounts of financial wealth and nonmortgage debt into equivalent bands. For each band of assets and debt, table 5.9 plots the sample proportions and the average amounts of cumulative HEW from 1993 to 2001.

The data on financial assets show a clear bifurcation of households. A substantial minority of households hold little or no financial assets. The next largest proportion is in the open-ended highest bracket. The figures on nonmortgage debt also show that a majority of households have very little debt, with just under 70 percent having less than £500 and just over 10 percent having debt in excess of £5,000.

The simple correlation between the level of financial assets and cumulative HEW is −0.01, and between nonmortgage debt and cumulative HEW −0.12. There is therefore no overall relationship between HEW and the level of financial wealth, although the 31 percent of the sample with over £50,000 of wealth have very low levels of equity withdrawal. There is a stronger relationship with unsecured debt, with an apparent negative correlation suggesting that higher HEW is associated with lower debt. However, the relationship is in fact nonlinear: A quadratic regression of equity withdrawal on debt and debt-squared gives highly significant coefficients on both the level and the square. Higher equity withdrawal between 1993 and 2001 is associated with increasing unsecured debt in 2000 (up to debt levels of £27,000), but beyond that, the association is negative. As table 5.9 shows, the least indebted (less than £500) have the lowest levels of HEW. Unfortunately, we do not know what their level of debt would have been in the absence of equity withdrawal.

It is possible to focus, however, on those who withdraw large amounts of equity and to examine their background characteristics. As suggested in table 5.8 and figure 5.7, these are mostly "downsizing" households, which we might surmise are older households who are retiring or where children are leaving home. This is broadly confirmed by a detailed analysis of this subset of households: The head of household is, on average, 12 years older than the sample as a whole, typically an outright owner (that is, without a mortgage) with no dependent children and often widowed (49 percent of the sample) and inactive, mostly retired (52 percent of the sample) with a high ratio (number of rooms to number in the household), which is typically a sign of housing size "disequilibrium" (see Feinstein and McFadden 1989; Disney, Henley, and Stears 2002). While these substantial flows contribute to the aggregate level of HEW, they are consistent with the life-cycle hypothesis of saving, suggesting that older households (who are increasing proportionately as the population ages) are engaging in consumption smoothing, which should not be a cause for concern.

5.5 Conclusion

As in several OECD countries, the United Kingdom has seen fluctuating house prices for several decades, coupled with changes in the level of secured and unsecured debt. In particular, since the late 1990s, there have been substantial rises in house prices, in levels of unsecured debt, and in home equity withdrawal, as illustrated in this chapter. The chapter has explored the theoretical links among home ownership, changing housing wealth, and levels of secured and unsecured debt. Its main novelty, however, is to examine the empirical relationships between these macroeconomic variables using two new household panel data sets for Britain.

The findings from the cross-section suggest that we must be cautious in drawing inferences from macroeconomic trends. Certainly, it has shown that home ownership is associated with access to certain types of unsecured debt, and home owners and tenants have different portfolios of credit arrangements. Home owners, for example, are typically more likely to have credit cards, whereas tenants are more likely to rely on catalogues and mail order purchases in order to obtain unsecured credit. Overall, however, total levels of household unsecured debt and arrears on debt and payments of bills tend to be negatively associated with home ownership. Higher-income families typically acquire more unsecured debt, and low-income families tend to run into difficulties with debt, but home ownership and housing equity play little part in these outcomes.

Concern over growing levels of housing equity withdrawal (HEW) in the United Kingdom suggests that it is the relationship between housing wealth and secured debt that is more significant. However, again using household data, the chapter suggests that the largest value of HEW is associated with the decumulation of assets later in the life cycle. The gradual aging of the population may increase the total value of HEW over time for this very reason. Whilst the value of remortgaging has increased substantially (which is a typical indicator of using rising housing wealth to secure debt), the proportion of households that have utilized remortgaging has remained roughly constant over time. More analysis is required, and, in particular, it would be useful to have household panel data that permit us to understand the trajectory of household debt over time, but the results here show that analyses from household data are essential if we are fully to understand the aggregate trends over time.

5A Appendix

Debt Questions—BHPS

Currently Owe Money?
I would like to ask you now about any other financial commitments you may have apart from mortgages and housing related loans. Do you currently owe any money on the things listed on this card? Please do not include credit cards or other bills being fully paid off in the current month.

Hire purchase?

Personal loan (from bank, building society, or other financial institution)?

Credit card(s) (including store card)?

Catalogue or mail order purchase?

DSS Social Fund loan?

Loans from individual?

Overdraft?

Student loan?

Anything else?

If Owes Money ...

About how much in total do you owe? Write in to nearest pound. If don't know, the following series of questions is asked to determine a band for debt.

Would it amount to

a. 500 or more? (If yes, ask b; if no, ask d)

b. 1,500 or more? (if yes ask c)

c. 5,000 or more?

d. 100 or more?

Debt/Arrears Questions—FACS

1. How much do you owe for each bill (see earlier)?

2. Over the past few years, a lot of different ways of buying things have been introduced and many people use them. Do you use any of the different ways of buying things listed on this card?

Credit cards (such as Access, Visa, and so forth)?

Charge cards (such as American Express, Diners Club)?

Shop or store cards (such as Marks and Spencer, John Lewis, and so forth)?

Catalogues/mail order schemes?

None of these?

3. Are you at the moment able to manage the repayments on the above cards? I mean, to meet the minimum amount you have to repay?

4. How much are you unable to repay at the moment?

5. There are also more and more ways of borrowing money these days. Over the past twelve months, have you used any of these ways to borrow money?

Bank overdraft?

Fixed-term loan from the bank or building society?

Loan from a finance company?

Loan from a moneylender or "tally man?"

Loan from a friend or relative?

Loan, or advance on wages, from your employer?

None of these?

6. Have you been able to keep up with the repayments for the above loans, or are you getting behind?

7. How much do you owe on these overdue payments?

8. How often would you say you have been worried about money during the last few weeks?

9. Is your rent paid up to date at the moment, or do you have some rent arrears that will have to be paid?

10. How much are your rent arrears at the moment?

11. Enter amount of rent arrears to the nearest £.

12. Enter number of weeks in arrears.

13. Enter number of months in arrears.

14. And may I just check, are you up to date with your loan or mortgage payments, or are you now behind with your loan or mortgage?

15. How much are your mortgage or loan arrears at the moment?

16. Enter amount of mortgage or loan that is in arrears.

17. Enter number of weeks in arrears.

18. Enter number of months in arrears.

Notes

1. Ausubel (1991) argues that a model based on rationing of credit market because interest rates are "too low" is inconsistent with empirical evidence that credit providers, especially credit card providers, tend to levy interest rates well above those that would exist in competitive markets. Chapter 6 further discusses why households borrow on credit cards (especially when they have assets earning lower interest rates).

2. However, under certain circumstances in the screening framework, Stiglitz and Weiss (1981) argue, requesting security on a debt may not help the lender—for example, if wealthier people are less risk averse (or projects differ in their "riskiness"), then those that put up the most collateral are prepared to take the greatest risk, and this may increase bank default risk. Collateral will deter the more risk-averse individuals who are less likely to default. See also Chan and Kanatos 1985.

3. Since "households" may include several family members that do not share resources, we follow standard practice and take as the household the "benefit unit"—that is, the household as defined for receipt of welfare benefits (this would also be the "tax unit," except that, in the United Kingdom, income tax is now individually assessed).

4. A similar specification is available on request from the authors using FACS. Although the sample size is far larger in FACS, there are no data on the value of housing equity, so we quote the results from BHPS. The key coefficients discussed in the text are similar.

5. The marginal effect using the FACS data ($n = 7{,}025$) is 21.8 percent.

References

Aoki, K., J. Proudman, and G. Vlieghe. 2002. "House Prices, Consumption, and Monetary Policy: A Financial Accelerator Approach." Mimeo., Bank of England, London.

Attanasio, O., and G. Weber. 1994. "The U.K. Consumption Boom of the Late 1980s: Aggregate Implications of Microeconomic Evidence." *Economic Journal* 104 (November): 1269–1302.

Ausubel, L. M. 1991. "The Failure of Competition in the Credit Card Market." *American Economic Review* 81 (March): 50–81.

Barnes, S., and G. Young. 2003. "The Rise in U.S. Household Debt: Assessing Its Causes and Sustainability." Bank of England Working Paper no. 206, London.

Ben-Shahar, D., and D. Feldman. 2003. "Signalling-Screening Equilibrium in the Mortgage Market." *Journal of Real Estate Finance and Economics* 26, nos. 2/3: 157–178.

Bester, H. 1985. "Screening vs. Rationing in Credit Markets with Imperfect Information." *American Economic Review* 75 (September): 850–855.

Black, J., D. de Meza, and D. Jeffreys. 1996. "House Prices, the Supply of Collateral and the Enterprise Economy." *Economic Journal* 106 (January): 60–75.

Borio, C., and P. McGuire. 2004. "Twin Peaks in Equity and House Prices?" Bank of International Settlements. *Quarterly Review* (March): 79–93.

Bridges, S., and R. Disney. 2004. "Use of Credit and Arrears on Debt among Low-income Families in the United Kingdom." *Fiscal Studies* 25 (March): 1–25.

Campbell, J., and N. G. Mankiw. 1989. "Consumption, Income and Interest Rates: Reinterpreting the Time Series Evidence." In *Macroeconomics Annual*, ed. J. O. Blanchard and S. Fischer, 185–216. Cambridge, Mass.: National Bureau of Economic Research.

Carroll, C. 2004. "Housing Wealth and Consumption Expenditure." Mimeo., Department of Economics, Johns Hopkins University, Baltimore, Md.

Case, K. 2000. "Real Estate and the Macroeconomy." *Brookings Papers on Economic Activity* 2: 119–162.

Chan, Y.-S., and G. Kanatas. 1985. "Asymmetric Valuations and the Role of Collateral in Loan Agreements." *Journal of Money, Credit and Banking* 17 (February): 84–95.

Davey, M. 2001. "Mortgage Equity Withdrawal and Consumption." *Bank of England Quarterly Bulletin* 41 (Spring): 100–103.

Debelle, G. 2004. "Household Debt and the Macroeconomy." *BIS Quarterly Review* (March): 51–63.

Disney, R., A. Henley, and D. Jevons. 2003. "House Price Shocks, Negative Equity and Household Consumption in the UK." Mimeo., University of Nottingham.

Disney, R., A. Henley, and G. Stears. 2002. "Housing Costs, House Price Shocks, and Savings Behavior among Older Households in Britain." *Regional Science and Urban Economics* 32 (September): 607–625.

Duca, J. V., and S. S. Rosenthal. 1993. "Borrowing Constraints, Household Debt, and Racial Discrimination in Labour Markets." *Journal of Financial Intermediation* 3: 77–103.

Farlow, A. 2004. "U.K. House Prices: A Critical Assessment." Credit Suisse First Boston, London.

Feinstein, J., and D. McFadden. 1989. "The Dynamics of Housing Demand by the Elderly: Wealth, Cash Flow and Demographic Effects." In *The Economics of Aging*, ed. D. A. Wise, 55–91. Chicago: Chicago University Press, for National Bureau of Economic Research.

HM Treasury. 2003. *EMU Study: Housing, Consumption and EMU.* London: HM Treasury.

Iacoviello, M. 2004. "Consumption, House Prices and Collateral Constraints: A Structural Econometric Analysis." Mimeo., Boston College, Chestnut Hill, Mass.

Meen, G. 1996. "Ten Propositions in U.K. Housing Macroeconomics: An Overview of the 1980s and early 1990s." *Urban Studies* 33, 3: 425–444.

Milde, H. and J. G. Riley. 1988. "Signalling in Credit Markets." *Quarterly Journal of Economics* 103 (February): 101–129.

Miles, D. 2004. "The U.K. Mortgage Market: Taking a Longer View." HM Treasury, London. http://www.hm-treasury.gov.uk/media/BF8/30/miles04_470%5B1%5D.pdf.

Muellbauer, J., and A. Murphy. 1990. "Is the UK Balance of Payments Sustainable?" *Economic Policy* 11: 345–383.

Paxson, C. 1990. "Borrowing Constraints and Portfolio Choice." *Quarterly Journal of Economics* 105 (May): 535–543.

Reserve Bank of Australia. 2003. "Housing Equity Withdrawal." *Bulletin* (February): 50–54.

Stiglitz, J. E., and A. Weiss. 1981. "Credit Rationing in Markets with Imperfect Information." *American Economic Review* 71 (June): 393–410.

6   Credit Cards: Facts and Theories

Carol C. Bertaut and Michael Haliassos

Access to consumer credit in the form of a credit card has grown rapidly to become one of the most frequently held financial instruments by households in the United States. Credit cards offer the convenience of cashless transactions and also allow for purchases over the telephone and, increasingly, via the Internet. Credit cards also offer consumers the flexibility of deferring payment to a future date, and thus can allow consumers to smooth spending over temporary liquidity shortfalls. However, invoking a credit card's revolving credit option typically results in paying high rates of interest not only on the existing balance but also on any new charges made on the card as well, and thus is a fairly costly form of credit, especially if the revolving credit feature is used frequently.

This chapter documents features of credit card and debit card ownership and use over time and across demographic groups in the U.S. population, using data from several waves of a high-quality and detailed survey of finances of U.S. households: the Federal Reserve Board's Survey of Consumer Finances (SCF). We consider household responses from the SCF to questions about access to and attitudes toward credit and debit cards, and explore portfolios of households with and without credit card balances.

Our analysis of the data, presented in sections 6.1–6.8, illustrates several puzzling features of credit card usage by U.S. households. In sections 6.9 and 6.10, we discuss recent theories of consumer behavior that may explain some of those puzzles. These include the choice to borrow at high rates of interest; the interplay between spending control problems, credit card borrowing, and personal bankruptcy filing; and the coexistence of credit card debt with considerable levels of liquid and retirement assets. We also explore the growing popularity of debit cards as either a supplement to or an alternative to credit card use. We offer concluding remarks in section 6.11.

6.1   Card Ownership over Time

Our primary source of information on the spread of credit and debit card use among U.S. households is from several waves of the SCF. The SCF has been conducted triennially since 1983, and recent waves have each consisted of about 3,000 households drawn from a standard representative sample, supplemented with about 1,500 high-wealth households selected on the basis of tax records. Sample weights are provided to make the data representative of the U.S. population as a whole. Each wave of the SCF provides detailed information on household-level holdings of a variety of financial assets as well as sources, terms, and uses of a wide range of consumer credit options, including credit cards. Data are also collected on household characteristics, including age, education, family structure, race, and income. Finally, the SCF also asks a number of questions on attitudes toward consumer borrowing, reasons for saving, and investment decisions.[1]

In 1983, 65 percent of U.S. households had a credit card of some kind, including store-specific cards and gas cards (table 6.1, column 1). Only 43 percent of households had a bank-type credit card such as a Visa or Mastercard (column 2)—that is, a card that is accepted at a broad range of retail establishments, and, after making a minimum required payment, allows the consumer to revolve the balance if so desired. By 1992, 62 percent of the U.S. population had a bank-type credit card, and by 2001, that percentage had risen to almost 73. Over the same period, the percentage of households with any type of credit card increased much less, and in 2001, that percentage was 76 percent, only slightly higher than the percentage with a bank-type card. There has also been an increase in the number of bank-type credit cards owned per household. In 1983, households with a bank-type card typically held only one such type card. By 2001, one-third of card-holding households still had only one bank-type card, one-third had two, and about one-fourth had three or four. A little more than 7 percent had five or more. In the remainder of our discussion here, we focus our attention on bank-type credit cards.

6.2   Trends in Card Ownership by Income, Education, and Age

Bank-type credit card ownership in the United States is strongly correlated with household income and with education, and this correlation has persisted over all waves of the SCF. However, the increase in

Table 6.1
Percentage of households by bank-type credit card payment pattern

	Has any credit card 1	Has bank-type card 2	Among those with a bank-type card			
			No balance and no new charges 3	No balance but has new charges 4	Carries balance 5	Hardly ever pays it off 6
1983	65.4	43.0	18.3	30.5	51.1	43.9
1992	72.0	62.3	10.7	36.8	52.6	48.9
1995	74.6	66.5	7.3	36.7	56.0	47.3
1998	72.2	67.2	8.3	36.9	54.8	47.6
2001	76.2	72.6	7.2	39.4	53.4	45.9
1983						
By age						
<35	57.2	34.0	14.9	24.5	60.6	49.2
35–54	73.7	52.0	14.4	24.8	60.8	43.0
55–64	75.0	53.1	21.0	35.6	43.4	42.4
65+	55.9	33.3	31.7	50.2	18.1	28.4
By education						
Less than high school	41.5	21.4	24.6	28.4	47.0	46.9
High school	65.1	39.2	22.7	22.9	54.5	45.9
Some college	73.1	49.4	18.4	28.9	52.7	46.4
College degree+	89.1	69.8	12.7	38.1	49.2	39.7
By income						
<$10,000	20.2	5.3	38.0	20.8	41.2	75.2
$10,000–$24,999	43.2	22.4	26.1	28.0	45.9	43.0
$25,000–$49,999	70.8	41.3	19.8	25.2	55.0	46.8
$50,000–$99,999	88.8	68.0	15.5	28.7	55.8	43.9
$100,000+	97.2	83.4	15.0	49.5	35.5	32.4
By marital status						
Unmarried	51.7	29.9	20.5	32.4	47.0	44.1
Married or partner	74.3	51.6	17.5	29.8	52.7	43.9
By race						
White non-Hispanic	70.3	46.8	19.3	32.5	48.2	42.4
Black	41.9	23.3	12.1	13.9	73.9	54.1
Hispanic	38.9	26.3	3.3	5.9	90.7	47.5
Other	60.7	46.3	11.1	28.4	60.4	55.6

Table 6.1
(continued)

	Has any credit card 1	Has bank-type card 2	Among those with a bank-type card			
			No balance and no new charges 3	No balance but has new charges 4	Carries balance 5	Hardly ever pays it off 6
1992						
By age						
<35	67.3	56.1	5.8	27.3	66.9	50.1
35–54	74.9	67.2	7.0	33.6	59.4	51.2
55–64	75.8	67.3	16.0	42.8	41.2	43.7
65+	70.1	57.9	20.1	49.9	30.0	41.9
By education						
Less than high school	39.6	27.5	22.5	28.0	49.6	70.7
High school	69.2	56.5	12.1	29.2	58.7	53.5
Some college	78.9	70.0	10.2	33.5	56.3	37.1
College degree+	91.5	85.6	7.6	44.8	47.6	47.3
By income						
<$10,000	28.5	18.9	23.1	25.0	51.9	70.4
$10,000–$24,999	60.6	47.4	18.1	31.1	50.8	54.0
$25,000–$49,999	77.7	66.1	10.2	29.2	60.7	49.0
$50,000–$99,999	91.0	84.3	6.9	38.1	54.9	47.9
$100,000+	95.9	93.5	7.0	59.1	33.9	34.4
By marital status						
Unmarried	58.7	49.0	13.1	35.5	51.4	50.7
Married or partner	81.9	72.2	9.4	37.4	53.2	48.1
By race						
White non-Hispanic	78.9	69.7	10.8	39.4	49.8	47.6
Black	47.0	35.5	9.6	13.1	77.4	47.7
Hispanic	43.6	33.7	9.5	16.0	74.5	77.8
Other	74.4	61.8	11.5	43.6	44.9	37.5
1995						
By age						
<35	67.6	58.8	6.0	25.2	68.8	49.5
35–54	78.2	71.9	5.1	28.7	66.2	46.5
55–64	78.7	72.0	6.3	45.9	47.8	43.5
65+	73.4	62.0	13.9	60.6	25.6	49.9

Table 6.1
(continued)

	Has any credit card 1	Has bank-type card 2	Among those with a bank-type card			
			No balance and no new charges 3	No balance but has new charges 4	Carries balance 5	Hardly ever pays it off 6
By education						
Less than high school	48.5	34.8	15.0	31.9	53.1	56.0
High school	70.8	61.8	9.0	29.7	61.4	48.0
Some college	79.3	71.2	7.2	28.8	63.6	49.2
College degree+	91.3	87.7	4.2	47.0	48.7	42.8
By income						
<$10,000	33.6	25.7	17.8	31.6	50.6	46.4
$10,000–$24,999	61.3	49.1	8.9	32.2	58.9	57.4
$25,000–$49,999	81.6	73.1	6.8	35.0	58.2	50.3
$50,000–$99,999	95.3	90.0	6.6	34.3	59.1	42.2
$100,000+	98.9	96.9	3.6	55.6	40.8	33.2
By marital status						
Unmarried	63.2	54.8	8.6	35.6	55.9	51.1
Married or partner	82.6	74.8	6.6	37.4	56.0	45.3
By race						
White non-Hispanic	79.4	71.9	7.6	40.2	52.2	46.4
Black	51.7	41.0	6.2	12.2	81.5	54.5
Hispanic	60.1	49.7	4.0	10.2	85.7	51.4
Other	75.5	67.6	5.2	40.9	53.9	37.1
1998						
By age						
<35	62.9	57.9	5.2	23.3	71.4	52.4
35–54	76.7	72.6	6.9	31.8	61.2	50.3
55–64	79.6	75.4	9.0	41.4	49.6	38.7
65+	69.0	61.6	14.1	59.3	26.8	31.4
By education						
Less than high school	42.5	34.7	14.8	26.0	59.2	53.7
High school	68.9	62.8	10.9	31.9	57.1	51.8
Some college	76.6	73.3	7.4	29.0	63.5	50.1
College degree+	91.6	88.2	5.4	46.4	48.2	41.0

Table 6.1
(continued)

	Has any credit card 1	Has bank-type card 2	Among those with a bank-type card			
			No balance and no new charges 3	No balance but has new charges 4	Carries balance 5	Hardly ever pays it off 6
By income						
<$10,000	29.4	23.5	8.6	29.7	61.7	51.1
$10,000–$24,999	54.8	47.7	14.1	30.4	55.4	44.4
$25,000–$49,999	77.0	71.0	9.4	32.8	57.8	52.6
$50,000–$99,999	91.0	87.7	6.5	34.7	58.8	47.5
$100,000+	98.9	98.0	3.6	59.1	37.3	35.3
By marital status						
Unmarried	59.3	54.9	10.7	35.1	54.2	46.5
Married or partner	81.5	76.1	7.0	37.8	55.1	48.1
By race						
White non-Hispanic	77.9	73.5	8.2	39.8	52.0	46.5
Black	48.2	39.7	10.3	15.6	74.2	57.6
Hispanic	54.2	48.4	7.7	15.6	76.6	48.1
Other	66.5	60.2	5.9	43.7	50.5	40.7

bank-card ownership over the past two decades was especially pronounced at lower-income and lower-education levels, reflecting in part improvements in industry credit-scoring techniques and risk analysis. In 1983, only 21 percent of households with less than a high school education and less than 23 percent of households with incomes between $10,000 and $25,000 owned a bank-type credit card.[2] By 2001, these percentages had doubled to 42 percent and 54 percent, respectively. Table 6.1 reports card ownership, both for credit cards generally and for bank-type credit cards, for various demographic groups over time. Such tabulation is useful for describing ownership patterns across demographic groups, but in the interest of brevity, we focus our discussion here on identifying how each characteristic contributes to ownership, controlling for other characteristics.

To help distinguish the relative importance of age, education, and income, as well as other factors that contribute to the likelihood of credit card ownership, table 6.2 presents results of probit regressions of the

Table 6.2
Probit estimation of credit card ownership in the United States (1983, 1992, 1995, 1998, and 2001 SCFs)

	Has at least one credit card			Has a bank-type credit card		
	Coeffi- cient	Stan- dard error	Signifi- cance	Coeffi- cient	Stan- dard error	Signifi- cance
Intercept	−0.007	0.074	0.920	−0.136	0.072	0.059
Married	0.412	0.036	<.0001	0.289	0.035	<.0001
Single female	0.267	0.039	<.0001	0.154	0.038	<.0001
Number of children	−0.039	0.009	<.0001	−0.036	0.009	<.0001
Nonwhite/Hispanic	−0.167	0.030	<.0001	−0.174	0.030	<.0001
Age <35	−0.210	0.038	<.0001	−0.153	0.036	<.0001
Age 35–49	−0.120	0.037	0.001	−0.061	0.033	0.065
Age 65–74	−0.022	0.047	0.641	−0.071	0.043	0.097
Age 75+	−0.469	0.049	<.0001	−0.551	0.047	<.0001
Less than HS diploma	−0.584	0.040	<.0001	−0.608	0.038	<.0001
High school diploma or equiv.	−0.257	0.035	<.0001	−0.261	0.033	<.0001
College degree or higher	0.269	0.039	<.0001	0.237	0.035	<.0001
Income <$10,000	−0.646	0.044	<.0001	−0.615	0.046	<.0001
Income $10,000–$24,999	−0.293	0.033	<.0001	−0.237	0.032	<.0001
Income $50,000–$99,999	0.256	0.037	<.0001	0.263	0.033	<.0001
Income $100,000+	0.380	0.054	<.0001	0.357	0.044	<.0001
ln (financial assets)	0.108	0.005	<.0001	0.116	0.005	<.0001
Self-employed	0.094	0.039	0.016	0.059	0.034	0.084
Not currently working	−0.240	0.054	<.0001	−0.192	0.055	0.001
Saver	0.056	0.027	0.036	0.028	0.025	0.252
Liquidity-constrained	−0.324	0.030	<.0001	−0.394	0.029	<.0001
Has checking account	0.317	0.063	<.0001	0.313	0.075	<.0001
d1983	−0.436	0.065	<.0001	−1.111	0.077	<.0001
d1992	0.014	0.040	0.731	−0.209	0.037	<.0001
d1995	0.088	0.039	0.026	−0.068	0.037	0.067
d1998	−0.079	0.039	0.040	−0.114	0.037	0.002
Number of observations	21,055			21,055		
−2 log likelihood	13,706.625			15,772.164		

probability of card ownership using the pooled sample of the 1983, 1992, 1995, 1998, and 2001 waves of the SCF. Columns 1–3 list results from a model where the dependent variable is the 0–1 dummy variable capturing ownership of any type of credit card (including store and gas cards). Columns 4–6 list results for ownership of at least one bank-type credit card.

Higher levels of both education and income contribute significantly and importantly to the probability of ownership of either type of credit card, even controlling for other household characteristics. The difference between the coefficients on having a high school degree but no further education and having a college degree or higher[3] implies an effect about as large as the difference between an income between $10,000 and $24,999 and an income of at least $50,000; both of these effects are about twice those of the difference in age from less than 35 to aged 50–65. A higher level of financial wealth also contributes positively to card ownership, although the relative contribution of this variable is less notable than that of increased income or education.

As these are reduced-form regressions, findings are the joint product of demand and supply considerations. On the demand side, education is likely to contribute to credit card ownership by increasing awareness of credit card instruments. Financial resources (both income and wealth) contribute in turn as scale variables determining the size of transactions, even though larger resources imply smaller needs for the borrowing feature of credit cards. Supply-side effects arise from the policy of credit card issuers to condition acceptance of applications on financial resources and to target specifically the more educated segments of the population.

Supply-side effects are likely to contribute to the findings on the race variable. Nonwhite or Hispanic households are found to be significantly less likely to own a credit card, even after controlling for education, income, and financial wealth, and even after including the measure of whether the household reports being liquidity-constrained.[4] More limited targeting of credit cards to minorities by credit card issuers may be the main factor behind this result. On the demand side, if future prospects for minorities are worse than what is implied by included controls, then this would tend to discourage both current spending and assumption of debt that would be difficult to repay later on.

In both regressions, age is a significant factor in predicting card ownership. Even after controlling for income and wealth, households with a head aged 35–49 are less likely to own either type of credit card than are those with a head aged 50–65 (the omitted dummy variable), and households aged under 35 are even less likely to be card owners. More limited participation at young ages is likely to arise from supply-side constraints rather than from demand considerations, as young households are more likely to want to have access to credit lines than their middle-aged counterparts. This is both because they expect to be earning more in the future and because they are less likely to be able to draw on accumulated assets. Households with a head 75 years or older are also significantly less likely to be card owners; indeed, the coefficient for age 75 or more is more than twice that of the coefficient for households aged under 35. More limited transaction needs and less familiarity with credit cards in their working years are likely to combine with less generous offers of credit cards to the elderly to produce this result.

The regressions also include dummy variables for each of the survey years (with 2001 as the omitted dummy variable). The relative sizes of the coefficients on these dummy variables in the bank-type card regression indicate significant year effects consistent with the spread of bank-type card ownership over the nearly twenty-year period from 1983 to 2001 that are not explained by changes in configuration of already included household characteristics. The coefficients on the year dummies in the regression of the broader class of credit cards are smaller and generally are less significant, consistent with the less dramatic spread in ownership of all types of credit cards taken together.

By applying the estimated coefficients from the probit models to characteristics of various "typical" households, we can explore how the probability of card ownership has changed over time for these representative households. Such calculations suggest that, in particular, young households and those with less education benefited from increased availability of bank-type credit cards.[5] For example, a single, nonwhite female aged less than 35 with a high school education and "typical" income and financial assets for that age and education bracket has only a 0.32 estimated probability of owning a bank-type credit card in 1983. By 1992, that estimated probability rises to 0.67, and by 2001, the estimated probability is 0.74.[6] A typical young college-educated white male has a notably higher estimated probability of bank-type credit card ownership in 1983 (0.60) and has a slightly smaller increase in the probability of card ownership by 2001 (to 0.91). For a middle-aged household, the rise in estimated probability of bank-type card ownership over time is less dramatic. For an individual who is 50–64 years old, married, in a college-educated household, the estimated probability of owning a bank-type card in 1983 is already 0.88; by 2001, the probability rises to 0.99.

Similar calculations for a typical elderly household (aged 75 or more) at various degrees of education also reveal a significant increase in the estimated probability of bank-type card ownership by 2001. However, especially for these older households, both year effects and cohort effects are present. For example, the typical married household aged 75 or more with some college education has an estimated probability of bank-type card ownership of 0.93 in 2001, an increase from 0.64 for elderly households in 1983. But the over-75 household in 2001 would likely have been aged 50–64 in 1983, and the estimated probability of bank-type card ownership for the household at that time would have been 0.73. Thus, the higher estimated ownership of elderly households by 2001 may largely reflect the continued ownership of households who had acquired cards when younger.

6.3   Trends in Debit Card Use

In 2001, 38 percent of households without a credit card responded that buying things on an installment plan was a "bad idea," compared with 27 percent of card-owner households. Although credit cards may lead to spending control problems, debit cards—that is, cards that are linked to a specific account and, when used, result in funds being withdrawn—can provide the same benefits of cashless transactions with a form of self-control, as will be discussed later. Credit card ownership has grown rapidly between 1983 and 2001, but debit card use has grown even more rapidly and over a shorter time period. As of the 1992 SCF, less than 10 percent of U.S. households owned a debit card (table 6.3, columns 2 and 6). By 1995, one-third of households reported using a debit card, and by 2001, close to half reported debit card use.[7] As debit cards have become more widespread, households that use debit cards but not credit cards appear increasingly willing to describe borrowing on credit as a "bad idea": In 1995, about 30 percent of households gave that response, and this fraction was about the same across credit card owners, debit card users, and noncard owners. By 2001, 40 percent of nonholders of credit cards who were debit card users gave the "bad idea" response, compared with 27 percent of credit cardholders.

Table 6.4 presents results from a probit regression of the probability of debit card use from the pooled sample of the 1992, 1995, 1998, and 2001 SCFs.[8] In contrast to the results on credit card ownership, younger households are much more likely to use debit cards than are older households, as the coefficient on households under age 35 is positive and significantly larger than that for age 35–49, which in turn is also positive and significantly different from zero. This result is likely to reflect the known tendency of banks to issue debit cards to younger households who have not yet acquired the financial resources or established the credit history needed for issuance of a credit card.

Higher education is associated with an increased likelihood of debit card use, although households with a college degree are no more likely to use a debit card than those with only some college. Households with higher incomes are also significantly more likely to use debit cards, except for those with incomes over $100,000; these households are actually slightly less likely to use debit cards than are households with incomes between $50,000 and $99,999. Greater financial asset holdings are associated with a small but significant effect on debit card use. Because higher education and financial resources tend to encourage provision of credit cards by issuers, these findings do not arise from lack of access to credit cards. Rather, they are likely to reflect a deliberate choice of more educated and well-to-do households to benefit from the ease of using debit cards for payments, as compared to using checks that are less widely acceptable. It is noteworthy that a tendency to use debit cards is observed despite the fact that use of credit cards for payments but not for borrowing usually contributes extra benefits, such as points or opportunities to float. We return to such issues later. Among other demographics, particularly interesting is the finding that although nonwhite/Hispanic households are significantly less likely than white households to have a credit card, they are no less likely to use a debit card.

As with bank-type card ownership, the year dummies are significant, with relative sizes and signs consistent with the spread in debit card use. Performing the same calculations for various "typical" households as we did for credit cards illustrates the adoption of debit cards over the 1990s, particularly by younger households, but also suggests that debit card use has not been universally or exclusively adopted by households who also are very likely to have access to a bank-type credit card. For the young, nonwhite, high school–educated female,

Table 6.3
Bank-type credit card and debit card use, by age, education, and income (1992, 1995, 1998, 2001 SCFs)

	Neither 1	Debit card but no credit card 2	Credit card but no debit card 3	Credit card, no debit card, no balance 4	Credit card, no debit card, has balance 5	Both debit and credit cards 6	Both debit and credit cards, no balance 7	Both debit and credit cards, has balance 8
1992								
All	36.3	1.4	54.6	25.8	28.8	7.8	3.8	4.0
By age								
<35	41.8	2.1	47.5	15.5	32.0	8.5	3.0	5.5
35–54	31.0	1.8	57.6	23.1	34.5	9.7	4.2	5.5
55–64	32.1	0.6	59.9	34.0	25.9	7.5	5.6	1.9
65+	41.7	0.5	54.3	37.6	16.7	3.5	2.9	0.6
By education								
Less than high school	72.5	0.0	26.5	13.3	13.2	1.0	0.6	0.4
High school	42.5	1.0	52.0	22.3	29.7	4.6	1.1	3.5
Some college	26.9	3.1	60.1	26.3	33.8	10.0	4.3	5.7
College degree+	12.6	1.8	71.9	36.8	35.1	13.8	8.1	5.7
By income								
<$10,000	79.9	1.3	16.5	7.8	8.7	2.4	1.3	1.1
$10,000–$24,999	51.5	1.1	43.7	21.0	22.7	3.8	2.4	1.4
$25,000–$49,999	32.5	1.4	59.5	24.0	35.5	6.6	2.0	4.6
$50,000–$99,999	13.8	1.9	72.7	32.5	40.2	11.6	5.5	6.1
$100,000+	5.1	1.4	74.8	50.4	24.4	18.7	11.4	7.3

1995								
All	30.4	3.1	52.0	23.8	28.2	14.6	5.5	9.1
By age								
<35	35.5	5.7	40.8	13.4	27.4	18.0	5.0	13.0
35–54	24.7	3.4	55.1	18.7	36.4	16.8	5.6	11.2
55–64	26.5	1.5	60.0	32.1	27.9	12.0	5.4	6.6
65+	37.4	0.6	54.2	40.4	13.8	7.7	5.7	2.0
By education								
Less than high school	61.8	3.4	30.0	14.6	15.4	4.9	1.8	3.1
High school	35.4	2.9	51.3	20.4	30.9	10.5	3.5	7.0
Some college	24.6	4.1	53.8	20.6	33.2	17.5	5.1	12.4
College degree+	9.8	2.5	65.0	35.0	30.0	22.8	10.0	12.8
By income								
<$10,000	71.7	2.7	22.5	12.1	10.4	3.2	0.6	2.6
$10,000–$24,999	48.0	2.9	40.6	16.9	23.7	8.5	3.3	5.2
$25,000–$49,999	22.7	4.3	57.3	25.6	31.7	15.8	5.0	10.8
$50,000–$99,999	6.7	3.3	67.2	28.4	38.8	22.9	8.5	14.4
$100,000+	2.9	0.2	73.5	44.4	29.1	23.5	13.0	10.5
1998								
All	25.7	7.2	40.7	20.8	19.9	26.5	9.6	16.9
By age								
<35	30.5	11.6	23.9	7.7	16.2	33.9	8.8	25.1
35–54	20.4	6.9	41.8	17.5	24.3	30.8	10.6	20.2
55–64	18.1	6.5	52.6	27.6	25.0	22.8	10.4	12.4
65+	35.3	3.2	49.7	37.5	12.2	11.9	7.7	4.2

Table 6.3
(continued)

	Neither 1	Debit card but no credit card 2	Credit card but no debit card 3	Credit card, no debit card, no balance 4	Credit card, no debit card, has balance 5	Both debit and credit cards 6	Both debit and credit cards, no balance 7	Both debit and credit cards, has balance 8
By education								
Less than high school	58.1	7.2	25.3	11.2	14.1	9.3	2.9	6.4
High school	27.6	9.6	41.6	20.1	21.5	21.2	6.8	14.4
Some college	17.8	8.9	42.0	18.3	23.7	31.4	8.5	22.9
College degree+	7.7	4.1	49.1	29.0	20.1	39.2	16.8	22.4
By income								
<$10,000	68.4	8.1	15.4	6.5	8.9	8.1	2.5	5.6
$10,000–$24,999	43.3	9.1	32.6	15.9	16.7	14.9	5.3	9.6
$25,000–$49,999	20.1	9.0	45.4	21.5	23.9	25.5	8.4	17.1
$50,000–$99,999	6.7	5.7	47.4	22.7	24.7	40.3	13.4	26.9
$100,000+	1.2	0.8	57.1	41.0	16.1	41.0	20.5	20.5
2001								
All	18.2	9.2	33.8	18.9	14.9	38.8	15.9	22.9
By age								
<35	20.8	15.1	17.4	6.1	11.3	46.7	14.3	32.4
35–54	12.0	9.7	34.3	15.3	19.0	44.1	16.3	27.8
55–64	17.3	6.6	42.0	23.8	18.2	34.1	15.6	18.5
65+	28.5	3.4	50.4	37.0	13.4	17.7	12.5	5.2

By education								
Less than high school	43.6	14.9	24.6	12.0	12.6	16.8	6.0	10.8
High school	20.8	9.0	37.3	16.6	20.7	32.9	9.9	23.0
Some college	11.5	10.0	34.0	15.3	18.7	44.6	15.2	29.4
College degree+	4.4	5.4	39.5	26.9	12.6	50.8	24.3	26.5
By income								
<$10,000	59.1	12.5	20.6	7.1	13.5	7.8	2.1	5.7
$10,000–$24,999	32.1	14.2	30.7	15.7	15.0	23.1	8.0	15.1
$25,000–$49,999	13.0	10.4	38.0	18.9	19.1	38.6	10.7	27.9
$50,000–$99,999	6.1	6.2	36.1	19.0	17.1	51.6	21.8	29.8
$100,000+	1.8	2.5	42.3	31.7	10.6	53.5	29.7	23.8

Notes: Variable definitions are as follows:

Debit card: In 1992, household owns a debit card; in 1995, 1998, and 2001, household uses a debit card.

Has balance: In all years, household has a bank-type credit card and had remaining balance after last bill was paid.

Table 6.4
Probit estimation of debit card use in the United States (1992, 1995, 1998, and 2001 SCFs)

	Uses a debit card*		
	Coefficient	Standard error	Significance
Intercept	−0.739	0.078	<.0001
Married	0.037	0.037	0.318
Single female	0.037	0.042	0.388
Number of children	−0.012	0.011	0.290
Nonwhite/Hispanic	−0.008	0.032	0.806
Age <35	0.510	0.037	<.0001
Age 35–49	0.307	0.031	<.0001
Age 65–74	−0.209	0.042	<.0001
Age 75+	−0.658	0.056	<.0001
Less than high school diploma	−0.327	0.046	<.0001
High school diploma or equivalent	−0.229	0.036	<.0001
College degree or higher	0.001	0.032	0.983
Income <$10,000	−0.346	0.057	<.0001
Income $10,000–$24,999	−0.149	0.040	0.000
Income $50,000–$99,999	0.127	0.035	0.000
Income $100,000+	0.036	0.041	0.382
ln J20(financial assets)	0.017	0.005	0.001
Self-employed	−0.240	0.029	<.0001
Not currently working	−0.130	0.058	0.024
Saver	0.462	0.034	<.0001
Liquidity-constrained	−0.042	0.026	0.113
Has checking account	0.213	0.031	<.0001
Buying on credit usually bad idea	0.083	0.024	0.001
d1983	−1.155	0.035	<.0001
d1992	−0.843	0.031	<.0001
d1995	−0.357	0.029	<.0001
d1998	−0.079	0.039	0.040

Notes: * for 1992, dependent variable is debit card ownership rather than use of a credit card; number of observations is 16,952; and −2 log likelihood is 16,470.584.

the estimated probability of having a debit card in 1992 is 0.22, less than the likelihood of having a bank-type card in 1992. By 2001, the estimated probability of using a debit card is 0.65, a sizable increase but still somewhat below that of having a bank-type card. For the single white college-educated male, the estimated probability of using a debit card is 0.21 in 1992 and increases to 0.64 in 2001, remaining well below the probability of bank-type card ownership. For the 50–64-year-old college-educated married household, the probability of using a debit card rises from 0.12 in 1992 and reaches only 0.50 in 2001.

6.4 Credit Card Use over Time and across Demographic Groups

Credit card ownership does not automatically imply that owners are paying the typically high interest rates associated with revolving credit card balances. Although the fraction of households with a bank-type card has increased, the SCF data indicate that the fraction of card holders who at any time revolve a credit card balance has changed relatively little over the past twenty years. In all of the SCF waves, a little over half of all bank-type credit card holders carried a balance on a card after making the most recent payment and before incurring new charges (table 6.1, column 5). The tendency of households to revolve credit card debt in combination with accumulation of assets, financial or real, has received considerable attention in current research on credit card behavior. As a prelude to discussing these theories, we present in this section statistics on the incidence of credit card debt revolving in various demographic groups.

In all years, much greater proportions of credit card debt revolvers are found among younger households than among older households. In contrast to the relation between level of education and card ownership, the relation between education and carrying a credit card balance, conditional on card ownership, is less pronounced, except that smaller proportions of college-educated households revolve a credit card balance than of households with either a high school degree or some college education.

The distribution of credit card revolvers by income shows a changing pattern over the SCF waves. In earlier waves, the proportion of credit card debt revolvers was smaller among cardholder households, who fell in the lowest income ranges, than for households in the next two income ranges. In 1998 and 2001, this relationship was reversed, and a larger fraction of low-income cardholders revolved credit than did middle-income cardholders. These simple statistics do not allow us to identify the reasons for the increase in low-income credit revolvers, but one likely explanation is that low-income households, who nonetheless qualified for credit cards in the earlier waves, were older and, consequently, may have had less need to borrow. Nearly half of cardholder households with incomes under $10,000 in 1983 were over 65, and less than 20 percent were under 35. By 2001, this age pattern had reversed, as households over 65 accounted for less than 30 percent of low-income cardholders, while more than a third were under 35.

In all the SCF waves, a much smaller percentage of cardholder households with incomes over $100,000 than of those with lower incomes carried a credit card balance. These higher-income households may have had less need or incentive to revolve credit card debt, or may have had better access to other sources of borrowing, particularly through tax-advantaged home equity lines. Indeed, over 90 percent of high-income families in 2001 had home equity against which they could borrow, with the median amount equal to about $130,000.[9] Nonetheless, a significant portion of relatively high-income households revolve credit: more than one-third of households in that income range were credit revolvers in all survey years.

6.5   Repeated versus Occasional Credit Revolvers

Simply being observed with credit card debt when the survey is conducted does not necessarily imply that debt revolving is a usual practice. For example, it may have resulted from an oversight or an unusual shock to household finances in the particular month. Establishing the behavioral pattern is important for theoretical analysis. Because the SCF is a cross-section sample for each survey year and not a panel, we cannot observe directly whether a card balance for a given household was a temporary event or whether that household had carried a balance in the previous months. However, it is possible to use self-reported information to help distinguish habitual revolvers from those whose card balance is temporary or accidental. In each of the survey waves, households with credit cards were asked whether they "always or almost always" paid off the card balance in full each month, whether they "sometimes" paid it off in full, or whether they "hardly ever" paid it off. The surveys also collect information on the new charges made on the bank-type card after payment of the last bill. We use these new charges data to get an idea of which households, who do not carry a balance on their credit cards, appear to actively use their cards.[10]

Table 6.1 shows the percentages in each survey year of households who had a bank-type credit card (column 2), those who had a card but had no balance on the card and incurred no new charges in the current month (column 3), those who had no balance but did incur new charges (column 4), and those who had a balance and hardly ever paid off the balance (column 6; the complementary percentage had a balance but claimed they usually or sometimes paid off the balance each month). Bearing in mind the difference in how these variables are constructed in the 1983 and later SCF waves, it nonetheless appears that the fraction of cardholders who had a card but did not actively use it has declined over time, from about 18 percent of cardholders in 1983 to less than 10 percent more recently. In all survey waves, the largest percentages of cardholder households who do not use their cards are among those who are over age 65, have no more than a high school education, and generally have incomes under $25,000. It is possible that these households are passive cardholders who have been issued a card without actively seeking one. Alternatively, they may be concerned about their ability to control their spending, and prefer to consider the card for emergency use only. Additional information available only from the 1998 and 2001 surveys indicates that households in this nonactive user category were about twice as likely to have ever declared bankruptcy as cardholders who did not carry a balance but did record active card use, suggesting some role for concerns about overspending and the social stigma of delinquency and bankruptcy.

A little less than 40 percent of cardholder households from the 1992–2001 waves had no outstanding balance on their credit card but did record new charges during the month (column 4). For the 1983 SCF, a comparable figure is 30 percent of cardholders who had no balance but claimed they used their card "often" or "sometimes." These households appear to use their credit cards for ease of transactions and perhaps to benefit from the float offered by deferring payment until the credit card bill is due. According to the 2001 survey, nearly all of these households report that they "always or almost always" pay off their balance in full each month. In all the SCF waves, the percentages of cardholder households that fall into this category are largest for older households and those with a college degree and at least $100,000 in income: households that presumably have less need to borrow, especially at high rates of interest, which are likely to face less income variability, and are more likely to have a sufficient buffer-stock of assets to tide them over income fluctuations. In 1998 and 2001, these households were also the least likely to have declared bankruptcy in the previous ten years.

About a quarter of all cardholders in 2001—and almost half of those who had a balance outstanding on their card—admitted to "hardly ever" paying off the balance each month (column 6). These fractions are relatively unchanged from earlier waves of the SCF. For the most part, this percentage is not much affected by age, education, or income, with the exception that smaller proportions of households with incomes over $100,000 fall into this category. The fact that this behavior cuts across many demographic and income groups suggests that frequent card revolvers may be motivated by factors other than simply a "need to borrow."[11]

Table 6.5 explores the relation between the percentage of U.S. households who have been denied credit and credit card ownership or card payment status. As explained in chapter 3 and in table 3.5, this "liquidity-constrained" information is taken from a series of questions asked in the SCF on whether the household, in the previous five years, had been turned down for credit or had not received as much credit as requested (and had not received the full credit amount on reapplying), or had not applied for credit because they thought they would be turned down. Roughly one-third of households without a bank-type credit card can be classified as "liquidity-constrained" according to this definition. Interestingly, as the fraction of households with at least one bank-type credit card has grown, so has the fraction of cardholder households that can be classified as "liquidity-constrained," from 12 percent in 1983 to 17 percent in 2001.

For 1992–2001, we can further distinguish the type of credit for which the household was turned down; roughly one-third of liquidity-constrained cardholders apparently had requested additional credit in the form of a credit card. Roughly one-third of the frequent credit card revolvers (those with a balance who hardly ever pay it off in full) can be classified as "liquidity-constrained," but only one-fifth identify the type of credit denied as other than for a credit card. In other words, about 80 percent of frequent card revolvers do not claim that they have been denied another form of credit. Although they do not appear to be revolving credit card debt by default, they may have decided that switching to lower cost forms of credit is too costly in terms of trans-

Table 6.5
Percentage of liquidity-constrained households, by bank-type credit card payment pattern (1983, 1992, 1995, 1998, and 2001 SCFs)

	1983	1992	1995	1998	2001
Percent with no bank-type credit card	57.0	37.7	33.5	32.8	27.4
of which: percent liquidity-constrained	27.9	34.0	39.3	34.0	34.3
of which: percent liquidity-constrained for credit other than credit card		25.6	30.6	27.2	27.3
Percent with bank-type credit card	43.0	62.3	66.5	67.2	72.6
of which: percent liquidity-constrained	12.4	14.8	15.0	16.9	17.0
of which: percent liquidity-constrained for credit other than credit card		10.0	10.1	10.5	11.2
Percent that has bank-type card but no balance and no new charges	18.3	10.7	7.3	8.3	7.2
of which: percent liquidity-constrained	6.9	9.7	10.7	8.8	7.5
of which: percent liquidity-constrained for credit other than credit card		6.6	8.2	6.6	6.7
Percent that has bank-type card; no balance but has new charges	30.5	36.8	36.7	36.9	39.4
of which: percent liquidity-constrained	4.4	5.2	5.6	6.1	6.4
of which: percent liquidity-constrained for credit other than credit card		3.4	3.9	3.9	4.3
Percent with bank-type card; balance but at least sometimes pays balance in full	56.1	51.1	52.7	52.4	54.1
of which: percent liquidity-constrained	10.3	17.7	14.7	18.0	18.5
of which: percent liquidity-constrained for credit other than credit card		11.5	10.1	11.7	13.6
Percent with bank-type card; balance and hardly ever pays balance in full	43.9	48.9	47.3	47.6	45.9
of which: percent liquidity-constrained	16.0	27.5	29.7	33.6	35.2
of which: percent liquidity-constrained for credit other than credit card		19.0	19.3	19.9	20.7

actions or time costs, or they may be unaware that other sources of credit, possibly at more attractive terms, are available, or they may be revolving credit card debt because doing so serves some additional purpose. In section 6.9, we explore a number of such possible purposes.

6.6 Credit Card Balances, Utilization, and Interest Rates

Recording an outstanding balance on the credit card, even if it reflects typical behavior, does not tell us anything about the quantitative importance of the balance, both in absolute terms and in relation to the credit limit faced by the household. Moreover, there is a clear difference between households revolving debt at low introductory rates or at the high interest rates typically associated with credit cards. This section reports typical sizes of credit card balances and the extent to which households in different demographic groups utilize their credit card limits.

6.6.1 Median Amounts Charged

Table 6.6 shows the median card balance of households who revolve credit, by each survey year, and differentiating between households who claim to "almost always" or "sometimes" pay off the balance each month from those who admit that they "hardly ever" pay off the balance.[12] Households who usually revolve credit tend, not surprisingly, to have larger balances on their credit cards than do households who indicate only occasional credit card revolving. The median amount of credit card debt outstanding for occasional revolvers increased from about $700 in 1983 to about $1,000 in 2001. The median balance for credit revolvers has increased by more, and, in recent years, has been more than twice as large: it has grown from $1,244 in 1983 to $2,800 in 2001.

Credit card balances of households that are occasional revolvers show less variation by age, education, and income than do the balances of households who usually revolve credit. Among households who usually carry a balance, the median credit card balance generally has been between $2,500 and $3,000 for households under 65, but only about $1,500 for older households. Although table 6.1 indicates that a smaller percentage of cardholding households with college education revolve credit card debt, those that do revolve their card debt tend to carry larger balances than do households with less education. Similarly, although a smaller percentage of higher-income households usually choose to revolve credit than do lower-income households, those that do typically carry larger balances than do households with lower incomes.

6.6.2 Credit Limits, Utilization Rates, and Interest Rates

To some extent, higher card balances of college-educated and higher-income credit revolvers reflects higher credit limits available to such households. Starting with the 1995 survey, data were collected on the total bank-type card limit—that is, the maximum amount that could be charged on all the bank-type credit cards owned by the household—as well as on the interest rate charged on the card with the highest balance (or the most frequently used card, if the balance on all cards was zero).

Table 6.6 indicates that credit limits are generally highest for households that have demonstrated that they can handle credit card accounts responsibly, and not necessarily those that have the greatest need to borrow. Credit limits tend to be highest for those that carry no balance but actively use their cards, or that carry a balance although they at least sometimes pay the balance in full. The median credit limit for these households ranges from $10,000 to $15,000, depending on the survey year. Households that either do not use their cards actively or usually revolve credit typically have credit limits of under $10,000 and often closer to $7,500. Credit limits are typically larger for households aged 35–64 than for households under 35, and are somewhat larger than for households over 65. Credit limits also tend to be higher for households with higher levels of education and higher income.

Table 6.6 also indicates that between 1995 and 2001, the median card limit declined for younger households, for those with less than high school education, and for those with incomes below $10,000. Multiple factors are likely to have contributed to the decline in the median card limit, but, in part, it may reflect the increase in card ownership by these demographic groups. The typical lower-education or lower-income household, who nonetheless qualified for a bank-type credit card in 1995, may have had a somewhat higher credit rating than the typical such household in 2001.

Columns 8 and 12 show the median credit card utilization rates of households that revolve credit, constructed as the balance remaining on the card after the last payment plus any new charges made on the card over the current month, divided by the available credit limit.[13] For households that carry a balance but at least sometimes pay it off, the median card utilization rate ranges between 15 percent and 20 percent. Households that hardly ever pay off balances have considerably higher median utilization rates of almost 40 percent in 1995 and about 50 percent in 1998 and 2001. These higher utilization rates reflect both the higher card balances of this group as well as the somewhat lower card limits these households face. In both 1998 and 2001, nearly one-tenth of cardholders and nearly one-fifth of those who revolved credit had a card utilization rate of 75 percent or higher. Proportions of such households were greater among the young and among those with less

Table 6.6
Credit card limits and interest rates charged on card with the highest balance (1995, 1998, and 2001 SCFs; all figures in 2001 dollars)

	No balance and no new charges		No balance but has new charges		Carries balance and at least sometimes pays it off in full				Carries balance and hardly ever pays it off			
	Credit limit on bank-type credit cards	Interest rate	Credit limit on bank-type credit cards	Interest rate	Median balance on bank-type cards	Credit limit on bank-type credit cards	Interest rate	Card utilization rate	Median balance on bank-type cards	Credit limit on bank-type credit cards	Interest rate	Card utilization rate
1995	6,679	15.0	13,359	16.0	1,162	13,359	14.0	15.1	2,905	9,351	15.0	38.3
1998	7,620	14.0	10,885	15.0	1,087	10,885	14.8	19.8	3,260	8,708	16.0	50.6
2001	7,500	16.0	15,000	15.0	1,000	10,000	13.0	17.5	2,800	7,500	16.0	50.0
1995												
By age												
<35	2,672	14.0	10,153	15.3	1,045	9,351	14.8	15.9	2,903	6,679	14.0	44.4
35–54	6,679	13.9	13,359	16.0	1,510	13,359	14.0	17.4	3,136	10,153	16.0	39.8
55–64	6,679	14.0	13,359	15.0	1,742	13,359	13.5	15.4	2,671	8,015	14.7	35.3
65+	6,679	16.0	12,023	17.0	325	12,023	14.4	6.7	1,161	9,351	15.9	16.8
By education												
Less than high school	6,679	15.0	8,015	17.0	592	11,622	15.9	10.9	1,510	6,679	15.0	27.3
High school	6,011	15.0	10,019	16.9	1,045	9,351	14.0	17.4	2,439	7,080	16.0	39.8
Some college	6,679	14.5	12,824	16.9	1,161	13,359	14.5	14.5	2,323	9,351	14.0	43.6
College degree+	6,679	14.5	14,694	16.5	1,510	16,030	14.0	14.6	3,252	13,359	15.0	36.9

By income												
<$10,000	3,473	15.0	6,679	18.0	290	8,015	13.9	9.9	1,743	6,679	15.9	57.8
$10,000–$24,999	4,008	17.0	9,351	17.9	813	7,247	16.5	20.6	2,208	6,679	16.0	46.9
$2,5000–$49,999	6,679	14.5	11,355	16.9	1,278	11,622	14.0	17.4	2,324	6,679	15.0	41.7
$50,000–$99,999	6,679	14.5	13,349	14.0	1,278	14,695	14.0	12.7	3,486	12,023	14.7	30.2
$100,000+	6,679	12.0	21,379	16.5	2,324	26,717	14.0	16.8	6,043	26,717	15.0	37.3
1998												
By age												
<35	3,810	12.9	10,885	14.0	1,042	6,531	15.0	28.9	2,498	5,769	16.0	60.9
35–54	9,361	13.5	16,328	14.9	1,194	10,885	14.0	18.6	3,258	10,885	15.9	45.4
55–64	10,885	14.0	13,062	14.9	1,086	14,151	15.0	14.4	3,801	10,885	18.0	57.7
65+	6,531	15.0	10,885	15.0	869	8,164	15.0	14.4	1,629	10,885	15.7	38.9
By education												
Less than high school	5,443	15.0	10,885	15.0	760	6,096	17.0	30.4	2,172	4,898	18.0	56.9
High school	7,293	13.0	8,708	15.0	869	8,164	15.0	17.6	2,715	7,946	16.0	46.8
Some college	10,885	14.9	10,885	14.0	1,194	8,708	14.5	24.9	3,475	7,620	17.0	47.4
College degree+	10,885	14.0	16,328	15.0	1,303	13,062	14.0	16.1	4,778	10,885	15.0	53.3
By income												
<$10,000	2,286	12.0	5,443	14.0	554	5,443	15.0	29.9	2,390	2,939	18.0	66.5
$10,000–$24,999	5,443	15.9	9,797	15.1	652	5,443	15.0	23.2	1,630	4,898	18.0	53.3
$2,5000–$49,999	7,620	12.5	10,885	15.0	1,087	8,164	14.5	22.4	3,260	7,620	16.9	50.9
$50,000–$99,999	13,062	14.0	13,062	14.8	1,087	11,974	14.0	15.4	3,803	11,974	14.0	44.5
$100,000+	10,855	13.0	21,770	15.0	2,173	20,682	14.0	20.0	5,433	16,328	15.9	51.9

Table 6.6
(continued)

	No balance and no new charges		No balance but has new charges		Carries balance and at least sometimes pays it off in full				Carries balance and hardly ever pays it off			
	Credit limit on bank-type credit cards	Interest rate	Credit limit on bank-type credit cards	Interest rate	Median balance on bank-type cards	Credit limit on bank-type credit cards	Interest rate	Card utilization rate	Median balance on bank-type cards	Credit limit on bank-type credit cards	Interest rate	Card utilization rate
2001												
By age												
<35	5,000	14.9	10,000	14.0	1,000	7,000	14.0	31.0	3,000	6,000	16.0	65.5
35–54	8,700	14.0	15,000	15.0	1,200	13,000	13.0	17.3	3,000	8,000	16.0	47.8
55–64	9,600	17.0	20,000	15.6	1,000	10,000	12.0	11.5	3,000	8,000	18.0	48.5
65+	8,000	17.0	15,000	16.0	600	10,000	14.9	8.8	1,500	9,000	14.9	35.4
By education												
Less than high school	6,000	16.3	10,000	16.7	500	5,500	15.0	20.8	1,200	5,000	17.0	47.0
High school	7,700	16.0	10,000	16.0	900	10,000	14.0	15.5	2,000	6,000	16.9	53.0
Some college	5,000	14.9	10,000	14.9	1,000	10,000	13.5	23.3	3,000	7,500	17.0	59.1
College degree+	7,500	15.0	20,000	15.5	1,500	15,000	12.5	16.4	4,000	11,000	14.0	49.5
By income												
<$10,000	8,500	15.0	5,000	15.0	710	2,500	18.0	40.0	1,000	2,500	18.9	50.0
$10,000–$24,999	5,000	17.0	6,500	17.0	500	5,000	14.5	21.2	1,800	4,500	16.0	60.0
$2,5000–$49,999	5,800	15.0	11,000	15.0	800	9,000	14.9	20.0	2,700	6,000	16.9	60.0
$50,000–$99,999	7,700	17.0	15,000	14.0	1,500	15,000	11.0	14.7	4,000	12,000	14.0	50.0
$100,000+	20,000	14.0	25,000	16.7	2,300	20,000	13.0	17.0	4,000	15,000	15.0	31.9

than college-level education. Most high-utilization households "hardly ever" pay off their card balance, and more than half (and over 70 percent of such young households) can be classified as "liquidity-constrained." Although the cross-section nature of the SCF prevents us from investigating the relation between current high card utilization rates and future default or bankruptcy filings—a topic we consider in more detail in section 6.9—greater proportions of high-utilization households exhibit indicators of financial difficulty: Nearly one-fifth of high-utilization households in 2001 indicated that, in the previous year, they had been two months or more behind in any type of installment loan payment, compared with only about 5 percent for all households.[14]

6.6.3 Average Interest Rates, New Charges, and Interest Expenses of Revolvers

Although low introductory or "teaser" interest rates of 1–5 percent can make the interest costs of carrying a balance on a credit card negligible, table 6.6 indicates that most habitual credit card revolvers pay relatively high rates of interest. For the typical household that sometimes paid off the balance in full, the median interest rate charged was 13–15 percent, depending on the survey year. For households that usually revolve debt, the typical interest rate was 15–16 percent, implying an annual interest rate cost of about $400, if the balance during the survey month and new charges recorded are representative of the normal monthly balance and charges. In 2001, less than 4 percent of frequent revolvers had interest rates of 5 percent or less on the bank-type card with the largest balance; nearly one-fifth faced interest rates above 20 percent.

6.7 Asset Holdings by Card Payment Patterns and Demographic Groups

In this section, we explore asset holdings of card owners and credit revolvers to highlight the puzzles of simultaneous accumulation of assets with high-cost credit card debt that have motivated a lot of recent credit card research reviewed in section 6.9. In all survey years, the highest levels of median liquid assets (defined as amounts held in checking accounts, savings accounts, money market deposit accounts, and call accounts at brokerages), median financial assets, and median total net worth are for those households that used their bank-type credit card to make new charges, but did not have a balance outstanding (table 6.7). This relative ranking holds for all survey years and for virtually all demographic subgroups, and, in fact, has become more pronounced over time.[15]

The next highest median asset levels are held by those who have a card but did not use it to make new charges. On average, their median asset holdings are about one-third to one-half as large as those of active card users without a balance. Households who have a balance but at least sometimes pay their balance off have asset levels a bit lower than those of card owners but nonusers, indicating that these households are able to accumulate financial assets. Households that hardly ever pay the card balance off have notably lower wealth levels, with median wealth averaging about half as large as for "sometimes" revolvers, and about one-fifth as large as for those who use cards but do not carry a balance. In all survey years, households without bank-type credit cards have the lowest amount of assets. The decline in median net worth of these households between 1983 and 2001 reflects the previously noted spread of card ownership to households with lower incomes.

6.8   Coexistence of Low-Interest Liquid Assets and High-Interest Credit Card Debt

Gross and Souleles (2002a) point out that over 90 percent of households with credit card debt in the 1995 SCF have some very liquid assets in checking and savings accounts, which usually yield at most 1–2 percent. One-third of credit card borrowers have more than one month's worth of gross total household income in liquid assets. Such large holdings of low-interest liquid assets are difficult to explain on the basis of transaction needs, and arbitrage considerations would call for them to be used to pay down, if not completely pay off, high-interest credit card debt.[16]

In our tabulations here, we take a more conservative stance that probably understates the puzzle. Table 6.8 shows the median card balances, liquid assets, financial assets, and net worth for households that carried a balance, differentiating between households that had liquid assets no larger than the credit card balance, and those that had liquid assets greater than the credit card balance (and at least $1,000 and at least half of total monthly income). Households that carry a credit card balance but appear to have more than enough liquid financial assets to pay off the balance in full are remarkably numerous. In 1995, 39 percent of credit card revolvers fell into this category; about 45 percent can be so classified in 1998 and 2001. In all years, the typical household that was a high-liquid-asset revolver had an unpaid bank-type credit card balance of about $1,000, while median liquid assets were six to eight times larger. These households also have fairly substantial holdings of total financial assets and net worth. Although some of these households may be accidental credit revolvers in the survey month, the majority claims only to "sometimes" pay of the balance in full, and about one-third admit to "hardly ever" paying off their card balance.

These households could potentially have greater liquid asset needs than do other households, but this seems unlikely. In comparison with assets held by other survey households on table 6.7, their liquid asset holdings appear somewhat larger than those that have a card but do not actively use it, but generally somewhat smaller than those of households that use cards but do not carry a balance.

6.9   Theories of Credit Card Behavior

Before reviewing theories of credit card behavior, it is useful to examine whether puzzling observed tendencies can be attributed simply to ignorance or limited understanding of the terms and conditions of credit card accounts. If so, it should be possible to restore optimal behavior through better information.

6.9.1   Are Households Unaware of Credit Card Terms?

Luckily, survey data make it possible to seek an answer to this question. In January 2000, the Credit Research Center sponsored a survey of nearly five hundred households (representative of the forty-eight contiguous U.S. states) that investigated consumers' attitudes toward credit cards. A more recent such survey was conducted in 2001, and their main findings are reported in Durkin (2000 for the older survey; 2002 for the newer). Durkin (2000) also contrasts them with findings from earlier SCFs in 1970 and 1977. We report Durkin's main findings in this section. Which terms of credit card agreements are regarded as important by consumers when opening a new or replacement card account? The January 2001 survey found that cost items predominate, mainly annual percentage rates and finance charges, as indicated by responses of about two-thirds of consumers. This percentage is not influenced by whether respondents did or did not possess a bank-type credit card. Three-fifths of those without cards thought that these were

Table 6.7
Median liquid assets, total financial assets, and bank-type credit card balances of U.S. households by credit card payment patterns (1983, 1992, 1995, 1998, and 2001 SCFs; all figures in 2001 dollars)

	Noncardholders			Cardholders with no balance and no new charges		
	Total liquid assets	Total finan-cial assets	Net worth	Total liquid assets	Total finan-cial assets	Net worth
1983	889	2,488	27,929	7,247	23,902	133,136
1992	252	884	13,330	3,787	25,246	133,425
1995	277	1,158	15,603	3,699	22,538	111,246
1998	435	1,401	13,661	4,278	33,961	117,776
2001	400	1,300	12,200	5,000	25,400	116,000
1983						
By age						
<35	480	968	6,140	5,247	10,766	29,850
35–54	967	3,199	48,506	7,002	20,081	138,611
55–64	2,388	6,719	71,448	7,642	43,786	184,441
65+	1,777	7,748	62,035	11,995	57,756	187,007
By education						
Less than high school	467	1,155	22,082	3,554	12,316	101,270
High school	1,022	3,554	32,119	6,398	23,902	128,858
Some college	1,066	2,844	17,423	8,352	22,557	119,011
College degree+	2,799	8,886	57,228	10,307	38,422	154,125
By income						
<$10,000	44	203	3,643			
$10,000–$24,999	467	1,066	10,570	3,879	8,823	86,165
$25,000–$49,999	1,422	3,764	35,761	7,528	22,557	93,280
$50,000–$99,999	3,377	19,255	111,089	8,175	27,719	138,220
$100,000+	20,661	106,760	345,287	38,826	159,531	382,833
1992						
By age						
<35	88	379	2,714	3,534	9,846	33,200
35–54	189	732	11,234	3,534	22,216	112,850
55–64	252	884	27,543	2,525	31,558	167,255
65+	1,262	4,418	53,080	5,302	34,208	148,825

Cardholders with no balance but made new charges				Cardholders who carry balance but "almost always" or "sometimes" pay off in full				Cardholders who carry balance but hardly ever pay off in full		
Total liquid assets	Total financial assets	Net worth	Median balance on bank-type cards	Total liquid assets	Total financial assets	Net worth	Median balance on bank-type cards	Total liquid assets	Total financial assets	Net worth
12,706	54,941	214,701	711	3,821	15,994	101,096	1,244	2,133	8,928	56,782
11,108	76,407	220,524	800	3,042	18,871	95,910	1,800	1,515	7,485	43,297
8,668	73,393	211,280	1,162	2,427	21,960	80,079	2,905	1,618	10,460	48,763
10,885	96,223	244,477	1,087	4,071	30,478	97,682	3,260	2,177	14,151	42,452
13,020	125,300	319,250	1,000	4,000	32,500	101,260	2,800	1,500	8,550	39,430
5,420	15,822	48,915	533	2,133	7,508	44,108	1,066	1,777	6,131	34,510
12,440	50,114	217,342	711	4,414	21,325	114,543	1,244	3,021	10,041	75,177
17,327	114,737	300,742	711	3,821	22,392	156,627	889	1,422	9,392	106,507
19,193	115,898	301,790	576	5,198	34,241	110,534	970	613	613	53,578
7,338	31,878	139,574	533	1,822	5,893	100,956	1,066	1,066	6,780	39,461
8,886	32,992	189,262	551	3,243	9,774	78,070	1,155	1,654	8,379	60,750
11,516	52,139	210,879	711	4,002	26,577	123,186	1,422	2,088	5,047	53,594
18,660	80,503	272,114	800	6,131	23,509	117,806	1,244	3,465	11,409	67,278
3,865	19,815	87,098	622	1,550	4,883	38,604	889	613	1,955	22,658
7,286	23,328	120,978	800	2,342	8,352	71,536	1,244	1,599	5,278	41,501
13,506	57,223	196,465	889	4,530	23,591	117,806	1,066	2,843	12,664	81,864
34,654	267,458	850,652	800	14,750	57,409	324,230	4,442	8,886	26,138	115,208
5,239	23,416	66,662	1,010	2,121	5,491	24,668	1,389	1,250	3,724	12,232
10,565	92,779	236,138	1,010	4,418	25,498	109,631	2,525	1,856	10,351	64,125
13,822	131,910	332,237	884	3,320	63,999	181,064	2,525	2,272	10,351	95,938
15,148	94,420	268,807	884	3,282	19,793	138,790	1,641	947	2,525	64,213

Table 6.7
(continued)

	Noncardholders			Cardholders with no balance and no new charges		
	Total liquid assets	Total financial assets	Net worth	Total liquid assets	Total financial assets	Net worth
By education						
Less than high school	126	265	10,704	2,146	13,254	89,245
High school	379	1,010	12,143	4,166	21,068	134,877
Some college	417	1,893	16,284	3,030	19,882	103,698
College degree+	985	4,355	31,558	5,807	35,445	151,615
By income						
<$10,000	13	126	1,893	947	4,671	38,412
$10,000–$24,999	153	631	10,843	3,787	15,021	103,130
$25,000–$49,999	631	2,903	23,100	3,661	22,216	133,425
$50,000–$99,999	2,146	13,393	70,891	6,690	39,131	138,853
$100,000+	12,623	30,926	177,984	7,826	96,541	257,295
1995						
By age						
<35	58	474	4,843	1,040	8,356	30,282
35–54	231	1,791	17,164	4,392	27,369	128,063
55–64	347	705	26,237	9,246	41,840	150,138
65+	925	2,196	55,733	5,548	23,232	131,414
By education						
Less than high school	59	347	12,275	4,623	21,036	121,914
High school	347	1,422	18,493	2,485	22,885	110,541
Some college	254	1,156	9,189	4,276	27,369	102,404
College degree+	1,156	7,513	31,022	3,999	23,116	103,213
By income						
<$10,000	0	69	2,520	2,312	8,091	76,664
$10,000–$24,999	347	1,156	13,338	3,467	14,101	102,404
$25,000–$49,999	578	3,467	26,930	2,890	34,443	131,414
$50,000–$99,999	2,219	18,527	59,061	3,699	21,960	110,541
$100,000+	5,652	34,096	112,979	22,307	96,278	415,048

Cardholders with no balance but made new charges			Cardholders who carry balance but "almost always" or "sometimes" pay off in full				Cardholders who carry balance but hardly ever pay off in full			
Total liquid assets	Total financial assets	Net worth	Median balance on bank-type cards	Total liquid assets	Total financial assets	Net worth	Median balance on bank-type cards	Total liquid assets	Total financial assets	Net worth
6,943	40,520	164,478	1,262	1,389	11,840	108,659	1,262	568	1,262	44,054
9,467	61,348	200,581	631	2,525	15,148	83,249	2,020	1,452	6,059	35,269
10,730	81,671	235,545	884	2,777	13,254	88,614	1,893	1,553	6,690	39,384
11,992	93,789	247,663	1,010	4,166	28,528	108,798	3,157	2,146	11,361	58,482
2,777	17,925	23,605	1,010	631	3,408	54,001	1,010	454	871	16,991
4,393	21,459	89,484	947	1,264	4,418	35,029	1,262	619	2,083	32,264
7,952	54,304	179,499	757	2,272	11,752	74,072	1,893	1,262	5,945	30,030
10,730	72,230	210,388	1,010	3,787	25,498	108,621	2,651	2,651	13,393	71,875
27,771	266,598	746,273	1,262	16,284	81,545	280,736	5,049	11,234	56,804	206,108
4,623	23,347	59,177	1,045	1,618	8,830	31,785	2,903	1,214	5,005	11,523
8,091	78,363	211,280	1,510	3,340	31,345	119,105	3,136	1,734	12,251	64,089
9,246	123,566	319,579	1,742	2,543	24,561	142,367	2,671	1,502	13,349	77,670
12,483	86,801	251,502	325	4,623	36,754	123,416	1,161	1,849	10,749	79,866
4,623	21,960	134,951	592	2,312	11,015	87,517	1,510	982	3,814	36,662
6,935	61,489	193,193	1,045	1,734	14,898	92,741	2,439	1,156	6,785	43,805
8,669	64,759	205,964	1,161	2,312	18,435	83,911	2,323	1,803	9,709	41,678
10,402	108,622	255,432	1,734	3,571	31,149	90,233	3,252	2,219	19,140	58,368
1,734	7,166	20,920	290	1,040	3,930	29,253	1,743	566	1,075	4,300
3,930	23,232	111,766	813	1,248	4,219	48,312	2,208	647	2,890	33,981
6,588	54,091	185,275	1,278	1,907	18,493	67,984	2,324	1,271	8,322	35,830
11,026	95,931	244,452	1,278	3,363	37,564	113,731	3,486	2,658	21,209	61,812
26,583	310,332	724,455	2,324	10,402	85,529	268,550	6,043	6,184	58,541	169,336

Table 6.7
(continued)

	Noncardholders			Cardholders with no balance and no new charges		
	Total liquid assets	Total finan-cial assets	Net worth	Total liquid assets	Total finan-cial assets	Net worth
1998						
By age						
<35	174	620	3,374	2,286	12,344	29,368
35–54	327	1,306	15,587	6,313	35,071	117,231
55–64	631	2,057	28,911	6,531	64,222	139,219
65+	1,306	5,029	72,930	4,354	34,832	146,948
By education						
Less than high school	109	490	8,708	2,286	30,228	91,358
High school	545	2,188	16,491	2,634	13,269	111,125
Some college	653	1,961	13,693	10,493	37,009	134,854
College degree+	1,089	10,450	46,098	6,096	85,121	187,331
By income						
<$10,000	1	131	1,959	762	1,056	91,358
$10,000–$24,999	327	795	6,640	2,286	15,892	80,549
$25,000–$49,999	980	5,660	29,477	4,191	29,934	100,501
$50,000–$99,999	1,959	16,437	58,942	8,164	47,132	176,555
$100,000+	12,572	291,577	378,852	17,971	174,444	279,702
2001						
By age						
<35	150	500	4,140	2,700	10,900	78,030
35–54	300	1,200	10,430	4,000	22,700	155,600
55–64	560	2,000	40,800	8,000	40,000	174,900
65+	1,500	4,400	66,000	10,901	25,400	114,840
By education						
Less than high school	100	300	8,400	4,500	17,500	112,500
High school	500	1,400	15,100	6,000	22,000	90,700
Some college	660	2,300	10,250	4,000	22,700	155,600
College degree+	1,600	12,670	41,500	8,000	43,900	179,000

Cardholders with no balance but made new charges			Cardholders who carry balance but "almost always" or "sometimes" pay off in full				Cardholders who carry balance but hardly ever pay off in full			
Total liquid assets	Total finan-cial assets	Net worth	Median balance on bank-type cards	Total liquid assets	Total finan-cial assets	Net worth	Median balance on bank-type cards	Total liquid assets	Total finan-cial assets	Net worth
4,354	23,610	54,654	1,042	2,395	8,545	31,828	2,498	1,252	4,572	8,675
10,885	93,938	258,519	1,194	4,898	38,206	118,973	3,258	2,286	23,839	66,594
13,062	138,240	316,862	1,086	5,225	47,415	148,744	3,801	3,048	23,457	74,203
12,953	130,337	278,656	869	3,472	24,165	114,510	1,629	2,068	9,579	85,382
7,837	40,819	152,259	760	1,850	6,967	67,552	2,172	1,089	11,974	31,817
9,361	83,325	206,869	869	2,482	21,389	78,274	2,715	1,742	9,426	43,257
9,034	72,385	214,761	1,194	4,354	30,478	97,040	3,475	2,068	13,334	41,766
12,300	141,505	294,004	1,303	5,987	53,337	125,221	4,778	3,113	25,374	50,561
2,504	8,708	92,991	554	1,143	2,612	21,639	2,390	218	958	8,588
3,461	40,819	152,259	652	1,089	2,743	30,707	1,630	1,034	1,948	11,135
8,817	42,854	173,126	1,087	2,504	19,038	79,069	3,260	1,306	9,165	28,192
11,429	114,510	265,812	1,087	5,606	53,380	142,463	3,803	3,277	31,131	76,739
27,212	350,323	756,834	2,173	12,017	124,415	287,689	5,433	6,966	115,381	204,856
6,000	32,505	69,550	1,000	2,190	7,590	19,390	3,000	1,420	4,350	7,700
12,700	114,500	297,000	1,200	4,350	45,500	133,100	3,000	2,000	13,320	53,620
17,000	283,300	542,002	1,000	5,360	40,740	177,379	3,000	1,500	13,150	76,580
17,200	179,600	405,300	600	7,500	26,700	147,700	1,500	1,110	4,150	74,000
11,100	46,000	196,820	500	2,000	9,000	59,200	1,200	1,000	2,800	23,110
7,000	69,700	197,800	900	3,000	23,330	87,800	2,000	1,200	6,800	34,800
12,400	122,000	304,600	1,000	3,700	19,320	71,070	3,000	1,520	9,200	34,050
17,200	218,300	465,300	1,500	5,820	60,950	178,001	4,000	2,400	22,460	69,500

Table 6.7
(continued)

	Noncardholders			Cardholders with no balance and no new charges		
	Total liquid assets	Total financial assets	Net worth	Total liquid assets	Total financial assets	Net worth
By income						
<$10,000	10	40	1,600	1,100	1,110	60,390
$10,000–$24,999	230	700	7,800	3,400	10,901	79,190
$25,000–$49,999	1,000	4,610	23,300	7,000	31,000	110,600
$50,000–$99,999	1,600	15,000	70,750	6,200	32,400	193,400
$100,000+	4,950	98,200	249,100	21,100	127,420	467,270

the most important terms, compared to slightly more than half of cardholders. The latter assign higher importance than do nonholders to annual fees, fixed versus variable rates, and frequent flier miles.

Respondents in the 2000 survey are "aware" of the annual percentage rates (APRs) charged on their revolving credit card debt. If we consider as "unaware" only those who state explicitly that they do not know the rate, then 91 percent of holders of bank-type credit cards are aware of their APR. If we also eliminate those who say that they know their rate but report too low an APR (i.e., an APR below 7.9 percent in 2000), then the proportion of aware holders falls to 85 percent.[17] Although awareness varies slightly across demographic groups, it exceeds 80 percent for all groups using either definition. Among groups with highest awareness of APRs were those with more than $1,500 in revolving debt and those reporting that they hardly ever pay off their balance in full. A major factor promoting awareness was the introduction of the Truth in Lending Act of 1969, which requires credit card companies to provide customers with written statements of credit costs, both at the opening of the account and on each monthly bill. After its introduction, awareness jumped from 27 percent of cardholders to 63 percent in 1970 and to 71 percent in 1977.

Not only are holders of bank-type credit cards aware of the terms, but two-thirds of them report that information about credit terms is

Cardholders with no balance but made new charges			Cardholders who carry balance but "almost always" or "sometimes" pay off in full				Cardholders who carry balance but hardly ever pay off in full			
Total liquid assets	Total financial assets	Net worth	Median balance on bank-type cards	Total liquid assets	Total financial assets	Net worth	Median balance on bank-type cards	Total liquid assets	Total financial assets	Net worth
2,000	14,540	67,000	710	645	800	14,900	1,000	250	650	6,300
4,400	37,900	137,400	500	1,500	4,500	41,280	1,800	720	1,400	9,975
7,300	63,820	197,420	800	2,500	13,650	49,700	2,700	1,400	6,590	24,100
12,200	118,900	304,100	1,500	5,500	49,000	130,000	4,000	2,950	29,000	74,240
38,500	452,200	980,500	2,300	10,300	148,300	382,129	4,000	6,430	79,300	189,700

easy to obtain; only 7 percent think that it is very difficult. Despite such responses, slightly less than half of bank-type card holders in 2000 agree that card issuers give holders enough information to enable them to use their credit cards wisely. Part of the additional information the rest ask for is already provided on the statements.

Interestingly, but perhaps not surprisingly, households are much more willing to declare negative attitudes regarding the use of credit cards made by others than by themselves. Holders of bank-type credit cards declared in 2000 that "other consumers" are confused about credit card practices, but approximately 90 percent of them declare satisfaction with their own card companies and say that it is easy to get another card if they are not treated fairly. In the 2001 survey, two-thirds respond that useful information on credit terms was very easy or somewhat easy to obtain for themselves, but fewer than half say so for others. The same percentages apply also to the question of whether credit card companies provided sufficient information to use credit cards wisely. All in all, these findings suggest that credit card holders are well-informed about the terms they face, especially if they revolve credit card debt, though they do not give much credit to their card issuers for providing the information, and they have little faith that others are equally well informed.

Table 6.8
Median liquid assets, total financial assets, and bank-type credit card balances of U.S. households that carried a credit card balance, by high liquid asset holding (1995, 1998, and 2001 SCFs; all figures in 2001 dollars)

	Households with bank-type card balance greater than liquid assets					Households with liquid assets greater than bank-type card balance (and at least $1,000 and at least one-half monthly income)					
	Percent of card-holders with balance	Median balance on bank-type cards	Liquid assets	Total financial assets	Total net worth	Percent of card-holders with balance	Median balance on bank-type cards	Liquid assets	Total financial assets	Total net worth	Percent that "hardly ever pay off" in full
1995	61.0	2,440	982	7,478	48,140	39.0	1,162	6,588	36,986	104,854	35.5
1998	53.0	3,260	1,089	10,341	38,391	47.0	1,087	7,837	37,009	107,587	33.8
2001	55.5	2,500	1,000	6,100	36,295	44.5	1,000	8,000	40,710	127,400	30.8
1995											
By age											
<35	67.7	2,324	867	3,699	12,367	32.3	1,081	4,635	18,435	45,423	35.5
35–54	60.3	3,138	1,156	11,292	68,851	39.7	1,394	7,975	42,649	123,093	34.9
55–64	58.2	2,324	809	7,165	88,176	41.8	1,743	6,993	44,787	159,385	35.8
65+	48.2	1,162	670	5,779	79,866	51.8	383	6,599	49,410	137,829	36.1
By education											
Less than high school	60.2	1,743	462	1,676	22,249	39.8	825	3,930	13,292	87,517	43.3
High school	67.3	2,092	751	5,328	45,585	32.7	1,162	6,761	37,564	113,765	31.1
Some college	60.5	2,324	982	6,704	40,834	39.5	1,046	5,779	36,986	95,226	41.1
College degree+	55.6	3,486	1,387	16,990	60,471	44.4	1,511	8,091	42,996	119,510	31.2

By income											
<$10,000	70.2	1,511	347	774	6,068	29.8	151	3,583	8,333	27,589	30.2
$10,000–$24,999	67.2	2,092	462	1,167	15,846	32.8	709	4,276	13,292	80,328	38.8
$2,5000–$49,999	63.8	2,557	925	7,166	36,489	36.2	1,162	4,623	24,561	83,067	37.7
$50,000–$99,999	57.4	3,138	1,503	16,644	72,550	42.6	1,511	7,859	51,433	134,951	34.7
$100,000+	45.0	5,810	3,514	47,041	169,336	55.0	2,440	21,960	134,304	337,378	23.4
1998											
By age											
<35	41.7	2,608	1,001	3,314	8,675	58.3	1,087	4,441	11,538	31,512	40.1
35–54	38.0	3,803	1,306	18,221	51,160	62.0	1,304	8,817	57,146	127,790	36.6
55–64	33.1	3,803	1,393	15,326	94,808	66.9	1,195	8,599	72,821	192,621	24.3
65+	21.0	3,368	577	2,112	64,232	79.0	760	6,749	35,921	130,903	21.0
By education											
Less than high school	61.8	2,282	435	2,112	31,022	38.2	761	5,443	22,314	98,455	41.7
High school	56.8	3,260	1,089	66,966	39,077	43.2	761	4,844	27,757	96,267	36.3
Some college	53.9	3,477	1,143	12,137	34,299	46.1	1,195	7,717	37,009	104,768	34.8
College degree+	46.9	4,781	1,524	20,028	47,676	53.1	1,521	9,666	63,133	125,221	29.1
By income											
<$10,000	72.3	1,956	218	675	9,285	27.7	272	2,558	5,769	15,402	16.5
$10,000–$24,999	57.1	1,956	381	925	5,693	42.9	652	3,048	9,579	48,003	34.7
$2,5000–$49,999	57.4	3,585	925	6,390	30,141	42.6	1,087	5,769	23,457	81,692	36.9
$50,000–$99,999	48.1	4,346	2,068	26,668	67,106	51.9	1,304	9,002	61,609	150,344	34.3
$100,000+	40.7	6,084	4,572	90,346	208,557	59.3	2,173	17,416	155,797	303,006	24.7

Table 6.8
(continued)

	Households with bank-type card balance greater than liquid assets					Households with liquid assets greater than bank-type card balance (and at least $1,000 and at least one-half monthly income)					
	Percent of card-holders with balance	Median balance on bank-type cards	Liquid assets	Total financial assets	Total net worth	Percent of card-holders with balance	Median balance on bank-type cards	Liquid assets	Total financial assets	Total net worth	Percent that "hardly ever pay off" in full
2001											
By age											
<35	66.6	2,500	950	2,850	7,180	33.4	1,000	5,000	19,420	38,350	35.5
35–54	55.5	2,600	1,200	11,500	53,960	44.5	1,500	8,000	52,400	146,800	31.2
55–64	44.1	3,080	600	6,100	43,260	55.9	1,200	10,000	75,720	196,730	30.2
65+	41.4	2,000	900	1,880	76,500	58.6	400	8,000	37,550	147,700	22.8
By education											
Less than high school	60.6	1,000	500	1,100	17,350	39.4	700	4,600	12,300	80,750	14.7
High school	60.0	2,000	910	5,030	36,800	40.0	700	7,100	33,630	96,720	28.8
Some college	59.7	2,900	1,000	5,750	22,840	40.3	800	8,000	27,950	121,250	22.3
College degree+	46.7	4,000	1,500	16,560	54,850	53.3	1,700	9,700	74,300	195,910	34.2
By income											
<$10,000	87.3	1,000	245	510	6,410	12.7	480	1,580	6,100	61,850	13.8
$10,000–$24,999	60.0	1,700	500	1,000	9,975	40.0	510	3,300	10,150	5,010	29.4
$2,5000–$49,999	58.1	2,900	870	3,300	17,350	41.9	700	5,300	25,360	81,860	41.2
$50,000–$99,999	51.7	4,000	2,000	22,910	69,400	48.3	1,200	9,300	58,600	169,150	28.1
$100,000+	40.4	4,000	4,000	79,300	223,500	59.6	2,500	17,200	165,000	399,050	19.5

6.9.2   Stickiness of Credit Card Interest Rates

In his seminal 1991 paper, Ausubel documents considerable stickiness of credit card rates despite extensive competition in the credit card market. This is all the more puzzling in view of the evidence presented earlier that credit card holders are generally aware of annual percentage rates, and they consider them very important. He points to the low concentration and considerable breadth of the industry, its freedom from interstate banking and branch banking restrictions, the nonresponsiveness of interest rates to fluctuations in the cost of funds to the banks, and to his finding that returns from the credit card business were several times higher than the ordinary rate of return in banking during the period he examines (1983–1988).[18] Ausubel considers search and switch costs that can make it difficult for consumers to move to different, lower-cost providers of credit cards.[19] He bases his adverse-selection theory on a class of consumers who do not intend to revolve credit card debt but find themselves doing so; and on another class of consumers that fully intend to borrow but are bad credit risks. In such a world, good customers exhibit some irrationality and are not particularly responsive to lower interest rates. Banks, on the other hand, do not want to lower interest rates, fearing that they will draw disproportionate numbers of bad risks. Thus, interest rates end up being sticky.[20]

Brito and Hartley (1995) argue that observed revolving of credit card debt need not be attributed to consumer irrationality, but to the ease of borrowing on the credit card compared to transactions costs involved in other types of loans. They construct a model in which relatively small costs of arranging for other types of loans can induce rational individuals to borrow on high-interest credit cards. Calem and Mester (1995) use data from the 1989 SCF to test for the presence of search and switch costs. Controlling for demand and for access to credit, they find that the level of credit card debt is greater among consumers who tend not to shop around for the best terms on loans or deposits. This tendency not to shop around can be attributed perhaps to an irrational belief that debt revolving is likely to be temporary, but it can also arise simply from higher search costs.

Calem and Mester also find that households with higher outstanding balances are more likely to be denied credit and to have experienced payment problems. Thus, customers with high balances face greater costs of switching to a provider that offers more attractive credit terms, because providers are likely to interpret their high balances as a signal of lack of creditworthiness. There may also be good credit risks who have been granted privileges by their existing credit card providers, such as large credit lines, and who therefore face switch costs of a different kind. More recent studies corroborate the view that the size of credit card debt influences the probability of declaring bankruptcy or delinquency. Domowitz and Sartain (1999) find that households with more credit card debt are more likely to file for bankruptcy. Gross and Souleles (2002b), who do not use survey data but an administrative set of credit card accounts, find that, even after controlling for account credit scores used by the credit card companies, accounts with larger balances and purchases, or smaller payments, are more likely to default.

Based on these findings, credit card issuers would be justified to regard high balances and purchases as bad signals, even after taking credit scores into account, despite the potential to earn more on consumers revolving large amounts of debt.[21] In the presence of search or switch costs, issuers would find that lowering interest rates does not attract many consumers whom revolve credit card debt but are good credit risks, and this could contribute to the stickiness of interest rates. Clearly, understanding the reasons and motives underlying bankruptcy and delinquency is central to understanding credit card behavior. It is to this that we now turn.

6.9.3 Strategic Default as an Explanation for Debt Revolving

In the late 1990s, there was a dramatic increase in the number of households filing for personal bankruptcy. Chapter 7 (especially section 7.2) contains a detailed discussion of U.S. bankruptcy law; hence, that material will not be discussed here. But we will discuss how it might impact credit card usage.

Recently, Dunn and Kim (2004) utilized Ohio data in the late 1990s from the Ohio Survey Research Center.[22] When the number of missed minimum credit card payments in the last six months is regressed on household financial and socioeconomic variables, three financial variables have a significant positive effect: the ratio of the total amount of required minimum payments on credit cards to household income; the number of credit cards on which the consumer has exhausted the credit limit; and the credit card utilization rate, measured as a percentage of the sum total of credit lines available to the consumer. Interestingly, education, income, and home ownership status are not found to influence default in the presence of these three financial variables. Such findings seem to provide support to the notion that ability to repay is an important factor behind delinquencies. The sample is then divided into "convenience users" who pay off the balance each month, borrowers with no default history, and borrowers with default history. Using tabulations, the authors find that the number of credit cards held increases on average from 2.5 to 4.6 as we move from convenience users to default borrowers, while the total credit line per card halves, from about $10,000 to about $5,000. The sum total of credit lines also drops from about $21,000 to about $18,000. Although no conclusive case can be made yet, these tabulations are consistent with "Ponzi scheme" practices of obtaining additional cards with small credit lines in order to pay off old credit card debt.

The widespread coexistence of credit card debt with substantial liquid assets in Survey of Consumer Finances data could derive, at least for some households, from strategic bankruptcy motives. If a household holds liquid assets and declares bankruptcy, it can take advantage of bankruptcy law provisions that exempt some assets from seizure, up to an exemption level. Thus, households who plan to declare bankruptcy have no incentive to pay off credit card debt with liquid assets. As pointed out by Lehnert and Maki (2002), a household can discharge a large part of unsecured debt based on Chapter 7 bankruptcy laws and may convert liquid assets to a bankruptcy-exempt asset category in its state of residence, such as housing for example. Lopes (2003) calibrates and solves a life-cycle model with uncollateralized borrowing and default, and finds that some consumers borrow with the intention of defaulting in the near future. Education matters for the incidence of default, because it affects the slope and level of the earnings profile, and hence the value attached to the loss of credit availability and stigma associated with bankruptcy in the model. Because of the exemption limit, savings can coexist with borrowing. Average simulated savings for those who borrow are higher in cases where the probability of default is higher (e.g., they monotonically drop with education).

As to empirical evidence, Lehnert and Maki (2002) find in Consumer Expenditure Survey data that households living in states with high bankruptcy exemption levels are 1–4.5 percentage points more likely to have both liquid assets and total unsecured debt in excess of a threshold ranging between $2,000 and $5,000 (in 1996 dollars). Lopes regresses liquid financial wealth for debt revolvers on exemption level for the household's region and on demographics, and finds a positive and significant coefficient on exemption level in the 1998 SCF. There is also evidence that links bankruptcy law, and its application, to the incidence of default. Fay, Hurst, and White (2002) found that state fixed effects are significant for the incidence of default. Indeed, they found that, even after controlling for state fixed effects, households are more likely to file for bankruptcy if they live in a district with higher aggregate bankruptcy rates, or with more lawyers per capita. Gross and Souleles (2002b) similarly found evidence that the tendency to declare bankruptcy is greater for households living in states with greater numbers of people whom have previously declared bankruptcy.

While a strategic bankruptcy motive can explain the behavior of some households, it is hard to believe that it does so for the majority of households with substantial liquid assets. For one thing, the phenomenon of portfolio coexistence seems too widespread relative to the still limited incidence of bankruptcies in the population. To suggest that all of these households, across all demographic groups, are motivated in their behavior by strategic bankruptcy motives, even though a miniscule portion of them actually default, and some of them not even strategically, seems unwarranted. Moreover, as pointed out by Gross and Souleles 2002a, even if strategic default motives were so widespread, strategic defaulters do not need to pay the interest costs of revolving high-rate balances and holding low-rate assets before they declare bankruptcy. They should instead run up their debts and buy exempt assets right before filing.

6.9.4 Debt Levels and Utilization Rates of Credit Lines

Gross and Souleles (2002a) use the same proprietary administrative data set of individual credit card accounts from different card issuers described above to estimate responses of credit card debt levels and utilization rates of credit lines to exogenous increases in credit lines and to changes in interest rates. By exogenous increases, they mean credit line increases initiated by the credit card providers themselves, and not by card holders.[23] They find that, over the year following an exogenous line increase, each extra $1,000 of liquidity (i.e., credit line) generates, on average, a $130 increase in credit card debt. Thus, liquidity matters, unlike what is implied by standard permanent income models. Estimates of this marginal propensity to consume (MPC) are significantly larger for accounts exhibiting greater utilization of credit lines, rising to about 50 percent for accounts with more than 90 percent utilization. The average long-run elasticity of debt to the interest rate on the account is estimated to be approximately -1.3, with less than half of this representing balance shifting across credit cards. The elasticity is larger than average for interest rate declines, providing a possible justification for the popularity of low introductory ("teaser") interest rates. It is also smaller among accounts with high utilization rates than among those with utilization rates between 50 and 90 percent. The authors uncover a remarkable response of credit card utilization rates to increases in credit lines initiated by banks. Regardless of the credit line utilization rate, the long-run cumulative response of utilization rates to an exogenous line increase is quite small, implying a return of utilization near to its initial level in about five months following the line increase. Although such behavior would be easier to understand had households themselves requested the line increase, it is less straightforward to interpret given that the initiative came from the banks themselves.

As the authors suggest, such behavior can be justified in the context of buffer stock models of asset accumulation. In such models, households face nondiversifiable income risk and choose, as a result, to hold a precautionary buffer of assets so as to be able to shield future consumption levels from shocks to their financial resources.[24] The same logic applies to available credit lines. Although these are not assets per se, they perform a similar function as a means to maintain consumption in the face of income shocks. Thus, households facing income uncertainty choose not to utilize their credit lines fully, but to leave a portion unused, adopting target utilization rates for credit cards.

6.9.5 Self-Control Explanations of Credit Card Debt

Alternative explanations of portfolio behavior by credit card holders depart from the standard framework by incorporating self-control problems. These models are part of a much broader literature based on psychology and marketing insights (for an excellent overview, see Shane, Loewenstein, and O'Donoghue 2002). Existing approaches differ, but all assume that the separation of consumption from payment made possible by credit leads to excessive expenditures, and that moderating these tendencies is possible, if costly, through the coexistence of revolving credit card debt and low-interest liquid assets and/or retirement. The types of coexistence that can be justified and the technical complications in solving such models depend crucially on the specific framework, as will be seen later.

6.9.5.1 Impulsive Behavior and Costly Self-Control

The idea that self-control matters for credit card behavior is not foreign to either the general public or to professionals in psychology and in marketing. Durkin (2000) reports that public opinion regarding credit cards seems more polarized in 2000 than in 1970, with the majority (51 percent) of all families declaring in 2000 that use of credit cards is "bad." Among credit card holders, such negative attitudes are more prevalent among those who typically revolve credit card debt.

Households are much more willing to declare negative attitudes regarding the use of credit cards made by others than by themselves. Durkin (2000) reports that holders of bank-type credit cards declared in 2000 that too much credit is available, and that "others" have difficulty getting out of credit card debt, while 90 percent of them recognized that overspending is the fault of "other consumers" and not of credit card companies. In the 2001 Survey of Consumers, only 10 percent of bank-type credit card holders responded that credit cards made managing finances more difficult for them, citing overspending and overextending financial resources as the main reasons. However, 40 percent felt that managing finances was made more difficult for "others," mainly because of overspending, too much debt, and a continuing cycle of debt (Durkin 2002).

Among researchers in marketing and in consumer psychology, self-control problems are known to occur when the benefits of consumption come earlier than the costs (Hoch and Loewenstein 1991). Credit cards do separate purchases and payments, and there is evidence that liquidity, of the type provided by the acceptability of credit cards, both makes it more likely that the consumer will buy a given item and increases the amount that the consumer is willing to pay for the item conditional on purchase (Shefrin and Thaler 1988; Prelec and Simester 2001; Wertenbroch 2003). Indeed, this may be a reason why sellers accept credit card payments despite the service charges this entails.

Imposing self-control is possible, if costly, and there is ample anecdotal evidence on precommitment and self-rationing strategies (see, e.g., Hoch and Loewenstein 1991; Schelling 1992; Thaler and Shefrin 1981; and Wertenbroch 2003). A telling example refers to deadlines that various people, including academics, impose on themselves to avoid procrastination even when missing them entails substantial costs (Thaler 1980; Ariely and Wertenbroch 2002). Another one refers to smokers who prefer to purchase small and more expensive packs of cigarettes rather than cartons, so as to discourage themselves from smoking too much. Ausubel (1991) cites the anecdotal example of card-holders who immerse their credit cards in trays of water and place them in the freezer, in an effort to avoid impulsive purchases.

Unfortunately, serious self-control problems are difficult to observe under controlled conditions, and therefore controlled empirical evidence on self-rationing is only now beginning to emerge (Wertenbroch 1998; Soman and Cheema 2002). Finally, while it is obviously awkward to ask survey participants directly whether they have self-control problems, some survey questions hint at impulsive behavior and other such problems. For example, respondents are sometimes asked whether they find it difficult to plan ahead, or to control their purchases, or whether they smoke, or whether they find it acceptable to borrow in order to buy frivolous luxury items. Still, such variables are not many and their interpretation is not always straightforward.

6.9.5.2 *Hyperbolic Discounting and Time Inconsistency*

Laibson, Repetto, and Tobacman (2003) study the coexistence of revolving credit card debt with substantial accumulation of assets for retirement in a calibrated model of a household with access to liquid and illiquid assets, and to borrowing through credit cards.[25] They show that a single rate of time preference cannot simultaneously match the level of accumulated assets upon transition to retirement and the observed level of revolving credit card debt at younger ages. Households appear to act impatiently with respect to short-term objectives facilitated by credit card borrowing, and much more patiently with respect to longer-term objectives regarding retirement planning. The authors propose hyperbolic discounting, under which the household should no longer be thought as a single entity, but as a sequence of temporally separated "selves" with possibly conflicting plans regarding future actions. When viewing two successive periods in the distant future, the two selves discount the second relative to the first differently. The current self is more patient with respect to longer-run objectives than he is with respect to current objectives, and also more patient than what he knows his future self will be close to the relevant date. The current self tries to "tie the hands" of future selves and to force them to accumulate more than what they are likely to do on their own. The instrument of self-control is irreversible investment in illiquid assets. The current self simultaneously borrows on the credit card to satisfy short-term objectives, and accumulates illiquid assets that the future self cannot liquidate to ensure that the household will have enough assets at retirement. Hence the observed coexistence of credit card debt and accumulation of retirement assets.

As recognized by the authors, this elegant model of temporally separated selves cannot also account for the observed coexistence of high-interest credit card debt and low-interest liquid assets. Specifically, the model does not imply that the current self should ignore arbitrage opportunities regarding current assets and debts. We now turn to a different model that incorporates self-control considerations between contemporaneous selves.

6.9.5.3   Accountant-Shopper Households

Bertaut and Haliassos (2002) propose an "accountant-shopper" model that can account for coexistence of high-interest credit card debt with substantial holdings of low-interest liquid assets. Haliassos and Reiter (2003) develop the underlying computational model of accountant and shopper interaction and showed that the model can also account for observed coexistence of credit card debt with considerable accumulation of retirement assets, as well as for target utilization rates of credit card lines found by Gross and Souleles (2002a) and discussed earlier. This framework splits each household into two units, which can either represent two distinct partners or two selves. In the case of a single person, it is a model of self-control, while in the other case, it should be thought of as a model of "partner-control." In either case, it is a model of contemporaneous self-control, unlike hyperbolic discounting in which the current self builds up illiquid retirement assets to control future selves. The accountant decides the size of payment into the credit card account each month as well as the overall household portfolio. The accountant is assumed to be fully rational and to solve a standard intertemporal expected utility maximization problem, taking into account all available information, the full implications of current actions for future outcomes, as well as the behavior of the shopper. The shopper goes to stores with credit card in hand and determines household consumption. The shopper's self-control problem is manifested in greater impatience compared to the accountant and in more limited understanding of the process governing future payments into the credit card account, which are ultimately influenced by the evolution of household assets and debts. Faced with uncertainty about future payments, the shopper typically refrains from exhausting the entire credit card line but maintains a buffer, consistent with the Gross and Souleles (2002a) empirical finding of target utilization rates. Even under shopper behavior that is fully predictable by the accountant, it is optimal for the accountant to leave part of the credit card balance unpaid so as to restrain the shopper. In equilibrium, the accountant brings about the desired consumption level but pays the interest cost of self-control, namely, the cost of not using low-interest assets to pay off high-interest debt.[26]

Because credit card debt is used as an instrument of self-control in addition to its traditional role of smoothing resources intertemporally, revolving debt does not conflict with holdings of either low-interest assets or retirement assets. Both types of assets are held for the usual precautionary and smoothing reasons associated with intertemporal maximization under uncertainty. Had the accountant decided to use some of these assets to lower the credit card balance, the shopper would have responded by charging more on the credit card, frustrating the accountant's attempt. Finally, although the model does not invoke hyperbolic discounting and control of temporally separated selves to justify portfolio coexistence, it seems flexible enough to be combined with intertemporal self-control considerations, if this is desired.

6.10 The Choice between Debit and Credit Cards

As we saw in the data sections, debit cards are a more recent medium than credit cards, but their use is spreading fast, and they are overtaking credit cards as the most prevalent form of electronic payment at the point of sale. Part of the usual motivation for debit cards is that they limit the potential for overspending associated with credit cards. Debit card transactions can either be made online, using a PIN, or offline using a signature and a process very similar to credit cards. Offline debit transactions have been aided by the Visa and Mastercard logos, and it is not an exaggeration that debit and credit cards enjoy comparable levels of acceptability today. Use of debit cards is not allowed only for items such as car rentals and some online purchases over the Internet. Moreover, debit and credit cards now offer essentially identical fraud protection (see also Zinman 2004). A major advantage of debit cards is that they do not allow overborrowing, as funds are immediately withdrawn from the account linked to the debit card (or withdrawn within three days in the case of offline purchases). Debit cards appear to be a natural way of solving self-control problems of relatively impatient and impulsive shoppers. It seems possible to impose discipline on a shopper by replacing the credit card with a debit card and limiting the funds available in the linked account. Indeed, observed usage of debit cards seems to reinforce this idea (Reda 2003).[27]

Still, use of debit cards is not a costless way of coping with a self-control problem. Debit card users forego the free-float offered by credit cards, since funds are (almost) immediately withdrawn from the linked account. Interest costs are not limited to those implied by the absence of free-floating, but also include the cost of keeping available balances in low-interest, linked checking accounts, instead of in higher-rate accounts and withdrawing funds only to cover the monthly payment on a credit card. This process can be quite complicated, especially if the debit card holder is not flush with liquid financial resources and tries to avoid overdraft costs and penalties associated with the linked account. Very often, credit card issuers offer additional rewards to credit card users but not to debit card users, such as frequent flier miles and other bonuses. Thus, using debit cards as instruments of self control is costly, although probably less so than revolving credit card debt to reduce the available credit line.[28]

Zinman (2004) questions the usual motivation for use of credit cards based on self-control considerations. He investigates whether choice of debit versus credit cards at the point of sale is in fact consistent with the relative cost of charging an extra dollar to the credit card compared to paying with the debit card. A key factor determining such relative costs is whether the consumer already revolves credit card debt, in which case, new purchases cannot benefit from the grace period and are thus subject to high interest rates.

Zinman formulates three testable hypotheses generated by a "canonical" model of consumer choice without self-control considerations. First, credit card debt revolvers should be more likely to use debit than those who do not, as they cannot take advantage of the grace period for new purchases. Second, revolvers who face binding credit constraints should be more likely to use debit than credit, for instance, because they are likely to be close to full utilization of the credit card line. Third, nonrevolving bank cardholders should be less likely to use debit than those without bank cards. The main rationale for this third prediction is increased likelihood that cardholders will want to take advantage of the free-float. Using data from the 2001 and other SCFs, Zinman finds economically and statistically significant effects on debit use of revolving status and of credit limit constraints in particular, supporting mainly the first two predictions of the canonical model.

However, these results and some stylized facts about debit card use may also be consistent with behavioral models. For example, results also seem consistent with the accountant-shopper model described earlier.[29]

Zinman illustrates problems of distinguishing between standard and behavioral explanations of debit card use using the Prelec and Loewenstein (1998) model of mental accounting. In that model, the act of paying produces cognitive transaction costs and incentives to decouple payments from consumption. The optimal decoupling strategy tends to favor delayed payment for durables but prepayment for instantaneous consumption. Credit cards serve as a decoupling device, because they delay payment and they also lump payments together. If there are convexities over losses associated with each distinct payment, both features attenuate "payment pain." Debit provides relatively instantaneous payment and thus less decoupling than credit. This additional decoupling motive in credit versus debit card use could rationalize, for example, the finding of Reda (2003) that debit cards tend to be used for smaller transactions involving instantaneous consumption, while credit cards are used for larger transactions of more durable items.

While it may be difficult to distinguish between traditional and behavioral models of credit versus debit card use by using solely data on choices at the point of sale, distinctions can be facilitated by reference to portfolios of credit card debt revolvers. Traditional models fail to explain coexistence of high-interest credit card debt with often substantial holdings of low-interest liquid assets. The existence of such "arbitrage" opportunities goes against the logic of models that stress rational calculation of interest and other transactions costs: if consumers are so careful about comparing costs of using debit versus credit for each purchase, how do they miss the interest cost of not paying off their outstanding balances? And if debit card use is motivated by nearly binding credit card limits, how is it optimal to keep enough money in the low-interest, linked account to finance purchases rather than using these funds to make more of the credit line available to the shopper and to take advantage of points, miles, and other advantages of credit card purchases? All in all, it seems that the shortcomings of standard models become apparent when these models are confronted with portfolios of credit card revolvers rather than simply with the payment margin between credit and debit cards.

6.11   Concluding Remarks

This chapter documented trends in credit card and debit card access
and usage in the United States using data from successive waves of
the SCF between 1983 and 2001. We documented the spread of access
and usage of such cards, examined trends exhibited by different demographic groups, and studied the widespread practice of revolving
high-interest credit card debt. The general picture is one of spreading
access and usage, but of a fairly stable proportion of bank card holders
who revolve credit card debt. Debt revolvers tend to exhibit partial utilization of credit card lines, and they often combine credit card debt
with substantial holdings of low-interest, liquid assets and with accumulation of retirement assets.

We then presented an overview of some of the most important re-.
cent theoretical and empirical contributions to the study of credit and
debit card behavior. Drawing on recent research, we dismissed the
possibility that there is widespread ignorance among credit card
holders of the terms governing their credit cards, including annual percentage rates. Despite lack of ignorance, there is considerable evidence
that credit card interest rates do not respond to competition in the
credit card market. This arises because consumers tend to be unrespon-
sive to changes in interest rates, probably as a result of search and
switching cost.

There is a rising trend in bankruptcy and delinquency in credit
cards, partly attributable to an increased tendency of households to declare bankruptcy, controlling for the quality of the cardholder pool and
for supply-side factors. To the extent that bankruptcy is now more
widespread and, presumably, more socially acceptable, it can influence
portfolio behavior. Strategic default motives may contribute to the
observed coexistence of credit card debt with low-interest, liquid
assets, though we doubt that this mechanism alone is sufficient to account for the widespread incidence of the phenomenon. Recent research on the determinants of the level of credit card debt and of the
extent of utilization of credit lines has found that credit line increases
initiated by banks themselves do contribute to increases in the amount
of debt revolved, such that credit line utilization returns in about five
months or so to its rate prior to the line increase. Credit card debt
revolvers appear to have target utilization rates of their credit lines,
and it is possible to justify such "buffer-stock" behavior in the context
of modern computational models of credit card behavior.

Credit and debit cards provide a natural means of testing the relevance of emerging self-control models of consumer preferences. A considerable fraction of card holders believe that credit cards create problems of self-control, mainly because of the probability of overspending, at least by others if not by themselves. Debit cards are widely regarded as instruments for self-control that reduce this possibility. Although the choice of debit versus credit cards at the point of sale can be largely justified by the relative costs of these two modes of transacting; portfolio coexistence of credit card debt with liquid and with retirement assets seems to require departures from the standard framework. Hyperbolic discounting has been shown to account for the first type of coexistence. An alternative framework of "accountant-shopper" households, in which a fully rational accountant tries to control an impulsive shopper, has been shown to be consistent with both types of coexistence and with buffer-stock utilization behavior.

Based on this survey of facts and of existing literature, we are led to the conclusion that credit cards provide a most fertile ground for analyzing consumption behavior, payment and repayment choice (including bankruptcy and delinquency), portfolio selection regarding both assets and debts, and the elusive nature of consumer preferences.

Notes

This chapter was written while Haliassos was visiting the Finance and Consumption Chair at the European University Institute, Florence, Italy. The authors thank the Chair for funding and for stimulating research interactions. Haliassos also thanks the European Community's Human Potential Program for partial research support under contract HPRN-CT-2002-00235, [AGE]. The views expressed in this chapter are those of the authors and do not necessarily represent those of the Board of Governors of the Federal Reserve System.

1. We use information from the 1983, 1992, 1995, 1998, and 2001 waves of the SCF. For a more complete discussion of features of the SCF as well as findings from the 2001 wave, see Aizcorbe, Kennickell, and Moore 2003.

2. For ease of comparison, all dollar figures are converted to 2001 prices using the urban consumers' all-items Consumer Price Index.

3. The omitted dummy variable is some college but not a four-year degree.

4. The probit regressions also include a number of other explanatory variables that have been found to be significant in explaining credit card ownership, including marital status, number of children, whether the household head is self-employed or not currently employed, whether the household can be considered "liquidity-constrained" because it has been turned down for credit or discouraged from applying for credit, whether the household over the past year spent less than its income, and whether the household had a checking account.

5. In estimating the probabilities of card ownership, income and financial assets were assigned using the median values for the age-education range under consideration. For a typical less-than-35-year-old with a high school education, the median income was slightly over $30,000 (in 2001 $), with about $1,900 in financial assets. For the same-aged household with a college degree, the median income is just under $45,000, and median financial assets were just under $10,000. For a household aged 50–64 with a college education, median income was just under $82,000, and median financial assets were slightly over $111,000. All representative households were assumed to be "savers," all were assumed to have a checking account, and none were assumed to be liquidity-constrained.

6. In comparison, the estimated probability that this same individual would have any type of credit card rises from 0.63 in 1983 to 0.78 in 2001.

7. In the 1992 SCF, the question was about debit card ownership. In subsequent surveys, the question was rephrased to elicit a response explicitly on debit card usage. Thus, the 1992 figure is an upper bound to actual debit card use in 1992.

8. For observations from the wave of the 1992 SCF, the dependent variable is debit card ownership instead of debit card use, as in the 1995–2001 waves. However, including the 1992 sample provides a useful base from which to measure the spread of debit card use, and size and significance of coefficients on the explanatory variables are little affected if the regression is run instead only on the 1995–2001 subset.

9. In contrast, about two-thirds of all U.S. households had home equity, and slightly over half of households with incomes under $50,000.

10. Information on new charges was not asked of households in 1983. We use instead a question that asked about frequency of use of the card in question. We consider households who had no balance on their bank-type card and answered that the card was used "hardly ever" or "never" to be nonactive card users.

11. One category of households that does seem to have increased slightly over time is cardholders who claim they "always or almost always" pay off the balance in full but nonetheless had a balance outstanding at the time of the survey. These households may be accidental revolvers who typically do pay off balances but for whatever reason carried a balance in the month preceding the survey. The percentage of "accidental users" has drifted upward from less than 10 percent of cardholders in 1992 (18 percent of those with a balance) to 12 percent in 2001 (22 percent of those with a balance).

12. As noted by Gross and Souleles (2002a, 151n) and others, SCF data are subject to the limitation that households substantially underreport their bank card debt. As an example, Gross and Souleles compare the average credit card debt (including retail store debt) across households with credit cards given by the 1995 SCF to that given by aggregate data on revolving consumer credit collected by the Board of Governors of the Federal Reserve System. The figures are around $2,000 and $5,000, respectively.

13. Because utilization rates are based on reported credit card balances, they are subject to the same underreporting that we noted in note 12 for credit card balances. Gross and Souleles (2002a) tend to find greater utilization rates based on administrative account data than those reported here, but their unit is an account rather than a household, and they have less information on demographics and on the overall household portfolio.

14. Less than 1 percent of cardholder households without a card balance were behind two months or more on any type of loan payment.

15. In 2001 dollars, median financial assets of households in this category in 2001 were $125,000, more than double the financial assets of such households in 1983, and median net worth at nearly $320,000 was about 50 percent higher. This increase in wealth can be explained in large part by the rise in the equity market over the 1990s and increased ownership of equities by these households: In 1983, less than half of households in this category were stockholders, but by 2001, that fraction was 75 percent.

16. This relationship between the size of the credit card balance to available liquid assets holds, even accounting for an understatement of credit card debt in the SCF as indicated in Gross and Souleles (2002a). Indeed, readily available resources to pay off the balance are somewhat understated, since the SCF does not collect data on cash held by respondents.

17. Note that some holders classified as "unaware" under the stricter criterion may be actually facing very low ("teaser") rates.

18. For example, Ausubel (1991) estimated that, while the ordinary pretax return on equity in banking for the fifty largest issuers of credit cards was on the order of 20 percent per year, these issuers earned annual returns of 60 percent to 100 percent or more on their credit card business during the period.

19. Examples include costs of locating other providers and of filling in new applications, and the perception that credit ratings and credit limits are functions of the length of time during which a particular credit card account is held, but he doubts that they are sufficiently important by themselves.

20. Although banks do not alter interest rates, they can be generous to creditworthy customers by providing grace periods, small or no annual fees, and points or miles—and strict with bad customers by imposing heavy penalties on those who miss their payments or exceed their limits.

21. As Brito and Hartley (1995) put it, "The most desirable customers are those who borrow a substantial amount on their cards and yet remain well within their credit limits and, therefore, are unlikely to default" (409).

22. This is a random household telephone survey conducted monthly by the Ohio State University Survey Research Center, and it includes variables unavailable in other surveys. The period is February 1998 through May 1999, with additional data from September 1999.

23. It is obvious that debt levels would rise more in response to any given increase if the customer had requested it with a specific expenditure in mind than if the bank initiated it.

24. Households exhibit such behavior when they are characterized by "prudence," usually identified with a positive third derivative of the felicity function.

25. The household has a finite lifetime of uncertain length, an effective size that varies over its life cycle, and a bequest motive. It is faced with a nondiversifiable income risk and age-income profile determined by its education level and estimated from PSID data.

26. This desired consumption level will not be the same in general as the level that would prevail in the absence of the problem of self-control. This is because the household bears costs in the effort to restrain the behavior of the shopper.

27. Reda, quoted in Zinman 2004, reports that debit cards tend to be used for smaller transactions involving instantaneous consumption, while credit cards are used for larger transactions of more durable items.

28. Haliassos and Reiter (2003) compare simulated costs of revolving credit card debt and of using a debit card to cope with a self-control problem. They find that, even if we abstract from bonuses and fraud protection offered by credit cards, the benefits from switching to debit cards are small for a household with a self-control problem. These can plausibly be eliminated by such additional benefits offered by credit cards and by any differential transaction fees or informational requirements in acquiring the newer instrument, debit cards.

29. Since, in that model, credit card debt is revolved mainly as an instrument of self-control, debt revolvers are more likely to exhibit self-control problems and to use debit cards as an additional measure to discipline impulsive shoppers. The same holds a fortiori for those with nearly binding credit card limits. To the extent that these arise from a desire to limit the resources available to the shopper, they will also be associated with a greater likelihood of encouraging the shopper to use a debit card for purchases.

References

Aizcorbe, Ana M., Arthur B. Kennickell, and Kevin B. Moore. 2003. "Recent Changes in U.S. Family Finances: Evidence from the 1998 and 2001 Survey of Consumer Finances." *Federal Reserve Bulletin* (January): 1–32.

Ariely, Dan, and Klaus Wertenbroch. 2002. "Procrastination, Deadlines, and Performance: Self-Control by Precommitment." *Psychological Science* 13: 219–224.

Ausubel, Lawrence. 1991. "The Failure of Competition in the Credit Card Market." *American Economic Review* 81: 50–81.

Bertaut, Carol C., and Michael Haliassos. 2002. "Debt Revolvers for Self-Control." University of Cyprus Working Papers in Economics 0208, Nicosia.

Brito, Dagobert L., and Peter R. Hartley. 1995. "Consumer Rationality and Credit Cards." *Journal of Political Economy* 103: 400–433.

Calem, Paul S., and Loretta J. Mester. 1995. "Consumer Behavior and the Stickiness of Credit-Card Interest Rates." *American Economic Review* 85: 1327–1336.

Domowitz, Ian, and R. Sartain. 1999. "Determinants of the Consumer Bankruptcy Decision." *Journal of Finance* 54: 403–420.

Dunn, Lucia F., and Tae-Hyung Kim. 2004. "An Empirical Investigation of Credit Card Default: Ponzi Schemes and Other Behaviors." Working paper, Ohio State University.

Durkin, Thomas. 2000. "Credit Cards: Use and Consumer Attitudes, 1970–2000." *Federal Reserve Bulletin* (September): 623–634.

Durkin, Thomas. 2002. "Consumers and Credit Disclosures: Credit Cards and Credit Insurance." *Federal Reserve Bulletin* (April): 201–213.

Fay, Scott, Eric Hurst, and Michelle White. 2002. "The Household Bankruptcy Decision." *American Economic Review* 92: 708–718.

Gross, David B., and Nicholas S. Souleles. 2002a. "Do Liquidity Constraints and Interest Rates Matter for Consumer Behavior? Evidence from Credit Card Data." *Quarterly Journal of Economics* 117: 149–185.

Gross, David B., and Nicholas S. Souleles. 2002b. "An Empirical Analysis of Personal Bankruptcy and Delinquency." *The Review of Financial Studies* 15: 319–347.

Haliassos, Michael, and Michael Reiter. 2003. "Credit Card Debt Puzzles." Mimeo., Department of Economics, University of Cyprus.

Hoch, Stephen J., and George F. Loewenstein. 1991. "Time-Inconsistent Preferences and Consumer Self-Control." *Journal of Consumer Research* 17, no. 4: 492–507.

Laibson, David, Andrea Repetto, and Jeremy Tobacman. 2003. "A Debt Puzzle." In *Knowledge, Information, and Expectations in Modern Microeconomics: Essays in Honor of Edmund S. Phelps*, ed. P. Aghion, R. Frydman, J. Stiglitz, and M. Woodford, 228–266. Princeton, N.J.: Princeton University Press.

Lehnert, Andreas, and Dean M. Maki. 2002. "Consumption, Debt and Portfolio Choice: Testing the Effect of Bankruptcy Law." Finance and Economics Discussion Paper 2002-14, Board of Governors Federal Reserve System.

Lopes, Paula. 2003. "Credit Card Debt and Default over the Life Cycle." Working paper, Financial Markets Group, London School of Economics.

Prelec, Drazen, and Duncan Simester. 2001. "Always Leave Home without It: A Further Investigation of the Credit-Card Effect on Willingness to Pay." *Marketing Letters* 12: 5–12.

Prelec, Drazen, and George Loewenstein. 1998. "The Red and the Black: Mental Accounting of Savings and Debt." *Marketing Science* 17: 4–28.

Reda, Susan. 2003. "2003 Consumer Credit Survey." *STORES Magazine* (November). Quoted in Zinman 2004.

Schelling, Thomas C. 1992. "Self-Command: A New Discipline." In *Choice Over Time*, ed. G. Loewenstein and J. Elster, 167–176. New York: Russell Sage Foundation.

Shane, Frederick, George Loewenstein, and Ted O'Donoghue. 2002. "Time Discounting and Time Preference: A Critical Review." *Journal of Economic Literature* 40: 351–401.

Shefrin, Hersch M., and Richard H. Thaler. 1988. "The Behavioral Life-Cycle Hypothesis." *Economic Inquiry* 26: 609–643.

Soman, Dilip, and Amar Cheema. 2002. "The Effect of Credit on Spending Decisions: The Role of the Credit Limit and Credibility." *Marketing Science* 21: 32–53.

Thaler, Richard H. 1980. "Toward a Positive Theory of Consumer Choice." *Journal of Economic Behavior and Organization* 1: 39–60.

Thaler, Richard H., and Hersch M. Shefrin. 1981. "An Economic Theory of Self-Control." *Journal of Political Economy* 89: 392–406.

Wertenbroch, Klaus. 1998. "Consumption Self-Control via Purchase Quantity Rationing of Virtue and Vice." *Marketing Science* 17: 317–337.

Wertenbroch, Klaus. 2003. "Self-Rationing: Self-Control in Consumer Choice." In *Time and Decision: Economic and Psychological Perspectives on Intertemporal Choice*, ed. George Loewenstein, Roy Baumeister, and Daniel Read, 491–516. New York: Russell Sage Foundation.

Zinman, Jonathan. 2004. "Why Use Debit Instead of Credit? Consumer Choice in a Trillion Dollar Market." Mimeo., Federal Reserve Bank of New York.

7   Bankruptcy and Consumer Behavior: Theory and U.S. Evidence

Michelle J. White

This chapter surveys theoretical research on personal bankruptcy, presents a model of optimal bankruptcy policy, discusses U.S. bankruptcy law, and surveys empirical evidence from the United States concerning how bankruptcy affects credit markets and other consumer behaviors. Bankruptcy law is an important factor affecting consumer credit markets, because whether consumers repay their loans or default depends on whether the legal system punishes defaulters and, if so, how severely. Bankruptcy law also affects other aspects of consumer behavior, including the decision to file for bankruptcy, the decision to become an entrepreneur, the number of hours worked, and how consumers allocate their portfolios.

Unlike most of European countries, the United States has separate bankruptcy laws for consumer debtors versus for corporations. The U.S. bankruptcy system is also unusual in how favorably its personal bankruptcy law treats debtors and how frequently consumers default and file for bankruptcy. U.S. consumers held about \$1,720 billion in unsecured debt in 2002, or about \$16,000 per household. The annual loss rate to creditors is about 7 percent, suggesting that losses on unsecured debt are about \$120 billion per year, or \$1,100 per household per year.[1] The number of personal bankruptcy filings per year in the United States increased fivefold between 1980 and 2003, from 300,000 filings to more than 1,500,000 (see table 7.1). This means that nearly 1.5 percent of U.S. households currently file for bankruptcy each year. Despite the increase in filing rates and the high rate of default on consumer loans, the proportion of U.S. households that would benefit financially from filing for bankruptcy is even higher than the proportion of households that currently files. Between 15 and 33 percent of households would benefit financially from filing for bankruptcy, depending on whether households take advantage of strategies that increase their financial

Table 7.1
Nonbusiness and business bankruptcies, 1980–present

Year	Number of nonbusiness bankruptcy filings	Number of business bankruptcy filings
1980	241,431	36,449
1985	297,885	66,651
1990	660,796	64,688
1995	806,816	51,878
2000	1,240,012	35,472
2002	1,539,111	38,540
2003	1,625,208	35,037

Source: Statistical Abstract of the United States, 2002, table 724, and 1988, table 837, and data from Administrative Office of the U.S. Courts.

benefit from filing, such as converting assets from nonexempt to exempt categories or moving to high exemption states (White 1998a).

Section 7.1 discusses the economic objectives of bankruptcy law generally and examines how the objectives of corporate and personal bankruptcy differ. Section 7.2 discusses U.S. personal bankruptcy law. Section 7.3 presents a model of optimal personal bankruptcy policy and discusses theoretical issues related to personal bankruptcy. Sections 7.4 and 7.5 survey empirical research on the effects of personal bankruptcy law on credit markets, and on the decision to file for bankruptcy and other aspects of consumer behavior. Section 7.6 concludes.

7.1   Objectives of Bankruptcy Law

Bankruptcy law applies to corporations, unincorporated businesses, and consumers. Economists have discussed five separate objectives of bankruptcy: (1) encouraging efficient investment decisions before and after bankruptcy; (2) encouraging efficient effort-level decisions before and after bankruptcy; (3) avoiding a race by creditors to be first that could cause businesses to shut down prematurely; (4) making an efficient choice between liquidation and reorganization once debtors are in bankruptcy; and (5) providing debtors with insurance against the consequences of adverse shocks to consumption, such as those caused by illness, job loss, or failure of the debtor's business.

Consider which of these objectives apply to personal bankruptcy. Note that personal bankruptcy law covers both consumer and small business bankruptcy, since most small businesses are unincorporated, and, therefore, business debts are legal obligations of the business owner.

The first objective does not apply to consumer debtors, because consumers generally borrow to finance consumption rather than investment, but it does apply to small business. The second objective applies mainly to consumer debtors. Outside of bankruptcy, consumer debtors are obliged to use part of both their earnings and their wealth to repay debt, and, if they default, creditors can collect by garnishing wages and/or claiming debtors' assets. After filing for bankruptcy, debtors may also be obliged to use their earnings and wealth to repay prebankruptcy debt. In both situations, the obligation to repay can discourage debtors from working hard. But under U.S. law, filing for bankruptcy ends debtors' obligation to use any of their earnings to repay debt. The Supreme Court has justified this policy—called the "fresh start"—on the grounds that it encourages debtors to work hard after bankruptcy. ("[F]rom the viewpoint of the wage earner, there is little difference between not earning at all and earning wholly for a creditor.")[2] A similar justification for the fresh start also applies to owners of small businesses, since their incentive to start new businesses and their ability to borrow after bankruptcy are higher if they are not required to use future profits to repay prebankruptcy business debts.[3] However, the fresh start also encourages opportunism, since it gives debtors incentives to borrow more and work less before bankruptcy, and to file for bankruptcy even when they are not in financial distress.

In contrast, objectives 3 and 4 are mainly relevant in the corporate bankruptcy context. These objectives arise because failing firms may either liquidate or continue to operate (reorganize) in bankruptcy, and inefficiencies occur when firms take the wrong path. A cost of creditors' racing to be first to collect is that it may cause corporations to liquidate when it would be economically more efficient for them to reorganize.[4] But in personal bankruptcy, true liquidation no longer occurs. This is because, while individual debtors' most valuable asset is generally their human capital, human capital can only be liquidated by selling debtors into slavery, as the Romans did, or confining them in debtors' prisons until someone else pays their debts, as the British did in Charles Dickens's time. Since slavery and debtors' prisons are no longer used, all personal bankruptcies are reorganizations. Bankrupt debtors retain ownership of their human capital and the right to continue using it, but some of their financial wealth/nonhuman capital may be liquidated, and they may face a tax on the post-bankruptcy return to their human capital. (Nonetheless, one of the two U.S. personal bankruptcy procedures is called liquidation.)

Finally, objective 5 applies mainly in personal bankruptcy. This is the objective of insuring debtors against the consequences of adverse shocks to consumption, such as those caused by illness, job loss, or failure of the debtor's business. When earnings or wealth turns out to be low, the obligation to repay debt makes a bad situation worse for debtors and may cause their consumption to fall to very low levels. But very low consumption levels can be costly even if they are temporary; debtors may lose their homes, develop permanent health problems because they cannot afford medical care to treat their illnesses, their children may drop out of school and not go back, and so forth. Sharp reductions in consumption by a large number of households may also cause or contribute to an economywide recession. Individual debtors can partially insure themselves against adverse consumption shocks by limiting their borrowing and diversifying their financial wealth. But they remain vulnerable, since they cannot diversify their human capital, which, for most debtors, constitutes most of their wealth. Personal bankruptcy provides partial consumption insurance to debtors by discharging some debts when adverse shocks occur, thereby freeing funds for consumption that would otherwise be used for debt repayment.[5]

Exemptions in personal bankruptcy are closely related to the insurance objective. When individual debtors file for bankruptcy, they are allowed to retain ownership of all their financial wealth up to the exemption level, plus their human capital. Higher wealth exemptions increase the level of insurance, because when the wealth exemption is higher, debtors file for bankruptcy and obtain debt relief in response to smaller adverse shocks to income or wealth. The 100 percent exemption for future wages—the fresh start—also provides insurance since debtors keep all of their post-bankruptcy wages in situations in which adverse shocks cause them to file for bankruptcy.

Exemptions also provide insurance to owners of noncorporate small businesses, since owners of failed firms can file for bankruptcy and obtain discharge of both the firm's debts and their own personal debts. In bankruptcy, they must use all of their nonexempt wealth to pay the firm's debts, but they keep their exempt wealth plus all of their post-bankruptcy earnings. Note that bankruptcy law provides owners of noncorporate firms with far less protection than that provided to corporate shareholders through the corporate form and limited liability, since corporate shareholders' liability for the corporation's losses is limited to loss of the value of their shares. In addition, corporate shareholders can further insure themselves by diversifying their shareholdings.

7.2   U.S. Personal Bankruptcy Law

In the United States, the Constitution reserves for the federal government the power to make laws concerning bankruptcy. This means that—with one important exception—personal bankruptcy law is uniform across the United States. When a debtor files for bankruptcy, creditors must cease their collection efforts and cease garnishing the debtor's wages.[6]

There are two different personal bankruptcy procedures and debtors are allowed to choose between them. The first procedure is called Chapter 7, whereby all unsecured debts are discharged. Unsecured debts are those for which the creditor does not have a claim on any particular asset owned by the debtor; they include credit card debt, installment debt, medical bills, and tort judgments. (Secured debts, such as mortgage and car loans, are not discharged in bankruptcy unless the debtor gives up the asset that secures the debt.) Debtors must surrender all of their nonexempt assets for repayment to creditors, but, under the fresh start, all of their future earnings are exempt from the obligation to repay. In 1978, the U.S. Congress adopted a uniform set of bankruptcy exemptions, but gave the states the right to opt out and adopt their own exemptions. About two-thirds of the states opted out by requiring that their residents use the state's exemptions in bankruptcy. The remaining one-third adopted their own exemptions, but allowed residents to choose between the states' exemptions and the federal exemption. As a result, exemption levels are the only feature of bankruptcy law that varies across the states.[7]

Table 7.2 gives information on bankruptcy exemptions by U.S. states as of 2001. The top panel gives exemptions for home equity ("homestead" exemptions), which vary widely. Texas, Florida, and five other states have unlimited exemptions for wealth in the form of home equity, which means that wealthy debtors in these states can file for bankruptcy and keep millions of dollars in wealth as long as it is invested in their homes. In contrast, Delaware and Maryland have no exemption at all for home equity. Some states allow married couples who file for bankruptcy to double the homestead exemption, and a few

Table 7.2

Personal bankruptcy exemptions in the United States, 2001

Homestead exemptions	State
$0–$7,500	Alabama, Delaware, District of Columbia, Georgia, Kentucky, Illinois, Indiana, Maine, Maryland, Michigan, New Jersey, Ohio, Pennsylvania, South Carolina, Tennessee, Virginia
$8,000–$30,000	Colorado, Hawaii, Louisiana, Missouri, Nebraska, New Hampshire, New Mexico, New York, Nebraska, North Carolina, Oregon, Utah, West Virginia, Wyoming, federal exemption
$40,000–$100,000	Arizona, California, Connecticut, Idaho, Massachusetts, Mississippi, Montana, North Dakota, Rhode Island, Vermont, Washington, Wisconsin
>$100,000–$250,000	Alaska, Minnesota, Nevada
Unlimited	Arkansas, Florida, Iowa, Kansas, Oklahoma, South Dakota, Texas

Personal property exemptions	State
$2,000–$4,500	Alabama, Florida, Indiana
$5,000–$8,700	Delaware, Illinois, Louisiana, Maryland, Massachusetts, Missouri, Nebraska, North Carolina, North Dakota, Ohio, South Dakota, Tennessee, Utah, Wyoming
≥$10,000	Alaska, Arizona, Arkansas, California, Colorado, Connecticut, District of Columbia, Georgia, Hawaii, Idaho, Iowa, Kansas, Kentucky, Maine, Michigan, Minnesota, Mississippi, Montana, Nevada, New Hampshire, New Jersey, New Mexico, New York, North Dakota, Oklahoma, Oregon, Pennsylvania, Rhode Island, South Carolina, Texas, Vermont, Virginia, Washington, West Virginia, Wisconsin, federal exemption

States that allow bankrupts to use either the state or the federal exemptions: Arkansas, Connecticut, District of Columbia, Hawaii, Massachusetts, Michigan, Minnesota, New Hampshire, New Jersey, New Mexico, Pennsylvania, Rhode Island, Texas, Vermont, Washington, Wisconsin.

Source: Author's calculations from data in Elias et al. 2001.

Notes: The exemptions given are for single filers. Some states allow married couples to double the homestead exemption, and some the elderly or disabled to take higher exemptions. States usually have a number of different personal property exemptions for items such as clothing, equity in cars, furniture, jewelry, tools of the trade, burial plots, or damage awards. These may be specified either as maximum dollar values or as blanket exemptions for the particular type of property. Some states also have a dollar-denominated "wildcard" exemption that applies to any type of property. The personal property exemptions listed are the sum of all personal property exemptions for which a maximum dollar value is given. In addition to these exemptions, some states have exemptions for retirement accounts and life insurance policies.

allow the elderly to take larger exemptions. The middle panel of table 7.2 gives exemptions for personal property. Exemptions for personal property may be specified either as maximum dollar values or as blanket exemptions for particular types of property. Most states have separate exemptions for clothing, equity in cars, furniture, jewelry, tools of the trade, and burial plots. Some states also have "wildcard" exemptions that apply to any type of property. The personal property exemptions listed in table 7.2 are the sum of nonhousing exemptions for which states specify a maximum dollar value. In addition to these exemptions, some states have exemptions for retirement accounts and life insurance policies. The bottom panel of table 7.2 lists states that allow their debtors to choose between the state's exemptions and the federal exemption. Compared to most state exemptions, the federal exemptions favor renters relative to home owners, since the federal personal property exemptions are relatively high, and renters can apply part of the federal homestead exemption to personal property.

The second personal bankruptcy procedure, called Chapter 13, is intended for wage earners. Under it, debtors in bankruptcy keep all of their assets in bankruptcy, but they must propose a multiyear plan to repay part of their unsecured debt from future earnings. If they fulfill the repayment plan, then the unpaid portion of the debt is discharged. Creditors are entitled to receive the same amount under Chapter 13 as they would receive if the debtor had filed under Chapter 7, but no more. This means that if all of a debtor's assets would be exempt under Chapter 7, the debtor can file under Chapter 13 and propose to repay only a token amount. Another reason why debtors sometimes file under Chapter 13 is that they are behind on their mortgage or car payments and filing under Chapter 13 delays the foreclosure process. Under Chapter 13, car lenders can be forced to reduce the principal value of the loan to the car's current market value, and mortgage lenders sometimes voluntarily agree to easier repayment terms.

Debtors can choose between using part of their future earnings but none of their wealth to repay debt under Chapter 13 or using part of their wealth but none of their future earnings to repay debt under Chapter 7. Although both wealth and future earnings are part of debtors' ability to repay, they are only obliged to use one or the other to repay, and the ability to choose the most favorable option is an important advantage for debtors. Because most debtors have no nonexempt wealth, they usually prefer to file under Chapter 7. In addition, debtors who have wealth that is nonexempt can often transfer it from nonexempt to exempt categories before filing for bankruptcy (such as by converting cash into home equity if their home equity is less than the homestead exemption). This allows them to file under Chapter 7 and avoid using either their future earnings or their wealth to repay their debt. About 70 percent of all bankruptcy filings occur under Chapter 7.[8]

7.3   Theory

This section discusses a model of optimal personal bankruptcy policy that emphasizes objectives 1, 2, and 5 from section 7.1.[9] I assume that individual debtors have no nonbankruptcy sources of consumption insurance, such as unemployment compensation or welfare. I also assume that there is only a single personal bankruptcy procedure, but the procedure incorporates variable exemptions for both financial wealth and future wages. (Current U.S. personal bankruptcy law either exempts all future wages under Chapter 7 or exempts all financial wealth under Chapter 13.)

The model has two periods. In period 1, a representative consumer borrows an amount B at interest rate r to be repaid in period 2. The loan can be used either for consumption or investment, including investment in an unincorporated business. Assume that the debt is unsecured and that it is the consumer's only loan.[10] The consumer also chooses her work hours in period 1, denoted N_1. Work hours are assumed to represent the consumer's effort level and/or investment in human capital. The wage rate per unit of time is assumed to be one. The consumer's wealth in period 1, W_1, is known with certainty.

At the beginning of period 2, the consumer chooses her period 2 labor supply, N_2. The wage rate per unit of time remains one. After making this choice, the consumer's period 2 wealth is determined by a draw from the wealth distribution, $f(W_2)$, where W_2 can take any real value. Finally, the consumer decides whether to file for bankruptcy.

The rules of bankruptcy are as follows. There is a fixed dollar cost of filing, denoted F, that includes lawyers' fees and court filing fees. In bankruptcy, the debt, $B(1+r)$, is discharged. There are two exemptions in bankruptcy, one for wealth and one for period 2 earnings. The wealth exemption, X, is assumed to be a fixed dollar amount that combines states' exemptions for homesteads and personal property. It can take any positive or negative value. The earnings exemption could either be a fraction of period 2 wages (a "bankruptcy tax") or a fixed dollar amount. But if the exemption were a fixed dollar amount, then consumers would either be subject to no bankruptcy tax at all, if their earnings were below the exemption, or would be subject to a 100 percent marginal bankruptcy tax on all of their earnings above the exemption. The latter situation would be extremely inefficient and would lead consumers who file for bankruptcy to reduce their earnings to the exemption level, which might involve quitting their jobs.[11] For this reason, I assume that the earnings exemption takes the form of a fixed fraction of period 2 earnings, x, where $0 \leq x \leq 1$. Consumers who file for bankruptcy must therefore repay $W_2 - X$ from their period 2 wealth plus $(1 - x)N_2$ from their period 2 earnings.

Consider the relationship between discharge of debt in bankruptcy and the two exemptions. Given the absence of nonfinancial penalties for bankruptcy, such as slavery or imprisonment, the two exemption levels and the filing cost, F, determine the price of discharge. If $X = \infty$ and $x = 1$ (the maximum values for both), then the price of discharge is F. Conversely, if X is large and negative and $x = 0$ (the minimum values for both), then there is no discharge of debt, that is, the price of discharge is complete impoverishment. The fresh start is represented by $x = 1$. The harshest exemption policy currently allowed in the United States is represented by $X = 0$ and $x = 1$, where the price of discharge is $F + W_2 - X$. This is an intermediate level, since debtors must use all of their wealth but none of their future earnings to repay their debt. In the model, we examine how the efficiency of personal bankruptcy is affected by varying the policy parameters X and x.

Now, consider the bankruptcy decision in period 2. If the consumer repays in full, period 2 consumption is $W_2 - B(1 + r) + N_2$, while if she files for bankruptcy, period 2 consumption is $X + xN_2$ (assuming that she pays the bankruptcy filing cost beforehand).[12] She is assumed to make the bankruptcy decision so as to maximize her period 2 consumption. This means that the condition for bankruptcy is

$$B(1 + r) \geq (W_2 - X) + (1 - x)N_2. \tag{1}$$

This says that the amount of debt discharged in bankruptcy must exceed the value of nonexempt wealth and earnings that the debtor must use to repay. Equation (1) implies that there is a threshold value of period 2 wealth, denoted $\hat{W}_2$, at which consumers are indifferent between filing or not filing, where $\hat{W}_2 = B(1 + r) + X - (1 - x)N_2$. Consumers file for bankruptcy if $W_2 \leq \hat{W}_2$ and do not file otherwise. Holding period 2 earnings constant, this expression implies that

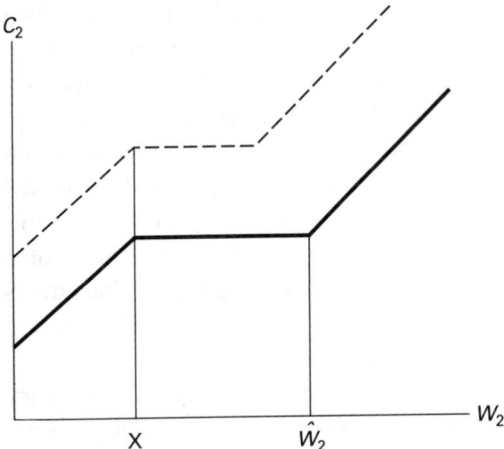

Figure 7.1
The insurance effect of bankruptcy

consumers' probability of filing for bankruptcy rises when either of the two exemptions increase.

The solid line in figure 7.1 graphs period 2 consumption, shown as the solid line, as a function of period 2 wealth, W_2. Period 2 earnings, N_2, are assumed to be constant. Consumption has three regions: the right-most, where $W_2 > \hat{W}_2$ and the debtor repays in full; the middle region, where the debtor files for bankruptcy, period 2 wealth is $X \leq W_2 \leq \hat{W}_2$, and period 2 consumption is $X + xN_2$; and the left-most, where the debtor files for bankruptcy, $W_2 < X$, and period 2 consumption is $W_2 + xN_2$.[13] The dashed line in figure 7.1 shows how the bankruptcy decision changes when period 2 labor supply increases.

Bankruptcy provides consumption insurance by shifting resources from higher to lower wealth states. Allowing consumers to file for bankruptcy and obtain debt discharge causes interest rates to rise and lowers consumption in the nonbankruptcy region, but increases consumption in bankruptcy. Higher levels of either exemption increase the amount of insurance by shifting the bankruptcy threshold $\hat{W}_2$ to the right so that consumers file for bankruptcy at higher wealth levels. However, while both exemptions provide consumption insurance, the insurance that each provides is slightly different. Raising the wealth exemption X transfers additional resources from good to medium draws of the wealth distribution, that is, from the right hand to the middle region of figure 7.1. In contrast, raising the earnings exemption, x, transfers additional resources from good to both medium and bad draws of the distribution, that is, from the right-hand region to the middle- and left-hand regions of figure 7.1. This difference between the two exemptions suggests a new justification for the "fresh start"—that a higher earnings exemption provides more valuable consumption insurance than a higher wealth exemption, because the former transfers consumption to the region where it is lowest.

Now, turn to lenders. Assume that there are many consumers who apply to borrow, and all are identical as of period 1. Lenders are willing to lend as long as there exists an interest rate at which expected repayment covers the opportunity cost of funds, denoted p. The condition under which lenders expect to make zero profits is

$$B(1+p) = \int_{-\infty}^{X} [(1-x)N_2 - F]f(W_2)\,dW_2$$

$$+ \int_{X}^{\hat{W}_2} [W_2 - X + (1-x)N_2 - F]f(W_2)\,dW_2$$

$$+ \int_{\hat{W}_2}^{\infty} B(1+r)f(W_2)\,dW_2. \tag{2}$$

The three terms on the right-hand side represented expected repayment in each of the three regions of figure 7.1. Equation (2) determines the market-clearing interest rate, r, as a function of the two exemption levels.

To determine how the interest rate varies with the exemption levels, differentiate equation (2) with respect to x and X. (We assume that B is fixed and that N_1 is independent of the two exemption levels.) The results are

$$\frac{dr}{dx} = \left(\frac{N_2}{B}\right) \frac{\left[\int_{-\infty}^{\hat{W}_2} f(W_2)\,dW_2 + Ff(\hat{W}_2)\right]\left[1 - \frac{(1-x)}{x}\varepsilon_X\right]}{\int_{\hat{W}_2}^{\infty} f(W_2)\,dW_2 - Ff(\hat{W}_2)} \tag{3}$$

and

$$\frac{dr}{dX} = \left(\frac{1}{B}\right) \frac{\left[\int_{X}^{\hat{W}_2} f(W_2)\,dW_2 + Ff(\hat{W}_2)\right] - \left[\int_{-\infty}^{\hat{W}_2} f(W_2)\,dW_2 + Ff(\hat{W}_2)\right]\left[\frac{N_2(1-x)}{X}\varepsilon_X\right]}{\int_{\hat{W}_2}^{\infty} f(W_2)\,dW_2 - Ff(\hat{W}_2)},$$

$$\tag{4}$$

where ε_x and ε_X denote the elasticities of N_2 with respect to x and X, respectively.

If $\varepsilon_x = 0$ ($\varepsilon_X = 0$), then dr/dx (dr/dX) must be positive as long as the cost of filing for bankruptcy, F, is not too high. Now, consider the possibility that ε_x is nonzero so that period 2 effort depends on the fraction of post-bankruptcy earnings that workers keep. Note that the expression $[1 - ((1 - x)/x)\varepsilon_x]$ must be positive for any reasonable values of ε_x.[14] Therefore, if ε_x shifts from zero to positive, dr/dx becomes smaller in size but remains positive. This is because the increase in the wage exemption causes consumers to work more in period 2, since the return to work effort is higher. As a result, they earn more and repay more so that lenders raise the interest rate by less in response to the same increase in x. If ε_x shifts from zero to negative, then dr/dx becomes more positive, since consumers work less and repay less when the exemption level rises. Finally, suppose ε_X is nonzero. Regardless of sign, it is likely to be small, since labor supply is not very responsive to changes in wealth.[15] And dr/dX must be positive as long as both ε_X and F are small.

Equations (3) and (4) are not always satisfied; in which case, lending markets may break down. When X increases, borrowers are more likely to file for bankruptcy. Lenders respond by raising the interest rate, but this only increases the amount that debtors repay if they do not file for bankruptcy. As a result, raising the interest rate becomes less and less effective as X rises. (While borrowers may also partially repay their debt in bankruptcy, the amount they repay is unaffected by the interest rate.) At very high levels of X, the probability of debtors repaying in full is so low that no interest rate clears the market and creditors cease lending. A similar argument applies to increases in x, since when x rises, debtors are more likely to file for bankruptcy and repay less when they do so. Because all potential borrowers are ex ante identical, lenders either lend to all or stop lending completely.[16]

To illustrate, suppose $f(W_2)$ is distributed normally with a mean of 2 and standard deviation of 0.25, and suppose $x = 1$, $B = 1$, $F = 0$, $\rho = 0.1$, and $\varepsilon_X = 0$. Then loan markets operate as long as X is less than 0.9 (or 90 percent of the loan amount), but they fail if X exceeds 0.9. However, if future wages are not entirely exempt, then loan markets can operate at even higher levels of X. Suppose $X = 0.95$ and $N_2 = 1 - 0.1x$, so that $\varepsilon_x = -0.1x/(1 - 0.1x)$. Then loan markets operate as long as $x \leq 0.4$, but fail if $x > 0.4$.

Now turn to consumers. Their utility in each period is assumed to depend positively on consumption and negatively on work hours, and they are assumed to be risk-averse. For simplicity, the discount rate is assumed to be zero. The representative consumer's expected utility function is therefore

$$U(W_1 + N_1 + B, N_1) + \int_{-\infty}^{X} U(W_2 + xN_2, N_2) f(W_2) \, dW_2$$

$$+ \int_{X}^{\hat{W}_2} U(X + xN_2, N_2) f(W_2) \, dW_2$$

$$+ \int_{\hat{W}_2}^{\infty} U(W_2 - B(1+r) + N_2, N_2) f(W_2) \, dW_2. \tag{5}$$

Because all consumers are identical in period 1, the social welfare function (SWF) is the same as the representative consumer's expected utility function.[17]

Individual consumers determine their period 1 and period 2 labor supply, N_1 and N_2, so as to maximize expected utility, treating the interest rate and the exemption levels as fixed. They increase N_1 until minus the ratio of the marginal disutility of effort to the marginal utility of consumption in period 1 equals unity. This means that N_1 is unaffected by the exemption variables as long as additional effort does not increase debtors' obligation to repay in bankruptcy. (This holds, for example, if consumers use all their additional wages for consumption.) Consumers increase N_2 until minus the ratio of the expected marginal disutility of effort to the expected marginal utility of consumption in period 2 equals the expected value of working an additional hour, or $1 - p(1 - x)$, where p denotes the probability of bankruptcy.

Now consider the determination of the optimal bankruptcy policy, denoted by X^* and x^*. For marginal changes in the two exemption variables, the conditions for an optimal bankruptcy policy are determined by differentiating equation (5) with respect to x and X.[18] The resulting first-order conditions are as follows:

$$\frac{dSWF}{dX} = U_1(X + xN_2, N_2) \int_{X}^{\hat{W}_2} f(W_2) \, dW_2$$

$$- \left[B \frac{dr}{dX} \right] \int_{\hat{W}_2}^{\infty} U_1(W_2 - B(1+r) + N_2, N_2) f(W_2) \, dW_2 \tag{6}$$

and

$$\frac{dSWF}{dx} = (N_2) \int_{-\infty}^{\hat{W}_2} U_1(\max[W_2, X] + xN_2, N_2) f(W_2) \, dW_2$$

$$- \left[B \frac{dr}{dx}\right] \int_{\hat{W}_2}^{\infty} U_1(W_2 - B(1+r) + N_2, N_2) f(W_2) \, dW_2, \qquad (7)$$

where U_1 denotes the marginal utility of consumption. The optimal exemption levels are determined by substituting equations (3) and (4) into equations (6) and (7), respectively, setting the resulting expressions equal to zero and solving.

It is easiest to interpret special cases of equations (6) and (7). Suppose filing costs, F, are zero and $\varepsilon_X = 0$. Then equation (6) becomes

$$\frac{dSWF}{dX} = \int_X^{\hat{W}_2} f(W_2) \, dW_2 \left[U_1(X + xN_2, N_2) \right.$$

$$\left. - \frac{\int_{\hat{W}_2}^{\infty} U_1(W_2 - B(1+r) + N_2, N_2) f(W_2) \, dW_2}{\int_{\hat{W}_2}^{\infty} f(W_2) \, dW_2} \right]. \qquad (8)$$

The term in square brackets is the marginal utility of consumption when consumers file for bankruptcy but use part of their wealth to repay (the middle region of figure 7.1) minus the average marginal utility of consumption when consumers avoid bankruptcy (the right-hand region of figure 7.1). At low levels of X, the marginal utility of consumption must be higher in bankruptcy than outside of bankruptcy, so the expression must be positive. As X rises, the average marginal utility of consumption in bankruptcy falls (because wealth is higher since more wealth is exempt), while the average marginal utility of consumption outside of bankruptcy rises (because interest rates rise). So the difference between the two terms gets smaller.

Nonetheless, equation (8) must remain positive so that the optimal wealth exemption level X^* is the highest level at which lenders are willing to lend. The intuition is that risk-averse consumers always want to purchase additional insurance as long as it is sold at a fair price. A higher wealth exemption provides additional consumption insurance, and lenders "sell" the insurance at a fair price because of the zero profit constraint. As a result, borrowers wish to buy as much insurance as possible, and the optimal wealth exemption X^* is the highest possible level.

Now suppose F is positive rather than zero. In this case, a third term whose sign is negative is added to equation (8). The additional term may either cause the optimal exemption level to fall or to remain unchanged. With $F > 0$, consumption insurance now costs consumers more than the fair price, since they pay both the fair price plus an additional cost when they file for bankruptcy. As a result, demand for consumption insurance falls, and even risk-averse consumers may not wish to purchase the maximum amount. The optimal exemption level falls by more as F rises and as consumers become less risk-averse.

Now, consider the case when $\varepsilon_X \neq 0$, but $F = 0$. Then the following third term is added to equation (8) in square brackets:

$$+ \frac{\int_{\hat{W}_2}^{\infty} U_1(W_2 - B(1+r) + N_2, N_2) f(W_2) \, dW_2}{\int_{\hat{W}_2}^{\infty} f(W_2) \, dW_2} \left(\frac{N_2(1-x)}{X} \right) \varepsilon_X. \qquad (8')$$

This term has the same sign as the sign of ε_X. Therefore if ε_X shifts from 0 to negative, then $dSWF/dX$ becomes negative at the old value of X^*. That is, the optimal exemption level X^* becomes smaller. This is because an increase in X now causes work effort to fall, so that borrowers repay less, and lenders raise interest rates by more than they did when work effort was fixed. As a result, consumption insurance is more expensive and the efficient amount of insurance falls. The opposite reasoning holds if ε_X shifts from zero to positive.

Now, turn to the earnings exemption. Suppose again that $F = 0$ and $\varepsilon_x = 0$. Then substituting equation (4) into equation (7), the resulting expression is

$$\left(N_2 \int_{-\infty}^{\hat{W}_2} f(W_2) \, dW_2 \right) \left[\frac{\int_{-\infty}^{\hat{W}_2} U_1(\max[W_2, X] + xN_2, N_2) f(W_2) \, dW_2}{\int_{-\infty}^{\hat{W}_2} f(W_2) \, dW_2} \right.$$

$$\left. - \frac{\int_{\hat{W}_2}^{\infty} U_1(W_2 - B(1+r) + N_2, N_2) f(W_2) \, dW_2}{\int_{\hat{W}_2}^{\infty} f(W_2) \, dW_2} \right]. \qquad (9)$$

The interpretation of equation (9) is similar to that of equation (8). The terms in square brackets in equation (9) are the average marginal utility of consumption in bankruptcy minus the average marginal utility of consumption outside of bankruptcy. For a given level of X, a higher earnings exemption provides consumers with additional consumption insurance. Because lenders "sell" the insurance at a fair price, risk-averse consumers wish to buy as much as possible, and the optimal exemption level x^* is the maximum level at which lenders are willing to lend. Additional insurance, in the form of a higher earnings exemption, is particularly valuable, since debtors must use part of their period 2 earnings to repay their debt, even when their wealth is in the lowest region in figure 7.1. Raising x therefore raises consumption where it is the most valuable.

When F is positive rather than zero, an additional term with a negative sign is added to equation (9), and the optimal earnings exemption is therefore lower. The intuition is the same as that given for the optimal wealth exemption. When ε_x is nonzero and $F = 0$, an additional term is added to equation (9) that has the same sign as the sign of ε_x. If ε_x is negative (positive), the optimal x^* falls (rises) relative to the optimal level when $\varepsilon_x = 0$. The reasoning is the same as before.

Wang and White (2000) simulated a parameterized version of this model. They assumed that the cost of filing for bankruptcy, F, was positive and that ε_x and ε_X were both negative. They found that the optimal earnings exemption level, x^*, was always one, a result that supports the U.S. fresh start policy. But in an extension of their model, Wang and White introduced an additional margin for moral hazard; consumers were allowed to choose whether to hide part of their non-exempt wealth when they filed for bankruptcy (in addition to choosing their effort level). Hiding a portion of wealth makes filing for bankruptcy more attractive, but drives up interest rates. In this situation, Wang and White found that the optimal wage exemption was sometimes less than 100 percent. A lower wage exemption improved efficiency by discouraging consumers from hiding wealth, since hiding wealth made them more likely to file for bankruptcy, and therefore, they paid the bankruptcy tax on earnings more often than consumers who did not hide wealth. (In contrast a lower wealth exemption encouraged consumers to hide wealth.) In Wang and White's model, the two exemptions were substitutes, since when the optimal wage exemption level was less than 100 percent, the optimal wealth exemption level increased.

What does the model imply in terms of testable hypotheses? First, it suggests that in jurisdictions with higher bankruptcy exemptions, consumption is more highly insured and, therefore, is more certain/ less variable. Second, higher wealth exemptions reduce the supply of credit, so that interest rates are predicted to be higher and credit rationing is predicted to be stronger in jurisdictions with higher exemptions. Third, if consumers' marginal utility conforms to standard assumptions, then jurisdictions with higher exemption levels will have higher credit demand, since prudent consumers demand more credit (at any given interest rate) when they have more consumption insurance; but debtors who are nearly risk-neutral may demand less credit when exemptions are higher, because the cost of the additional wealth insurance is larger than what they are willing to pay. Fourth, if potential entrepreneurs are risk-averse, then jurisdictions that have higher bankruptcy exemptions will tend to have higher entrepreneurship rates. This is because potential entrepreneurs are more willing to take the risk of going into business if a generous bankruptcy exemption reduces the downside risk of business failure. Finally, the model suggests that the predicted change in work effort following bankruptcy is ambiguous, since the income and substitution effects pull in opposite directions.

Some of these predictions have been tested. Before reviewing the empirical literature, however, the remainder of this section discusses other theoretical issues in personal bankruptcy.

7.3.1 Bankruptcy and Incentives for Strategic Behavior

A problem with U.S. personal bankruptcy procedures is that they encourage debtors to engage in strategic behavior in order to increase their financial gain from filing. Using the same notation as above, consumers' financial benefit from filing for bankruptcy under Chapter 7 can be expressed as follows:

$$\text{Financial benefit} = \max[B(1+r) - \max[W_2 - X, 0], 0] - F. \tag{10}$$

Here the fresh start policy is assumed to be in effect so that future earnings are exempt from the obligation to repay. Consumers' financial benefit from filing for bankruptcy is the amount of debt discharged, $B(1+r)$, minus the value of nonexempt assets that they must give up in bankruptcy, which is the maximum of $[W_2 - X, 0]$. (Bankruptcy costs are ignored.) Although this expression gives the financial benefit from filing under Chapter 7, it also approximates the financial benefit from filing under Chapter 13, since debtors' obligations to repay under the two are closely related.

White (1998a, 1998b) calculated the proportion of U.S. households that would benefit from filing for bankruptcy, using data from the Survey of Consumer Finances (SCF), which includes detailed information on households' wealth as well as the financial benefit of filing for bankruptcy on the survey date. She found that approximately one-sixth of U.S. households had positive financial benefit and would therefore benefit from filing.

White also examined how the results would change if consumers pursued various strategies to increase their financial gain from bankruptcy, including (1) debtors converting assets from nonexempt to exempt by using them to repay part or all of their mortgages (assuming that additional home equity would be exempt in bankruptcy); (2) debtors moving to a more valuable house, if doing so would allow them to shelter additional wealth in bankruptcy; and (3) debtors charging all of their credit cards to the limit (but not obtaining new credit cards). These strategies together increased the proportion of households that benefited from bankruptcy from one-sixth to one-third. A final strategy involved debtors moving to Texas before filing for bankruptcy, since Texas has the most favorable exemptions (recall table 7.2). Combining all of these strategies, 61 percent of all U.S. households could benefit from filing for bankruptcy. These results suggest that, even with the high bankruptcy filing rate in the United States, many more households could benefit from filing for bankruptcy than actually choose to file. Thus, the bankruptcy filing rate may well continue to increase in the future, although sections 7.3.2 and 7.3.3 explain why filing rates are lower than a third.

7.3.2 Default without Bankruptcy

The model discussed above did not consider the possibility that consumers might default on their debt but not file for bankruptcy. White (1998b) investigated an asymmetric information game in which the decision to default is separate from the decision to file for bankruptcy. Debtors first decide whether to default, and, following default, creditors decide whether to attempt to collect the debt by obtaining a court order to garnish the debtor's wages. If creditors attempt to collect, then debtors choose whether to file for bankruptcy. There are two types of debtors. Type 1 debtors are assumed to have low wealth, and they always default. If creditors attempt to collect, then these debtors always file for bankruptcy, and creditors receive nothing. Type 2 debtors have higher wealth, and they may or may not default. If creditors attempt to collect following default, type 2 debtors always repay in full. Creditors are assumed to be unable to identify individual debtors' types at the time of default. Attempting to collect is assumed to be costly for creditors, while filing for bankruptcy imposes a cost on debtors.

White shows that, in equilibrium, type 1 debtors always default, but type 2 debtors and creditors both play mixed strategies. This means that some debtors of both types obtain the benefit of debt discharge without bearing the costs of filing for bankruptcy, because they default and creditors never attempt to collect. The model therefore suggests that, even though U.S. bankruptcy filing rates are high, additional households would benefit from filing for bankruptcy but do not actually file because they default, and creditors never attempt to collect.

7.3.3 The Option Value of Bankruptcy

Consumers' right to file for bankruptcy can be expressed as a put option with an exercise price equal to the exemption level. Debtors' future wealth is uncertain. If it turns out to exceed the wealth exemption plus the amount owed, then they pay off the debt in full. But if debtors' wealth turns out to be less than this amount, then they exercise their option to "sell" the debt to creditors for a price equal to $\min[X, W_2]$, that is, they file for bankruptcy.

White (1998a) calculated the value of debtors' option to file for bankruptcy. She used household-level data from the Panel Study of Income Dynamics (PSID), which asks respondents questions concerning their wealth every five years. The calculations were done separately for households at various points in the wealth distribution. The results showed that the value of the option to file for bankruptcy is high for some households in all portions of the wealth distribution. The high value of the bankruptcy option suggests that many households who would not benefit from filing for bankruptcy immediately nonetheless have a positive option value and may find it worthwhile to file for bankruptcy in the future.

7.3.4 The Crisis Model of Bankruptcy

The economic view of bankruptcy and credit markets is controversial and many sociologists and law academics reject it completely. Their view of bankruptcy, as discussed in Sullivan, Westbrook, and Warren 1989 and 2000, is that consumers file for bankruptcy only when unanticipated adverse events—such as illness, divorce, or job loss—occur that make it impossible for them to repay. In this model, debtors do not plan in advance for the possibility of bankruptcy, but file only when adverse events leave them with no choice. (Chapter 2 discusses some of the reported causes of default for several different countries.)

The crisis model leads to several testable hypotheses. One is that credit availability and interest rates are predicted to be unrelated to bankruptcy exemption levels, because debtors do not take into account the possibility of filing for bankruptcy when deciding whether and how much to borrow. Another testable implication is that whether consumers file for bankruptcy will depend on whether adverse events have occurred and on income, since income affects ability to repay. But bankruptcy decisions will not depend on the financial benefit from filing for bankruptcy. In theory, these differing predictions should allow the economic model of bankruptcy and the crisis model of bankruptcy to be tested against each other empirically.

7.3.5 "Overlending"
Policymakers in the United States often argue that creditors rather than debtors are responsible for high bankruptcy filing rates, because creditors lend too much and debtors therefore find it difficult to repay, an argument also made in Sullivan, Westbrook, and Warren 1989. One important issue is that U.S. bankruptcy rules make it difficult for lenders to predict whether potential borrowers will repay, since debtors are obliged to use both earnings and wealth to repay outside of bankruptcy, but are only obliged to use their nonexempt wealth to repay in bankruptcy. As a result, lenders must predict both debtors' ability to repay and their probability of filing for bankruptcy. And if debtors decide to behave opportunistically, then they have an incentive to borrow as much as possible before filing.

Another factor is that competition among lenders may create a prisoner's dilemma situation. Suppose there are two credit card lenders, A and B, and each must decide whether to offer credit cards to the other's customers. Suppose S_a equals 1 if A solicits B's customers and equals 0 otherwise, and S_b equals 1 if B solicits A's customers and equals 0 otherwise. A's profits are $P_a(S_a, S_b)Q_a(S_a) - C(Q_a(S_a))$, and B's profits are $P_b(S_b, S_a)Q_b(S_b) - C(Q_b(S_b))$. Here $P_a(S_a, S_b)$ and $P_b(S_b, S_a)$ are A's and B's average revenue per cardholder, respectively. Suppose that, before any solicitation occurs, A and B have the same average revenue per cardholders, or $P_a(0,0) = P_b(0,0)$. Soliciting by either lender is assumed to lower both lenders' average revenue so that $P_a(1,0) < P_a(0,0)$, $P_a(1,1) < P_a(0,1)$, $P_b(1,1) < P_b(0,0)$, and $P_b(1,1) < P_b(0,1)$. One explanation for the decline in average revenue is that adverse selection occurs in the response to solicitations (Ausubel 1999). Thus, when A solicits B's customers, those who respond are of lower quality than the average among B's customers, and vice versa. Another explanation is that soliciting increases the total credit available to borrowers who accept the new card, and additional credit increases the probability of default (Domowitz and Sartain 1999). Either explanation implies that soliciting by either lender lowers average revenue for both lenders. $Q_a(S_a)$ and $Q_b(S_b)$ are the total number of cards that A and B issue, which is assumed to depend only on own soliciting. Thus, $Q_a(1) > Q_a(0)$ and $Q_b(1) > Q_b(0)$. Finally, $C(Q_a(S_a))$ and $C(Q_b(S_b))$ are A's and B's total cost functions, where average costs are assumed to fall with number of cards issued.

The payoffs of the game are as follows:

A	B Solicit	No
Solicit	$P_a(1,1)Q_a(1) - C(Q_a(1))$, $P_b(1,1)Q_b(1) - C(Q_b(1))$.	$P_a(1,0)Q_a(1) - C(Q_a(1))$, $P_b(0,1)Q_b(0) - C(Q_b(0))$.
No	$P_a(0,1)Q_a(0) - C(Q_a(0))$, $P_b(1,0)Q_b(1) - C(Q_b(1))$.	$P_a(0,0)Q_a(S_a) - C(Q_a(0))$, $P_b(0,0)Q_b(0) - C(Q_b(0))$.

Consider whether A and B choose to solicit or not. The dominant strategy equilibrium is for both to solicit if the following two conditions hold for A and analogous conditions hold for B:

$$P_a(1,1)Q_a(1) - P_s(0,1)Q_a(0) > C(Q_a(1)) - C(Q_a(0)), \tag{11}$$

$$P_a(1,0)Q_a(1) - P_s(0,0)Q_a(0) > C(Q_a(1)) - C(Q_a(0)). \tag{12}$$

The right side of both conditions is the change in total costs that occurs as a result of A soliciting. The left-hand side of equation (12) gives the increase in A's total revenue from soliciting, assuming that B does not solicit; while the left-hand side of equation (11) gives the increase in A's total revenue from soliciting, assuming that B also solicits. Both lenders are more likely to solicit each others' customers if there are substantial economies of scale in soliciting, if the number of customers that respond to a solicitation increases, and/or if adverse selection is not too severe (i.e., new customers are not much lower in quality than old customers).

Is the mutual soliciting equilibrium inefficient compared to the alternative of no soliciting, that is, does "overlending" occur? Competition among lenders gives consumers an opportunity to borrow more, but opportunistic behavior raises interest rates and makes those who repay worse off. Competition among lenders also may increase or decrease lenders' profits. Whether the "overlending" equilibrium is more or less efficient compared to the no soliciting equilibrium depends on all of these factors.

7.3.6 Bankruptcy as Protection for Governments

Finally, another function of the bankruptcy system is to protect the government from the obligation to use the social safety net to bail out consumers who borrow too much and/or turn out to have low wealth in period 2. In the absence of bankruptcy, these debtors would be obliged to repay their debts, and, as a result, their consumption might fall so low that they qualify for government assistance. Posner (1995) has argued that bankruptcy benefits the government by transferring some of these costs from the public sector to private lenders.

7.4 Empirical Evidence: Credit Markets

7.4.1 Bankruptcy Effects on Empirical Supply and Demand

Section 7.3 argued that bankruptcy exemptions both reduce the supply of credit and increase the demand for credit, although the increase in demand may be reversed at high exemption levels. The first paper to test these predictions was Gropp, Scholz, and White (1997). They used data from the 1983 SCF to examine how bankruptcy exemptions affect supply and demand for consumer credit. The SCF gives detailed information on debts and assets for a representative sample of U.S. households, and it also indicates whether households have been turned down for credit and what interest rates they pay. The Gropp, Scholz, and White study did not distinguish between different types of debt or different types of exemptions, so that their debt variable included both secured and unsecured debt, and their bankruptcy exemption variable was the sum of homestead and personal property exemptions. The authors found that borrowers are more likely to be turned down for credit and paid higher interest rates in states with higher bankruptcy exemptions—evidence of a reduction in the supply of credit in high-exemption states. In particular, borrowers were 5.5 percentage points more likely to be turned down for credit if they lived in a state in the highest quartile of the exemption distribution, rather than in a state in the lowest quartile of the exemption distribution. In addition, borrowers in the second quartile of the wealth distribution paid an interest rate that was 2.3 percentage points higher if they lived in a state with combined bankruptcy exemptions of $50,000 rather than $5,000. But borrowers in the third and fourth quartile of the wealth distribution paid interest rates that were not significantly different in high versus low exemption states.

The authors also examined how the amount of debt held by households varied between high- versus low-exemption states. Although supply and demand for credit cannot be separately identified, a finding that households hold more debt in high-exemption than low-exemption states suggests that the increase in demand for credit more than offsets the reduction in the supply of credit, and vice versa. The authors found that high-asset households held more debt in high-exemption states, while low-asset households held less. Thus when high-asset households increased their credit demand in response to higher exemption levels, lenders accommodated them by lending more. But when low-asset households increased their credit demand, lenders responded with tighter credit rationing. Gropp, Scholz, and White (1997) calculated that, holding everything else constant, a household whose assets placed it in the highest quartile of the asset distribution would hold $36,000 more debt if it resided in a state with combined bankruptcy exemptions of $50,000 rather than $6,000; while a household whose assets placed it in the second to lowest quartile of the asset distribution would hold $18,000 less debt. Thus, higher exemption levels were associated with a large redistribution of credit from low-asset to high-asset households.

The results of the study suggest that, while policymakers often think that high bankruptcy exemptions help the poor, in fact, they cause lenders to redistribute credit from low-asset to high-asset borrowers and raise the interest rates they charge to low-asset borrowers.

7.4.2 Secured versus Unsecured Credit
More recent papers on bankruptcy and credit markets distinguished between secured versus unsecured loans, and between homestead and personal property exemptions. Berkowitz and Hynes (1999) and

Lin and White (2001) both used the Home Mortgage Disclosure Act (HMDA) data to investigate the effect of bankruptcy exemptions on mortgage credit. The HMDA data give information on whether applicants for mortgages and home improvement loans were turned down, as well as the location and some characteristics of the potential borrower. While mortgage loans are always secured, home improvement loans may either be unsecured or take the form of second mortgages. This means that they represent a mixture of secured and unsecured loans.

Berkowitz and Hynes (1999) argued that higher homestead exemptions reduce rather than increase default and, therefore, lead to an increase in the supply of mortgage credit. Their argument is that, if debtors have defaulted on their mortgages and are in danger of losing their homes, they can file for bankruptcy, obtain discharge of their nonmortgage debts, and use funds that would otherwise go to nonmortgage creditors to pay the mortgage. The higher the exemption levels, the more of debtors' wealth is protected in bankruptcy and, therefore, the lower the probability that they will default on their mortgages. Berkowitz and Hynes found support for their hypothesis that higher bankruptcy exemptions lead to an increase in mortgage availability.

Lin and White (2001) extended the bankruptcy decision model discussed earlier to include two separate decisions by debtors: whether to default on an unsecured loan and whether to default on a mortgage.[19] If debtors default on an unsecured loan, then they are assumed to file for bankruptcy. If debtors default on a mortgage, lenders have the right to foreclose on the house and sell it, regardless of whether the debtor has filed for bankruptcy. The proceeds of selling the house net of transactions costs are used, first, to repay the mortgage; second, to repay the second mortgage (if any); and, third, to give the debtor the homestead exemption. Any remaining funds are used to repay unsecured creditors. In the extended model, debtors face uncertainty concerning both their period 2 wealth and their period 2 housing value.

There are several distinct cases, corresponding to different levels of period 2 housing value. In one case, the value of the house is so low that housing equity is more negative than the cost of moving so that debtors prefer to default on their mortgages regardless of the value of their period 2 wealth, W_2. Debtors also default on their unsecured debt and file for bankruptcy if W_2 turns out to be low, that is, the bankruptcy decision is the same as in the model just discussed. In other cases, housing value is higher, and so debtors would prefer to repay their mortgages and keep their houses. But whether they can do so depends on their realizations of period 2 wealth, W_2. This is the case emphasized by Berkowitz and Hynes (1999), in which debtors' ability to repay their mortgages may be enhanced by filing for bankruptcy and obtaining discharge of their unsecured debt. Finally, housing value may be so high that debtors never default on their mortgages and never file for bankruptcy. If W_2 turns out to be too low to repay the unsecured debts, then debtors sell their houses and use the proceeds to repay both loans.

Lin and White show that, first, if the transaction cost of foreclosure is fixed, then neither the homestead nor the personal property exemption level affects the supply of mortgage loans. This is because when debtors default on their mortgages, lenders foreclose on the house and are repaid before the debtor receives the homestead exemption. So mortgage repayment is independent of both exemption levels.[20] However, a more realistic assumption is that the transactions cost of foreclosure is higher when the debtor files for bankruptcy, because filing for bankruptcy delays the foreclosure process.[21] Then a rise in either exemption reduces the supply of mortgage credit, because debtors' probability of filing for bankruptcy rises, and mortgage lenders' return falls when debtors file for bankruptcy. These predictions hold even if borrowers are assumed to file for bankruptcy as a means of increasing their ability to repay their mortgages, as discussed earlier. Finally, increases in either the homestead or the personal property exemption are predicted to reduce the supply of unsecured credit.

Since the HMDA data cover a series of years in the 1990s, Lin and White (2001) tested their model both with and without state-fixed effects. The results without state-fixed effects rely on cross-state variation in exemption levels. They show that applicants for both mortgage and home improvement loans were significantly more likely to be turned down in states with higher homestead exemptions. When applicants live in states with homestead exemptions that are unlimited rather than in the lowest quartile of the distribution, their probability of being turned down for mortgage loans rises by 2 percentage points, and their probability of being turned down for home improvement loans rises by 5 percentage points. When applicants live in states with personal property exemptions of $10,000 rather than $1,000, their probability of being turned down for mortgage loans rises by 1 percentage point, and their probability of being turned down for home improvement loans rises by 0.4 percentage points. All of these results are statistically significant. Because the availability of mortgage loans is influenced by exemption levels, the results suggest that the costs of foreclosure are higher when borrowers file for bankruptcy.

When state-fixed effects are introduced, the exemption variables capture only the effects of changes in exemption levels that occur during the period covered by the data. In this specification, Lin and White again found that applicants are more likely to be turned down for mortgage and home improvement loans, although the mortgage loan coefficient is only significant at the 10 percent level. But the relationships between the personal property exemption and the probability of applicants being turned down for either type of loan were insignificant. Because few changes in exemption levels occurred in the years covered by the HMDA data, more years of data will be needed to definitely answer the question of whether there is a relationship between credit availability and bankruptcy exemptions.

7.4.3 Bankruptcy and Small Business Credit

In the United States, personal bankruptcy law is the bankruptcy procedure applicable to small businesses as well as to consumers. Owners of unincorporated businesses are legally liable for their businesses' debts. This means that, if the business fails, owners have an incentive to file for personal bankruptcy because both their business and personal debts will be discharged. In contrast, owners of corporations are not legally liable for their corporations' debts, so that personal bankruptcy law, in theory, is irrelevant to small corporations. But in practice, lenders to small corporations often require the corporation's owner to personally guarantee the loan and/or to give the lender a second mortgage on the owner's house. This muddies the corporate/noncorporate distinction and makes personal bankruptcy law applicable to small corporations as well. About one in five personal bankruptcy filings in the United States list some business debt, suggesting the importance of bankruptcy law to small business owners (Sullivan, Westbrook, and Warren 1989).

Berkowitz and White (2004) used the National Survey of Small Business Finance to examine how bankruptcy exemptions affect small business credit. They found that if small businesses are located in states with high rather than low homestead exemptions, they are more likely to be turned down for credit, and, if they receive loans, interest rates are higher and loan sizes are smaller. For noncorporate firms, the probability of being credit-rationed rises by 32 percent if firms are located in states with unlimited rather than low homestead exemptions; while for corporate firms, the increase is 30 percent. Both relationships are statistically significant. Conditional on receiving a loan, noncorporate firms paid 2 percentage points more in interest and corporate firms paid 0.83 percentage points more if they were located in states with homestead exemptions at the seventy-fifth versus the twenty-fifth percentiles of the distribution. Both types of firms receive about $70,000 less credit if they are located in states with homestead exemptions at the seventy-fifth rather than the twenty-fifth percentiles of the distribution. Thus higher bankruptcy exemptions also reduce the supply of credit to small businesses, both noncorporate and corporate.

7.5 Empirical Evidence: Consumer Behavior

Now, turn to the empirical studies of the consumer bankruptcy decision. As previously discussed, the economic model of bankruptcy predicts that consumers plan in advance for the possibility of bankruptcy, and their probability of filing depends on the financial benefit from doing so. This model implies that the important factors affecting the bankruptcy decision are consumers' assets and debts and the bankruptcy exemption in their state, since these factors combine to determine the financial benefit from filing. The sociological model of bankruptcy assumes that consumers do not plan in advance for bankruptcy, and they file only when adverse events reduce their ability to repay. This model implies that the important determinants of the bankruptcy decision are measures of households' ability to repay, including income and whether adverse events—such as illness, job loss, or divorce—have recently occurred. An important additional issue is the role of social disapproval, or stigma, in the bankruptcy filing decision. Although the bankruptcy procedure in the United States is very favorable to individual debtors, they may hesitate to file if social disapproval is strong.[22]

7.5.1 Bankruptcy Stigma
Several papers used aggregate bankruptcy filing data to test the relationship between bankruptcy exemption levels and consumers' probability of filing for bankruptcy. White (1987) used county-level aggregate data from the early 1980s to test this relationship and found a positive and significant relationship between exemption levels and

county-level bankruptcy filing rates. Buckley and Brinig (1998) did a similar study using state-level data from the 1980s, but did not find a significant relationship between the filing rate and exemption levels. The Buckley-Brinig results for exemption levels are not surprising, since they included state dummy variables in their analysis. In this specification, the state dummy variables capture the effect of states' initial exemption levels, while the exemption variables themselves capture the effect of changes in exemption levels. Because few states changed their exemption levels during the period, Buckley and Brinig found no relationship between exemption levels and the probability of filing.

Efforts to estimate models of the bankruptcy filing decision using household-level data were initially hampered by the lack of survey data on whether individual households have filed for bankruptcy. In an innovative study, Domowitz and Sartain (1999) got around this limitation by combining two data sources: a sample of households that filed for bankruptcy under Chapter 7 in the early 1980s and a representative sample of U.S. households—the 1983 SCF—that included information on households' income and wealth. They found that households were more likely to file for bankruptcy if they had greater medical and credit card debt and less likely to file if they owned a home. Domowitz and Sartain did not examine the effect of financial benefit or exemptions on the bankruptcy filing decision.

Fay, Hurst, and White (2002) were the first to use microdata to estimate a model of the bankruptcy filing decision; they used panel data from the PSID. In 1996, the PSID asked respondents whether they filed for bankruptcy during the period 1984–1995 and, if so, in which year. Using the results of the survey and other data collected each year by the PSID, Fay, Hurst, and White calculated households' financial benefit from filing for bankruptcy each year. For each year, they also had information concerning households' income, homeowner status, demographic characteristics, and whether particular adverse events had occurred during the previous year. They found that consumers are significantly more likely to file for bankruptcy as their financial benefit from filing increases: If financial benefit increased by $1,000 for all households, then the results imply that the national bankruptcy filing rate will increase by 7 percent each year. Thus the evidence supports the hypothesis that consumers treat filing for bankruptcy as an economic decision. Fay, Hurst, and White also found that ability to pay affects the bankruptcy decision, since households with higher income were found to be significantly less likely to file. However, they were not able to cleanly test the economic versus the sociological models of bankruptcy against each other. This is because financial benefit is measured with error, since the PSID does not collect data on wealth every year, and, as a result, measured financial benefit is correlated with income. This means that Fay, Hurst, and White's finding that income is significantly related to the probability of filing for bankruptcy could support either the sociological model (because income itself affects the bankruptcy decision) or the economic model (because financial benefit affects the bankruptcy decision, and income is correlated with measured financial benefit). Finally, Fay, Hurst, and White also examined whether recent adverse events affected the bankruptcy decision by including measures of whether the household head or spouse experienced job loss or a serious illness during the previous year or whether divorce occurred during the previous year. They found that all three variables were positively related to the probability of filing for bankruptcy, but the job loss and illness variables were insignificant, and the divorce variable was only marginally significant. Thus, the results provide little support for the sociological model of bankruptcy.

Consider next the role of bankruptcy stigma in the decision to file for bankruptcy. Gross and Souleles (2002) used a dataset of credit card accounts from 1995 to 1997 to model the decision to default on credit card loans and to file for bankruptcy. They controlled for variables such as the cardholder's riskiness and the length of time since the account was opened. They treat the residual of their model as a measure of the effect of bankruptcy stigma. Gross and Souleles found that, over the two-year period of their data, the probability of filing for bankruptcy rose by 1 percentage point, and the probability of default rose by 3 percentage points, holding everything else constant. The authors interpret their results as evidence that bankruptcy stigma fell during their time period.

Fay, Hurst, and White (2002) used a more direct approach to measuring bankruptcy stigma; they used the aggregate bankruptcy filing rate in the local region during the previous year as an inverse proxy for the level of bankruptcy stigma. Surveys of bankruptcy filers show that they usually learn about bankruptcy from friends and relatives. Filers learn that the bankruptcy process is quick and easy, which reduces their fear of filing. They also learn that friends and relatives view bankruptcy in a favorable rather than a judgmental light; that is, the level of bankruptcy stigma is lower than they thought. Fay, Hurst, and White hypothesized that in a region with more bankruptcy filings, people are more likely to learn firsthand about bankruptcy, which reduces their perception of the level of bankruptcy stigma and makes them more likely to file. They tested this by including in their bankruptcy filing model the aggregate bankruptcy filing rate in the household's bankruptcy court district during the previous year. They found that in districts with higher aggregate filing rates (lower bankruptcy stigma), the probability of filing for bankruptcy was significantly higher.

7.5.2 Entrepreneurship and Work Effort

Fan and White (2003) examined whether debtors who live in states with higher bankruptcy exemptions are more likely to own businesses, using panel data from the Survey of Income and Program Participation. They focused on the effect of the homestead exemption, since it is the largest and most variable of the bankruptcy exemptions, and they distinguished between the effects of the homestead exemption on the behavior of home owners versus renters, since only the former can take the homestead exemption. Fan and White found that home owners are 35 percent more likely to own businesses if they live in states with high or unlimited rather than low homestead exemptions, while the difference for renters was 29 percent. Both differences are statistically significant. (The fact that exemptions have a large effect on renters' probability of owning businesses may be due to the fact that most renters expect to become home owners by the time they face the prospect of bankruptcy.) Fan and White also examined the effect of bankruptcy exemptions on decisions to start and end businesses, in which starting a business is measured by not owning a business in one year and owning one in the next, while ending a business is the opposite. They found that home owners are 28 percent more likely to start businesses if they live in states with unlimited rather than low homestead exemptions, although the relationship is only marginally significant. But they did not find a significant relationship ending a business and the exemption level.

As discussed earlier, policymakers justify the fresh start in bankruptcy (the 100 percent exemption for post-bankruptcy earnings) on the grounds that debtors work harder after bankruptcy if they are not required to use part of their earnings to repay old debt. But the previously discussed model implies that the fresh start, in fact, has an ambiguous effect on post-bankruptcy labor supply. Outside of bankruptcy, creditors may garnish part of debtors' wages if debtors default. Then, if debtors file for bankruptcy, garnishment ends and debtors keep all of their post-bankruptcy earnings. The substitution effect of keeping all their earnings implies that debtors will work more after bankruptcy. But discharge of debt in bankruptcy also increases debtors' wealth, and the income effect implies that they will work less after bankruptcy. Overall, bankruptcy could therefore be associated with either an increase or a decrease in work effort.

Han and Li (2004) used the PSID's special bankruptcy survey to test whether consumers work more or less after bankruptcy. They found that filing for bankruptcy is associated with a large (17 percent) reduction in the number of hours worked by the household head, but the relationship was not statistically significant. Their results suggest that the income effect of debt discharge in bankruptcy is quantitatively more important than the substitution effect of ending a debtor's obligation to repay. These results, although tentative, suggest support for reforms that would reduce the exemption for post-bankruptcy earnings to less than 100 percent, since these reforms are more likely to be economically efficient if labor supply falls when debtors file for bankruptcy.

7.5.3 Bankruptcy and Consumption Insurance

The model discussed earlier emphasized the insurance role of bankruptcy and the fact that higher exemption levels are associated with additional insurance.[23] Grant (2003) tested this hypothesis using data from the U.S. Consumer Expenditure Survey. This dataset gives microlevel information for a rotating panel of households, each of which is interviewed quarterly over a one-year period. To measure the insurance effect of bankruptcy, Grant computed the average variance of household consumption for each stateyear covered by the dataset. Then he regressed the change in the variance of consumption from one year to the next on the bankruptcy exemption level, control variables, and state-fixed effects. The data have the advantage of covering a twenty-year period, so that the number of changes in bankruptcy exemption levels is maximized. In this formulation, the hypothesis is that the coefficient of the exemption variable will have a negative sign, which implies that higher exemptions are associated with lower-consumption variance/higher-consumption insurance. Grant found that both the exemption variable and a dummy variable for states with unlimited homestead exemptions have the predicted negative signs, and the results were statistically significant. Thus, the empirical results provide support at a macrolevel for the hypothesis that higher bankruptcy exemptions are associated with an increase in the level of consumers' certainty concerning their future consumption.[24]

7.6   Conclusion

The results of the studies surveyed in this chapter suggest that bankruptcy has important and wide-ranging effects on both credit markets and on other aspects of consumer behavior. On the credit market side, generous bankruptcy exemptions increase consumers' demand for credit by providing partial consumption insurance, but cause lenders to reduce the supply of credit by increasing the probability of default. In states with higher bankruptcy exemptions, consumers are turned down for credit more often and pay higher interest rates. If they have high assets, they hold more credit in high-exemption states; if they have low assets, they hold less credit in high-exemption states. Small businesses are also more likely to be turned down for credit, pay higher interest rates, and hold less credit if they are located in high-exemption states. These results apply to both noncorporate or corporate small businesses. Overall, the bankruptcy system causes credit to be redistributed from high-exemption to low-exemption states and from low-asset to high-asset borrowers. High bankruptcy exemptions also have other effects on consumer behavior—for example, they cause debtors to behave more opportunistically, reallocate their portfolios toward more unsecured debt and more liquid assets, file for bankruptcy more often, work fewer hours after filing for bankruptcy, and become self-employed more often. But higher bankruptcy exemptions benefit consumers by reducing the variance of consumption, that is, they provide partial consumption insurance.

Notes

I am grateful to Charles Grant and Giuseppe Bertola for helpful comments and to the Economics Program at NSF for research support under grant number 0212444.

1. See table 7.1 for the source of data on number of bankruptcy filings. Data on consumer debt are taken from *Economic Report of the President* (2003), and from "Effect of U.S. Economy on Credit Card Loss Rates," *S&P Business Wire*, December 18, 2002.

2. *Local Loan Co. v. Hunt*, 202 US 234 (1934).

3. Other countries do not generally apply the fresh start in bankruptcy, and they treat debtors much more harshly. For example, in Germany, individual debtors are not

allowed to file for bankruptcy voluntarily, and their debts are not discharged in bankruptcy, although creditors' efforts to collect are stayed. Debtors are required to repay from future earnings. See White 1996 and Domowitz and Alexopoulos 1998 for discussion. Note that, in the United States, not all debt is discharged in bankruptcy, so that in practice debtors receive only a partial fresh start.

4. See White 1994 for a model of objectives 3 and 4.

5. Rea (1984) and Jackson (1986) were the first to discuss the insurance aspect of personal bankruptcy. See Olson 1999 and Athreya 2002 for discussion in the macroeconomic context.

6. To garnish wages, creditors must obtain a court order allowing them to collect a portion of the debtor's wages from the debtor's employer. Federal law allows creditors to garnish up to 25 percent of debtors' wages, but some states restrict garnishment further, and a few prohibit it completely.

7. See Hynes, Malani, and Posner 2004 for discussion of the political economy of exemption laws. All of the states opted out between 1978 and 1982, and, since then, relatively few changes in exemption levels have occurred.

8. For a more detailed discussion of the differences between Chapters 7 and 13 and special circumstances that might lead debtors to file under Chapter 13, see White 1998a.

9. This section draws on Bebchuk and White 2006 and on Fan and White 2003. For other models of bankruptcy that emphasize its macroeconomic effects, see Domowitz and Alexopoulos 1998 and Athreya 2002.

10. Because the consumer has only a single loan, the model does not consider priority rules in bankruptcy. See section 7.4.2 for discussion of secured versus unsecured loans in the personal bankruptcy context.

11. Another reason for assuming a fractional wage exemption is that wage garnishment exemptions take this form (normally, 75 percent of wages are exempt from garnishment). Nonetheless, the proposed bankruptcy reform currently pending in the U.S. Congress imposes a fixed dollar wage exemption on certain types of debtors.

12. This assumes that the consumer pays the cost of filing, F, beforehand so that the cost is passed on to creditors. Also, the model assumes that creditors never garnish debtors' wages, since debtors always file for bankruptcy if they default. See section 7.3.2 for a discussion of wage garnishment and the possibility that debtors might default but not file for bankruptcy.

13. If consumers' wages are subject to garnishment in period 1 (because they have defaulted on an earlier debt), then $\hat{W}_2$ shifts to the left since an additional benefit of filing for bankruptcy is that garnishment ends. See section 7.3.1 for further discussion of the relationship between default and bankruptcy.

14. For example, if $x = 0.5$, then ε_x must be less than 1.

15. While the stereotype is that wealthy people work less, empirical evidence suggests that the probability of owning a business increases with wealth. See Holtz-Eakin, Joulfaian, and Rosen 1994 and Fan and White 2003.

16. If borrowers varied along some credit-relevant dimension that lenders could observe in period 1, then lenders would gradually cease lending to more creditworthy borrowers as the bankruptcy exemption level increased.

17. The model assumes that wages are not subject to garnishment in period 1. It could be modified to consider this possibility.

18. By the envelope theorem, the effect on consumers' optimal labor supply is irrelevant as long as changes in the exemption variables are small.

19. See Brueckner 2000 for a model of mortgage default that is similar to the model discussed earlier of the bankruptcy decision.

20. This result assumes that mortgage lenders have no claim on other assets of the debtor, even if the proceeds of selling the house are less than the amount of the mortgage.

21. Borrowers who are behind on their mortgage payments and expect lenders to foreclose often file for bankruptcy under Chapter 13. Doing so allows them to delay the foreclosure proceeding, although they must eventually repay their mortgage arrears in order to avoid foreclosure.

22. Another reason why consumers might avoid filing for bankruptcy is that they may not be able to obtain credit after filing. However, a survey by Staten (1993) finds that three-quarters of debtors are able to obtain new credit within a year of filing for bankruptcy, although they tend to pay high interest rates. Some lenders feel that debtors are better credit risks after filing for bankruptcy, since they cannot file again under Chapter 7 for six years.

23. Because unsecured debts are discharged under Chapter 7 bankruptcy but some assets are exempt, debtors who contemplate filing for bankruptcy have strategic incentive to borrow—even at high interest rates—in order to acquire liquid assets when such assets will be exempt in bankruptcy. See chapter 6 for a discussion of empirical evidence of such behavior.

24. Lehnert and Maki (2002) have also examined the relationship between bankruptcy and consumption smoothing.

References

Athreya, Kartik B. 2002. "Welfare Implications of the Bankruptcy Reform Act of 1999." *Journal of Monetary Economics* 49: 1567–1595.

Ausubel, Lawrence M. 1999. "Adverse Selection in the Credit Card Market." Working paper, Department of Economics, University of Maryland.

Bebchuk, L. A., and Michelle J. White. 2006. "Bankruptcy Law." In *Handbook of Law and Economics*, ed. A. M. Polinsky and S. Shavell. Amsterdam: Elsevier.

Berkowitz, Jeremy, and Richard Hynes. 1999. "Bankruptcy Exemptions and the Market for Mortgage Loans." *Journal of Law and Economics* 42: 908–930.

Berkowitz, Jeremy, and Michelle J. White. 2004. "Bankruptcy and Small Firms' Access to Credit." *RAND Journal of Economics* 35, no. 1: 69–84.

Brueckner, Jan K. 2000. "Mortgage Default with Asymmetric Information." *Journal of Urban Economics* 20: 251–274.

Buckley, F. H., and F. M. Brining. 1998. "The Bankruptcy Puzzle." *Journal of Legal Studies* 27: 187–208.

Domowitz, Ian, and Michelle Alexopoulos. 1998. "Personal Liabilities and Bankruptcy Reform: An International Perspective." *International Finance* 1: 127–159.

Domowitz, Ian, and Robert Sartain. 1999. "Determinants of the Consumer Bankruptcy Decision." *Journal of Finance* 54: 403–420.

Elias, S., A. Renauer, R. Leonard, and K. Michon. 2001. *How to File for Bankruptcy*, 9th ed. Berkeley, Calif.: Nolo Press.

Fan, Wei, and Michelle J. White. 2003. "Personal Bankruptcy and the Level of Entrepreneurial Activity." *Journal of Law & Economics* 46, no. 2 (October): 543–568.

Fay, Scott, Erik Hurst, and Michelle J. White. 2002. "The Household Bankruptcy Decision." *American Economic Review* 92, no. 3 (June): 706–718.

Grant, Charles. 2003. "Evidence on the Effect of U.S. Bankruptcy Exemptions." Working paper, EUI, Florence.

Gropp, Reint, John K. Scholz, and Michelle J. White. 1997. "Personal Bankruptcy and Credit Supply and Demand." *Quarterly Journal of Economics*: 217–251.

Gross, David, and Nicholas Souleles. 2002. "An Empirical Analysis of Personal Bankruptcy and Delinquency." *Review of Financial Studies* 15, no. 1: 319–347.

Han, Song, and Wenli Li. 2004. "The Effect of Filing for Personal Bankruptcy on Labor Supply: Evidence from Micro Data." Working paper, Federal Reserve Bank of Philadelphia.

Holtz-Eakin, Douglas, David Joulfaian, and Harvey Rosen. 1994. "Sticking It Out: Entrepreneurial Survival and Liquidity Constraints." *Journal of Political Economy* 102: 53–75.

Hynes, Richard M., Anup Malani, and Eric A. Posner. 2004. "The Political Economy of Property Exemption Laws." *Journal of Law and Economics* 47: 19–43.

Jackson, Thomas H. 1986. *The Logic and Limits of Bankruptcy Law*. Cambridge, Mass.: Harvard University Press.

Lehnert, Andreas, and Dean M. Maki. 2002. "Consumption, Debt and Portfolio Choice: Testing the Effects of Bankruptcy Law." Working paper, Board of Governors.

Lin, Emily Y., and Michelle J. White. 2001. "Bankruptcy and the Market for Mortgage and Home Improvement Loans." *Journal of Urban Economics* 50, no. 1: 138–162.

Olson, Martha L. 1999. "Avoiding Default: The Role of Credit in the Consumption Collapse of 1930." *Quarterly Journal of Economics*: 319–335.

Posner, Eric A. 1995. "Contract Law in the Welfare State: A Defense of the Unconscionability Doctrine, Usury Laws, and Related Limitations on the Freedom to Contract." *Journal of Legal Studies* 24, no. 2: 283–319.

Rea, Samuel A. 1984. "Arm-Breaking, Consumer Credit and Personal Bankruptcy." *Economic Inquiry* 22: 188–208.

Staten, Michael. 1993. "The Impact of Post-Bankruptcy Credit on the Number of Personal Bankruptcies." Working paper no. 58, Credit Research Center, Purdue University.

Sullivan, Theresa, J. L. Westbrook, and Elizabeth Warren. 1989. *As We Forgive Our Debtors: Bankruptcy and Consumer Credit in America*. New York: Oxford University Press.

Sullivan, Theresa, J. L. Westbrook, and Elizabeth Warren. 2000. *The Fragile Middle Class: Americans in Debt*. New Haven: Yale University Press.

Wang, Hung-Jen, and Michelle J. White. 2000. "An Optimal Personal Bankruptcy System and Proposed Reforms." *Journal of Legal Studies* 29, no. 1: 255–286.

White, Michelle J. 1987. "Personal Bankruptcy under the 1978 Bankruptcy Code: An Economic Analysis." *Indiana Law Journal* 63 (fall): 1–57.

White, Michelle J. 1994. "Corporate Bankruptcy as a Filtering Device: Chapter 11 Reorganizations and Out-of-Court Debt Restructurings." *Journal of Law, Economics and Organization* 10 (October): 268–295.

White, Michelle J. 1996. "The Costs of Corporate Bankruptcy: A U.S.-European Comparison." In *Corporate Bankruptcy: Economic and Legal Perspectives*, ed. J. Bhandari and L. Weiss, 467–500. Cambridge: Cambridge University Press.

White, Michelle J. 1998a. "Why It Pays to File for Bankruptcy: A Critical Look at Incentives under U.S. Bankruptcy Laws and a Proposal for Change." *University of Chicago Law Review* 65: 685–732.

White, Michelle J. 1998b. "Why Don't More Households File for Bankruptcy?" *Journal of Law, Economics, and Organization* 14, no. 2 (October): 205–231.

8 The Evolution of the Credit Counseling Industry in the United States

Michael Staten

The personal insolvency industry has become a big business in the United States. In 2003, over 1.6 million American households filed for personal bankruptcy relief. Over the past decade, over 10 percent of all U.S. households did the same. Consequently, providing assistance to financially troubled consumers has become a growth industry. In addition to formal legal services offered by bankruptcy attorneys, consumers have increasingly sought assistance from credit counseling agencies, most of which are established as nonprofit entities. Beginning in the 1960s as a network of small, locally controlled nonprofit agencies, credit counseling has evolved into an industry in its own right. Although no comprehensive industry statistics exist, a conservative estimate based on available data suggests that between 5 and 6 million consumers sought advice from credit counseling organizations in 2002.[1]

From the outset, credit counseling was conceived as a creditor-sponsored effort to advise financially troubled consumers on alternatives to personal bankruptcy. A network of nonprofit counseling agencies was established to offer in-person, individualized counseling sessions through which consumers received budgeting analysis and advice. A core service of each agency was to negotiate with creditors on behalf of eligible consumer clients to set up voluntary repayment plans, concessions on finance charges and repayment terms, and a halt to collection efforts. When successful, these agency-administered repayment plans provide a valuable service for consumers by helping them to avoid the stigma associated with filing for bankruptcy.

They also help creditors. The oldest network of nonprofit credit counseling agencies, those operating as members of the National Foundation for Credit Counseling (NFCC), returned $2.3 billion to creditors in 2002 through the voluntary repayment plans structured for their consumer clients. Industrywide statistics are elusive, but payments to all credit grantors in 2002 through counseling agency repayment plans may have totaled as much as $8 billion. In terms of credit card receivables, up to $22 billion in outstanding balances from major national card issuers were being serviced through credit counseling debt repayment plans in 2002.[2] To put this in perspective, total credit card charge-offs industrywide in 2002 were $35 billion.

The rapid expansion in both credit availability and serious loan delinquencies during the 1990s caused demand for counseling services to soar, and led to the entry of hundreds of new competitors. The number of credit counseling agencies mushroomed from fewer than 250 agencies operating between 700 and 800 offices in 1992 to over 900 agencies operating as many as 2,000 offices by the end of 2003.[3] Unlike the traditional agencies that provided face-to-face counseling, many of the new entrants offered telephone counseling only and could serve clients nationwide from a single call center.

Some of these new entrants adopted deceptive and abusive practices that have tarnished the positive public image of the counseling industry that had been cultivated over the previous thirty years. The Internal Revenue Service (IRS), the Federal Trade Commission (FTC) and the U.S. Senate all launched investigations into the industry practices during 2003. In October 2003, the FTC and the IRS joined with state regulators to issue a joint press release urging consumers to be cautious when considering use of a credit counseling agency, offering tips on how to choose a reputable organization.[4] At least five state attorneys general have filed lawsuits against one of the largest credit counseling agencies in recent years (U.S. Senate 2004, 30–31). Legislation is pending in Congress and in various states that would impose new regulations to curtail abusive practices. In short, despite serving millions of consumers annually, the credit counseling industry has developed a serious reputational problem.

How did a social service-oriented industry comprised mostly of nonprofit firms go so far astray? The following sections will describe the evolution of the credit counseling industry in the United States, an industry that began as a market-driven alternative to personal bankruptcy. The industry's birth, subsequent growth, and eventual reputational crisis are readily explainable through simple economic analysis. With the industry now at an evolutionary crossroads, facing stricter regulation and skeptical clients, its future is less clear. The subsequent sections will discuss the central issues facing public policymakers.

8.1   Historical Origins and Growth of Credit Counseling

For as long as there has been a consumer credit industry, there have also been overextended borrowers in need of advice and assistance. During the first half of the twentieth century, financially troubled consumers who had difficulty making payments to multiple creditors would sometimes turn to commercial debt poolers for assistance. A debt pooler was typically a for-profit company that would act as an intermediary between a borrower and his creditors. The primary objective of the debt pooler was to negotiate a repayment arrangement acceptable to most or all of the creditors. The repayment plans would generally entail either a reduction of the outstanding balance and interest charges or a longer payout period, or both. The debtor would make regular payments to the debt pooler, who would then distribute the proceeds to the creditors according to the plan. For this service, the debt pooler typically received a fee from the borrower.

When these plans worked well, debtors were able to utilize the creditor concessions to resolve their debts and avoid bankruptcy. Bankruptcy in the first half of the twentieth century was a relatively rare event and carried considerable social stigma. Negotiation with multiple creditors to arrange and administer repayment plans took considerable effort and expertise, and so represented a valuable service to a struggling debtor. However, when these plans worked badly, unscrupulous poolers took advantage of borrowers and generally gave the entire business an unsavory reputation. In words that ring familiar today, Milstein and Ratner (1981) describe some of the problems: "Preying on a clientele that generally is legally unsophisticated and willing to believe exaggerated claims of ready cures for their overwhelming financial burdens, debt poolers have, for example, charged exorbitant fees and collected these fees before paying amounts owed to creditors. There have been instances in which creditors have simply not received the payments made to the debt pooler, and debtors have been unable to recover their money. Further, debt poolers have often established repayment plans that are clearly not feasible" (980).

Legislative steps to curtail deceptive practices and exploitation of borrowers by debt poolers began as early as 1935 when Minnesota and Wisconsin established licensing requirements for poolers (Milstein and Ratner 1981, 982). The pace of legislation accelerated during the 1950s as states either prohibited for-profit debt pooling or regulated its operation. By 1980, twenty-nine states and the District of Columbia had prohibited commercial debt pooling. An additional sixteen states allowed commercial debt pooling but imposed a variety of regulations to curtail abusive practices. These measures included licensing requirements, the posting of a bond or cash deposit by debt pooling companies, established ceilings on fees charged to consumers and maximum time limits for forwarding consumer payments to creditor accounts. At the same time, many of these regulations exempted categories of institutions that provided debt pooling services, presumably because they were structured to operate in the consumer's best interest. Exempted institutions included (1) the debtor's attorney, or other agent working on the debtor's behalf; and (2) organizations or parties whose loyalty to creditor interests was clearly disclosed, such as representatives of one or more creditors (984). Some states specifically exempted nonprofit debt poolers, presumably because they lacked the commercial, for-profit motive that spawned abusive practices.

Perhaps in response to both the rising numbers of delinquent accounts as well as to an increasingly constrained "pooling" industry, in the late 1960s, the credit-granting industry supported a reconstitution of the existing National Foundation for Consumer Credit (NFCC), which was originally established in 1951 to promote borrower education about how to handle credit wisely. In 1967, creditor and community service representatives were added to the NFCC's board of trustees, and the organization's mission was redirected so as to establish and promote credit counseling agencies across the country. Over the next fifteen years, a national network of nonprofit credit counseling agencies evolved under the sponsoring and licensing umbrella of the NFCC. By 1980, NFCC-member agencies operated in over two hundred cities in forty-seven states, generally under the trademarked name Consumer Credit Counseling Service (Milstein and Ratner 1981, 981).

There is little doubt that creditors supported the NFCC's counseling initiative in order to promote an alternative to bankruptcy for debtors.[5] Unlike the earlier commercial debt pooling business, in which debtors bore the cost of hiring intermediaries to negotiate on their behalf, credit counseling evolved as a market-driven alternative to bankruptcy funded mostly by creditors. From the beginning, the centerpiece of the credit counseling industry has been the administration of a Debt Management Plan (DMP). A DMP is a voluntary agreement between a consumer and her creditors that resembles the earlier debt pooling arrangements. In the absence of the CCCS-administered DMP, the typical experience of a financially troubled consumer would be as the recipient of each creditor's individual collection efforts. In fact, at the first sign of serious trouble, a race would ensue to squeeze the consumer first so as not to be left outside when the consumer's income and assets were exhausted. However, creditors recognized that through mutual forbearance, they could collect more as a group, perhaps much more if by suspending their individual collection efforts they could avoid pushing the consumer into the bankruptcy court. The incentive to participate in a DMP is greatest for unsecured creditors who would typically collect nothing (or almost nothing) in a Chapter 7 bankruptcy liquidation.[6] Mortgage holders and auto lenders worry less about recovery of principle, given the value of the collateral, so are less likely to participate in DMPs. Consequently, the concept of the Debt Management Plan administered by a credit counseling agency originally had the strongest backing from retail creditors, and later by bank credit card issuers as general-purpose credit card debt expanded rapidly through the 1980s.

Of course, consumers also valued an alternative to bankruptcy. Many consumers wished to avoid the social and economic stigma associated with filing for bankruptcy and had sufficient income to repay their debts over a three-to-four-year period. But, a DMP wasn't appropriate for everyone. NFCC-member agencies provided advice and financial/budgeting education to their consumer clients, in addition to setting up a formal DMP. Much of the education regarding budgeting and wise use of credit was an outgrowth of the process of screening borrowers to determine the extent of their credit problems, beginning with an initial, face-to-face interview.

According to NFCC data, during 1992 (the last year in which NFCC-member agencies constituted nearly the entire credit counseling industry in the United States), member agencies conducted individual budget counseling sessions with 549,116 consumers. A large majority of these individuals received advice and assistance without being set up on a DMP. On average, about 30 percent of CCCS clients nationwide were advised after the initial interview that they could handle their debt problems on their own, armed with the information resulting from the budget review and perhaps with some recommended adjustments to spending and incomes. Another 36 percent were referred elsewhere for legal or other assistance (e.g., to handle problems such as substance abuse, child support, and so forth), including legal advice regarding bankruptcy options. Only about 35 percent were placed in debt management plans. Over the past twenty-five years,

NFCC statistics reveal that these percentages have been remarkably consistent.[7]

In setting up a DMP, the counseling agency negotiates with creditors on behalf of the consumer to lower monthly payments as well as obtain waivers or reductions in finance charges and fees. The objective is to structure a repayment plan out of the client's available monthly income that repays all creditors within three to four years. The average DMP negotiated in 1992 involved nine creditors and $12,548 of debt to be repaid. It called for a monthly payment from the client to the agency of $349, on average, to be distributed to the client's creditors (almost exclusively unsecured). The average scheduled plan length was forty-two months. Repayment plans were strictly voluntary between the consumer and creditors: not all creditors need participate (though the successful negotiation of a plan hinges on convincing as many to participate as possible), and the consumer could back out at any time. Participating creditors agreed to suspend collection efforts, and often reage accounts (i.e., reinstate them as current), so long as plan payments continued. These plans returned nearly $1 billion to creditors nationwide in 1992.

The DMP product was at the heart of the service provided by the agency, and provided the revenue that supported most of the agency's operations. A peculiar funding arrangement evolved in which the creditors that participated in DMPs voluntarily contributed to the CCCS agency a percentage of the debt recovered. This contribution, known in the industry as "fair share," originally was about 15 percent of amount recovered through DMP payments, on average, but has fallen through the years for reasons to be discussed in the following section. The linkage of the fair-share contribution to the dollars recovered through DMPs makes clear that the credit-granting industry viewed their investment in the credit counseling network as supporting an alternative to courthouse remedies for insolvency.[8] However, given the fact that, year after year, the majority of consumers passing through the counseling interviews were not placed on DMPs, the fair-share contribution that derived from payments made by only 30–40 percent of all clients included a sizeable subsidy to support the rest of the agency's operations. A breakdown of NFCC agency revenue in 1992 reveals that 76 percent derived from creditor fair-share contributions. Another 15 percent derived from consumer clients on DMPs (monthly payments that averaged $9.48 plus one-time plan set-up fees that averaged about $14 at the minority of agencies that levied the fee).

Table 8.1
NFCC agency locations, 1982–2003

Year	Number of agencies	Number of locations	Number of locations per agency
1982	128	191	1.5
1983	139	237	1.7
1984	136	251	1.8
1985	140	277	2.0
1986	145	297	2.0
1987	156	353	2.3
1988	168	415	2.5
1989	171	479	2.8
1990	182	582	3.2
1991	190	718	3.8
1992	198	745	3.8
1993	202	831	4.1
1994	197	1,012	5.1
1995	200	1,197	6.0
1996	195	1,297	6.7
1997	193	1,374	7.1
1998	190	1,414	7.4
1999	184	1,429	7.8
2000	175	1,418	8.1
2001	155	1,295	8.4
2002	143	1,180	8.3
2003	129	1,091	8.5

Source: NFCC Annual Member Activity Reports, various years.

Clearly, the DMP product was supporting nearly all of each agency's operation.

8.2   New Entrants, Competition, and Erosion of Services

Between 1986 and 1992, personal bankruptcies in the United States more than doubled, with about 900,000 households filing for bankruptcy relief in 1992 alone. If we interpret rising bankruptcies as a sign of rising incidence of households with repayment problems, it is not surprising that NFCC-member counseling agencies experienced enormous growth during the same period. Table 8.1 illustrates the expansion in office locations, with over four hundred locations added to the NFCC network between 1986 and 1992. Dollars returned to creditors through DMPs leaped by 33 percent in 1992 from the previous year.

DMPs grew even faster than bankruptcies during this period. In 1986, there were 68,000 new DMPs started at NFCC agencies, compared to 121,000 personal bankruptcy petitions filed under Chapter 13 and 324,000 filed under Chapter 7. In 2002, NFCC agencies opened over 202,000 new DMPs, an increase of 197 percent, compared to 254,000 Chapter 13 petitions and 643,000 Chapter 7 petitions the same year. Indeed, the volume of new DMPs began to rival the volume of Chapter 13 petitions filed.

Creditors considered the counseling DMP option an important substitute for both Chapter 13 and Chapter 7 bankruptcies (see chapter 7 for a discussion of the two bankruptcy procedures, and of debtors' choices between them). The large majority of Chapter 7 filers have debts that far exceed their capacity to pay.[9] Chapter 13 is the more relevant comparison point. It is in fact a close cousin to the debt management plan and offers some advantages to borrowers whose income suffices to repay a significant portion of their debts. Court-supervised debt repayment plans are binding on creditors and can be set up to repay less (often far less) than 100 percent of the outstanding debts. All creditors are compelled to participate and required to halt collection activity. Even secured creditors (with the exception of mortgage lenders) are required to accept "cram down" of the balance to be repaid under a plan to an amount equal to the value of the collateral. On the other hand, the use of Chapter 13 carries a price: borrowers must pay attorney fees, and must bear whatever social stigma attaches to the filing of bankruptcy, as well as the economic stigma resulting from the record of bankruptcy attaching to the borrower's credit report for ten years. A voluntary DMP allows the borrower to avoid the stigma (social and economic) associated with bankruptcy, although it may require the repayment of more debt than under a Chapter 13 bankruptcy filing.

Apparently, in the late 1980s and into the early 1990s, many borrowers found this to be an acceptable tradeoff. Figure 8.1 displays the growth of new DMPs at NFCC-member agencies versus Chapter 13 bankruptcy petitions, both against the backdrop of the much larger volume of Chapter 7 petitions.

Yet, even as NFCC agencies were expanding, the volume of calls from troubled consumers was growing faster. Creditors complained of growing backlogs at agencies and waits of one to two weeks before borrowers could get an appointment with a counselor. As bankruptcies resumed a path of rapid growth in 1995–1996, creditors began

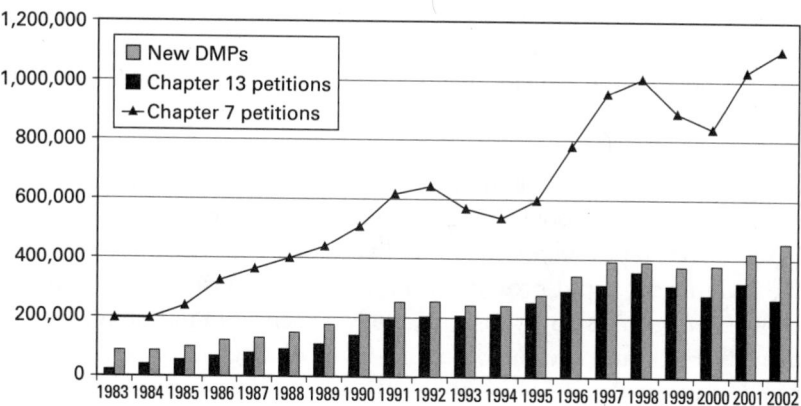

Figure 8.1

Nonbusiness bankruptcy filings versus new DMPs at NFCC-member agencies

viewing counseling as triage: Quick assessment of, and response to, repayment problems was deemed necessary to prevent even more debtors from resorting to bankruptcy for relief. As a consequence, creditors were amenable to cooperating with new entrants who could deal quickly and efficiently with the rising tide of enquires from borrowers in trouble. Their willingness to deal with non-NFCC competitors increased further as a result of the Garden State Credit Counseling lawsuit, a key antitrust case filed against the NFCC and several major creditors. The outcome of the lawsuit forced creditors to cooperate with a much broader range of agencies in addition to NFCC members.

NFCC-member agencies retained the exclusive rights to use the CCCS trademark, but no longer had claim to what, in many cities, had amounted to an exclusive geographic territory in which they were the only counseling agency that could effectively negotiate with creditors. Still, the CCCS brand name was well-established and had even greater visibility with creditors than consumers. New competitors hoping to deal with large national creditors on behalf of consumers had to adopt business models that negated the brand name advantage.

Established NFCC agencies had evolved over twenty-five years as quasi-social service agencies, specializing in providing resource-intensive, face-to-face budgeting and financial counseling from brick and mortar offices, with little or no competition due to the exclusive territorial licensing arrangement that accompanied the permission to use the CCCS brand. Many NFCC agencies were slow to adopt new technology and unaccustomed to the need for business plans, price competition, or the development of alternative products and revenue streams.[10]

These were the margins that the new entrants exploited. Given the demand by creditors for quick assessment of their delinquent customers' repayment problems, the most successful of the new firms recognized that rapid response and delivery of a core DMP product was the formula for rapid growth in the counseling business. Technology allowed new firms to bypass relatively expensive (and slow) investment in brick and mortar offices in favor of large "call centers" that could support the delivery of telephone counseling. Moreover, telephone counseling coupled with an effective national advertising campaign made a nationwide service possible, and little time was needed to launch a new business. The new entrants could begin competing with virtually every established NFCC agency, regardless of geographic location.

To a new entrant aspiring to rapid growth, there was little point in specializing in providing a service that did not generate revenue. So, competition from the new firms occurred at the one margin of the bundle of counseling services that was actually priced: the DMP. New entrants employed technology to deliver the DMP product faster (shorter queues for consumers), more cheaply (telephone delivery instead of face-to-face interviews at brick and mortar offices), and with greater back-office efficiency (electronic payment processing and accounting). The quicker turnaround, more efficient administration, and national reach appealed to creditors at a time when excess demand for counseling was peaking. Because the new entrants' costs were lower (partly through efficiency, and partly because they offered a more limited service), they could undercut the full-service NFCC agency pricing structure. This triggered downward pressure on prices, namely, on the "fair share" (agency revenue from creditors as a percentage of DMP dollars disbursed to creditors).

Competitors rapidly entered the counseling market. Because most states required credit counseling agencies that administer debt repayment plans to be structured as nonprofit entities, one of the best metrics for tracking the entry of new competitors is the number of applications to the IRS for tax-exempt status under Section 501(c)(3) of

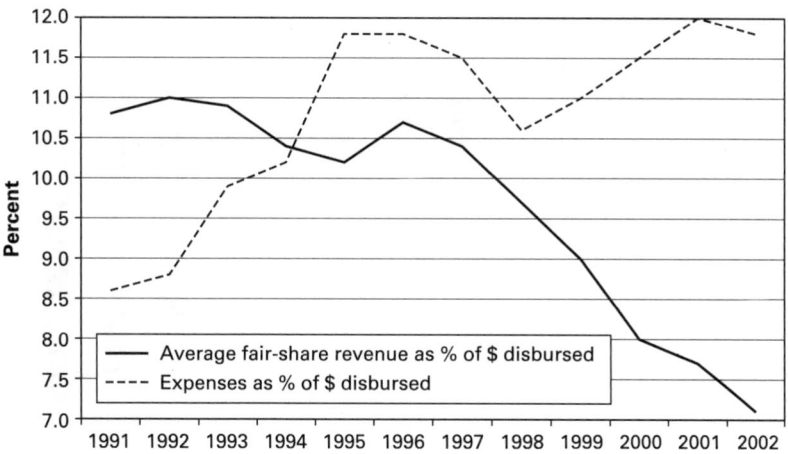

Figure 8.2
Trend in NFCC agency fair-share revenue and expenses

the IRS code. According to the IRS, 1,215 credit counseling agencies have applied for tax-exempt status since 1994. Over 800 of those applications were received between 2000 and 2003. As of early 2004, the IRS reported that 872 tax-exempt credit counseling organizations were operating in the United States (United States Senate 2004, 3). Of this number, approximately 126 were NFCC members.

Figures 8.2 and 8.3 illustrate the impact on NFCC agency income statements. Just prior to the wave of new entrants, between 1991 and 1994, NFCC agency revenue exceeded operating expenses, largely because of the increased fair-share revenue that derived from the rapid escalation in dollars disbursed to creditors from existing DMPs. However, as competition from new entrants drove down the "price" that creditors were willing to pay to support DMPs, between 1996 and 2002, the fair-share rate steadily eroded, falling from about 10.6 percent to about 7 percent. At the same time, operating expenses as a percentage of dollars disbursed continued to fluctuate between 10.5 percent and 12 percent. Figure 8.3 illustrates the resulting funding gap collectively experienced by NFCC-member agencies. By 2002, the agencies' primary revenue source, the fair-share payments from creditors in conjunction with DMPs, was generating $110 million less than total agency operating expenses. Fair-share revenue comprised just 58.3 percent of NFCC total revenues, down from nearly 76 percent a decade earlier. Clearly, NFCC agencies were experiencing acute pressure to generate other revenue streams, as well as pressure to cut costs.

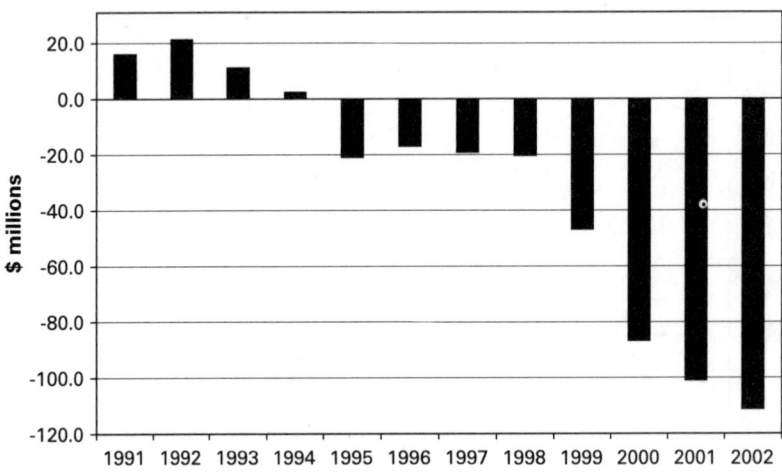

Figure 8.3
NFCC agency funding gap (fair-share revenue − expenses)

Increased fees on borrowers made up most of the difference. According to the NFCC, in 2002, client DMP fees rose to 29.6 percent of total NFCC-member agency revenues, up from 23.9 percent just one year earlier. Nearly all agencies (96 percent) charged a monthly fee for DMP clients, averaging $14 per month, and 61.4 percent charged a one-time enrollment fee that averaged $23. As for counseling in the absence of a DMP (i.e., the initial counseling session), 34 percent of agencies were charging a fee that averaged $12.94.

However much the entry of new firms may have boosted the number of consumers on DMPs, it generally did not enhance the delivery of counseling services to non-DMP clients. The reliance on price competition to attract creditor cooperation (and referrals) increased the incentive of new entrants to cut the quality and quantity of nonpriced services (education) and to maximize the number of consumers enrolled in DMPs, regardless of qualifications. Both of these margins were difficult for creditors to monitor.

The new entrants benefited from an information asymmetry. The intake interview allowed the agency to know more about the client than did the creditor. Consequently, creditors could not easily determine if some clients were being placed on DMPs and (given concessions on finance charges and fees) when they could actually handle their debts on their own.[11] And the effectiveness of the counseling session and advice given was very difficult for a creditor to monitor. Consequently, the quality of the DMP product, as well as general education and counseling, was subject to erosion because some of the key dimensions of the product were not easily observed by the payor. Over time, poor agency follow-up on the DMP and "cherry picking" (i.e., putting clients on plans who didn't need them) led to distrust on the part of creditors and much closer scrutiny of agency DMP proposals and practices; it also probably contributed to further erosion of the fair share percentage. Quite literally, the new entrants that had effectively become large "debt plan mills," specializing in fifteen-minute counseling sessions over the telephone to set up DMPs, were driving out full-service counseling. The continued erosion of the fair-share rate increased the pressure on the established agencies to cut costs and increasingly emphasize the service that was explicitly priced: the DMP.[12]

Not all of the newcomers followed this strategy, and not all of the new competition was detrimental. The Consumer Federation of America and the National Consumer Law Center, hereafter CFA, noted that newcomer agencies "pioneered more business-like methods of making debt management plans convenient for consumers, including flexible hours, phone and Internet counseling, and electronic payments. These improvements, in turn, have forced the old guard to be more responsive to their clients" (2003, 8). Aggressive advertising on the Internet and through telemarketing and television ads has raised consumer awareness of counseling options, which has been a long-standing objective of the credit-granting industry and the NFCC.

Nevertheless, the CFA report also noted a number of problems associated with the operations of some of the largest of the new entrants. The lack of face-to-face contact inherent in telephone-based counseling raises questions about the education value associated with the "counseling" session. In many cases, the telephone "counseling" appears to be nothing more than a screening interview for DMP eligibility. A CFA survey of non-NFCC agencies found that only five of the forty agencies surveyed offered services unrelated to DMPs. The CFA authors noted that "nearly all of the counselors at non-NFCC agencies we contacted by phone were surprised by inquiries about courses or other consumer education resources. When asked this question, one counselor simply said, 'We consolidate credit cards. That's it'" (2003, 19).

The CFA report also noted that NFCC-member agencies have struggled to continue providing a full range of personal financial education services to their clients. In addition to conducting 1.15 million individual counseling sessions in 2002, NFCC-member agencies also conducted 37,368 in-person educational presentations (mostly focused on budgeting) for schools, employers, and religious and community organizations. However, the number of such presentations was down 28 percent from 1999. CFA concluded that "despite these efforts, multi-service agencies are a dying breed" (2003, 19).

Some of the largest newcomers that advertise most aggressively also appear to have engaged in deceptive and misleading practices. Federal Trade Commission testimony before Congress in 2004 stated that "our greatest concern is deception by credit counseling agencies about the nature and costs of the services they offer to consumers" (U.S. Federal Trade Commission 2004, 6). The agency cited the following practices as ones that may violate the FTC Act or other statutes enforced by the FTC:

• *Mispresentations about fees or "voluntary contributions"*   Some agencies were charging large fees, often characterized as donations or voluntary contributions that are hidden from consumers. One example would be when an agency retains the consumer's first monthly payment instead of forwarding it to the client's creditors. Such practices may not be adequately disclosed to the consumer up front.

• *Promising results that cannot be delivered*   The aggressive advertising employed by some agencies suggests that they will lower consumers' interest rates, monthly payments, or overall debt by an "unrealistic or unattainable amount." Some also falsely promise to eliminate negative (but accurate) information from a consumer's credit report.

• *Abuse of nonprofit status*   Some agencies use their nonprofit designation to convince consumers to pay fees disguised as "donations." These agencies "may, for example, claim that consumers' donations will be used simply to defray the [agency's] expenses. Instead the bulk of the money may be passed through to individuals or for-profit entities with which the [agencies] are closely affiliated. Tax-exempt status also may tend to give these fraudulent [agencies] a veneer of respectability by implying that the [agency] is serving a charitable or public purpose. Finally, some consumers may believe that a nonprofit [agency] will charge lower fees than a similar for-profit entity" (6).

• *False advertising regarding credit counseling services*   Masquerading as "counseling" agencies that purport to provide advice and education, some of these firms may be enrolling "all clients indiscriminately in DMPs without any actual counseling" (6).

• *Failure to pay creditors in a timely manner or at all* These charges sound remarkably similar to the regulatory concerns about commercial debt poolers that prompted sharp regulation of that industry nearly fifty years earlier. It seems that after well-intentioned beginnings, the credit counseling industry is in danger of devolving back to the "pooling" industry that fell into disrepute a half century earlier.

8.3   What Really Caused the Industry to Devolve?

8.3.1   For-Profits versus Nonprofits

Some observers have blamed the for-profit orientation of many of the new entrants for the demise of the educational component of counseling services, and the emergence of the DMP as the sole agency product. Of course, almost all of the major new competitors in the counseling industry were organized as nonprofit firms. A 2004 U.S. Senate investigative report found that many of the new entrants "have developed a completely different business model, using a for-profit model designed so that their nonprofit credit counseling agencies generate massive revenues for a for-profit affiliate for advertising, marketing, executive salaries, and any number of other activities other than credit counseling. The new model looks to the consumer to provide those revenues" (U.S. Senate 2004, 1). The report further notes that "the primary effect of the for-profit model has been to corrupt the original purpose of the credit counseling industry—to provide advice, counseling, and education to indebted consumers free of charge or at a minimal charge, and place consumers on debt management programs only if they are otherwise unable to pay their debts. Some of the new entrants practice the reverse—provide no bona fide education or counseling and place every consumer onto a debt management program at unreasonable or exorbitant charge" (2).

As noted previously, the idea that nonprofit status would insulate a counseling agency from competitive pressures and align agency incentives more closely with the consumer apparently led most states to enact laws that required organizations providing credit counseling services to be nonprofit.

Administration of DMPs by nonprofit credit counseling agencies was validated in 1969 when the IRS affirmed that 501(c)(3) tax-exempt status was properly granted to an "organization that provides information to the public on budgeting, buying practices, and the sound use of consumer credit through the use of films, speakers, and publications."

It also ruled that such an organization may enroll debtors in "budget plans," where the debtor makes fixed payments to the organization and the organization disburses payments to each of the debtor's creditors (U.S. Senate 2004, 3–4). But this ruling, coupled with the requirement by most states that counseling agencies be nonprofit, has had the unintended negative consequence of giving less scrupulous agencies the positive glow of a charitable enterprise, thereby lowering consumer caution and possibly aggravating the damage done by false claims and deceptive advertising. Clearly, a credit counseling agency's "nonprofit" status has lost whatever value it may once have had as a signal of quality and integrity of operation. Equally clear is the fact that nonprofit organizations can compete with each other just as aggressively as for-profit firms.

But, even if the IRS cracks down on the for-profits masquerading as nonprofits, is there any reason to think that the incentives of nonprofits will always align more closely with the consumer than a commercial, for-profit counseling firm? This is especially relevant now that technology allows counseling agencies to compete with each other nationally for clients, without necessarily investing in brick and mortar offices. In other words, is the requirement that a counseling agency be nonprofit necessary or even helpful? As noted earlier, one of the positive effects of new entry into the counseling business was that it forced existing agencies to adopt new technologies for delivering services to consumers and payments to creditors, and be more responsive to both. We know that nonprofit (tax-exempt) credit unions and for-profit banks and savings institutions coexist effectively in providing consumers with a full range of financial services, and consumers trust both. In the context of personal insolvency advice, lawyers who dispense bankruptcy advice are most definitely operating on a for-profit basis. Why is it reasonable to expect them to be unbiased sources of recommendations, but that for-profit counseling firms would not be?

8.3.2   Dependence on Creditor Revenues

The reliance of the counseling industry on creditors for the majority of their revenue has been cited by industry critics as compromising the agencies' promise to act in consumers' best interests (Milstein and Ratner 1981; Gardner 2002; CFA 2003). The most frequent criticism is that the typical counseling agency in today's market serves as little more than a collection agency for creditors, does not fully inform the borrower regarding all the available options for handling debts, especially those options that involve something other than full payment, and does not adequately disclose to the consumer its financial links to the credit industry. An obsession with enrolling clients on DMPs, at the expense of genuine education and sound advice, has been ascribed to agencies that are dependent on DMP-generated revenue.

It is true that most agencies do not purport to offer comprehensive legal advice on insolvency options, although many will refer debtors for bankruptcy assistance when appropriate. But it does not seem reasonable to expect counseling agencies to offer a full range of legal options, since a well-established market for debtor insolvency attorneys already exists to provide those services. The unique purpose of the creditor-supported counseling agency was and is to offer first-tier budget advice but also to offer a brokered debt repayment plan that coordinates collective sacrifice on the part of creditors in exchange for a borrower's "good faith" effort to repay. Counseling agencies offer a form of personal-finance triage, a way for borrowers who want to pay their debts in full to handle their repayment problems outside the formal bankruptcy system. That is the essence of the product offered. So long as there is sufficient disclosure so that consumers recognize this, the claim that creditor support generates an inferior experience for consumers seems to be a red herring.[13]

In fact, there is plenty of evidence that, when done properly, credit counseling by agencies that do depend on creditors for revenue (which is nearly all of them) can genuinely help consumers. A recent report by the U.S. Senate Committee on Investigations (U.S. Senate 2004) and the already mentioned report published jointly by the Consumer Federation of America and the National Consumer Law Center (CFA 2003) each suggested that NFCC-member agencies are generally providing a broad range of education and counseling services for their clients, in keeping with their original mission, as opposed to indiscriminately enrolling clients on DMPs. In particular, the Senate report commended the NFCC for setting accreditation standards for agency membership, suggesting that "if applied throughout the industry ..., these professionals standards would go a long way toward addressing the abusive practices identified in this Report" (23–24).

Consequently, it is reasonable to examine the conduct of NFCC-member agencies in evaluating how well credit counseling can work in what has become a very competitive marketplace.

An analysis of NFCC agency experience with clients quickly refutes the suggestion that its member agencies routinely place consumers on

Table 8.2
NFCC DMP closings in 2002

Reasons cases were closed	% of cases	Months on plan
Successful completion	24.5	42.6
Self administration	22.7	26.2
Nonpayment	42.5	16.5
Noncompliance	3.0	17.8
Unauthorized new credit	0.3	19.1
Late or partial payment	2.7	16.5
Bankruptcy	4.8	13.4
Unknown	2.6	19.3
N = 304,701		

DMPs when bankruptcy would have been the better option for the consumer, even though the majority of agency revenue derive from DMP payments. Table 8.2 displays data on over 300,000 DMPs closed during 2002.

Nearly one quarter of the closed plans (74,651) were successfully completed, averaging 42.6 months in length. An additional 22 percent (69,167) of plans were closed because the borrowers had recovered sufficiently to handle repayment on their own. Even the plans closed for nonpayment lasted an average of sixteen months. In short, the closed-case breakdown suggests that the large majority of the plans set up for consumers involved an extended period of repayment, even for those plans that ultimately failed. On average, these plans appear to be the result of good-faith assessments by agencies of the likelihood that the repayment option would resolve financial difficulties, and good-faith attempts by consumer clients to see the plans through.

Additional evidence from a study published by Visa USA (1998) indicates that agencies do screen and categorize debtors reasonably accurately according to severity of financial difficulty and likelihood of bankruptcy. The study tracked 129,556 consumer clients of eleven NFCC-member agencies that participated in counseling sessions from January 1996 through July 1998. Counseling was defined as a comprehensive one-on-one money management interview with a trained counselor. Each interview included a detailed discussion of the client's financial situation, the development of a monthly budget, and a written action plan defining steps to be taken. Subsequently, clients were matched to Visa's proprietary Bankruptcy Notification Service database to determine the frequency of bankruptcy by outcome of the counseling session.

Of the clients who were deemed able to handle their debts on their own (e.g., no need for a DMP and creditor concessions), 5 percent filed for bankruptcy within one year of counseling. For those clients who enrolled in DMPs, 7.4 percent declared bankruptcy within one year of counseling. Among clients who were referred for legal advice (e.g., income insufficient to support a DMP), 32.2 percent declared bankruptcy within one year. Of the clients who were referred for other assistance (e.g., referral to another social service agency to address unstable family issues or addictions such as gambling, alcohol, or drug abuse), 12.6 percent declared bankruptcy within one year. Keeping in mind that agency clients are self-selecting into counseling sessions because they are experiencing credit problems, these statistics on subsequent bankruptcy further refute the charge that, as "glorified collection agencies," the NFCC-member agencies are routinely funneling borrowers into DMPs, regardless of the kind of assistance they really need.

Another recent study documents the value of full-service counseling experience for consumers who do not enroll in DMPs. Staten, Elliehausen, and Lundquist (2002) found that one-on-one credit counseling has a positive impact on borrower behavior over an extended period. The study examined the impact of individual credit counseling sessions for 14,000 consumers during 1997, none of whom were subsequently enrolled in DMPs. Credit bureau data provided objective measures of credit performance for these clients over a three-year period following their initial counseling session, as well as for a large sample of borrowers with similar risk profiles and geographic residences in 1997 who did not receive counseling. Using nine different measures of borrower credit performance, the empirical analysis found that borrowers who received counseling generally improved their credit profile over the subsequent three years, relative to observationally similar borrowers who did not receive counseling. Perhaps not surprisingly, the benefit from counseling was greatest for borrowers with the poorest initial risk profile.

At least two conclusions emerge from this brief review of the operations of one large group of similarly structured counseling agencies. First, creditor support of agency operations does not have to compromise value to consumers. Moreover, if creditors are not permitted to help underwrite agency operations, who will? The same industry critics who advocate that agencies move away from creditor funding (or at least deemphasize reliance on fair-share revenue tied to DMP payments) have also condemned many of the new entrants for charging excessive fees to consumers. Given that creditors and consumers are the two primary beneficiaries of successful counseling, who should pay for the service if they do not?

The second conclusion is that the business model followed by virtually all credit counseling agencies today fails to capitalize on some important dimensions of their product by failing to document and price the educational components of their services. For NFCC-member agencies, over two-thirds of the clients who undergo individualized counseling sessions receive training and information of some value but generate little or no revenue. Both creditors and consumers benefit from this service, and presumably both are in a position to pay something for those services. Again, the relevant business issue is not whether creditors should support these agencies at all, but how to diversify agency revenue so as to insulate a broad range of educational services from the impact of price competition on the DMP product.

8.3.3 Informational Asymmetry

The prevailing revenue structure on which the industry is based is flawed and primarily responsible for the ongoing erosion in the quality and range of services offered by counseling agencies. To understand the essence of the problem, it is helpful to think about the incentives created under the current revenue structure and its variations. Keep in mind that agencies gain an informational advantage because they deal directly with consumers, see a fuller picture of their overall debt exposure, and have the benefit of the data gathered at the initial counseling interview. Consequently, they can better assess a consumer's financial situation than can creditors.

Agencies that rely more on fair share from creditors and less on initial plan set-up fees from consumers engage in risk sharing with creditors. That is, both the agency and the creditor recover more if the consumer stays on the plan. This arrangement gives the agency increased incentive to work with debtors (follow-up calls and interviews, when warranted) to keep them on a plan, and to enroll them on plans that have a good chance of being successful.[14]

However, it also increases the agency's incentive to sign up lower-risk/less needy consumers for DMPs, to increase the probability that they'll stay on plan (cherry picking). Creditor concern over this development was noted in a previous section.[15] The information asymmetry makes it difficult for creditors to know whether consumers who enroll in DMPs actually need the assistance. In other words, are they actually trying to avoid bankruptcy as opposed to trying to save money in interest and fees? Coupled with the explosion in the number of agencies submitting proposals, differing standards used across agencies, and uneven success rates of the resulting plans, the administrative costs to issuers of evaluating DMP proposals have soared, as has distrust. As a result, creditor willingness to continue funding agencies at traditional levels has eroded.

Alternatively, agencies that rely more on up-front fees paid by the consumer have no less incentive to indiscriminately place people on DMPs (to the extent that the up-front fees include one-time setup charges for plans) and have less incentive to follow up with the consumer and shepherd clients through plans. In addition, the higher fees charged to financially stressed consumers probably increase the likelihood that these consumers will default.

However, if techniques such as statistical scoring models could be developed that would give both agency and creditor a similar indication of who is at greater risk of bankruptcy, then the cherry-picking problem could be reduced or eliminated. Moreover, the same models could then be used to calibrate the payment to the agency. That is, payment would include an appropriate base amount for every client (to compensate for the interview/evaluation process and the resulting educational value), but then a graduated payment scale for those that go on DMPs, depending on the initial score. The same model could also be used to determine an appropriate amount of concessions (i.e., reduced finance charges and fees). This approach would preserve the agency's incentive to keep debtors on plans, at the same time reducing the risk of cherry picking and the resulting distrust by creditors.

There is already some indication that the market is moving in this direction. Creditors have begun to utilize performance-based, fair-share rules that take into account an agency's overall plan completion rate when determining the appropriate fair-share percentage (U.S. Senate 2004, 27–29). One very large card issuer (Citigroup) has dropped the fair-share concept altogether in favor of a grants-based approach in which agencies would apply (quarterly) for fixed amounts of funding. Presumably, this could result in some payment to compensate the agency for the educational value of counseling sessions outside of DMP enrollment, and many creditors are reacting to the findings of recent investigative reports by imposing minimum standards on agencies as a condition of dealing with them at all. This may be a faster and more effective incentive for policing agency performance than reliance on relatively slow-moving legislative solutions, although the independently derived rules will lack standardization.

With the application of scoring techniques to counseling data, we are likely to see both payment to the agency and concessions to consumers driven by "need," as judged by the totality of information available at the time of the counseling session. By reducing the information asymmetry between creditor and agency, statistical scoring should eventually establish the linkage of higher compensation to better service. To the extent that creditors can discern a measurable value even to non-DMP consumers who receive counseling, revenue streams can be created to sustain the full-service dimension of the traditional counseling agency. So, a competitive market can work after all.

8.4 Conclusions

Many of the abusive and deceptive practices identified in recent investigations of the credit counseling industry boil down to poor disclosures and poorly informed consumers. These could occur regardless of whether agencies were supported exclusively by creditor payments or were completely independent of creditor financial support. Consequently, the existence of financial ties between creditors and the counseling industry does not appear to be a fundamental problem. In addition, all of these abuses could occur in both for-profit and nonprofit agencies, so the focus on for-profit rather than nonprofit entities appears misplaced. Consumers have to adjust to the reality of a competitive market for counseling services that requires them to shop across all types of providers, just as they would shop for other financial services. In the absence of large-scale government funding or an outpouring of philanthropic support, neither of which seem likely, the viability of a geographically broad-based credit counseling industry will remain dependent on support from the credit-granting industry.

At its core, it appears that the basic problem plaguing the counseling industry is neither the dependence on creditor funding nor the aggressive competition among agencies. Rather, it is the information asymmetry between creditors and counseling agencies that creates incentive problems, increases distrust, and prevents the explicit valuation of the full range of agency services. Reducing the information asymmetry about the financial condition of clients would enable pricing schemes that bring creditor, agency, and consumer interests in closer alignment. Furthermore, to the extent that the value of counseling itself can be documented independent of the DMP recovery function, agencies should be able to collect revenue on every eligible client in order to fund the continued provision of a broad range of educational services for all clients.

Notes

1. The National Foundation for Credit Counseling (NFCC) is the umbrella organization for the oldest network of nonprofit credit counseling agencies in the United States. The NFCC (2003) reports that 1.3 million households contacted one or more of their 140 agencies (1,040 offices) in 2002. The NFCC estimates that its agencies' share of the counseling market has declined from 90 percent in the early 1990s to between 25 percent and 30 percent by 2002.

2. Furletti 2003 (2) and author's calculations based on top ten receivables as reported in *Card Industry Directory, 2004 edition* (New York: Thomson Financial Media, 2003).

3. NFCC member activity reports; U.S. Senate 2004, 3.

4. See FTC Press Release, "FTC, IRS and State Regulators Urge Care When Seeking Help from Credit Counseling Organizations," October 14, 2003, http://www.ftc.gov/opa/2003/10/ftcirs.htm.

5. Milstein and Ratner (1981, 986) refer to a 1980 NFCC pamphlet that states that CCCS was started in response to the rising number of personal bankruptcies. NFCC listed the reduction in the number of bankruptcies first among the benefits of having a CCCS organization.

6. The vice president of the American Association of Creditor Attorneys said in an interview, "Most of my clients take the position that we'd rather have the debtor go into consumer credit counseling and accept the proposed repayment plan than have the debtor go into Chapter 7" (Daly 1993, 46).

7. According to NFCC annual member activity reports, in 1980, approximately 40 percent of consumers who participated in a counseling "intake" interview were placed on a DMP. By 2002, 30 percent of NFCC interviewees were placed on DMPs.

8. As a case in point, an article published in 1995 in an industry trade publication summarizes the results of a study conducted by one company to see if the fair-share payments and foregone finance charges on behalf of DMP clients were "worth it," relative to handling similarly situated customers through standard collection procedures. The company concluded that it was, indeed, worth it—just in terms of recoveries on DMPs alone. See Spurgin 1995.

9. See Staten 1999 for a summary of the findings of various studies of the capacity to repay debt among Chapter 7 petitioners.

10. Even as recently as 2001, a Consumer Reports study of credit counseling found that NFCC member agencies suffered from "an excess of stodginess" and had been slow to adopt efficient communication and debt repayment methods" (Consumer Reports 2001).

11. In a workshop on credit counseling sponsored by the Federal Reserve Bank of Philadelphia, the managing director of collections for Juniper Bank remarked that credit card issuers were "particularly alarmed by recent trends in [counseling] agency marketing strategies. In addition to targeting 'credit stressed' consumers, some agencies market their services to any consumer who believes he or she is paying too much in finance charges. This makes it difficult for card issuers to know whether consumers who enroll in DMPs are actually trying to avoid bankruptcy or trying to save money in interest and fees" (Furletti 2003, 3).

12. An analogy to competition from new entrants in the airline industry seems appropriate. In 1980, deregulation brought new entrants and price competition. Between 1985 and 1998, price competition drove down the quality of service. Incumbent airlines shifted toward the "no frills" approach adopted by the startups. This period saw the demise of airline meals, and the installation of additional rows of seats at the expense of leg room.

13. Following an investigation by the Federal Trade Commission, the NFCC agreed in 1997 to require its member agencies to prominently disclose their funding relationship to the credit-granting industry in correspondence with consumer clients, although there is no such requirement on non-NFCC agencies.

14. At least one of the largest new entrants to the counseling business, Cambridge Credit Counseling, has devised a different pricing scheme that also gives consumers extra incentive to continue on their DMPs by promising to rebate a certain proportion of client's fees when they reach certain milestones in the plan.

15. See note 12.

References

Consumer Federation of America and National Consumer Law Center (CFA). 2003. "Credit Counseling in Crisis: The Impact on Consumers of Funding Cuts, Higher Fees and Aggressive New Market Entrants." http://www.consumerfed.org/credit_counseling_report.pdf.

Consumer Reports. 2001. "Pushed Off the Financial Cliff." July.

Daly, James J. 1993. "The Boom in Credit Counseling." *Credit Card Management* (July): 44–48.

Furletti, Mark. 2003. "Consumer Credit Counseling: Credit Card Issuers' Perspectives." Discussion paper, Payment Cards Center, Federal Reserve Bank of Philadelphia, September.

Gardner, Stephen. 2002. "Consumer Credit Counseling Services: The Need for Reform and Some Proposals for Change." *Advancing the Consumer Interest* 13, nos. 1 and 2: 30–35.

Milstein, Abby Sniderman, and Bruce C. Ratner. 1981. "Consumer Credit Counseling Service: A Consumer-Oriented View." *New York University Law Review* 56 (November–December): 978–998.

National Foundation for Credit Counseling (NFCC). 2003. "2002 Member Activity Report."

Spurgin, Ralph E. 1995. "Are They Worth It? Credit Counseling Agencies." *Credit World* (March–April): 17–18.

Staten, Michael E. 1999. "Evidence on Bankrupt Debtors' Ability to Pay." Testimony before the U.S. House of Representatives, Committee on the Judiciary, Subcommittee on Commercial and Administrative Law, March 17.

Staten, Michael E., Gregory Elliehausen, and E. Christopher Lundquist. 2002. "The Impact of Credit Counseling on Subsequent Borrower Credit Usage and Payment Behavior." Monograph No. 36, Credit Research Center, McDonough School of Business, Georgetown University.

U.S. Federal Trade Commission. 2004. Prepared statement before the Permanent Subcommittee on Investigations, Committee on Governmental Affairs, U.S. Senate, March 24.

U.S. Senate. 2004. "Profiteering in a Non-Profit Industry: Abusive Practices in Credit Counseling." Staff report, Permanent Subcommittee on Investigations, March 24.

Visa USA. 1998. "The Impact of Credit Counseling on Bankruptcies."

9 Development and Regulation of Consumer Credit Reporting in the United States

Robert M. Hunt

Consumer credit bureaus are organizations that compile and disseminate reports on the creditworthiness of consumers. Firms that lend to consumers provide the underlying data to the bureaus. In the United States today, there is at least one credit bureau file, and probably three, for every credit-using individual in the country. Over two billion items of information are added to these files every month, obtained from thirty thousand lenders and other sources, and over three million credit reports are issued every day. In many instances, real-time access to credit bureau information has reduced the time required to approve a loan from a few weeks to just a few minutes.

This chapter describes how the consumer credit reporting industry evolved from a few joint ventures of local retailers around 1900 to a high-technology industry that plays a supporting role in America's trillion-dollar consumer credit market. In many ways, the development of the industry reflects the intuition developed in the theoretical literature on information-sharing arrangements. But the story is richer than the models. Credit bureaus have changed as retail and lending markets changed, and the impressive gains in productivity at credit bureaus are the result of their substantial investments in technology.

A consumer credit report typically includes four kinds of information.[1] First, there is identifying information, such as the person's name, current and previous addresses, Social Security number, date of birth, and current and previous employers. Next, there is a list of credit information that includes accounts at banks, retailers, and lenders. The accounts are listed by type, the date opened, the credit limit or loan amount, outstanding balances, and the timeliness of payments on the account. There may also be information gleaned from public records, including bankruptcy filings, tax liens, judgments, and possibly arrests or convictions. The file will typically include a count of the number of inquiries authorized by the consumer but will not contain any information about applications for credit or insurance that were denied.

In 2002, Americans held more than 1.5 billion credit cards, used them to spend $1.6 trillion, and maintained balances in excess of $750 billion.[2] Information provided by credit bureaus is an important ingredient in the vast expansion of unsecured consumer credit in the United States over the last century. This information is used to decide who is offered credit and on what terms. Credit bureau data are used to monitor fraud. The existence of credit bureaus is an inducement to honor one's debts. Information shared through credit bureaus can increase competition among providers of financial services, resulting in more credit offered on better terms.

But this does not mean that private credit bureaus necessarily maximize social welfare. There are plausible reasons why credit bureaus may make more mistakes than would otherwise be efficient. Nor would their choice of the relative frequency of mistakes (including inaccurate derogatory information versus excluding positive information) necessarily be efficient. In the United States, credit bureaus have a tarnished reputation and are subject to regulation at the federal and state levels. The regulatory regime adopted in the United States was clearly shaped by an attempt to balance the social benefits and costs of information sharing. How this balance can be improved is the subject of ongoing debate.

Section 9.1 reviews briefly the economic insights and international evidence relevant to voluntary information-sharing arrangements (see chapter 10 in this volume for a more detailed discussion). Section 9.2 describes how consumer credit reporting evolved in the United States over the last century in response to legal, economic, and technological changes. Section 9.3 reviews the most commonly articulated rationale for regulation of the industry, based on inadequate precaution with respect to consumer privacy and the accuracy of data contained in credit files. Section 9.4 reviews the American scheme for regulating the industry (see chapter 2 for a review of international data-protection arrangements). Section 9.5 reviews the American scheme for regulating the industry, including the changes introduced by the Fair and Accurate Credit Transactions Act of 2003. Section 9.6 concludes by examining two of the leading challenges facing the industry in the United States: ongoing security breaches among data repositories and consolidation of the credit card industry.

9.1   The Economics of Credit Bureaus

Adverse selection is an important problem in the market for unsecured credit in the United States, as reviewed in chapter 1. Ausubel (1999) found that individuals who responded to a given credit card solicitation were, on average, worse credit risks than those who did not respond. Also, customer pools resulting from credit card solicitations offering inferior terms (e.g., higher interest rates) had a higher average risk of default than pools resulting from solicitations offering better terms.[3] Ausubel's earlier finding that credit card rates in the United States are sticky—that is, they do not change very much in response to a change in banks' cost of funds—can be interpreted as another indicator of adverse selection (Ausubel 1991). If lenders respond through credit rationing, marginal increases in the supply of loanable funds would not reduce interest rates until the excess demand is entirely eliminated (Stiglitz and Weiss 1981).[4]

The significance of moral hazard in credit card markets is, of course, a central topic in the ongoing debate over bankruptcy reform in the United States. Throughout 2001–2002, credit card delinquency and charge-off rates, as well as the consumer bankruptcy rate, were at or near record highs. (They have since declined.) Empirical research suggests that many factors contribute to bankruptcy filings (Sullivan, Warren, and Westbrook 2000), and some economists wonder why Americans do not file more than they do (White 1998).[5]

By providing timely information about the characteristics and behavior of potential borrowers, credit bureaus mitigate adverse selection and moral hazard problems. Because that information is retained for a considerable time (seven years for most derogatory credit information in the United States), credit bureaus enable the maintenance of reputation effects in a market consisting of millions of otherwise anonymous borrowers (Klein 1997). In the United States, credit bureau data can be used to generate lists of consumers who are offered preapproved lines of credit (prescreening). The availability of data on a universe of credit users also makes it possible to develop sophisticated models to select and price credit risk for unsecured consumer loans.

Given the evident benefits to lenders, it seems natural to expect information sharing to emerge through credit bureaus. The benefits of information sharing, however, depend on many features of the economic environment (see also chapter 10). Information sharing becomes more attractive when good customers are harder to find and it becomes relatively more efficient to pool information than for each firm to generate its own information (Wilson 1990). The incentive to join a credit bureau also depends on how frequently lenders expect to encounter new potential borrowers, which depends on the geographic mobility of consumers and possibly the geographic reach of a lender's operations, and on the nature of competition among lenders. For competition, consider two possible lending environments: one in which consumers do all their borrowing from a single lender and one in which borrowers are able to obtain loans from many different lenders. In the latter case, lenders would clearly be willing to incur some expense in order to obtain a better idea of a borrower's total indebtedness, both before and after making a loan.

On the cost side, economies of scale can play a role in determining the establishment and growth of credit bureaus. The fixed cost of information sharing arrangements can be prohibitive if fixed costs are high and relatively little lending is going on, but it is easier to absorb when lenders are making a higher volume of loans. The volume of consumer lending also affects the information advantage that a credit bureau enjoys over the information held by any given lender. And when there is a high volume of applications for loans of modest size, as is typical for consumer credit relative to business loans, lenders cannot afford to invest a lot of resources evaluating each loan application. Once established, a credit bureau can help lenders to substitute more costly screening techniques (credit scoring) with timely credit history information, without incurring an unacceptable increase in overall credit risk. These techniques need not depend on the information contained in one lender's files. Rather, they are often refined and calibrated using credit history information gathered from all participating lenders (e.g., credit scores, sometimes called FICO scores). Network effects are also important: Credit bureaus become more useful to lenders as the coverage of potential customers increases, and a credit bureau with better coverage of lenders is more highly valued because any lender that relies on the bureau's data can be more confident it knows the totality of a borrower's credit activity. Both of these mechanisms can mitigate adverse selection. They may also reduce moral hazard if borrowers are aware that their credit lines and payment history are reported by, and can be disclosed to, a larger share of potential creditors. Finally, additional membership helps to amortize a bureau's fixed costs.

These factors suggest the possibility of multiple equilibria. Without some form of coordination, a credit bureau may not attain a sufficient scale to be self-sustaining. But if a sufficient scale is reached, band-wagon effects might easily lead to universal membership. In that case, when we observe credit bureaus, we would expect to observe only a few of them, perhaps only one, serving each particular market. But network effects may not be so strong as to imply universal participation by creditors or a monopoly credit bureau. For example, there may be a point where increases in credit bureau membership yields relatively little new information but creates more competition for a relatively fixed pool of borrowers (Wilson 1990). Alternatively, a lender that is more worried about moral hazard than adverse selection may be tempted not to join the credit bureau, essentially free riding on the deterrent effect created by the information sharing of its fellow lenders. This is less likely as the cost of participating in a credit bureau falls. Finally, creditors may choose to share information with more than one bureau in order to stimulate competition and innovation for such services.

As to market structure, in a more concentrated lending market, a given bank will have information about a larger share of the universe of borrowers than would a bank in a less concentrated market (Marquez 2002). This suggests credit bureaus may enjoy a larger informational advantage over individual banks when lending is less concentrated. Moreover, when there are many lenders, they are likely to be more concerned about the current indebtedness of any prospective borrower. To the extent that subsequent indebtedness may reduce the likelihood that existing loans will be repaid, lenders will also be concerned about any additional borrowing done by their existing customers at other institutions.[6] This argument suggests that credit bureaus should be more likely to emerge more often when there are more lenders, each of whom accounts for a smaller share of the borrowing population.

Market concentration, however, is also related to the intensity of competition among lenders. More competition reduces the likelihood that lenders will join a credit bureau because doing so reduces the information asymmetry between a borrower's current lender and its competitors (Wilson 1990; Pagano and Jappelli 1993; chapter 10, this volume). The question is whether a bank can earn enough profits on customers it attracts from other lenders to offset the decline in profits that results from having to offer more competitive terms to its existing customers. If the only barrier to competition is the lack of information on rivals' customers, establishing a credit bureau might reduce profits.

In that case, it is less likely that information sharing would be voluntarily adopted by the industry.

Padilla and Pagano (1997) suggest another possible inducement to the formation of credit bureaus. If banks can extract significant rents from borrowers and cannot commit to avoid this, borrowers may have too little incentive to avoid default. In this environment, disclosing information about one's borrowers is a way to commit not to extract too much rent. Banks will agree to share information if they gain more by reducing the default rate than they lose in profits on loans that would otherwise be repaid.

Information sharing, however, need not be an all-or-nothing discrete choice. It is possible these trade-offs could result in an equilibrium where some, but not all, information about customers is shared. For example, lenders might share only negative information about their customers (delinquencies and defaults) but not positive credit information (such as the size of a credit line, its utilization, or other information relevant to a customer's ability to repay). Several papers show that disclosing limited information may be superior to disclosing all available information about borrowers. In Padilla and Pagano 2000, there is a trade-off between the benefits of reducing adverse selection via full disclosure and reducing moral hazard by limiting disclosure, which induces borrowers to signal their type by avoiding defaults. The result is more lending, at lower interest rates, and with less frequent defaults than a policy of sharing all available information. In Vercammen 1995, a similar intuition can be used to justify limiting the length of borrowers' credit history, a practice regularly observed in the credit reporting industry.[7]

Theoretical insights appear very relevant to the limited cross-country empirical evidence available (see Pagano and Jappelli 1993; Jappelli and Pagano 1999; chapter 10, this volume). Credit bureaus tend to emerge in countries where people are relatively mobile and, to a lesser extent, where the ratio of consumer borrowing to consumption is higher. The relationship between these variables and the annual per capita volume of consumer credit reports is even stronger. In most developed countries, only a handful of credit bureaus are responsible for generating the vast majority of credit reports, and at least one of those bureaus will enjoy nearly complete coverage of consumers who borrow money (Jappelli and Pagano 1999). It appears that credit bureaus are more likely to emerge as a joint venture of local retailers or lenders than they are from collaborations of firms with a national reach

(Pagano and Jappelli 1993). But once a credit bureau is created, its scope tends to grow with the scope of its members. In addition, bureaus that evolved in this way tend to share more positive credit information than bureaus initially established to serve lenders with a national reach. In several developed countries, the sharing of consumer credit information did not exist until it was mandated by law. In these countries, the volume of consumer credit tended to be smaller, and there were fewer regulatory restrictions limiting competition between lenders (Pagano and Jappelli 1993). These patterns are consistent with the argument that voluntary information sharing is more difficult to initiate when doing so might contribute to intense competition among lenders, but that once established, credit bureaus enjoy significant network effects.

Can we quantify the benefits that consumer credit bureaus provide? A lower bound of the gross benefits should be reflected in the revenue earned by credit bureaus and firms, such as Fair Isaac, which develop scorecards for consumer loans. For the United States, this lower bound is at least several billion dollars. McCorkell (2002) argues that using scorecards built with data supplied by credit bureaus results in delinquency rates 20–30 percent lower than lending decisions based solely on judgmental evaluation of applications for credit. Conversely, holding the expected default rate constant, using scorecards yields a comparable increase in the acceptance rate (Chandler and Parker 1989; Chandler and Johnson 1992). Similar claims have been made about the efficacy of scorecards for auto insurance.[8]

If we suppose for the moment that this technology disappeared and that lenders did not adjust the volume of their credit card lending, a simple estimate of the resulting increase in loan losses for the United States would be about $5 billion a year. Conversely, suppose that lenders responded to the loss of this technology by trying to hold the delinquency rate constant. The resulting decline in outstanding revolving loans would be about $120 billion.[9] These obviously crude calculations bound a region of potential gains, as banks would obviously adjust to any change in their screening technology.

9.2   The Evolution of the American Consumer Credit Reporting Industry

International evidence is consistent with the argument that voluntary information sharing is more difficult to initiate when doing so might contribute to intense competition among lenders, but that once established, credit bureaus enjoy significant network effects. How well does the history of U.S. credit bureaus conform to the relevant theory?

Consumer credit bureaus emerged in the United States in the late nineteenth century. Other early adopters include Austria, Sweden, Finland, South Africa, Canada, Germany, and Australia (Jappelli and Pagano 1999). In the United States, most of the early credit bureaus were cooperatives or nonprofit ventures set up by local merchants to pool the credit histories of their customers and to assist in collection activities. Others were established by local finance companies or the local chamber of commerce (Cole and Mishler 1998).

The next step for this industry was the formation of a mechanism to share consumer credit information in different cities and regions of the country. This was accomplished through a trade association established in 1906. For most of its existence, this organization was known as Associated Credit Bureaus, Inc., or ACB.[10] ACB developed the procedures, formats, and definitions that enabled the sharing of credit files between agencies across the country. ACB even introduced a form of scrip, which members purchased from the association, that was used as a currency to pay for credit reports obtained from fellow members in other cities.

Membership of ACB grew rapidly from fewer than 100 bureaus in 1916 to 800 in 1927, and doubled again by 1955. According to ACB, its members collectively attained universal coverage of consumer borrowers by 1960. But even in that year, the largest of the credit bureaus maintained files on consumers in, at most, a handful of cities. At a time when the technology was limited to filing cabinets, the postage meter, and the telephone, American credit bureaus issued sixty million credit reports in a single year.

9.2.1 Economic and Technological Change

Credit bureaus emerged at a time when the primary source of consumer credit was offered by retailers; other important sources were pawnbrokers, small loan companies, and, of course, friends and family. One reason that retailers were so dominant in this period was that state usury laws made it difficult to earn profits on small loans lent at legal rates (Caldor 1999; Gelpi and Julien-Labruyere 2000). Retailers, on the other hand, were able to earn a profit because they simply charged more for goods purchased on credit. This advantage became less important after 1916, when many states relaxed their usury laws.

Even so, in 1929, retailers financed one-third of all retail sales. Among retailers who offered credit, credit sales accounted for a little more than half of their sales.[11]

The share of retail sales carried on open accounts—a form of revolving credit—ranged from 20 to 22 percent in the business censuses conducted from 1929 to 1948. In 1935, open account sales represented 21 percent of sales at food stores, 19 percent at clothing stores, 26 percent at department stores, 24 percent at furniture stores, 22 percent at gas stations, and 52 percent at fuel and ice dealers. But the share of sales accounted for by installment contracts financed by retailers declined from 13 percent in 1929 to less than 6 percent in 1948, as finance companies and banks took up more of that business.

Over the course of the last century, credit bureaus benefited from the increasing importance of consumer credit in the economy, but they also had to adapt to changes in the market for consumer credit. In the half-century beginning in 1919, consumer credit grew four times more rapidly than did total consumer spending. But consumer credit held by retailers grew only as rapidly as consumer spending. As a result, the share of consumer credit held by retailers fell by half (from 80 percent to 40 percent) between 1919 and 1941. By 1965, it had fallen by nearly half again (figures 9.1 and 9.2).[12] In 2000, nonfinancial businesses held only 5 percent of outstanding consumer credit. Thus, the

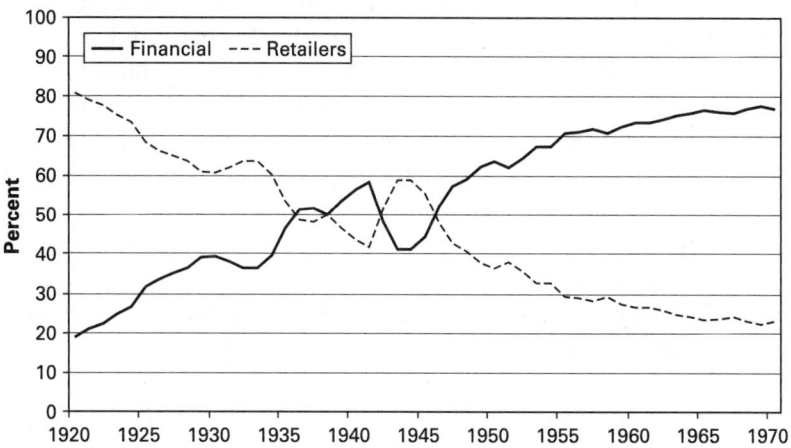

Figure 9.1
Shares of consumer credit (old series)
Sources: Federal Reserve Board, Banking and Monetary Statistics, 1941–1970, and author's calculations. See the appendix for details.

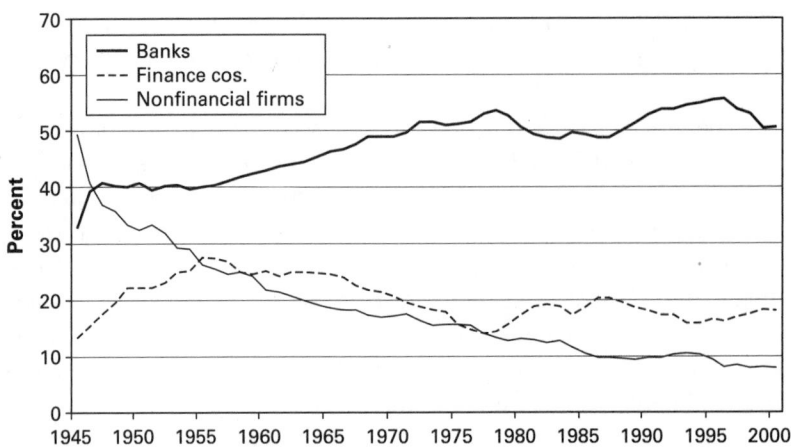

Figure 9.2
Shares of consumer credit
Sources: Federal Reserve Board, *Consumer Credit (G 19),* and author's calculations. See the appendix for details.

rapid growth in consumer debt over this period did not end up on the books of retailers, but rather on the balance sheets of financial institutions, primarily banks and finance companies.

Another significant change in this period was that retail and consumer credit markets got bigger. At the turn of the century, for all but a handful of retailers and catalogue sellers, the market was limited to a single city or just part of a city. But this gradually changed. For example, regional or national department store chains accounted for less than 15 percent of department store sales in 1929. By 1972, they accounted for nearly 80 percent of sales. If we examine retail sales as a whole, which includes the sales of tens of thousands of independent restaurants and gasoline stations, the share of sales by regional or national chains rose from 13 percent in 1929 to 31 percent in 1972 (figure 9.3). Over time, larger chains removed their credit operations from individual stores and consolidated them at the headquarters. Membership and information sharing at the local credit bureau became less important, while cooperation with the larger and more comprehensive credit bureaus became more important.

For a long time, banks' geographic expansion was constrained by restrictive branching laws. For consumer credit, however, branching restrictions became less important once bank-issued credit cards were introduced in the late 1950s and widely adopted in the late 1960s

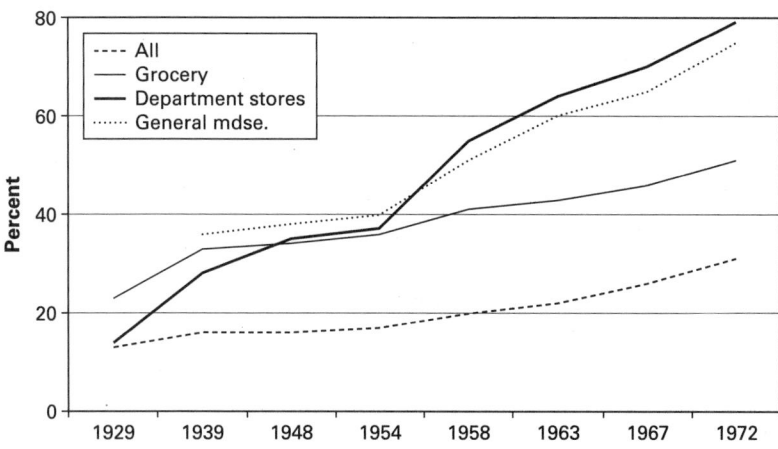

Figure 9.3
Share of retail sales by regional or national chains
Sources: Census of Retail Trade and author's calculations. See the appendix for details.

(Nocera 1994; Evans and Schmalensee 1999). Eventually, among the banks with the largest number of credit card accounts, the vast majority of these customers were not served through their traditional branch operations.

Once credit cards offered by banks were widely adopted, many retailers opted to accept these cards while dropping their in-house credit programs. Many retailers, especially smaller ones, had offered credit plans simply to compete with other retailers. Merchants paid a price for accepting the bank cards—the merchant discount (6 percent of the purchase price at that time)—but they avoided other expenses, such as bookkeeping and collections activity, to say nothing of the cost of financing these receivables themselves. Larger retailers have maintained their store cards; even today there are more store card accounts than bankcard accounts, and the largest issuers include retailers such as Sears. In other instances, retailers have subcontracted their store card operations to financial firms and no longer carry the receivables on their own balance sheets.

These changes occurred rapidly after the late 1960s. In 1968, the amount of revolving credit held by retailers was nearly six times higher than bank card balances and outstanding check credit. Ten years later (1978), banks and retailers held roughly equal amounts of revolving credit (figure 9.4). Another fifteen years later (1993), revolving credit

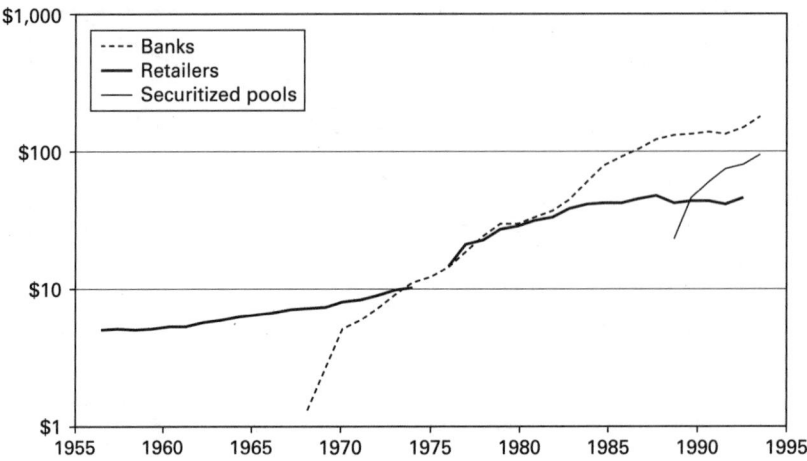

Figure 9.4
Revolving credit (U.S.$ billions, log scale)
Sources: Federal Reserve Board, *Consumer Credit (G 19),* and author's calculations. See the appendix for details.

held at banks was more than three times higher than balances held by retailers.[13]

The rapid development of the credit card industry presented both opportunities and challenges to credit bureaus in the early 1970s. On the one hand, card-issuing banks were a source of new business to credit bureaus. "Prescreening services"—the process by which a card issuer would specify a set of characteristics of potential borrowers, used to generate a mailing list of people to whom the issuer extends firm offers of credit—became a significant source of revenue to the industry. On the other hand, lenders were interested in offering credit cards on a regional or national scale, which required access to credit files that no single bureau held in the late 1960s. In addition, banks were rapidly automating their systems and soon expected to share and obtain data with credit bureaus through electronic rather than paper means. To meet these changes, credit bureaus had to automate, and they had to get larger. And that is exactly what happened. The largest credit bureaus already enjoyed coverage of one or more large cities, and they soon began to expand their scope by acquiring credit bureaus in other cities. ACB membership declined from a peak of around 2,200 in 1965 to only about 500 today. After rising for decades, the number of credit bureau offices also began to decline, falling 20 percent between 1972 and 1997.

Credit bureaus in the largest cities were automated first, beginning with Los Angeles in 1965, followed by New York and San Francisco in 1967.[14] Shortly thereafter, the largest bureaus established networks to access files in any of their automated bureaus across the country. As member banks and retailers built up national credit franchises, their data made it possible for the largest bureaus to progress toward the goal of in-house universal coverage of borrowers. The three largest credit bureaus (today they are called TransUnion, Experian, and Equifax) attained universal coverage in the 1980s.

Most credit bureaus were simply too small to afford the high fixed cost of automating with the technology then available. In 1975, two-thirds of ACB-member bureaus were located in towns with populations of 20,000 or less. As recently as 1989, more than a third of ACB-member bureaus had not yet automated and relied upon an ACB service to obtain access to information provided by regional and national creditors. Nearly 500 independent credit bureaus had automated, but they relied on contracts with one or more of the top three bureaus to obtain information provided by larger creditors.

9.2.2   The Consumer Credit Reporting Industry Today

In 1997, there were just under 1,000 active consumer credit reporting agencies in the United States, employing about 22,000 people and generating $2.8 billion in sales (rising to $3.5 billion in 2002).[15] Virtually all of this revenue is derived from charges for access to consumer credit reports. Controlling for inflation, industry revenue has quadrupled since 1972, twice the increase in the overall economy and two-thirds faster than the rate of increase in the stock of outstanding consumer credit. The number of credit reports issued today is ten times higher than thirty years ago, yet industry employment is essentially unchanged. Few industries can boast such impressive gains in labor productivity.

The industry is segmented into small and big firms. A typical credit bureau has just one office and employs ten people. Nine-tenths of all firms have annual sales of less than $2.5 million. In 1997, only fourteen companies had more than five offices. Yet these firms accounted for more than a fifth of all offices, half of industry employment, and two-thirds of industry receipts. The four largest firms alone account for over half of industry receipts. These larger firms concentrate on high-volume businesses—those firms seeking credit file information thousands or even millions of times a year. They also conduct most of the prescreening services that result in the billions of solicitations for credit cards or insurance delivered by mail each year. Smaller firms, on the other hand, concentrate on low-volume and one-time customers. For these customers, the automated technology of the large bureaus has been too costly to justify for such a low volume. But with cheap, powerful PCs and Internet-based delivery, such costs are falling, and this may put additional pressure on the smaller independent bureaus.

There are also a number of smaller, less well-known credit bureaus that serve particular niche markets. Many personal finance companies participate in associations (called lenders' exchanges) that maintain records of credit extended to an individual from members in the association. There is a medical credit bureau that primarily serves doctors and dentists. Another bureau (the Medical Information Bureau) pools certain health information of applicants for life insurance. There are a number of highly automated credit bureaus that serve retailers that accept personal checks and banks that seek information on customers opening checking accounts (Telecredit, SCAN, and Chexsystems). There are a variety of bureaus that serve landlords evaluating prospective tenants (Landlord Connections, for example), and there is even a bureau that serves telephone companies (the National Consumer Telecommunications Exchange).

Outside the United States, consumer credit bureaus are on the rise. A recent World Bank survey found at least twenty-five new private bureaus were created in Europe, Asia, and Latin America during the 1990s (Miller 2003). Quite a few public credit registries were also created, especially in Latin America. The big American bureaus have begun to expand abroad. Experian, now owned by a British firm, has concentrated on Europe, while Equifax has acquired a number of bureaus in Latin America.

9.3   The Accuracy of Credit Bureau Information

The American consumer credit reporting industry has a poor reputation in the eyes of many consumers. To some degree, credit bureaus are victims of their own success. Few people stop to think about the role a credit bureau played in their successfully obtaining credit, insurance, or even employment. But when they are denied such things on the basis of information contained in a credit report, the credit bureau often gets the blame. Perhaps no issue about this industry generates more heated debate than the accuracy of credit reports: even a small error rate, given the volume of activity involved, would result in millions of inaccuracies each year. For all of this heat, until very recently, there was very little data available to study this problem.[16]

9.3.1   Economic Intuition

Credit bureaus obtain account history data from member institutions, sort and aggregate these data into personal credit histories, and disseminate this information to members at their request. The benefit to members from sharing this information clearly depends on its accuracy and timeliness. But members also share in the cost of providing information to the bureau. The more costly it is to provide this information, the less attractive it will be for a lender to join a bureau.

The level of quality maintained by credit bureaus should of course depend on a balancing of the costs and benefits to their member institutions. This depends, in turn, on the relative costs of making and correcting mistakes. Naturally, lenders wish to minimize the cost of processing and transmitting the information they are obliged to provide to credit bureaus. This is not to say that lenders do not care about the quality of this information—after all, the data are typically a direct output of their own internal information systems.

When using credit bureau data, lenders are concerned about two types of errors: A type I error grants credit to a person based on erroneous information; a type II error denies credit to a person based on erroneous information. For lenders, the expected loss associated with a type I error (the principal lost) is likely to be higher than the expected loss from a type II error (forgone profits on a loan). So given that lenders are both the providers and beneficiaries of credit history information, one might expect that credit bureau files are more likely to contain erroneous references to delinquencies or defaults than they are to mistakenly omit actual delinquencies or defaults. To borrowers, of course, the cost of not being able to obtain a loan could well be higher than the cost to a lender of not being able to make a loan to that person. To the extent that borrowers' losses are not fully reflected in bureaus' decision making, there could be too many errors and, in particular, too many type II errors.

When potential borrowers become aware of erroneous information in their credit reports, they will have an incentive to dispute it if they can.[17] In fact, borrowers enjoy a comparative advantage in identifying such errors. One way to improve the accuracy of credit reports is to encourage consumers to dispute errors in their reports, setting in motion a process for rechecking the source and accuracy of the data reported. Given there is a mutual interest in improving the accuracy of the data, it is not surprising to find that credit bureaus encourage consumers to correct errors in their files and devote considerable resources (customer service staffing, fee waivers, and so on) to the process.[18] In a cross-country survey, Miller (2003) found that twenty-five of forty-three private bureaus offered free credit reports to consumers as a means of correcting errors. Less than half reported using statistical or modeling techniques to identify errors.

Both consumers and lenders share the benefits of any reduction in type II errors that result from an efficient dispute process. Of course, they also share in the costs of that process. But it is likely that consumers enjoy relatively more of the benefits while lenders bear relatively more of the cost of administering the dispute resolution process. As a result, from the standpoint of society, credit bureaus may devote too few resources to the error correction process.[19] Moreover, there may be disagreement over the extent of proof required in order to reject a consumer's dispute, how rapidly the dispute must be resolved, and so forth. These issues suggest a possible role for government regulation.

9.3.2 Consumers' Views on Credit Report Errors

One approach is to document errors identified when consumers examine their own credit reports. This approach benefits from the consumer's knowledge about his or her own credit behavior, but most studies of this sort are based on small and usually unrepresentative samples. Such studies typically find a high incidence of errors (in 20–40 percent of reports), but it is unclear whether most of these errors would have a significant effect on the consumer's access to credit or insurance (see the following).[20]

In 1989, ACB presented some aggregate statistics about its members. In that year, consumers requested some 9 million credit reports, which is about 2 percent of the 450 million reports generated annually at that time. Consumers disputed about one-third or 3 million of those reports. In about 2 million cases, or two-thirds of disputed files, credit reports were altered in the reverification process. But not all these changes were the result of an error in the report. Some were the result of the routine updating of files with the most current information. More recently, the Government Accountability Office, then known as the General Accounting Office, described a recent analysis of consumer disputes received by the three national reporting agencies during 2002.[21] The vast majority of disputes were in response to an adverse action notice received by a consumer. About 10 percent of the disputed items were deemed inaccurate by the information provider, and another 16 percent of items were deleted because the investigation could not be completed within the time limit specified by the FCRA (see the following).

Sometimes a credit report will include references to the accounts of other people. These errors occur because creditors do not report information on individuals so much as they do on accounts. The credit bureau assembles a report on an individual by linking the accounts with the same names, addresses, birthdays, Social Security numbers, and other information that is presumably unique to the individual. But this is not a simple exercise in a country with many thousands of lenders, and where consumers move frequently and are also ambivalent about adopting a universal, unique ID number.

Credit bureaus have developed sophisticated processes to aggregate account information into borrower profiles, but they are not perfect. In an older study, Williams (1989) was able to identify errors of this sort in credit reports a little over 10 percent of the time. Such errors are not always innocuous: If the erroneous information includes someone else's delinquencies, for example, a person's credit rating will be adversely affected. Even if the erroneous accounts are in good standing, they make it appear that the applicant has more open credit lines than he or she actually does.

9.3.3 Taking a Peek into Credit Bureau Files

Another approach is to examine a large quantity of credit bureau files. This has the advantage of working with representative samples, but the disadvantage of not having the consumer's judgment about the accuracy of particular items in a report. In this section, we review two recent studies.

Statistics on the contents of files at one of the large U.S. credit bureaus, in 1999, are found in Avery et al. 2003. The dynamism of the U.S. credit market is reflected in even the most cursory statistics presented. There are more than 1.4 billion separate credit accounts, amounting to $6.7 trillion in debts, as reported by some 23,000 creditors and other organizations. About three-quarters of all accounts had recently been updated by the information provider. Among these accounts, only 43 percent were currently open.[22] Among those accounts not currently reported, 70 percent had a zero balance. Two-thirds of all currently open accounts had a positive balance. The majority of all the accounts (63 percent) involved some form of revolving credit (e.g., a credit card). While these statistics are influenced by variations in reporting practices, they also illustrate the long memory of credit bureau files (typically seven years), the ease with which most borrowers move their business from one lender to another (e.g., changing credit cards or refinancing a mortgage), and the effects of changes in industry structure (e.g., mergers and acquisitions).

Avery et al. (2003) describe four concerns about the quality of data they analyzed. First, about 8 percent of accounts were not currently reported but carried a positive balance at the time of the last report. Some of these accounts were likely closed, but this information was not reported to the bureau. As a result, some consumers will appear to have more open accounts, and a higher total indebtedness, than they actually have. Second, some lenders (accounting for 1 percent of accounts) reported accounts only when they were past due. For borrowers with a relatively short credit history, the omission of an account in good standing might reduce their credit score. Third, there was clear evidence of duplicate and stale public record information and accounts in collection. Finally, about a third of all revolving accounts were reported without a credit limit (40 percent among banks). Most consumers in their data (70 percent) had at least one account with an omitted credit limit on a revolving account. Such omissions tend to increase estimates of borrowers' account utilization. That is because the industry convention is to substitute the highest balance reported for the credit limit when the actual credit limit is not reported. Less than 20 percent of revolving accounts reported with a credit limit by banks showed a balance representing 75 percent or more of the available line. Among revolving accounts reported without a credit limit by banks, more than half had an estimated utilization (current balance/ highest balance) in excess of 75 percent. Higher utilization tends to depress credit scores.

Avery, Calem, and Canner (2004) revisit this problem by examining the files of a large credit bureau as of June 2003. They found credit limits were omitted on a smaller share of revolving accounts (14 percent) and that such omissions affected 46 percent of consumers in the files. While this represents a significant improvement, it is clear that reporting an actual credit limit is hardly a universal practice (see section 9.6).

In 2002, the Consumer Federation of America (CFA) released a study of a large sample of credit reports generated in the process of underwriting mortgages for about 1,500 consumers in twenty-two states. Mortgage brokers often work with a local reseller of credit reports, who obtains data, including credit scores, from all three national bureaus. This made it possible to compare all three reports drawn for a consumer at exactly the same time and to calculate the variance in credit scores generated by these reports. The study found that, for a significant share of consumers (29 percent), the difference between the highest and lowest credit score was fifty points or more.[23] A smaller share (16 percent) had one score in the "prime" range (620 or above) and another in the "subprime" range (below 620). Variation in the contents of reports from the three national bureaus is hardly unexpected. Even when drawn at the same time, the credit reports of each bureau are often based on different vintages of data reported by the same creditors at slightly different times and processed at different speeds. Each bureau also processes the underlying data somewhat differently. And given the possibility of merge errors (described previously), drawing three reports increases the probability of observing a material error of this sort.

If borrowers and lenders do not take into account this variation in scores, it is possible that a significant number of borrowers might have difficulty obtaining a mortgage on the best terms. But borrowers and lenders often take this risk into account. For example, many mortgage applicants examine their credit reports prior to applying for a loan. Some mortgage lenders take the average of the three credit scores, which reduces the effect of outliers. The resellers that work with mortgage lenders offer an expedited review, or rescoring, to correct erroneous information and obtain updated scores in a few days. Of course, this service does not come without a cost—typically $10 per trade line corrected, plus the borrower's time in examining his or her credit reports.

An important question, then, is whether it is more cost effective to address errors in this way or, instead, to insist on further improvements in the quality of information reported by the three national bureaus. And if the system is to rely significantly on the precaution of consumers, it is important to know how well most consumers understand credit reports and their rights under the Fair Credit Reporting Act. Recent surveys suggest that many consumers understand the basics, but not much more (Government Accountability Office 2005).

9.3.4   The Economic Importance of Credit Report Errors

Sometimes errors in credit bureau information affect credit decisions. The key question is how often does this happen? In this section, we examine two studies. One is the only study that actually examines changes in credit-granting decisions that result from correcting errors in reports. The other, based on much more recent data, simulates the effect on credit scores of various changes in contents of credit bureau files at one of the national bureaus.

In the early 1990s, ACB released summary statistics from a study based on a sample of nearly 16,000 applicants, all of whom were denied credit (Connelly 1992). Relatively few people requested a copy of their credit report, but a quarter of those who did disputed something in their report. In about 14 percent of the disputed reports, the resulting changes were significant enough to reverse the credit decision. In the study, there were only thirty-six such instances (0.2 percent of the sample). A simple extrapolation, based on the previously cited statistics provided by ACB, suggests that, in the early 1990s, the number of applications for credit mistakenly denied could have been large—in the tens if not hundreds of thousands each year.[24]

In their 2004 study, Avery, Calem, and Canner constructed a credit-scoring model that is a reasonable approximation to ones used by many lenders. The model was built using a large representative sample drawn from the credit records of one of the large credit bureaus in 2003. They evaluated the sensitivity of their scoring model to the kinds of data issues they raised in their 2003 article (stale information, non-reporting of accounts in good status, failure to disclose actual credit limits, and problems with public records and collections accounts). They explored the distribution of any effects by calculating the sensitivity of scores for borrowers in three risk groups (low-, medium-, and high-credit risk) and separately for borrowers with relatively short credit histories (thin files).

In most of their simulations, the average effect on credit scores was relatively modest. For example, reporting as closed an account paid as agreed raised the scores of a majority of consumers, but only by an average of four points. Reclassifying a stale account (not recently reported) from a major derogatory to closed had no affect on scores for 82 percent of consumers and raised the scores of other consumers by only one point. Deleting an erroneous collection agency account had no effect on 41 percent of borrowers and raised the scores of another 51 percent, but only by an average six points. Deleting a duplicate public record had no affect for 39 percent of consumers and raised the scores of other consumers by only one point.

Avery, Calem, and Canner (2004) also found that, for 32 percent of consumers, omitting a credit limit on a single revolving account would have no effect on their scores. Unlike in the other simulations, they found clear evidence of a bias resulting from an omitted credit line. Reporting the actual credit limit almost never hurt a consumer's score, but it would raise the scores of two-thirds of consumers. Still, the average improvement was small, about six points.[25]

An important qualification is that the simulated effects were larger for consumers with either lower credit scores or with relatively thin credit files. For example, adding an actual credit limit to a revolving account for a consumer with an initial score below 660 raised the scores of three-quarters of this group by an average of thirteen points. A similar effect was observed for consumers with thin credit files. The effects of correcting erroneous collections or public record information were also much larger.

There appear to be a number of reasons for these modest effects. First, changes in the contents of credit bureau files tended to increase the scores of some individuals while reducing the scores of others.[26] Second, the scoring model itself places less weight on credit file attributes that exhibit more "noise." That is a natural outcome of a process whose purpose is to produce reliable forecasts of the probability of default. For example, stale accounts reported in derogatory status sometimes occur when a loan is refinanced. Given that this has little to do with the prospects for default, it is not surprising that scoring models place little weight on such information. On the other hand, where the scoring models have less precision (e.g., for consumers with thin files), the effects of noise are indeed larger.

9.4 Privacy Concerns and Identity Theft

Credit bureaus are information-sharing arrangements that help to reduce the problems of adverse selection and moral hazard in credit, insurance, and other markets. The flip side of information sharing is necessarily a loss of consumer privacy. It is likely that sharing a little information about borrowers, such as their payment history, generates benefits that exceed the losses associated with any loss of privacy, especially if consumers are aware that such information is being shared and access to the information is limited. When access is less well-regulated, consumers are less well-informed, or information is used for purposes not envisioned by consumers, this case becomes harder to make. This is only compounded when access to these data increases the risk of identity theft—obtaining credit and other benefits under another's name.[27] The Federal Trade Commission (2003) estimates that identity theft contributes to $5 billion in consumer losses and $33 billion in business losses each year.

The American credit-reporting industry has been embarrassed on several occasions by the ease with which people have obtained credit reports when they should not have. Green (1991) found about a third of the bureaus contacted were willing to provide credit reports without complying with the requirements of the Fair Credit Reporting Act. In 1989, Dan Quayle's credit report was obtained by a reporter under the pretext of making a job offer to the vice president. Certainly, some deception was required in order to obtain the reports.[28] But it does seem that, at least at the time, a little deception went a long way.

Direct access to the files of the largest credit bureaus is relatively difficult to obtain. These companies operate automated systems that serve high-volume customers. Their size makes it possible for them to afford elaborate and expensive security arrangements for their systems. Their customers are primarily lenders who regularly provide information on their customers in addition to being frequent users of information contained in credit bureau reports. It is relatively easy to police this stable customer base.

At many of the smaller bureaus, the clientele consists of infrequent or one-time users of credit reports. These users are less likely to be providers of credit information to the bureau. Some of these bureaus are really just resellers of credit information compiled by one or more of the large bureaus. Those bureaus may have a more difficult time policing their customers and may not have an adequate incentive to do so.

On the other hand, it is the larger bureaus that are more likely to market information products that have little or nothing to do with applications for credit, insurance, or even employment. For example, the largest bureaus offer databases that make it possible to match a person's name or other identifying information to an address or phone number (called individual reference services). They also prepare targeted mailing lists of potential customers for nonfinancial products based on a set of characteristics specified by the buyer of the list—for example, a catalogue company. Credit bureaus are not the only firms offering these services, but they are the most controversial. At a minimum, such activities create at least the impression that a person's personal information and payment history are being used for purposes completely unrelated to evaluating an application for credit.

In 2001, the FTC succeeded in restricting the use of certain data in consumer credit reports to generate target-marketing lists used to sell nonfinancial products to consumers. The FTC also succeeded in applying the financial privacy requirements of the Gramm-Leach-Bliley Act to credit bureaus' "look-up" services, whereby a person's name and other identifying information are matched with a current address or phone number contained in credit files.[29] Credit bureaus may also be affected by the European Privacy Directive, which is generally more restrictive than U.S. law (Cate 1997).

9.5 The Regulation of Consumer Credit Bureaus

In deciding how to regulate the credit reporting industry, policymakers must decide whether to mandate information sharing by creditors and other firms or, instead, to adopt rules that attempt to improve upon the voluntary information-sharing arrangements established by the private sector. The American system of regulation is an example of the latter approach, but other countries have adopted the former (see chapter 2 of this volume). The key is to increase the quality of information provided to credit bureaus without creating a disincentive to sharing the information in the first place. This is essential as long as the basic design of the American system of information sharing remains a voluntary one.

9.5.1 The Fair Credit Reporting Act

The primary mechanism for regulating the activities of consumer credit bureaus in the United States is the Fair Credit Reporting Act (hereafter FCRA).[30] It was enacted in 1970 and amended several times since, most notably in 1996 and 2003. The FCRA creates obligations for credit bureaus, users of credit reports, and organizations that provide information to credit bureaus. The principal agency responsible for enforcing the FCRA is the Federal Trade Commission (FTC), but other federal agencies (including the Federal Reserve Board) are also responsible for enforcing the act among firms they regulate.[31]

In many ways, this law was designed to refine the balance between the obvious benefits credit bureaus generate and consumers' legitimate concerns over accuracy and privacy. The FCRA creates obligations for credit bureaus, users of credit reports, and credit bureau members. But it also limits their potential liability and prevents the states from enacting legislation affecting many aspects of credit reporting (see appendix 9A).

Traditionally, the duties of lenders and other information providers have been relatively modest: to avoid furnishing information known to be erroneous and to participate in the process of correcting errors identified by consumers. In fact, these are the only instances under the FCRA where an information provider can be sued by consumers. All their other obligations under the FCRA are enforced by a federal agency. Still, over time, Congress has increased the responsibilities of information providers, most notably in 2003.

Similarly, the existence of inaccuracies in credit files does not, in itself, constitute a violation of the FCRA. Rather, the act requires credit bureaus to use reasonable procedures to ensure maximum possible accuracy. This standard is satisfied if the bureau adopts procedures a reasonably prudent person would use under the circumstances. Historically, the courts have interpreted this standard in light of the incremental benefits and costs of attaining higher levels of accuracy.[32] This balancing of benefits and costs may change over time, as advances in technology make it easier for bureaus to adopt ever more powerful computers and software and as lenders change how they make credit decisions.

The FCRA also encourages consumers to correct errors in their reports. The cost to consumers of obtaining their own reports is limited by regulation. And since 1970, the cost of obtaining a credit report has been free whenever information contained in a credit report has contributed to an adverse decision affecting the consumer—precisely the circumstance in which an error may be more costly. The FCRA requires users of credit bureau information to remind consumers of their right to obtain and, if necessary, correct their credit reports. The act sets a time limit for reinvestigations to be completed, at no cost to the consumer, and includes a number of mechanisms for ensuring that any corrections are disseminated to other credit bureaus and users of the report in question. This is not to say that the FCRA has attained the ideal balancing of benefits and costs that might be achieved. Consumer groups remain concerned about the problems of accuracy and privacy and, in some areas, question whether the act is adequate (Golinger and Mierzwinski 1998).[33] Numerous congressional hearings in the late 1980s and early 1990s culminated in amendments, enacted in 1996, that significantly strengthened consumer protections. Thereafter, the FTC sued a number of credit bureaus, alleging they were devoting inadequate resources to the consumer-dispute process. After extensive hearings in 2003, Congress enacted many significant changes to the Fair Credit Reporting Act. Many of these are still being implemented.

At the same time, continued improvements in computer and communications technology have reduced the average cost of investigating alleged errors and correcting them when found. The industry argues, however, that any benefit from the reduction in the unit cost of resolving consumer disputes is being offset by rapid growth in the number of reports being disputed. A conservative estimate of the industrywide cost of labor devoted to resolving consumer disputes and instances of identity theft would easily exceed $10 million.

9.5.2   The Fair and Accurate Credit Transactions Act of 2003 (FACTA)

The latest amendments to the FCRA also reflect a balancing of costs and benefits. On the one hand, a temporary prohibition on new state regulation of certain aspects of consumer credit reporting was made permanent. The industry had argued strenuously that this is necessary to avoid the balkanization of information in credit bureau files and a significant increase in costs. On the other hand, Congress significantly increased the obligations of credit bureaus, users of credit reports, and information providers. The direct cost of these new obligations is not trivial: A rough estimate is that they will exceed at least $100 million.[34]

The amendments are far-ranging.[35] They institute a system of fraud alerts to assist victims of identity theft in cleaning up their credit reports and protecting them from additional losses. Consumers can obtain a free copy of their credit report each year from each of the national bureaus. Consumers will also be able to obtain a credit score, based on the contents of their credit reports, more easily and at a cost limited by regulation. Consumers can choose to dispute inaccuracies in their reports either with the bureau itself, or directly with the firm that provided the information to the bureau. Within credit reports, accounts arising from medical services will be coded so as not to disclose the nature of the medical treatment provided. Consumers' rights to opt out of lists for prescreened offers of credit or marketing solicitations by affiliated companies were also enhanced.

Information providers face a number of additional obligations. For example, the amendments call for the FTC and financial regulators to establish guidelines to ensure the accuracy and integrity of information provided to credit bureaus. Information providers will be required to establish procedures to ensure compliance with these guidelines.[36] Also, if a firm regularly shares information with a national credit bureau, it must inform its customers that it reports negative information on repayment behavior to credit bureaus. This disclosure can be made at any time, but not later than thirty days after the first time the lender reports derogatory information on the consumer's account.

One of the most interesting changes made to the FCRA is an expansion in the definition of adverse action. In the past, a consumer denied credit must be told if this negative outcome was due at least in part to information contained in a credit report, and, if so, the consumer may request a free copy of his or her report from the bureau used by the lender. In an age of risk-based pricing, however, negative information in a credit report may not result in a denial of credit, but rather to credit granted on less favorable terms (e.g., higher rates or more fees). Under the 2003 amendments, an adverse action has occurred if those terms are materially less favorable than those the creditor grants to many of its customers.

9.6 What Lies Ahead?

In the United States, the two-tier industry structure—that is, a few giant credit bureaus with national coverage serving high-volume customers, and many smaller bureaus serving specific niches or reselling data to low-volume customers—is likely to mature while adapting to new forms of delivery, for example, the Internet. Advances in predictive modeling, such as credit scoring, will likely increase the value of information contained in credit bureau files. But the industry also faces new challenges from governments as well as their own customers.

9.6.1 Regulation of Commercial Data Brokers

Within a year of the passage of FACTA, a series of new data breaches has resulted in calls for additional regulation of information-sharing arrangements. In late 2004, the data broker ChoicePoint discovered that a number of its customers had established sham businesses to gain access to the records of approximately 145,000 consumers.[37] The breach has already been linked to at least 750 instances of identity theft. Also in 2004, LexisNexis discovered that the passwords of many clients of a newly acquired subsidiary had been compromised. Hackers had obtained access to information (names, addresses, Social Security numbers, driver's license numbers, and public records) on nearly 300,000 consumers.[38] These incidents are especially noteworthy because not all the data these firms sell qualify as a credit report, and consequently, they do not fall under the regulation of the FCRA.

These, and other incidents, are receiving considerable media attention because a 2002 law enacted by the state of California (S.B. 1386) requires firms to disclose security breaches to California residents. So far in 2005, six states have enacted similar legislation. A number of customer notification bills have also been introduced in Congress. These would augment an existing requirement created by the Gramm-Leach-Bliley Act of 1999. That law requires banks and "thrift" organizations to disclose instances of unauthorized access to sensitive customer information if the information has been misused, or such misuse is reasonably possible (OCC 2005).

Despite the extended preemptions enacted by FACTA, state legislatures have been active in considering new regulations affecting credit reporting. A 2005 Washington law (S.B. 5418) permits victims of identity theft to place a "security freeze" on their credit reports. The Maine legislature passed a bill that would permit any consumer to pay a fee to the credit bureau in order to initiate a security freeze.[39] A stronger form of the identity theft protections is available under FACTA: A security freeze would permit access to a consumer's credit report only with the consumer's prior consent.

9.6.2   Limited Information Sharing by Lenders

While credit bureaus are dealing with the problem of too much information being disclosed, they must also confront the opposite problem—the reluctance of some lenders to share information that is extremely useful for assessing a consumer's risk of default.

For a brief period in the late 1990s, lenders accounting for one-half of all consumer credit ceased reporting certain information (credit limits and high balances) on at least some of their credit card accounts (Fickensher 1999a and 1999b; Lazarony 2000). Financial regulators warned lenders their underwriting systems might be compromised by incomplete credit bureau information (Federal Financial Institutions Examination Council 2000). The leading credit bureaus responded by announcing they would limit access to their databases for lenders

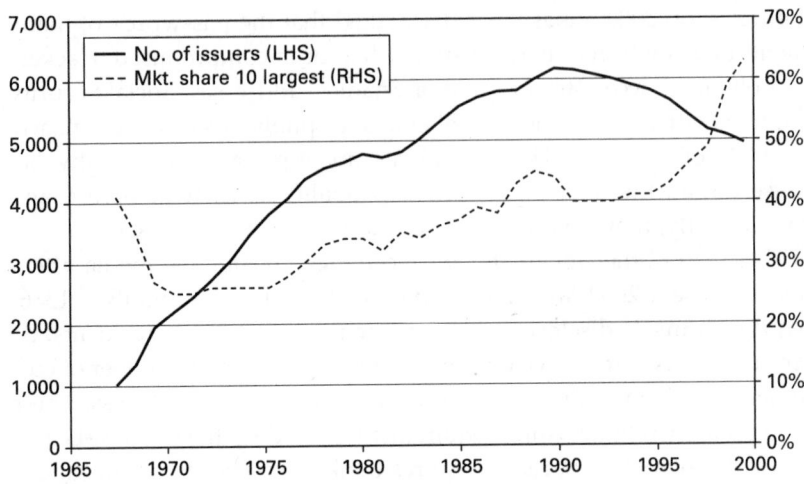

Figure 9.5
Consolidation in the U.S. credit card industry
Sources: Call report data and author's calculations.

providing incomplete credit histories. Thereafter, a number of lenders began to send more complete credit information to the bureaus.[40]

Still, as recently as 2003, at least one large credit card lender continued to omit the size of its credit lines in data it shares with credit bureaus.[41] In that same year, one of the leading purchasers of government-guaranteed student loans (Sallie Mae) stopped reporting repayment information to two of the three national credit bureaus (Singletary 2003, 2004).

Such behavior might reflect an increase in competition for new customers by credit card and other lenders. During this period, an increasing share of consumers' unsecured debt was held on the books of a few lenders. Between 1994 and 2004, the share of credit card balances held by the top ten banking institutions increased from 48 percent to 90 percent (figure 9.5), while the number of issuers fell more than 40 percent.[42] These banks are the principal source of information about consumers' payment habits for bank cards, as well as the principal source of potential new customers. During this period, consumers were inundated with offers of credit card accounts that carried low introductory interest rates on balances transferred from other banks. Such episodes are a clear reminder that, in the United States at least, information sharing remains a voluntary activity. Creditors and other information providers are sensitive to the costs and benefits of participating. This voluntary equilibrium need not continue if there are significant changes in the economic or legal environment.

9A Appendix

An Overview of the Fair Credit Reporting Act

Limitations on Disclosure of Credit Bureau Data
Credit reports may be furnished only for purposes authorized in the act, for example, to lenders making a loan decision, insurers underwriting a policy, or employers considering a person for employment. A credit report may also be issued to any person with a legitimate business need arising from a transaction initiated by the consumer or with an existing account with a consumer. An example might be a credit check performed by a prospective landlord.

A credit report may be used in an employment decision but only with the potential employee's prior consent, (although there is a national security exception for federal government agencies). If the employer takes an adverse action against the employee on the basis of information obtained in a credit report, it must inform the consumer that some of the information obtained was derived from a credit report.

Medical information about a consumer cannot be shared with affiliates, creditors, insurers, or employers without the consumer's consent. Providers of medical services and products that share information with credit bureaus must identify themselves as such to bureaus so that their information can be coded in a way that the nature of the medical services provided is not inadvertently disclosed. Lenders are prohibited from obtaining or using medical information (other than the dollar amount and payment status of an account) to make credit decisions.

The FCRA was initially interpreted and later modified to explicitly permit a process called prescreening. This is the process of generating lists of customers to be sent firm offers of credit or insurance, based on criteria specified by a lender or insurance company, without obtaining the prior consent of the consumers. Consumers can call a single 1-800 number to opt out of prescreening services provided by the three national credit bureaus. Businesses that send prescreened offers to consumers must tell consumers of their right to opt out of such offers.

The 2003 amendments also require the FTC and financial regulators to issue rules governing consumers' rights to opt out of marketing solicitations made by affiliated entities that rely on consumer information that would otherwise be considered a credit report.

Under the FCRA, credit bureaus must use reasonable procedures to prevent disclosures of consumers' information that violate the act. Users of credit bureau information must identify themselves and the reason why a credit report is being sought. Credit bureaus must make a reasonable effort to verify this information when dealing with new customers. When a consumer report is purchased for resale to an end user, the identity of the end user and the proposed use of that report must be provided to the credit bureau.

The FCRA specifies penalties for violations of consumers' privacy. A credit bureau or a user of a credit report found to be in negligent noncompliance with the act is responsible for the consumer's actual damages plus his or her reasonable legal expenses. Punitive damages may be awarded in instances of willful noncompliance. Officers or employees of a credit bureau who knowingly or willfully disclose consumer information to a person not authorized to receive it can be prosecuted. Any person who obtains a consumer report under false pretenses is subject to criminal prosecution and can be sued by the credit bureau for actual damages.

Identity Theft Reports

The 2003 amendments permit consumers to notify national credit bureaus they are victims of identity theft. The national bureaus must share this information with each other. An initial fraud alert lasts for ninety days. Consumers can place a long-term alert (seven years) on their credit file by submitting to the bureau a copy of a police report (which subjects the consumer to criminal sanctions for false reporting). This also permits consumers to block the disclosure of certain information in their credit reports, such as delinquent accounts opened by an identity thief. Consumers may request that their purged credit reports be sent to users who recently accessed their reports. These must be provided at no cost to the consumer. Within a year of filing a fraud alert, the consumer may receive two free reports from each of the national credit reporting agencies.

Fraud alerts can remain on a consumer's report for up to seven years. Creditors accessing credit reports containing a fraud alert must take additional steps to verify the identity of the consumer prior to extending or increasing credit to that consumer. Unless the consumer stipulates otherwise, he or she may not be included in lists used to make prescreened offers of credit for a period of five years.

Accuracy of Credit Bureau Data

Duties of Credit Bureaus

Credit bureaus must use reasonable procedures to assure maximum possible accuracy of the information contained in credit reports. This standard is satisfied if the bureau adopts procedures similar to those a reasonably prudent person would use under the circumstances.

Credit reports may not include negative credit information that is more than seven years old or bankruptcies that are more than ten years old. Suits or unpaid judgments may not be included after seven years unless the relevant statute of limitations runs longer, although these limitations do not apply in cases in which a credit report is used for the purposes of an application for credit or life insurance exceeding $150,000, or for a position with a salary that exceeds $75,000. Also, there is no limitation on the reporting of criminal convictions.

Under the 2003 amendments, consumers may request one free credit report each year from each of the national credit bureaus. Consumers may purchase additional reports for a fee that is capped by regulation (currently $9.50). A consumer is also entitled to a free credit report if he or she experiences an adverse decision on the basis of information contained in a credit report (see p. 333).

Under the 2003 amendments, if a bureau generates a credit score for use by their customers, the bureau must also provide a credit score to consumers who request them. The score provided to the consumer need not be the same one used by its customers. Bureaus may charge a fee for these scores, subject to a cap set by the FTC. The amendments void contract provisions that prohibit the disclosure of credit scores by bureaus or lenders.

Duties of Lenders and Other Information Providers

A provider of information to a credit bureau may not be sued by a consumer for noncompliance with the FCRA unless it failed to review all the information provided to it by the credit bureau when reinvestigating a file at the request of the consumer.

An information provider may not furnish credit bureaus with information it knows, or has reasonable cause to believe, is inaccurate. This is defined as specific knowledge that would lead a reasonable person to have substantial doubts about the accuracy of the information.

If an organization regularly furnishes information to a credit bureau and discovers an inaccuracy, it must notify the bureau of the error and correct the information. Lenders must notify credit bureaus of accounts that are voluntarily closed by a customer. If a consumer has contacted the firm to dispute information it has provided to a credit bureau, the dispute must be noted when that information is subsequently reported to the credit bureau.

The 2003 amendments call for the FTC and financial regulators to establish guidelines to ensure the accuracy and integrity of information provided to credit bureaus. Information providers are required to establish procedures to ensure compliance with these guidelines. Consumers may now direct their disputes directly to information providers, who must respond and correct any erroneous information previously sent to a credit bureau (except disputes submitted by credit repair organizations). The FTC and financial regulators are charged with developing regulatory standards that apply to the dispute process among information providers.

Under the 2003 amendments, when a firm that regularly shares information with a national credit bureau reports negative information on a consumer's account for the first time, it must also notify the consumer. The notice requirement can be satisfied by giving the consumer a disclosure indicating the lender may report future negative payment performance to a credit bureau.

If, on the basis of information obtained from a credit report, a lender grants credit to a consumer on terms materially less favorable than the best terms it offers a substantial proportion of consumers, the lender must disclose this fact to the consumer. Such disclosures are not required when a consumer applies for credit on specific terms and was granted those terms.

Procedures for Dispute Resolution

Anyone who makes an adverse decision—such as denying an application for credit, insurance, or employment—on the basis of information contained in a credit report must inform the consumer and provide the name, address, and phone number of the bureau that furnished the report. If the adverse decision pertains to an extension of credit but is based on information other than a credit report, the consumer has a right to request an explanation for this decision. The creditor must respond to such a request within sixty days. The consumer must be given a disclosure describing his or her rights under the FCRA, including the right to obtain a free credit report after experiencing an adverse action. The 2003 amendments expanded the definition of adverse action to include instances in which a lender provides credit on terms materially less favorable than it makes available to many of its customers.

Consumers must receive all the information in their file, including any medical information, and the sources of the underlying data must also be reported. The consumer must also be given the identity of any person who procured his or her credit report in the past year, two years if the purpose was employment-related.

Consumers may dispute an item in their credit report simply by writing to the credit bureau, or the firm that provided it with the information, and explaining why the information in question is inaccurate. At a minimum, the bureau must forward this complaint to the provider of the information in question, which must then investigate the item. The information provider must report back to the bureau, which in turn informs the consumer of the outcome of the investigation. If the information provider had previously sent the erroneous information to one of the national credit bureaus, it must also send the corrected information to them.

If the result is a change in the credit report, the consumer receives a free copy of the revised report and may request that it be sent to anyone who recently obtained a copy of his or her report. If the investigation does not resolve the dispute, the consumer may insert a brief statement about the item in his or her file.

A credit bureau must remove or correct inaccurate information from its files within thirty days after it is disputed (or forty-five days if the complaint arises from examination of the free copy of their credit report that consumers are entitled to each year). The FCRA does not require credit bureaus to remove accurate data from a file unless it is either outdated or cannot be verified. If a dispute results in a change in the credit report, the disputed information cannot be reinserted unless it is reverified by the information source and the consumer is given notice of the change in his or her file.

Preemption of State Law
The FCRA prohibits consumers from suing for defamation, invasion of privacy, or negligence (under state law) resulting from information

that is contained in their credit report. This prohibition applies to suits against credit bureaus, users of credit reports, and information providers. This prohibition does not apply, however, where false information is furnished with malice or willful intent to injure a consumer.

The 1996 amendments to the act temporarily prohibited states from enacting new legislation regulating certain aspects of credit reporting. These include limits on the amount of time that derogatory information can be retained in credit reports, the amount of time allowed for credit bureaus to respond to a consumer dispute, additional duties of firms that provide information to credit bureaus, or new restrictions on the ability of credit bureaus to offer prescreening services to companies making firm offers of credit or insurance.

The 2003 amendments make those prohibitions permanent. They also created additional preemptions against new state legislation in the following areas: how frequently consumers can obtain a free copy of their credit report; mandatory disclosure of credit scores used for credit decisions (except insurance decisions); the opt-out process for exchanges of information among affiliates that would otherwise be treated as a credit report; or the duties of lenders to notify consumers that they received credit on less than the most favorable terms as a result of information contained in their credit report. The amendments also preempt new state laws that would conflict with the identity theft provisions contained in the new law.

Consumer Credit Extended by Retailers and Financial Institutions

The share of retail sales financed via retailer credit in 1929 is derived from the 1930 *Census of Business*. This calculation excludes paper, primarily automobile loans, financed or purchased by finance companies. The shares of open account sales for various categories of stores in 1935 are from a reprint of the 1935 survey in the 1939 *Survey of Business*.

Calculations for the growth of consumer credit held by retailers and financial companies and the respective shares of consumer credit held by these categories are based on data contained in *Banking and Monetary Statistics, 1941–1970* (1976).

The shares of consumer credit for more recent years are derived from the Federal Reserve Board's statistical release *Consumer Credit (G 19)*, published monthly. The edition used, together with the most recent version of the historical series (found at the board's Web site), is from April 2005. The shares depicted in figure 9.2 are net of securitized assets. This tends to understate the share of consumer credit underwritten by commercial banks beginning in the early 1990s.

It should be noted that survey coverage, categories of lenders (including retailers), and categories of loans vary depending on the vintage of data being used. For example, consumer credit is sometimes divided into installment credit and other credit, but how that is done varies over time. Also, a separate breakdown for retailers disappears in releases after the mid-1990s. Thereafter, a breakdown for nonfinancial companies (mostly retailers) is reported.

Comparisons of the growth rate of consumer credit relative to consumer spending rely on the most recent version of the National Income and Product Accounts for years after 1928. For the period 1919 to 1928, these calculations are based on series E 135 (CPI all items) and G 470 (personal consumption expenditures) in the *Historical Statistics of the United States, Colonial Times to 1970.*

The statistics on revolving credit held by retailers and commercial banks (figure 9.4) are based on a variety of tabulations published by the Federal Reserve System. These include the *Annual Statistical Digest* (1970–1979, 1980–1989, 1991, 1992, 1993, and 1994), *The Federal Reserve Bulletin* (December 1968, October 1972, and December 1975), and revisions to the *Consumer Installment Credit* series published in April 1986 and May 1993. After 1970, banks' revolving credit includes check credit. Revolving credit at retailers includes gasoline stations. Because of changes in reporting of the series, there are no consistent data for revolving credit at retailers for 1975. The year-end number for 1976 is derived from the January 1977 number for revolving credit at retailers, less the proportionate share of the increase in credit held by retailers.

The measures of bank credit card concentration (presented in figure 9.5) are derived from Call Report data. The number of issuers and market shares are calculated at the holding company level. The number of issuers is determined by identifying banks that report unused commitments on credit card loans (schedule RC-L).

Shares of Retail Sales Accounted for by Regional and National Chains
For 1929, the shares are calculated using the Census Bureau's categories of "sectional or national" chains as reported in the 1930 *Census of Business.* Shares for later years are calculated using firms with twenty-six or more stores, as reported in the 1939 *Census of Business* and the *Census of Retail Trade* thereafter. The 1939 census also reports data

categorized as sectional or national chains, and for most categories of retailers, these are comparable to the numbers reported for firms with twenty-six or more stores.

Consumer Credit Reporting Agencies

Data on the number of offices, employment, receipts, and concentration ratios are from the *Census of Service Industries* as reported in 1972 and more recent editions. The numbers for 1997 are for the industry code 5614501 in the new North American Industry Classification System (NAICS). The numbers reported for previous years are based on the old Standard Industrial Classification System (SICS) industry group 7323, but only where information about consumer credit reporting agencies is broken out separately from mercantile credit reporting agencies. Unfortunately, there is not enough publicly available information to calculate concentration ratios in years prior to, or after, 1997.

Data on the number of credit reports issued, the number of credit bureaus, and the composition of ACB membership are from testimony provided by the organization in the transcripts of the 1970 and 1975 hearings in the House of Representatives. Numbers on credit bureau activity today are from the testimony in the 2003 hearings in the House of Representatives. Information on the organization of credit bureaus and the extent of automation in the late 1980s is from ACB testimony contained in the transcripts of the 1989 hearings in the House of Representatives. The most recent data on the number of members and indicators of activity are from ACB's Web site, as reported in October 2001. Information about the major credit bureaus' other lines of businesses were found on the companies' Web sites.

Errors in Consumer Credit Reports

The aggregate statistics from ACB are from its response to questions printed in the transcripts of the September 1989 hearings in the House of Representatives (855). The same hearings report statistics for TRW that are comparable (796, 801–802).

The statistic on the frequency of mismerge errors is from the study prepared by James R. Williams in 1989. Williams identified errors in the rating of an account (satisfactory or delinquent, for example) in about 13 percent of 350 credit reports. This report was reprinted in the transcripts to the June 1990 hearings in the House of Representatives (517–539).

This chapter refers to surveys conducted by two consumers groups. The Consumers Union survey is reprinted in the transcripts of the June 1991 hearings in the House of Representatives (425–435). The other is the Public Interest Research Group's 1998 study, which can be found at http://www.pirg.org/reports/consumer/mistakes/index.htm. The samples in these surveys are quite small, 57 and 131, respectively, and were not drawn randomly from the population of credit users.

The statistics from the Arthur Andersen study are from the National Press Club speech by D. Barry Connelly, executive vice president of ACB. While the sample size of the Andersen study is quite large— over 15,000 applicants who were denied credit—the results are based on a small set of those applicants. About 1,200 requested copies of their credit report, and about 300 of those disputed their reports. In thirty-six of 267 instances analyzed, the lender reversed the credit decision.

Notes

The idea for this chapter originated in discussions with the Federal Reserve Bank of Philadelphia's Payment Cards Center. Thanks to James DiSalvo for his assistance in assembling data for this paper. Thanks to Mark Furletti for help with fact checking. Any remaining errors are my own.

The chapter benefited from discussions with Robert Avery, Mitchell Berlin, Tony Capaldi, John Caskey, Paul Calem, Satyajit Chatterjee, Richard Disney, Nicola Jentzsch, Nick Souleles, and Todd Zywicki and seminar participants at Butler University, the European University Institute, the Federal Trade Commission, Riksbank, and the Southern Finance Association. I also thank the referees and editors for many helpful suggestions.

The views expressed here are those of the author and do not necessarily represent the views of the Federal Reserve Bank of Philadelphia or the Federal Reserve System.

1. This chapter focuses on what the Fair Credit Reporting Act (FCRA) calls consumer reports and not investigative consumer reports. The latter are sometimes used for employment, insurance, and other decisions, are based in part on information gathered from personal interviews, and are governed differently under the FCRA. Investigative reports engendered significant controversy in the late 1960s and early 1970s, in part because consumers were not always informed they were being done or that information based on them was maintained in credit bureau files. See Miller 1971 and Privacy Protection Study Commission 1977.

2. These numbers are from *The Nilson Report*, as reprinted in U.S. Bureau of the Census, 2004b.

3. Additional empirical evidence is found in Calem and Mester 1995.

4. Adverse selection can lead to sticky prices through mechanisms other than credit rationing. For example, Mester (1994) describes how reductions in banks' costs of funds may result in an increase in the average riskiness of credit card borrowers.

5. For reviews of the recent literature, see Congressional Budget Office 2000, Mester 2002, and chapter 7 of this volume. After many legislative attempts, a bankruptcy reform law was enacted in 2005 (Public Law no. 109-8).

6. Shaffer (1998) posits another argument that is relevant here—the winner's curse associated with being the lender who grants a loan to a borrower previously rejected by many other banks.

7. Such limitations are usually imposed by law and typically apply only to derogatory credit information.

8. See the 2003 testimony by Kevin Sullivan. For extensive materials on the use and effectiveness of scores for insurance underwriting, see the 2003 testimony by Cheri St. John.

9. This number is 20 percent of the product of the charge-off rate on banks' credit card loans (4.38 percent) times outstanding revolving credit ($613 billion) in the first quarter of 2000. That was the recent low for delinquencies and charge offs on U.S. banks' credit card loans. See Barron and Staten 2003 for a comparable exercise in which they ask what would be the decline in the discriminatory power of a scorecard when it is constructed only with derogatory credit information. Jappelli and Pagano (1999) use a cross-national sample with macroeconomic data to identify some preliminary evidence of the effect of credit bureaus on default rates.

10. This association was originally called the National Federation of Retail Credit Agencies. Today it is called the Consumer Data Industry Association, or CDIA, but I will refer to its historic name throughout this paper. Some of the information presented in this section is drawn from the organization's website.

11. These numbers exclude credit arranged through separate finance companies. For details on the historical statistics cited in this section, see the appendix.

12. To span the century, two sets of data are required. See the appendix for details.

13. If we include securitized revolving credit, mostly issued by banks at the time (described in chapter 1) but not carried on their balance sheets, the ratio would be 5:1 rather than 3:1.

14. In 1969, only four ACB-member bureaus were partially or fully automated. Six years later, 80 member bureaus had automated.

15. These statistics are from the *Census of Service Industries* (U.S. Bureau of the Census, various years). See the appendix for details.

16. See the 2003 testimony of Richard Hillman.

17. But consumers are less likely to dispute errors in their favor (e.g., unreported delinquencies) than they are errors that might adversely affect their access to credit.

18. Prior to the passage of the FCRA, some credit bureaus in the United States were less receptive to the idea of encouraging consumers to investigate their files. Some bureaus actively discouraged lenders from disclosing to consumers the name of the bureau, or even that a credit report had been obtained.

19. This problem is aggravated if some consumers use the dispute process strategically, namely, by disputing accurate derogatory information in the hope it will be erroneously removed. A recent estimate is that about one-third of disputes received by credit bureaus are generated by credit repair organizations attempting to do just this. See the 2003 testimony of Stuart Pratt.

20. See, for example, the study by Consumers Union (in Michelle Meier's 1991 testimony) and several studies by the Public Interest Research Group (Golinger and Mierzwinski 1998; Cassady and Mierzwinski 2004).

21. See the 2003 testimony by Richard Hillman.

22. The authors define "recently updated" as an account either reported within the past two months or reported as paid down and closed. A higher proportion of revolving accounts currently reported (71 percent) were open.

23. The mean deviation between the highest and lowest scores was 43 points; the median deviation was 36 points.

24. Thirteen and a half percent of 3 million disputed reports is 405,000. But that number is likely an overestimate for two reasons. First, the frequency of the most egregious mistakes is almost certainly higher in a sample of consumers denied credit than for the population as a whole. (We don't know how serious the selection problem was because the study, prepared by Arthur Andersen, was never published.) Second, not all of the 3 million reports disputed in 1989 occurred after a denial of credit. So the 405,000 number is probably too high. The question is, by how much?

25. The borrower must score at least 660 to qualify as a "good credit risk," while a score of below 620 makes it difficult to obtain credit. A description of FICO scores is available at the Credit Report Site (http://www.consumerfed.org/consumerinf.cfm).

26. In most simulations, the mean change in score (in either direction) was twelve points or lower.

27. For a discussion of the different kinds of identity theft, see Cheney 2003. The 2003 Federal Trade Commission survey provides some evidence on the extent of this problem for U.S. consumers.

28. The reporter was writing the article "Is Nothing Private?" on credit bureaus for *Business Week*, published by McGraw-Hill. In 1998, McGraw-Hill was ordered to pay $7,500 in damages, resulting from a deliberate breach of contract, to the credit bureau that provided the information.

29. See *TransUnion Corp. v. Federal Trade Commission*, and *Individual Reference Services Group, Inc. (IRSG) v. Federal Trade Commission et al.*

30. A review of the legal and regulatory evolution of this law is found in the 2003 testimony of Commissioner Beales.

31. Under the act, state attorneys general may sue on behalf of their residents. In addition, certain state laws provide consumers with additional rights.

32. See, for example, *Bryant v. TRW, Inc* (1982) and *Houston v. TRW Information Services, Inc.* (1989).

33. See also the 2001 testimony of Edmund Mierzwinski.

34. See the Congressional Budget Office unfunded mandates estimate in Senate Report no. 108-166.

35. Public Law no. 108-159. The text of the act, as well as an updated version of the U.S. Code reflecting these amendments, can be downloaded from the FTC's Web site (http://www.ftc.gov/os/statutes/ferajump.htm).

36. The legislative history suggests the standard is not exceptional; the procedures should ensure that firms have a reasonable belief that the information they provide to credit bureaus is accurate. See House Report no. 108-263.

37. See the Congressional Budget Office unfunded mandates estimate in Senate Report no. 108-166.

38. See the 2005 testimony of Derek Smith and Kurt Sanford. In 1997, Equifax spun off its insurance- and employment-screening business, which became ChoicePoint.

39. Information on state legislative is from the National Conference of State Legislatures website (http://www.ncsl.org).

40. Statistics on the improvement in reporting of credit limits are discussed in section 3.3.

41. See the 2003 hearings before the Senate Committee on Banking, Housing and Urban Affairs (533–538) and Dash 2005.

42. This market share calculation includes only banks. Between 1970 and 1990, the market share of the top ten banks rose gradually from about 25 percent to about 40 percent. As the figure shows, taking into account securitization, activity increases the concentration measure.

References

Books and Articles

Annual Statistical Digest. Various years. Washington, DC: Board of Governors of the Federal Reserve System.

Ausubel, Lawrence M. 1991. "The Failure of Competition in the Credit Card Market." *American Economic Review* 81: 50–81.

Ausubel, Lawrence M. 1999. "Adverse Selection in the Credit Card Market." Mimeo., Department of Economics, University of Maryland.

Avery, Robert B., Raphael W. Bostic, Paul S. Calem, and Glenn B. Canner. 2003. "An Overview of Consumer Data and Credit Reporting." *Federal Reserve Bulletin*: 47–73.

Avery, Robert B., Paul S. Calem, and Glenn B. Canner. 2004. "Credit Report Accuracy and Access to Credit." *Federal Reserve Bulletin*: 297–322.

Banking and Monetary Statistics, 1941–1970. 1976. Washington, DC: Board of Governors of the Federal Reserve System.

Barron, John M., and Michael Staten. 2003. "The Value of Comprehensive Credit Reports: Lessons from U.S. Experience." In *Credit Reporting Systems and the International Economy*, ed. Margaret Miller, 273–310. Cambridge, MA: The MIT Press.

Caldor, Lendol. 1999. *Financing the American Dream: A Cultural History of Consumer Credit.* Princeton, NJ: Princeton University Press.

Calem, Paul S., and Loretta J. Mester. 1995. "Consumer Behavior and the Stickiness of Credit-Card Interest Rates." *American Economic Review* 85: 1327–1336.

Cassady, Alison, and Edwin Mierzwinski. 2004. *Mistakes Do Happen: A Look at Errors in Consumer Credit Reports.* Washington, D.C.: National Association of Public Interest Research Groups.

Cate, Fred H. 1997. *Privacy in the Information Age*. Washington, D.C.: Brookings Institutions Press.

Chandler, Gary G., and Robert W. Johnson. 1992. "The Benefit to Consumers From Generic Scoring Models Based on Credit Reports." *IMA Journal of Mathematics Applied in Business and Industry* 4: 61–72.

Chandler, Gary G., and Lee E. Parker. 1989. "Predictive Value of Credit Bureau Reports." *Journal of Retail Banking* 11: 47–54.

Cheney, Julia. 2003. "Identity Theft: A Pernicious and Costly Fraud." Discussion paper, Federal Reserve Bank of Philadelphia Payment Cards Center.

Cole, Robert H., and Lon Mishler. 1998. *Consumer and Commercial Credit Management*, 11th ed. Boston: McGraw-Hill.

Congressional Budget Office. 2000. *Personal Bankruptcy: A Literature Review*. Washington, D.C.: Congressional Budget Office.

Connelly, D. Barry. 1992. "Announcement of the Credit Report Reliability Study." Text of speech before the National Press Club, February 4.

Consumer Credit (G 19). Various years. Washington, D.C.: Board of Governors of the Federal Reserve System.

Consumer Installment Credit, Revision Sheets (January 1975–January 1986). 1986. Washington, D.C.: U.S. Department of Commerce, National Technical Information Service.

Credit Score Accuracy and Implications for Consumers. 2002. Washington, D.C.: Consumer Federation of America.

Dash, Eric. 2005. "Up Against the Plastic Wall." *New York Times* (May 21): 5.

Evans, David S., and Richard Schmalensee. 1999. *Paying with Plastic: The Digital Revolution in Buying and Borrowing*. Cambridge, Mass.: The MIT Press.

Federal Financial Institutions Examination Council. 2000. "Consumer Credit Reporting Practices." Advisory letter, January 18.

Federal Reserve Bulletin. Various years. Washington, D.C.: Board of Governors of the Federal Reserve System.

Federal Trade Commission. 2003. *Identity Theft Survey Report*. Washington, D.C.: Federal Trade Commission.

Fickensher, Lisa. 1999a. "Lenders Hiding Credit Data and Regulators Object." *American Banker* 149 (July 7): 1,7.

Fickenscher, Lisa. 1999b. "Credit Bureaus Move Against Lenders That Withhold Info." *American Banker* 149 (December 30): 1.

Gelpi, Rosa-Maria, and Francois Julien-Labruyere. 2000. *The History of Consumer Credit: Doctrines and Practices*. New York: St. Martin's Press.

Government Accountability Office. 2005. *Credit Reporting Literacy*. Report no. 05-223. Washington, D.C.: U.S. Government Accountability Office.

Golinger, Jon, and Edmund Mierzwinski. 1998. "Mistakes Do Happen: Credit Report Errors Mean Consumers Lose." Washington, D.C.: Public Interest Research Group. http://www.pirg.org/reports/mistakes (accessed 10/15/2001).

Green, Mark. 1991. "Prying Eyes: An Investigation into Privacy Abuses by Credit Reporting Agencies." Mimeo., New York City Department of Consumer Affairs.

"Is Nothing Private?" 1989. *Business Week* (September 4): 74–82.

Jappelli, Tulio, and Marco Pagano. 1999. "Information Sharing, Lending and Defaults: Cross Country Evidence." CEPR Working Paper no. 2184.

Jentzsch, Nicola. 2004. *The Economics and Regulation of Credit Reporting: The United States and Europe.* PhD dissertation, Freie Universität Berlin.

Klein, Daniel B. 1997. "Promise Keeping in the Great Society: A Model of Credit Information Sharing." In *Reputation: Studies in the Voluntary Elicitation of Good Conduct,* ed. Daniel B. Klein, 267–287. Ann Arbor: University of Michigan Press.

Lazarony, Lucy. 2000. "Lenders Defy Credit-Reporting Crackdown, Hoarding Data That Could Save You Money." *Bankrate.com,* April 28, 2000 (accessed September 28, 2001).

Marquez, Robert. 2002. "Competition, Adverse Selection, and Information Dispersion in the Banking Industry." *Review of Financial Studies* 15: 901–926.

McCorkell, Peter L. 2002. "The Impact of Credit Scoring and Automated Underwriting on Credit Availability." In *The Impact of Public Policy on Consumer Credit,* ed. Thomas A. Durkin and Michael E. Staten, 209–219. Boston: Kluwer Academic Publishers.

Mester, Loretta J. 1994. "Why Are Credit Card Rates Sticky?" *Economic Theory* 4: 505–530.

Mester, Loretta J. 2002. "Is the Personal Bankruptcy System Bankrupt?" *Federal Reserve Bank of Philadelphia Business Review* (1st Quarter): 31–44.

Miller, Arthur R. 1971. *The Assault on Privacy: Computers, Data Banks, and Dossiers.* Ann Arbor, Mich.: University of Michigan Press.

Miller, Margaret. 2003. "Credit Reporting Systems around the Globe: The State of the Art in Public and Private Credit Registries." In *Credit Reporting Systems and the International Economy,* ed. Margaret Miller, 25–80. Cambridge, Mass.: The MIT Press.

Nocera, Joseph. 1994. *A Piece of the Action: How the Middle Class Joined the Money Class.* New York: Simon & Schuster.

Padilla, A. Jorge, and Marco Pagano. 1997. "Endogenous Communication among Lenders and Entrepreneurial Incentives." *The Review of Financial Studies* 10: 205–236.

Padilla, A. Jorge, and Marco Pagano. 2000. "Sharing Default Information as a Borrower Discipline Device." *European Economic Review* 44: 1951–1980.

Pagano, Marco, and Tullio Jappelli. 1993. "Information Sharing in Credit Markets." *Journal of Finance* 48: 1693–1718.

Privacy Protection Study Commission. 1977. *Personal Privacy in an Information Society.* Washington, D.C.: U.S. Government Printing Office.

Shaffer Sherill. 1998. "The Winner's Curse in Banking." *Journal of Financial Intermediation* 7: 359–392.

Singletary, Michelle. 2003. "No Altruism Here." *Washington Post* (October 19): F01.

Singletary, Michelle. 2004. "Sallie Mae, Moving in Slo-Mo." *Washington Post* (February 29): F01.

Stiglitz, Joseph E., and Andrew Weiss. 1981. "Credit Rationing in Markets with Imperfect Information." *American Economic Review* 71: 393–410.

Sullivan, Teresa A., Elizabeth Warren, and Jay L. Westbrook. 2000. *The Fragile Middle Class: Americans in Debt*. New Haven: Yale University Press.

U.S. Bureau of the Census. 2004a. *2002 Economic Census, Administrative and Support and Waste Management and Remediation Services*. Washington, D.C.: U.S. Government Printing Office.

U.S. Bureau of the Census. 2004b. *Statistical Abstract of the United States: 2004–2005*. Washington, D.C.: U.S. Government Printing Office.

U.S. Bureau of the Census. 2001a. *1997 Economic Census, Administrative and Support and Waste Management and Remediation Services*. Washington, D.C.: U.S. Government Printing Office.

U.S. Bureau of the Census. 2001b. *Current Business Reports, Service Annual Survey: 1999*. Washington, D.C.: U.S. Government Printing Office.

U.S. Bureau of the Census. 2001c. *Statistical Abstract of the United States: 2001*. Washington, D.C.: U.S. Government Printing Office.

U.S. Bureau of the Census. 1975. *Historical Statistics of the United States, Colonial Times to 1970, Bicentennial Edition*. Washington, D.C.: U.S. Government Printing Office.

U.S. Bureau of the Census. Various years. *Census of Service Industries*. Washington, D.C.: U.S. Government Printing Office.

Vercammen, James A. 1995. "Credit Bureau Policy and Sustainable Reputation." *Economica* 62: 461–478.

White, Michele J. 1998. "Why Don't More Households File for Bankruptcy?" *Journal of Law, Economics, and Organization* 14: 205–231.

Williams, James R. 1989. "Credit File Errors: A Report." Mimeo, Consolidated Information Services, August 7.

Wilson, James A. 1990. "Fishing for Knowledge." *Land Economics* 66: 12–29.

Hearings and Testimony

Statement of Howard Beales, Director of the Bureau of Consumer Protection, Federal Trade Commission, in U.S. House of Representatives, *Fair Credit Reporting Act: How It Functions for Consumers and the Economy*, Hearings before the Financial Institutions and Consumer Credit Subcommittee of the Financial Services Committee, 108th Congress, 2nd Session (June 4, 2003).

Statement of Richard J. Hillman, Director, Financial Markets and Community Investment, General Accounting Office, in U.S. Senate, *The Fair Credit Reporting Act and Issues Presented by Reauthorization of The Expiring Preemption Provisions*, Hearings before the Committee on Banking, Housing, and Urban Affairs, 108th Congress, 2nd Session (July 31, 2003).

Statement of Michelle Meier, Counsel for Government Affairs, Consumers Union, in U.S. House of Representatives, *Fair Credit Reporting Act*, Hearings before the Subcommittee on Consumer Affairs and Coinage of the Committee on Banking, Finance and Urban Affairs, and Currency, 102nd Congress, 1st Session (June 6, 1991).

Statement of Edmund Mierzwinski, Consumer Program Director, U.S. Public Interest Group, in U.S. House of Representatives, *An Examination of Existing Federal Statutes Addressing Information Privacy*, Hearings before the Subcommittee on Commerce, Trade, and Consumer Protection of the Committee on Energy and Commerce, 107th Congress, 1st Session (April 3, 2001).

Statement of Stuart Pratt, President of the Consumer Data Industry Association, in U.S. Senate, *The Fair Credit Reporting Act and Issues Presented by Reauthorization of the Expiring Preemption Provisions*, Hearings before the Committee on Banking, Housing and Urban Affairs, 108th Congress, 1st Session (June 19, 2003).

Statement of Kurt P. Sanford, President and CEO of LexisNexis, Inc., in U.S. Senate, *Securing Electronic Personal Data: Striking a Balance between Privacy and Commercial and Governmental Use*, Hearings before the Committee on the Judiciary, 109th Congress, 1st Session (April 13, 2005).

Statement of Derek Smith, Chairman and CEO of ChoicePoint, in U.S. House of Representatives, Hearings before the Commerce, Trade, and Consumer Protection Subcommittee of the Committee on Energy and Commerce, 109th Congress, 1st Session (March 15, 2005).

Statement of Cheri St. John, Vice President, Fair Isaac Corporation, in U.S. House of Representatives, *Fair Credit Reporting Act: How It Functions for Consumers and the Economy*, Hearings before the Financial Institutions and Consumer Credit Subcommittee of the Financial Services Committee, 108th Congress, 2nd Session (June 4, 2003).

Statement of Kevin T. Sullivan, Vice President and Deputy General Counsel, Allstate Insurance Company, in U.S. House of Representatives, *Fair Credit Reporting Act: How It Functions for Consumers and the Economy*, Hearings before the Financial Institutions and Consumer Credit Subcommittee of the Financial Services Committee, 108th Congress, 2nd Session (June 4, 2003).

U.S. House of Representatives. *Amendments to the Fair Credit Reporting Act*, Hearings before the Subcommittee on Consumer Affairs and Coinage of the Committee on Banking, Finance and Urban Affairs. 101st Congress, 2nd Session (June 12, 1990).

U.S. House of Representatives. *Fair Credit Reporting*, Hearings before the Subcommittee on Consumer Affairs of the Committee on Banking and Currency, 91st Congress, 2nd Session (1970).

U.S. House of Representatives. *Fair Credit Reporting Act*, Hearings before the Subcommittee on Consumer Affairs and Coinage of the Committee on Banking, Finance and Urban Affairs. 102nd Congress, 1st Session (October 24, 1991).

U.S. House of Representatives. *Fair Credit Reporting Act*, Hearings before the Subcommittee on Consumer Affairs and Coinage of the Committee on Banking, Finance and Urban Affairs, and Currency, 102nd Congress, 1st Session (June 6, 1991).

U.S. House of Representatives. *Fair Credit Reporting Act*, Hearings before the Subcommittee on Consumer Affairs and Coinage of the Committee on Banking, Finance and Urban Affairs. 101st Congress, 1st Session (September 13, 1989).

U.S. House of Representatives. *Fair Credit Reporting Act and Issues Presented by Reauthorization of the Expiring Preemption Provisions*, Hearings before the Committee on Banking, Housing, and Urban Affairs, 108th Congress, 1st Session (May 20; June 19, 26; July 10, 29, and 31, 2003).

U.S. House of Representatives. Committee on Financial Services, "Fair and Accurate Credit Transactions Act of 2003," House Report no. 108-263, 108th Congress, 1st Session (September 4, 2003).

U.S. Senate. Committee on Banking, Housing, and Urban Affairs, "Amending Fair Credit Reporting Act," Senate Report no. 108-166, 108th Congress, 1st Session (October 17, 2003).

Cases

Bryant v. TRW, Inc. 689 F.2d 72 (1982).

Houston v. TRW Information Services, Inc. 707 F. Supp. 689 (1989).

Individual Reference Services Group, Inc. (IRSG), v. Federal Trade Commission et al., 145 F. Supp. 2d6 (2001).

TransUnion Corp. v. Federal Trade Commission, 245 F.3d 809 (2001).

Websites

Consumer Data Industry Association (formally ACB): http://www.cdiaonline.org

ChexSystems: http://www.chexhelp.com

Credit Report Site: http://www.thecreditreportsite.com/credit_scoring.asp#scoreranges

Equifax: http://www.equifax.com/

Experian: http://www.experian.com

Fair Isaac Corporation: http://www.fairisaac.com

Federal Trade Commission: http://www.ftc.gov

Medical Information Bureau: http://www.mib.com/

Public Interest Research Group: http://www.pirg.org/

Shared Check Authorization Network (SCAN): http://www.arjaydata.com

TeleCheck: http://www.telecheck.com

TransUnion, LLC: http://www.tuc.com

The U.D. Registry, Inc.: http://www.udregistry.com

10

The Role and Effects of Credit Information Sharing

Tullio Jappelli and Marco Pagano

Information sharing about borrowers' characteristics and their indebtedness can have important effects on credit markets activity. First, it improves the banks' knowledge of applicants' characteristics and permits a more accurate prediction of their repayment probabilities. Second, it reduces the informational rents that banks could otherwise extract from their customers. Third, it can operate as a borrower discipline device. Finally, it eliminates borrowers' incentive to become overindebted by drawing credit simultaneously from many banks without any of them realizing.

This chapter provides a brief account of models that capture these four effects of information sharing on credit market performance, and reviews the growing body of empirical studies that have attempted to investigate the various dimensions and effects of credit-reporting activity. Understanding the effects of information sharing also helps to shed light on some key issues in the design of a credit information system, such as the relationship between public and private mechanisms, the dosage between black and white information sharing, and the "memory" of the system. By merging the insights from theoretical models with the lessons of experience, one can avoid serious pitfalls in the design of credit information systems.

In many countries, lenders routinely share information on the creditworthiness of their borrowers. This can happen either on a voluntary basis through credit bureaus that are set up by the lenders themselves or operated independently by a third party, or on a mandatory basis through public credit registers (PCRs) operated by central banks.

Private credit bureaus receive data about borrowers from the respective lenders. They collate this information with data from other sources (courts, public registers, tax authorities, and so forth) and compile a file on each borrower. Lenders can obtain a return flow of consolidated data about a credit applicant by requesting a "credit report" from the bureau.

Lenders who provide their private information to credit bureaus are granted access to the common database insofar as the data provided are timely and accurate. Credit bureaus are exposed to a potential conflict of interest, especially when they are owned by the lenders themselves: Each lender would like to exploit the information provided by other lenders without disclosing its own. This explains why sanctions are invariably threatened to any credit granter that fails to supply data or provides inaccurate information. Sanctions range from fines to loss of membership and hence denial of access to the bureau's files. In other words, credit bureaus are based on the principle of reciprocity, which is generally stated in the contractual agreement between the bureau and credit grantors.

A private credit bureau can issue several kinds of credit reports, depending on the information gathered, the type of credit application (consumer credit, house mortgage, business loan, and so forth), and, most importantly, the amount of detail requested by the lender. Reports range from simple statements of past defaults or arrears ("negative" data) to detailed reports on the applicant's assets and liabilities, guarantees, debt maturity structure, pattern of repayments, employment and family history ("positive" data). The more sophisticated credit bureaus also use statistical models to produce and sell "credit scoring" services, by which they rate borrowers according to their characteristics and credit history. Such scores were initially developed by credit granters, mainly for assessing credit applications. Where positive information is also available, the models are now intensively also utilized to promote financial instruments, price loans, and to set and manage credit limits.

In several countries, government authorities have taken an active role in fostering the exchange of information among lenders, creating public credit PCRs that operate in many respects like credit bureaus. The PCRs are generally managed by central banks, and access is granted only to authorized central bank staff (mainly for surveillance reasons and under tight confidentiality rules) and to the reporting financial institutions. This creates a two-way flow of data between credit granters and the PCR, as in the case of private credit bureaus.

The key difference is that participation in a PCR is compulsory, and its rules are not contracted but imposed by regulation. This implies a second important difference, namely that PCRs have universal coverage (all loans above a threshold amount must be reported at specified intervals), but the information consists mainly of credit data and is disseminated in consolidated form (giving the total loan exposure of each borrower, but no details on individual loans). Credit bureaus are less complete in their coverage but offer details on individual loans and merge credit information with other data.

The reporting threshold of PCRs varies considerably. Clearly, the higher the threshold, the fewer the number of borrowers covered and credit reports issued. The threshold also demarcates the segment in which private credit bureaus operate without competition from the PCR: Above the threshold, credit bureaus have to take into account that lenders can also turn to the public register's reports. The data reported by PCRs also varies considerably across countries. For instance, in Argentina, lenders are required to report data on defaults, arrears, loan exposure, interest rates, and guarantees. In Germany, only loan exposure and guarantees are reported; in Belgium, only defaults and arrears.

Given the lack of official statistics that exists on credit bureaus and PCRs, the only cross-country information is based on specially designed surveys. Two such surveys have been carried out in recent years. The first was conducted by Jappelli and Pagano 2002 on a sample of forty-nine countries, and concerns both private credit bureaus as well as PCRs. The second, a large-scale World Bank project described in Miller 2003, assembled data for seventy-seven countries, with extremely detailed statistics on the operation of PCRs.

Both surveys document the impressive growth and international diffusion of information sharing among lenders. Figure 10.1 shows the fraction of countries where either a PCR or a private credit bureau operated in each decade, based on data drawn from Jappelli and Pagano 2002 for private credit bureaus and from Miller 2003 for PCRs. Less than 20 percent of the countries featured a private credit bureau before 1950 and less than 5 percent had a PCR. By contrast, by the turn of the century, 50 percent of the countries surveyed by Miller 2003 had a PCRs, and over 60 percent of the countries surveyed by Jappelli and Pagano 2002 had a private credit bureau.

This impressive overall growth in credit reporting activity, fostered both by market forces and regulatory intervention alike, hides considerable heterogeneity in the operating rules, data collected, and feedback to financial intermediaries. The surveys just mentioned provide detailed information on several of these dimensions.

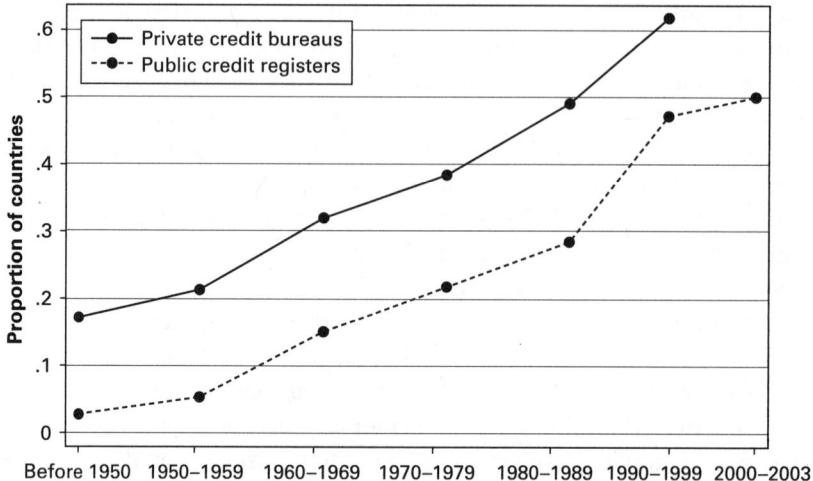

Figure 10.1
Credit reporting around the world
Sources: Miller 2003 and Jappelli and Pagano 2003.

The spread of information sharing in credit markets begs important positive and normative questions: What is the effect of information sharing on credit market performance? Why and under which circumstances are lenders willing to share private credit data? Should the government intervene in this activity, and how? If it does, how should the rules of a PCR be designed? Do special issues arise in the case of developing countries, where informal credit is widespread?

10.1 The Role of Credit Information Systems

In this section, we elucidate the various roles that information sharing can have in credit markets, bring out the predictions that can be drawn from the models that have formalized them, and compare these predictions with the available evidence. We then turn to examine the empirical evidence, bringing it to bear on the theories' predictions.

10.1.1 Theoretical Issues and Empirical Predictions
In principle, exchanging information about borrowers can have four effects: 1. improve banks' knowledge of applicants' characteristics, easing adverse selection problems; 2. reduce the "informational rents" that banks could otherwise extract from their customers; 3. act as a bor-

rower discipline device, by cutting insolvent debtors off from credit; 4. eliminate or reduce the borrowers' incentive to become "overindebted" by drawing credit simultaneously from many banks without any of them realizing.

Pagano and Jappelli (1993) show that information sharing reduces adverse selection by improving the pool of borrowers. In their model, each bank has private information about local credit applicants but has no information about nonlocal credit applicants. The latter therefore face adverse selection. However, if banks exchange their information about their clients' quality, they can also assess the quality of nonlocal credit seekers, and lend to them as safely as they do with local clients.[1] As a result, the default rate decreases. In contrast, the effect on lending is ambiguous, because when banks exchange information about borrowers' types, the implied increase in lending to safe borrowers may fail to compensate for the reduction in lending to risky types. Banking competition strengthens the positive effect of information sharing on lending: When credit markets are contestable, information sharing reduces informational rents and increases banking competition, which in turn leads to greater lending.

The exchange of information between banks may also reduce the informational rents that banks can extract from their clients within lending relationships, as shown by Padilla and Pagano 1997, in the context of a two-period model in which banks have private information about their borrowers. This informational advantage confers to banks some market power over their customers, and generates a hold-up problem: Anticipating that banks will charge predatory rates in the future, borrowers exert low effort to perform, resulting in high default and interest rates, and possibly market collapse. If they commit themselves to exchange information about borrowers' types, however, banks restrain their own future ability to extract informational rents, leaving a larger portion of the surplus to entrepreneurs. As a result, these will invest greater effort in their project, resulting in a lower default probability, lower interest rates, and greater lending relative to the regime without information sharing.[2]

An effect on incentives exists, even when there is no holdup problem, if banks communicate to each other data about past defaults rather than information about borrowers' quality. Padilla and Pagano (2000) show that this creates a disciplinary effect. When banks share default information, default becomes a signal of bad quality for outside banks and carries the penalty of higher interest rates. To avoid this penalty, borrowers exert more effort, leading to lower default and interest rates and to more lending.[3] In contrast with the result of Padilla and Pagano (1997), disclosing information about borrowers' quality has no effect on default or interest rates in this model. Ex ante competition is assumed to eliminate the informational rents of banks so that their customers' overall interest burden cannot be reduced further. As a result, when information about their quality is shared, borrowers have no reason to change their effort level, and equilibrium default and interest rates remain unchanged. And since lending to risky borrowers is a costly investment in useful quality information, lending can be reduced when such information is shared: Banks that cannot offset the costs of default by low-quality borrowers by earning informational rents on future lending to high-quality borrowers require a higher probability of repayment to be willing to lend, and the credit market may collapse in situations in which it would be viable without information sharing.

This suggests that communicating default data and disclosing borrowers' characteristics can have quite different effects on the probability of default. The disciplinary effect arises only from the exchange of default information. If banks also share data on borrowers' characteristics, they actually reduce the disciplinary effect of information sharing: A high-quality borrower will not be concerned about his default being reported to outside banks if they are also told that he is a high-quality client. But, as discussed earlier, exchanging information about borrowers' characteristics may reduce adverse selection or temper holdup problems in credit markets, and thereby reduce default rates.

The previous three effects arise even if households and firms apply for credit with only one lender at any time. Exclusive lending is a maintained assumption in all the models mentioned so far. But in practice, credit seekers may apply for credit from several lenders at the same time, and this is often granted. For instance, a consumer may simultaneously draw on several credit cards and/or credit lines at different financial intermediaries; it also common among companies, especially large ones (Ongena and Smith 2000).

Maintaining multiple lending relationships creates informational problems for lenders if each potential lender has no clear information about how much credit the borrower has already obtained or will be able to obtain from other lenders. A borrower's default risk, from the viewpoint of a given lender, depends on the overall indebtedness of the borrower when his obligation toward that lender will mature. If this information is unavailable to the lender, however, the borrower has the incentive to overborrow. To understand why, consider a consumer seeking credit from a credit card company and from a bank that do not tell each other how much the consumer borrows from each. Assume that the probability of default is an increasing function of total debt. When the consumer applies for a loan from the bank, each additional dollar he borrows reduces the probability of repayment of the capital and interest to the credit card company. Thus, the consumer's expected repayment per dollar of debt is a decreasing function of his total debt, and he has the incentive to overborrow. Anticipating this moral hazard, both lenders will ration the amount of credit supplied and/or require a higher interest rate, or even deny credit unless assisted by collateral or covenants restricting total debt.[4] This moral hazard problem disappears if the bank and the credit card company agree to reveal to each other the magnitude of the credit extended to the client. So, when lenders share information about outstanding loans, they can be expected to increase the supply of lending and/or improve the interest rates offered to credit seekers.

The models mentioned so far show that, by exchanging different types of information, lenders may control different informational problems. Exchanging information about borrower characteristics relieves adverse selection and holdup problems. Pooling default information tends to correct moral hazard problems, and its ability to do so is actually reduced if borrower characteristics are also disclosed. Finally, exchanging information about borrowers' debt exposure removes the particular form of moral hazard deriving from borrowers' ability to borrow from multiple lenders.

Despite the variety of the informational problems considered, overall some of the predicted effects of information sharing are similar. All the models predict that information sharing (in one form or another) reduces default rates, whereas the prediction concerning its effect on lending is less clear-cut. However, the prediction about default is unambiguous only if referred to the probability of default of an individual borrower. When one considers the average default rate, composition effects may overturn the prediction. Suppose that information sharing gives lower-grade borrowers access to credit. Even if each borrower's probability of default is reduced, the aggregate default rate may increase because the relative weight of lower-grade borrowers increases in the total pool. If empirical tests rely on aggregate measures of the default rate, this composition effect may introduce a bias against the models' prediction.

10.1.2 Macroeconomic Evidence

The predictions about the effects of information sharing are tested in Jappelli and Pagano 2002 on cross-country data. As shown by the regression results reported in the first two columns of table 10.1, the breadth of credit markets is associated with information sharing. Total bank lending to the private sector scaled by GNP is indeed larger in

Table 10.1
Effect of information sharing on Bank lending/GDP and on credit risk

Variable	Bank lending/GDP		Credit risk	
	OLS	Robust	OLS	Robust
GDP growth rate	2.17	−1.19	−0.56	−0.61
	(0.62)	(−0.68)	(−1.97)	(−2.06)
Log GDP	2.23	5.34	−0.34	−0.21
	(0.61)	(2.00)	(−0.74)	(−0.43)
Rule of law	7.72	4.87	−1.67	−1.71
	(3.64)	(2.89)	(−4.74)	(−5.45)
Creditor rights	5.27	9.96	−0.09	−0.09
	(1.07)	(3.23)	(−0.17)	(−0.17)
French origin	−7.01	2.46	0.90	1.04
	(−0.65)	(0.31)	(0.73)	(0.70)
German origin	26.67	14.66	−2.76	−2.46
	(1.24)	(1.42)	(−2.32)	(−1.41)
Scandinavian origin	−44.46	−29.22	2.19	2.23
	(−3.18)	(−2.59)	(1.42)	(1.18)
Negative information only	29.38	36.46	−4.54	−3.78
	(1.82)	(3.50)	(−2.15)	(−1.89)
Positive and negative information	15.65	27.23	−2.40	−2.22
	(1.43)	(2.92)	(−1.37)	(−1.23)
Constant	−42.65	−60.64	27.51	26.49
	(−1.22)	(−2.96)	(8.90)	(7.09)
Adjusted R^2	0.67	−.−	0.84	−.−
Number of countries	40	40	35	35

Note: This table is based on Jappelli and Pagano 2003. Negative information only is 1 if prior to 1994 private credit bureaus and/or PCRs exchange black information, and 0 otherwise. Negative and positive information is 1 if prior to 1994 credit bureaus or PCRs exchange black and white information. See the appendix for sources and definition of the other variables. t-statistics are reported in parentheses. White-corrected standard errors are used in the OLS estimates.

countries where information sharing is more solidly established and extensive. This relation persists even controlling for other economic and institutional determinants of bank lending, such as country size and growth rate, and variables capturing respect for the law and protection of creditor rights. The third and fourth columns of table 10.1 show that public and private information sharing also mitigates credit risk, in accordance with the theory.

The literature also sheds light on the incentives to create private and public information-sharing arrangements. As for private credit bureaus, Pagano and Jappelli (1993) show that lenders should have a greater incentive to share information when the mobility of credit seekers is high. Intuitively, a society where borrowers are very mobile is one where banks must often assess the credit risk of nonlocal credit applicants, on which some other bank possesses private information. Indeed, figure 10.2 shows that countries that feature greater residential mobility (such as Canada, Australia, Sweden, and the United States)

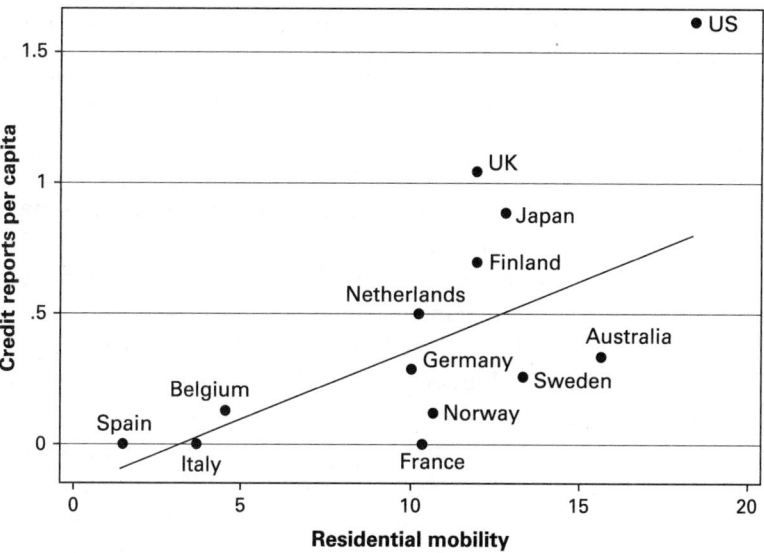

Figure 10.2
Credit reporting and borrowers' mobility
Source: Pagano and Jappelli 1993.
Note: The number of credit reports refers to 1989 for the United States, the United Kingdom, Germany, France, and Spain, to 1988 for Japan, and to 1990 for all other countries. Private consumption is drawn from the OECD National Accounts. Residential mobility is the household's probability of changing residence in a year.

Table 10.2
Determinants of the presence of public credit registers

Variable	Probit	Tobit
Creditor rights	−0.07	2,204.75
	(−0.81)	(0.95)
Rule of law	−0.01	361.37
	(−0.09)	(0.36)
Preexistence of a private credit bureau	−0.41	13,169.54
	(−2.04)	(2.13)
French origin	0.49	−11,998.97
	(3.35)	(−1.65)
German origin	0.566	−15,803.28
	(1.77)	(−1.72)
Scandinavian origin	0.476	−10,200.36
	(1.16)	(−0.96)
Number of countries	43	41

Note: This table is based on Jappelli and Pagano 2003. Countries are divided according to the presence of public credit registers. Presence of a PCR is 1 if the register is operating in 1998, and 0 otherwise. Preexistence of a private credit bureau is 1 if at least one private credit bureau was in operation before the establishment of the PCR, 0 otherwise. See the appendix for sources and definition of the other variables. In the probit regression, the dependent variable is the presence of a PCR prior to 1998, and the coefficients indicate the effect of the variable on the probability of establishment of a PCR. In the tobit regression, the dependent variable is the PCR minimum reporting threshold; t-statistics are reported in parentheses.

have comparatively extensive private credit-reporting activity, as measured by the number of credit reports per capita.

As for PCRs, the incentive to establish them should be stronger where similar private arrangements have not yet arisen, and where creditor rights are poorly protected. Table 10.2 shows that, indeed, PCRs were more often established in countries without preexisting private credit bureaus and in countries where the legal system is based on the Napoleonic code, which is associated with poorer creditor protection. In the first column, the probability of finding a PCR is negatively associated to the preexistence of a private credit bureau; in the second, the PCR's reporting threshold is positively associated to the preexistence of private credit bureaus, implying that, where credit bureaus already exist, the PCR's coverage is restricted to large loans. This indicates that not only the existence but also the design of PCRs responds to the presence of credit bureaus. The association between the presence of a PCR and the legal origin dummies suggests that PCRs are introduced to compensate, at least partly, for the weak protection that the state offers to creditors' interests, and thus to remedy heightened moral hazard in lending.

10.1.3 Microeconomic Evidence

Recent studies based on individual-level data on consumers or banks have shed further light on several interesting effects of information-sharing arrangements in credit markets. Contributions have been especially produced as part of two international research projects by the Inter-American Development Bank (IADB) and the World Bank, see Pagano 2001 and Miller 2003. However, this work is still piecemeal: A systematic analysis of the impact of these arrangements on lending activity, defaults, and interest rates is still missing.

Some papers analyze the effectiveness of credit bureaus and generally find that credit reports are an important tool to assess consumer credit risk (Chandler and Parker 1989; Barron and Staten 2003). This is confirmed by Kallberg and Udell (2003), who document that trade credit history in Dun & Bradstreet's reports improves default predictions relative to financial statements alone. Also Cowan and De Gregorio (2003) find that, in Chile, positive and negative information in credit reports contributes to predict defaults.

This improved assessment of credit risk appears to translate into higher lending. Galindo and Miller (2001) find a positive relation between access to finance (debt) and an index of information sharing in the Worldscope database, using the firm-level sensitivity of investment to cash flow as a proxy of credit constraints. They find that well-performing credit reporting systems reduce the sensitivity of investment to cash flows. Love and Mylenko (2003) combine firm-level data from the World Bank Business Environment Survey with aggregate data on private and public registers collected in Miller (2003) and find that private credit bureaus are associated with lower perceived financing constraints and a higher share of bank financing. However, the existence of public credit registers does not have a significant effect on financing constraints.

In addition, the individual country studies of the IADB and World Bank projects brim with interesting evidence on the effect of information sharing on specific credit markets, highlighting particularly its "disciplinary role." Castelar Pinheiro and Cabral (2001) report that, in Brazil, the whole postdated check market (whose size is of the same order of magnitude as the stock of household credit) operates without collateral, without personal guarantees, and without legal sanctions of any type. Its only foundation is its information-sharing mechanism: a "black list" of people issuing checks without funds. This mechanism alone also explains why the interest rate charged by factoring companies that operate in this market is much lower than that charged by credit card companies. Similar evidence is reported for Chile, where department stores seeking to collect an unpaid loan send the relevant information both to a collection agency and to the main Chilean credit bureau, DICOM. Apparently, notifying DICOM is a very effective way of securing immediate repayment, since delinquent customers see their credit dry up with all the stores that they patronize.

Moreover, the degree and sophistication of information-sharing arrangements appear to be synchronized with those of the financial system as a whole. For instance, Costa Rica, which has one of the most sophisticated credit markets in the region, also has an impressive and keenly competing set of private credit bureaus covering the majority of the population of the country, with different bureaus specializing in different services. The development of information-sharing mechanisms appears in turn to prompt lenders to move toward more refined screening and monitoring practices. This is witnessed by the central role that information-sharing systems have taken in borrower selection in Peru, especially after the development of a public rating register in that country. As explained by Trivelli, Alvarado, and Galarza 2001, this has encouraged lenders to shift away from exclusive reliance on collateral toward information-based lending.

10.2   Issues and Pitfalls in the Architecture of Credit Information Systems

Under which circumstances should public policy create a credit-reporting system by mandating banks to disclose their private information? And if so, which information should be pooled and which should be kept confidential? For how long should information remain available in a credit-reporting system? These are just some of the many policy issues that arise in the creation, design, and regulation of information exchange in credit markets. In this section we take up the most salient of such issues, building on the prior discussion of the effects of information sharing on the performance of credit markets.

10.2.1   Relationship between Private and Public Systems

Information-sharing arrangements are often created spontaneously by groups of lenders or individual entrepreneurs in the form of credit bureaus or of rating agencies. The design of a public credit registry cannot disregard how much information sharing the private sector is already exchanging spontaneously. Clearly, the case for the introduction of a PCR is comparatively stronger in countries where private information-sharing arrangements among lenders do not exist, or are primitive and limited in coverage and scope. In fact, as mentioned in section 10.1.2, empirically, the probability that a PCR is introduced is lower in countries with preexisting private information-sharing arrangements. Private and public arrangements are substitutes in this area.

By the same token, however, public arrangements can "crowd out" private ones. The introduction of a cost-effective PCR can put existing credit bureaus out of business or discourage the creation of new ones. In this sense, the crucial parameter in the design of a PCR is the minimum reporting threshold, since it effectively delimits the market segment left to the operation of private credit bureaus. In countries where an effective PCR operates, credit bureaus tend to specialize in loans to households and to small businesses, whose size is typically below the reporting threshold of the PCR. The higher this threshold, the larger the scope for private initiative in the industry.

The substitutability between public and private information-sharing arrangements, however, should not be exaggerated. There are also reasons why the two sources of information may be complements. For instance, credit bureaus may provide a greater degree of detail than PCRs, may merge other types of information with banking records, or may provide credit-scoring services to lenders. Therefore, a lender may obtain a clearer assessment of a credit applicant's solvency by accessing both the relevant PCR and a credit bureau than by confining himself to only one of these two sources of information.

10.2.2   Dosage of Negative and Positive Information

The type of data reported is another key element in the design of a credit information system. The simplest and most inexpensive systems are "blacklists," that contain information only on defaulters. These are most effective in correcting moral hazard problems in the credit market, owing to their disciplinary effect via reputational mechanisms.

Intermediate systems also include reporting of loan amounts so that lenders may form a more precise estimate of the total indebtedness of credit seekers. Such information helps to correct the moral hazard problems that may arise if loan contracts are nonexclusive, as explained in section 10.1.1.

The most sophisticated systems also include other forms of positive information about borrowers' characteristics, such as demographic information for households and accounting information for firms. As explained in section 10.1.1, however, in this area, "more" is not always "better." A system that provides much information about borrowers' characteristics may lead banks to identify high-quality borrowers more easily, but by the same token, such borrowers will be less worried that they will be reported as defaulters, trusting that their reputation will not be stained by such an event. As a result, they may exert less effort to avoid default.

10.2.3 Memory of the System

The number of years a credit information system "remembers" default or arrears by a given borrower is another important parameter in the design of a credit information system. More specifically, in setting the memory of the system, one has to ask two distinct but related questions. First, how long are default records kept? Second, are they removed after (late) repayment? Both of these features impinge on what we will call the "forgiveness" (or forgetfulness) of the system.

At one extreme, a system with infinite memory, in which borrowers have no chance to exit from the "blacklist," even after late repayment, may create a high incentive to repay on time, but may ex ante deter the decision to take any debt. The risk of being eternally blacklisted in case of default may be so large as to deter from borrowing even individuals with relatively solid prospects. Ex post, a blacklist with an extremely long memory may prevent defaulted debtors from ever making a comeback. Upon default, entrepreneurs may never have a chance to get new loans and start a new business and, therefore, to repay their past debts. Furthermore, even if a borrower has the money to repay a defaulted loan, he may have little incentive to do so because in any event his reputation is permanently marred. In this sense, a blacklist with a very long memory can contribute to the well-known problem of "debt overhang," by which defaulted debt becomes a permanent obstacle to the resumption of subsequent economic activity. At the other extreme, a system in which records are kept for a very short time and immediately erased upon late repayment would exert very little discipline on borrowers and correspondingly provide very little information on their track record to lenders.

The desirable degree of memory and "forgiveness" of the system lies between these two extremes. The system should trade off the need to discipline borrowers and the need to give them a "second chance." The optimal degree of forgiveness depends on many features of reality—including, for example, the persistence of default-inducing shocks—and generally differs from country to country. Where creditor rights are less well-protected—for instance, because of poor judicial enforcement—the need to discipline borrowers may be more pressing than elsewhere, and therefore, one may want to make the memory of the system longer and less forgiving.

A particularly interesting memory design is found in the Belgian Central Office for Credit to Private Individuals, a PCR that records only default information concerning household debt. Borrowers who redeem their debt disappear more quickly from the register than borrowers for whom a repayment commitment continues to exist. If arrears are repaid, then the information is automatically removed after one year; if the debt is repaid after default, it is removed only after two years. Irrespective of the type and status of the obligation, the database does not keep any record for more than ten years. So "punishment" is stricter for more serious misconduct (defaults are punished more than arrears), but eventually, there is forgiveness for everybody.

Apart from its role in the design of a PCR, this parameter is also a public policy variable, insofar as policymakers may limit the memory of private credit bureaus by regulation. For instance, Danish credit bureaus are entitled to register and distribute, at most, five years of data that is relevant to assess the financial situation of businesses or individuals; the 1970 U.S. Fair Credit Reporting Act, as amended in 1996, prohibits dissemination of adverse information after more than seven years.

10.2.4   Monopolistic Dangers of Private Information Sharing

The literature on Industrial Organization (IO) highlights that information sharing between firms may either increase or decrease the degree of market competition and the surplus enjoyed by consumers. This literature generally considers firms rather than financial intermediaries, and, therefore, typically abstracts from the effects that information sharing may have on adverse selection or moral hazard problems in downstream relationships with customers. Vives (1990) and Kuhn and Vives (1995) show that the effects of the production of information by an oligopolistic firm on the profits of its competitors and on consumer surplus are, in general, ambiguous and depend on the nature of the information produced (aggregate demand, individual demand, production cost) and on the type of strategic variables chosen by competitors (price or quantity competition).

In the context of an oligopolistic market with a homogeneous product and price competition, firms may try to collude to set prices above the competitive level and thereby earn extra profits. The collusive agreement is sustained by each firm's implicit threat of competing aggressively in the future against any potential deviant. But such deviations from collusion can be punished only if detected: For collusion to be sustainable, each firm must be able to observe the prices set by its competitors. Therefore, sustaining collusion requires a certain degree of price disclosure by competitors. On this basis, in recent times, competition authorities have often come to regard information-sharing agreements as automatic evidence of collusive practices (Kuhn 2001).

This contrasts with the literature surveyed in section 10.1.1, the general thrust of which is that, in credit markets, information sharing tends to increase competition by making the information set of lenders more homogeneous and thereby reducing lenders' information rents. The main difference between the traditional IO standpoint and this new banking literature on information sharing has to do with the type of information exchanged. In the banking literature, lenders share information about the characteristics or behavior of their customers rather than about prices, sales, and costs, as assumed by the traditional IO literature.[5]

Indeed, information sharing among banks has never been a concern of competition authorities: Governments often mandate information sharing as a way to enhance competition in the financial sector. This does not rule out, however, that even information-sharing arrangements in the financial sector may be designed to stifle competition. This can be achieved by setting up a credit bureau as a closed membership "club of incumbents." By refusing to admit potential entrants, incumbents erect an informational barrier to entry: Without access to the club's database, entrants are less informed than are incumbents.

This is exemplified by the Mexican case, where, in recent years, the Mexican Bank Association formed a private credit bureau ("Buro de

Credito") in partnership with Dun & Bradstreet and Trans-union. Two attempts to set up competing credit bureaus were unsuccessful because it proved impossible to obtain information from the banks. This happens whenever banks are vertically integrated with a monopolistic credit bureau, with which they have an exclusive relationship. This strategy allows banks to use the bureau as a collective entry prevention device against potential entrants in the credit market, illustrating a potential danger of information sharing arrangements even in credit markets.

This suggests that credit bureaus should be open-access so that any actual or potential lender can access the same information at nondiscriminatory costs. Alternatively, public policy should foster competition among private credit bureaus.[6] In some cases, the only way to create sufficient competition is to set a very low—possibly zero—threshold in public credit registers, as indeed is the case in several Latin American countries.

10.2.5 Pooling Information across Company Groups and Countries

If a credit information system must go beyond negative information and provide data about the overall indebtedness of each debtor, it must identify debtors and their liabilities unambiguously. For households, this is relatively simple, but it is worth mentioning that it may be much more difficult for firms belonging to company groups. A subsidiary may have a very limited debt exposure, but the group may be greatly overindebted. In fact, a distressed group will want to disguise its true leverage by borrowing new funds via relatively healthy subsidiaries.

Consolidating debt for companies linked by complex pyramidal structures and cross-shareholdings is very difficult, and even large PCRs may be ill-equipped to do so. The loans to the various subsidiaries may go undetected to a PCR because each of them does not exceed the reporting threshold. While this is unlikely to happen for large corporations, whose loan sizes are quite large anyway; in some European countries, the group structure is commonplace even for small and medium-sized enterprises (see Barca and Becht 2001). And corporate groups often transcend national borders. If a group takes large amounts of debt via its foreign subsidiaries, both the PCR of the country where the group's holding company is incorporated, and banks, will be unable to get reliable and complete data about the company's overall exposure.[7]

The problems created by access of companies to foreign credit, however, do not arise solely due to the possibility of borrowing via foreign subsidiaries. A multinational group structure compounds the problem, but even when a company borrows directly from foreign banks, its debt may go unreported to the domestic PCR. Hence, the roots of this information-sharing problem lie in the phenomenon of cross-border lending: not only companies, but also individuals (see chapter 2, this volume, for a discussion of European national and cross-border information-sharing regulation) increasingly access foreign credit markets via their foreign subsidiaries, and use such credit to diversify their sources of funds, reduce their cost of capital, or overcome domestic credit constraints. As borrowers become integrated into the world capital market, national credit information systems become unable to identify their total indebtedness.

So far, credit bureaus have adopted one of two alternative strategies to respond to this challenge: direct entry into foreign markets or alliances with foreign bureaus. Direct entry can be implemented by setting up local branches in foreign countries or by taking over national credit bureaus.[8] Other bureaus have created a web of transnational alliances to resist this wave of consolidation. Several European credit bureaus have linked up with each other in recent years. By creating a two-way flow of information between each other, these bureaus are trying to provide the same services as truly multinational entities without surrendering their independence. The same problems arise for PCRs. Again, a possible solution is to coordinate national public registers and create interfaces between their information systems. Of course, this may not be easy to implement. Apart from the fact that, in some countries, PCRs do not exist, the existing registers often feature different designs regarding coverage, reporting thresholds, type of information reported, and privacy protection clauses, posing formidable problems to their integration. These substantive problems are compounded by the inertia that is so often typical of bureaucratic organizations that operate under a soft budget constraint and lack the competitive pressure under which private organizations operate.

Does this make national PCRs obsolete organizations, bound to be displaced by the growth of private transnational private credit bureaus? The answer probably hinges on how many years ago a PCR was established. In Europe, where national PCRs are quite old and feature deeply ingrained differences, the seven countries that have them find it difficult to agree on a common set of rules so that the danger of their displacement by private multinational bureaus is increasing (Jappelli and Pagano 2003). By the same token, however, countries that are just establishing a public credit register for the first time have the opportunity of designing them so as to ensure compatibility with the systems of their main commercial partners. In this dimension, late-comers may be better positioned than their predecessors.

10.2.6 Privacy Protection

Credit information provision finds an obvious limit in the set of legal provisions designed to protect confidential information, or individual privacy. Such provisions differ widely both within Europe and be-tween the United States and European countries, and these differences appear to have had profound effects on the development of credit in-formation systems (see chapter 2, this volume; Jappelli and Pagano 2003). For instance, France's strict privacy protection laws have pre-vented the development of private credit bureaus in that country.

The degree of privacy protection accorded to prospective borrowers has historically affected the development of credit bureaus. The activ-ities of credit bureaus are regulated almost everywhere so as to pre-vent violation of privacy and civil liberties. Privacy laws effect a wide range of consumer guarantees, such as limits on access to files by po-tential users, bans on white information (e.g., in Finland and Austra-lia), compulsory elimination of individual files after a set time (e.g., seven years in the United States, five years in Australia), bans on gath-ering certain kinds of information (race, religion, political views, and so forth), and the right to access, check, and correct one's own file.[9]

However, one should not necessarily take a negative view of the ef-fect of privacy laws on credit information systems. As already pointed out in our discussion of the desirable memory of such systems in sec-tion 10.2.3, divulging certain types of information may lead people to become "too cautious"—that is, it may reduce risk taking and entre-preneurship below the socially desirable level. Therefore, a moderate concern for privacy may also indirectly serve economic efficiency.

In addition, there is one privacy protection rule that directly improves the accuracy of the data stored by credit information sys-tems: entitling individuals with the right to inspect and correct mis-taken information about them. Such feedback not only improves the quality of information but also helps to correct the negative bias in reporting for which credit bureaus are often blamed (see also the dis-cussion in chapter 9). Such bias is easily explained: When a negative credit report is mistakenly filed, the lender will generally deny credit and, therefore, is unlikely to ever find out about the mistaken information, while the opposite would happen if a positive report was filed for a bad credit risk. Therefore, credit bureaus prefer to err on the negative side.

10.2.7   Designing Information Sharing Systems in Developing Countries

Some issues in the design of credit information systems are particularly relevant for developing countries, where these systems are often still being designed.

First, in most developing countries, the role of informal lending is much larger than in developed economies. Since, typically, both credit bureaus and PCRs base their information on data reported by formal lenders, their utility is much reduced in these countries. This limitation of information-sharing systems could be overcome by allowing informal lenders—such as the nongovernmental organizations (NGOs) that manage microcredit programs—to access PCRs. For instance, Trivelli, Alvarado, and Galarza (2001) report that one of the main limitations of the Peruvian PCR is its insufficient coverage of data about debts with informal and rural lenders, because the majority of such lenders have never had any relation with the formal system.

A second issue is that PCRs are more important in countries where creditor rights receive relatively poor protection, and the law is less effectively enforced, as documented in section 10.1.2. In this sense, PCRs appear to act as a partial substitute for the lack of good judicial enforcement. Credit bureaus can, of course, play this role too. The disciplinary role of negative information can be particularly important in this respect. For instance, in Brazil, information-sharing mechanisms allow widespread reliance on postdated checks. Castelar Pinheiro and Cabral (2001) report, "Easy, low-cost information on the person writing the check and the high cost to the consumer of being placed on a 'blacklist' for writing a check without funds have made postdated checks the most widely used form of consumption financing" (179).

Third, in LDCs the availability of information provided by PCRs can effectively induce changes in banks' lending policies, shifting from a collateral-based lending policy to an information-based one. In many developing economies, it is often complained that formal lenders request their loans to be assisted by collateral whose value greatly exceeds the loan and pay little attention to the prospective cash flows of the project they are financing. The availability of more readily usable information, together with knowledge of credit-scoring techniques, may contribute to a shift in lending strategies.

Finally, in developing countries, credit information systems should be designed so as to be accessible by relatively unsophisticated bank personnel and avoid importing too-sophisticated systems, which presuppose very detailed positive information or rely on complex scoring techniques. Most LDCs may usefully start with simple negative information systems, possibly complemented by data on loan exposure, and later proceed to enrich them with additional data on corporate accounts and management and personal information.

10.3 Conclusions

This chapter offers a comprehensive overview of the economic effects of information-sharing systems, drawing together theory and empirical evidence, with an eye to obtaining directions for the design of credit information systems. Information sharing about borrowers' characteristics and their indebtedness can have important effects on credit markets activity. First, it improves the banks' knowledge of applicants' characteristics and permits a more accurate prediction of their repayment probabilities. Second, it reduces the informational rents that banks could otherwise extract from their customers. Third, it can operate as a borrower discipline device. Finally, it eliminates borrowers' incentive to become "overindebted" by drawing credit simultaneously from many banks without any of them realizing. This chapter provides a brief account of models that capture these four effects of information sharing on credit market performance, as well as of the growing body of empirical studies that have attempted to investigate the various dimensions and effects of credit reporting activity.

One of the insights from the literature is that the design of the mechanism used to share credit information matter at least as much as the decision to set up an information-sharing mechanism. The theoretical insights of the literature help to identify key issues in the design of credit information systems: the relationship between public and private mechanisms, the dosage between negative and positive information sharing, the "memory" of the system, and several others. This can provide guidance about possible pitfalls in the design of credit information systems, which are of particular relevance to developing countries, where such systems are often still being engineered.

10A   Appendix

Definition of Variables Used in Tables 10.1 and 10.2

Bank lending   Claims of banks on private sector, 1994–1995 average.
Source: International Financial Statistics (line 32d).

Credit risk   The index is based on the International Country Risk
Guide Financial Indicator (ICRGF) and refers to October 1995. The
index is constructed on the basis of a survey of leading international
bankers, who are asked to rate each country on a scale of zero to ten
each of the following five risks: default or unfavorable loan restructuring, delayed payment of suppliers' credits, repudiation of contracts by
governments, losses from exchange controls, expropriation of private
investments. The original index scales from zero to fifty (maximum
creditworthiness). We define credit risk as fifty minus the original
index, so that fifty represents maximum risk.
Source: Erb, Harvey, and Viskanta 1996, Table 4, Series ICRGF.

Creditor rights   An index aggregating creditor rights. The index
aggregates various rights that secured creditors might have in bankruptcy, liquidation, and reorganization. Restrictions on the managers'
ability to seek unilateral protection from creditors, mandatory dis-
missal of management in reorganizations, lack of automatic stay on
assets, and absolute priority for secured creditors all contribute to this
index. The index ranges from zero to four.
Source: La Porta et al. 1997.

Log GDP   Logarithm of the gross domestic product in 1992–1993.
Gross domestic product is expressed in 1990 million dollars.
Source: International Financial Statistics, line 99b for GDP and *aa* for ex-
change rates.

GDP growth   Average annual percent growth of per capita gross domestic product for the period 1970–1993.
Source: International Financial Statistics.

Legal origin   Identifies the legal origin (English, German, French, Scan-
dinavian) of the company law or commercial code of each country.
Source: La Porta et al. 1997.

Rule of law   Assessment of the law-and-order tradition in the country. Average of the 1982–1995 period. Scale from zero to ten, with
lower scores for less tradition of law and order.
Source: La Porta et al. 1997.

Notes

1. Kallberg and Udell (2003) also point out that information exchange from multiple sources improves the precision of the signal about the quality of the borrower.

2. Gehrig and Stenbacka (2005) consider a similar model but assume that banks compete ex ante for clients and that customers face switching costs. Under these assumptions, future informational rents are a stimulus to competition. Since information sharing reduces these rents, in their model, it reduces competition, in contrast with what is predicted by Padilla and Pagano (1997). This shows that under some assumptions, information sharing can act as an anticompetitive device, a point that we shall return to in section 10.2.4.

3. In this model, there is no holdup problem because initially banks have no private information about credit seekers, and ex ante competition dissipates any rents from information acquired in the lending relation.

4. A lender is not only threatened by the borrower's prior debt commitments but also by those that he may contract in the future, as shown by Bizer and DeMarzo 1992.

5. Even when they share information about loans, credit bureaus do not reveal the identity of the lender associated with a particular loan.

6. This may not always be possible due to the strong economies of scale that characterize the industry, which, in fact, has undergone a process of dramatic concentration (Jappelli and Pagano 1993).

7. This is exemplified by two conspicuous Italian cases, the Ferruzzi and the Parmalat scandals. In both cases, the huge debt buildup in the early 1990s was facilitated by an incomplete perception of the group's total exposure. In 1992, the Ferruzzi group was the second industrial group in Italy and had a hugely complex financial structure, with an Italian holding company and nearly 300 controlled companies, of which only 100 registered in Italy. The group borrowed heavily both in Italy and abroad via its many subsidiaries, and in 1993, it entered a state of financial distress. Its total indebtedness was almost U.S. $20 billion, an amount that "exceeded the entire private external debt of the Philippines ($14 billion), and was not far from that of Malaysia ($28 billion) at the end of 1997" (Penati and Zingales 1998, 2). About one-quarter of its total unsecured bank debt ($15 billion) was owed to foreign banks. Much of this debt had been transferred within the group from one company to another via a complex set of intragroup loans. A similar story appears to explain the buildup of debt carried out by Calisto Tanzi, the controlling shareholder of Parmalat. Although in this case a precise account must await the verdict of ongoing trials, there is substantial evidence that much of the undetected debt was raised by the foreign subsidiaries of the group.

8. Of course, this is unlikely be the only reason for the strategy of credit bureaus' foreign acquisitions. Other reasons are economies of scale, superior technical knowledge accumulated by large bureaus, and desire to diversify revenue structure.

9. As far as access limits are concerned, there appear to be three levels of privacy protection. There are low-protection countries, such as Argentina, where anyone can access all debtors' data, regardless of the purpose of investigation. In medium-protection countries, such as the United States, data can be accessed only for an "admissible purpose," essentially the granting of credit. A higher level of privacy protection may be embodied in the further requirement of the borrower's explicit consent to access his file. This principle is enshrined in the legislation of several European countries and in the Directive 95/46 of the European Parliament on "the protection of individuals with regard to the

processing of personal data and on the free movement of such data." In some countries (such as France, Israel, and Thailand), safeguards for consumer privacy are so strong that regulation has impeded the emergence of private credit bureaus.

References

Barca, Fabrizio, and Marco Becht, eds. 2001. *The Control of Corporate Europe*. Oxford: Oxford University Press.

Barron, John M., and Michael Staten. 2003. "The Value of Comprehensive Credit Reports: Lessons from the U.S. Experience." In *Credit Reporting Systems and the International Economy*, ed. Margaret Miller, 273–310. Cambridge, Mass.: The MIT Press.

Bizer, David S., and Peter M. DeMarzo. 1992. "Sequential Banking." *Journal of Political Economy* 100, no. 1 (February): 41–61.

Castelar Pinheiro, Armando, and Célia Cabral. 1999. "Credit Markets in Brazil: The Role of Judicial Enforcement and Other Institutions." In *Defusing Default: Incentives and Institutions*, ed. Marco Pagano, 157–188. Washington, D.C.: Johns Hopkins University Press.

Chandler Gary G., and Lee E. Parker. 1989. "Predictive Value of Credit Bureau Reports." *Journal of Retail Banking* 11: 47–54.

Cowan, Kevin, and Jose De Gregorio. 2003. "Credit Information and Market Performance: The Case of Chile." In *Credit Reporting Systems and the International Economy*, ed. Margaret Miller, 163–201. Cambridge, Mass.: The MIT Press.

Erb, B. Claude, Campbell R. Harvey, and Tadas E. Viskanta. 1996. "Political Risk, Economic Risk, and Financial Risk." *Financial Analyst Journal* (November–December): 29–45.

Galindo, Arturo, and Margaret J. Miller. 2001. "Can Credit Registries Reduce Credit Constraints? Empirical Evidence on the Role of Credit Registries in Firm Investment Decisions." Paper prepared for the Annual Meetings of the Inter-American Development Bank, Santiago, Chile, March.

Gehrig, Thomas, and Rune Stenbacka. 2005. "Information Sharing and Lending Market Competition with Switching Costs and Poaching." University of Freiburg: unpublished manuscript, http://www.shh.fi/~stenback/infoshar-r94.pdf, February.

Jappelli, Tullio, and Marco Pagano. 2002. "Information Sharing, Lending and Defaults: Cross-Country Evidence." *Journal of Banking and Finance* 26, no. 10 (October): 2017–2045.

Jappelli, Tullio, and Marco Pagano. 2003. "Public Credit Information: A European Perspective." In *Credit Reporting Systems and the International Economy*, ed. Margaret Miller, 81–114. Cambridge, Mass.: The MIT Press.

Kallberg, Jarl G., and Gregory F. Udell. 2003. "The Value of Private Sector Credit Information: the U.S. Case." *Journal of Banking and Finance* 27, no. 3: 449–469.

Kuhn, Kai-Uwe. 2001. "Fighting Collusion by Regulating Communication Between Firms." *Economic Policy* 32: 168–204.

Kuhn, Kai-Uwe, and Xavier Vives. 1995. *Information Exchanges among Firms and Their Impact on Competition*. Luxembourg: Office for Official Publication of the European Community.

La Porta, Rafael, Florencio Lopez-de-Silanes, Andrei Shleifer, and Robert W. Vishny. 1997. "Legal Determinants of External Finance." *Journal of Finance* 52, no. 3 (July): 1131–1150.

Love, Inessa, and Nataliya Mylenko. 2003. "Credit Reporting and Financing Constraints." World Bank Policy Research Working Paper 3142, October.

Miller, Margaret J., ed. 2003. *Credit Reporting Systems and the International Economy*. Cambridge, Mass.: The MIT Press.

Ongena, Steven, and David C. Smith. 2000. "Bank Relationships: A Review." December. In *The Performance of Financial Institutions*, ed. P. Harker and S. A. Zenios, 221–258. Cambridge: Cambridge University Press.

Padilla, A. Jorge, and Marco Pagano. 1997. "Endogenous Communication among Lenders and Entrepreneurial Incentives." *The Review of Financial Studies* 10, no. 1 (winter): 205–236.

Padilla, A. Jorge, and Marco Pagano. 2000. "Sharing Default Information as a Borrower Discipline Device." *European Economic Review* 44, no. 10: 1951–1980.

Pagano, Marco, ed. 2001. *Defusing Default: Incentives and Institutions*. Washington, D.C.: Johns Hopkins University Press.

Pagano, Marco, and Tullio Jappelli. 1993. "Information Sharing in Credit Markets." *The Journal of Finance* 43, no. 5 (December): 1,693–1,718.

Penati, Alessandro, and Luigi Zingales. 1998. "Efficiency and Distribution in Financial Restructuring: The Case of the Ferruzzi Group." Unpublished manuscript, University of Chicago, October, http://gsblgz.uchicago.edu.

Trivelli, Carolina, Javier Alvarado, and Francisco Galarza. 2001. "Growing Indebtedness, Institutional Change and Credit Contracts in Peru." In *Defusing Default: Incentives and Institutions*, ed. Marco Pagano, 319–351. Washington, D.C.: Johns Hopkins University Press.

Vives, Xavier. 1990. "Trade Association Disclosure Rules, Incentives to Share Information and Welfare." *Rand Journal of Economics* 21: 409–430.

N/A

Contributors

Carol C. Bertaut
Board of Governors of the
Federal Reserve System

Giuseppe Bertola
Università di Torino and Finance
and Consumption
EUI

Sarah Bridges
Experian Centre for Economic
Modelling and School of
Economics
University of Nottingham

Luca Casolaro
Bank of Italy

Jonathan N. Crook
Credit Research Centre
University of Edinburgh

Richard Disney
Experian Centre for Economic
Modelling and School of
Economics
University of Nottingham

Leonardo Gambacorta
Bank of Italy

Charles Grant
University of Reading and
Finance and Consumption
EUI

Luigi Guiso
University of Sassari
Ente "Luigi Einaudi" and CEPR

Michael Haliassos
School of Economics and
Business
Goethe University
Frankfurt

Andrew Henley
School of Business and
Economics
University College of Wales
Swansea

Robert M. Hunt
Federal Reserve Bank of
Philadelphia

Tullio Jappelli
University of Salerno
CSEF and CEPR

Nicola Jentzsch
Free University of Berlin

Marco Pagano
University of Naples Federico II
CSEF and CEPR

Amparo San José Riestra
IESE Business School
University of Navarra

Michael Staten
McDonough School of Business
Georgetown University

Michelle J. White
University of California,
San Diego, and NBER

Index